EDUCATIONAL PSYCHOLOGY

Dr. S. K. Chatterjee

CELEBRATING 50 YEARS 1960-2010

Since 1960

[*For B.Ed., M.Ed., B.A./B.Sc. (Education), M.A./M.Sc. (Education) & M.Phil Students.*]

EDUCATIONAL PSYCHOLOGY

Dr. Saroj Kr. Chatterjee

M.A., M.Ed., M.Sc., Ph.D.

Principal (Retd.), Govt. B.Ed. College, Banipur,
and Govt. Hindi Teachers' Training College, Calcutta.
Ex-Reader, State Council of Educational Research & Training, W.B.
Ex-Asst. Professor, Govt. B.Ed. College, Hooghly,
State Institute of Education, Banipur,
and Surendra Nath College, Calcutta.

BOOKS AND ALLIED (P) Ltd.

No. 1-E(1), "Shubham Plaza" (1st Floor)
83/1, Beliaghata Main Road, Kolkata 700010 (India)
Tel : (+91-33)6535-3844 • ***Fax*** : (033)2358-2127
e-mail : books1960@ymail.com • booksandallied1960@gmail.com

EDUCATIONAL PSYCHOLOGY

First Published : December, 2000
Reprinted : 2002
Reprinted (with Corrections) : 2009
Reprinted : 2010, 2012
Reprinted : 2015

Publisher : Arunabha Sen
BOOKS & ALLIED (P) LTD.
8/1 Chintamoni Das Lane, Kolkata 700009

Typesetter : BOOKS & ALLIED (P) LTD.
8/1 Chintamoni Das Lane, Kolkata 700009

Printer : EUREKA
91/A, Baithakkhana Road, Kolkata 700009

ISBN 81-87134-87-9

Price : **₹ 295.00**

Dedicated to

Prof. Rajeswari

and

Prof. Sisir Chatterjee

Indian Institute of Science, Bangalore

Preface

Like other branches of knowledge, *Educational Psychology* has also advanced with considerable rapidity in recent years. But it is felt that though there are a number of text books available on this subject, there is a great dearth of suitable advanced level text books, which can satisfy the needs of the students pursuing higher courses in Educational Psychology. This book, *Advanced Educational Psychology*, is expected to fill the gap. It provides up-to-date information to the students of B.Ed., M.Ed., B.A./B.Sc. (Education), M.A./M.Sc. (Education) and M. Phil. of different Indian Universities.

The book comprises a general view of current knowledge in Educational Psychology and its application to teaching learning process. Along with the common topics some new topics such as suicide and educational system, microteaching and educational technology have been included in this book. Juvenile Delinquency has been dealt with in detail, as because the problem is eating into the vitals of our society. To help the students particularly of M.Ed. and M.Phil., a topic on Educational Research has been incorporated.

In fact, the text book has a vast coverage of topics and it includes the latest development in the various fields of Educational Psychology. Besides, the book has been profusely illustrated with charts, diagrams, flow charts and tables.

At the end of each chapter a brief Summary, References, Questions and Assignments have been inserted for the benefit of students.

I wish to express my profound gratitude to my brother, Prof. Sisir Chatterjee, who inspired me to write a book on Advanced Educational Psychology in English.

I have necessarily drawn on the writings of several authors on Educational Psychology and I record here my sense of indebtedness to all of them.

I am thankful to Mr. Samir Chakravarty, Librarian, David Hare Training College, Calcutta and Miss Mala Sur, Librarian, State Council of Educational Research and Training, West Bengal for their help and cooperation.

Besides, I would like to thank Sri Arunabha Sen, Executive Director of Books & Allied (Pvt.) Ltd., Calcutta for his careful processing of the manuscript and other necessary assistance.

Any suggestion for the improvement of the book would be warmly accepted.

MAHALAYA, 2000
278-B Rashbehari Avenue
Calcutta 700 019

Dr. Saroj Chatterjee

Contents

Chapter 1

Psychology—Meaning, Nature and Scope

Introduction : Educational psychology applies the general principles of psychology to the practical needs of education. It studies those principles of psychology which will help the improvement of educational process. Psychology helps the educator to know the innate abilities of the pupil and the laws of his mental development. This undoubtedly facilitates the teaching-learning process.

In fact, psychology provides a strong foundation to education. This is why teaching of psychological principles has become part and parcel of teachers' training program at all levels today.

1.1 What is psychology?

Psychology is the study of problems concerning human behaviour. It should not be confused with spiritualism, mental telepathy or fortune-telling. Various definitions of psychology are briefly discussed below:

1.1.1 Psychology is the science of soul

The term Psychology is derived from the Greek words Psyche and Logos. Psyche means Soul and Logos means Science. Thus the word psychology literally means, Science of the soul.

Formerly, psychology was a part of Philosophy, which deals with different aspects of soul. But soul cannot be observed nor can we experiment with it. Therefore, this definition cannot be accepted because modern psychology is purely empirical.

1.1.2 Psychology is the science of mind

Psychology deals with mental processes (Mill). So, psychology is defined as the Science of Mind.

But, like soul, mind has also no material existence. Therefore, the definition of psychology as the science of mind is misleading and unacceptable.

1.1.3 Psychology is the science of consciousness

Some modern psychologists define psychology as the science of consciousness. William James (1892) defined psychology as the description and explanation of state of consciousness as such. Wundt and Titchener (1892) also defined psychology as the science of consciousness. But this definition is too narrow and subjective. The modern behaviourists discard consciousness because the factual data required for a natural science cannot be provided by it.

1.1.4 Psychology is the science of behaviour

The Behaviourist School of psychology regards psychology as the science of conduct or behaviour.

McDougall defines psychology as the positive science of the behaviour of living things. Psychology relies on the method of investigation common to all natural sciences.

J.B. Watson (1913) also defines psychology as the science of human behaviour. It is the science of investigation of human conduct. But to McDougall, behaviour of living things are always purposeful. However, Watson regards behaviour as mechanical response of an organism to the stimulus. Hence the behaviourists reduce psychology to a biological science.

Thus, in course of time ,the definition and concept of psychology underwent complete change. First psychology lost its soul, then it lost its mind, then it lost consciousness, it still has behaviour of a kind (Woodworth). In fact, this change has brought about a great advancement in the subject.

In 1879 Prof. Wundt first established a psychological laboratory at Leipzig University in Germany. Here experiments were conducted on various mental processes and psychologists from America and other parts of the world joined Wundt in the endeavour. Because Wilhelm Wundt founded a laboratory of psychology, he is considered as father of scientific psychology.

Conclusion : From the above discussion on the definition of psychology we see that the concept of the subject has changed frequently. However, to be brief, psychology is the science of experience and purposive behaviour of individuals in relation to their environment. This standpoint has been taken by most of the modern psychologists.

1.2 Nature of psychology

McDougall, Pillsbury, Watson and other modern psychologists consider psychology as the science of human behaviour.

But what is meant by science and behaviour? Why psychology should be called a science?

1.2.1 Meaning of science

A science is a systematic body of knowledge relating to a subject. Briefly it should have the following characteristics :

1. A science seeks truth.
2. A science seeks to explain the phenomena within its scope.
3. A science believes in cause and effect relation.
4. Scientific results are systematic and self-consistent.
5. A science adopts observation, experiment, comparison, classification and measurement as methods of investigation.
6. Scientific laws help future prediction.
7. Scientific results are applicable to future researches.

1.2.2 Why psychology be called a science?

Let us examine how far psychology fulfils the above criteria of science:

1. Psychology adopts scientific methods to find out new truths. It deals with behaviour of an individual and establishes facts by objective and reliable methods. Psychology is empirical. It is based on experiments and surveys.
2. Psychology tries to explain mental processes by the laws of mind. For example, it assumes the existence of unconscious to explain the phenomena of retention or dream. The explanation of mental processes given by psychology takes the form of generalisation and framing hypotheses.
3. Psychology does not believe in subjective ideas. It emphasises the cause and effect relationships in behaviour of an individual. It encourages critical thinking.
4. The methods employed in the study of human behaviour in psychology are systematic. It analyses behaviour, formulates hypotheses and generalises the results by framing laws.

5. Psychology observes mental processes under controlled condition, compares them with one another and classifies them. It conducts experiments with the help of scientific instruments. Psychology has discovered a number of scales to measure intelligence, personality and other human characteristics.

6. Psychology helps to predict behaviour. The results of the study of behaviour can be verified under similar conditions. So, we can make reliable predictions about the individual in the light of his studied behaviour.

7. Psychological findings about human behaviour are consistent and applicable to future researches.

1.2.3 What kind of science is Psychology?

Physical sciences, such as Physics, Chemistry, Mathematics or Astronomy deal with the phenomena of matter. Botany, Zoology, Physiology deal with phenomena of life. They are called biological sciences. Psychology is closely related to physical and biological sciences. Physical sciences study the nature of physical phenomena. They help psychology to explain behaviour of an organism, which are reactions to physical stimuli. There are close connections between psychic performances and the organisation of the brain (E.R. Hess). In fact, there is a close relation between nervous system and glandular system with the behaviour of an individual. Thus it is obvious that psychology and biological sciences are intimately related.

Psychology deals with the behaviour of an organism. It is the science of experience and telic behaviour. McDougall defined Psychology as a positive science of the conduct of the living creatures. Psychology studies the behaviour of an individual in groups. It investigates how an individual interacts in a social group. As a social science psychology studies scientifically various social problems. Thus psychology is a biological, sociological as well as behavioural science.

Some argue that psychology cannot be equalled with those Physical and Biological sciences, because psychology is not so perfect and accurate. But no scientific theories are perfect, stable and unchangeable for ever.

1.3 Meaning of behaviour

Behaviour is the outward organic expression of mental processes. Watson defined behaviour as an act which can be observed and measured objectively. According to him psychology studies the response pattern of an organism in reaction to the stimuli coming from the environment. The behaviourists consider behaviour as a mechanical response of the organism to a stimulus. They reject the notions of mind or consciousness altogether.

But this doctrine of Behaviourism cannot be fully accepted. It is true that psychology deals with human behaviour and animal behaviour. It investigates different aspects of human behaviour at different stages of development. It deals with normal as well as abnormal behaviour. It deals with both the individual and collective behaviour.

1.3.1 Psychology is the science of Experience and Behaviour

Behaviour is inexplicable without conscious experience. Behaviour without mental process is absurd. The behaviour of an organism is not like that of a machine. The organism has ability for abstract thinking, reasoning, imagining and his behaviour involves purposiveness. The individual is a psychophysical organism and possesses decision-making ability on the basis of previous experiences.

Thus in brief, psychology is the positive science of experience and purposive behaviour of an individual.

1.4 Applications of psychology

Today almost in every sphere of human life, psychology is widely applied. In fact, wherever living organisms exist, psychology attempts to study and describe their activities.

Psychology is the science of mental processes and purposive behaviour. So all kinds of purposive behaviour of human being come within the scope of psychology.

Again, mental processes such as learning, sensation, perception etc. are accompanied by physiological processes. So, physiological processes also fall within the domain of psychology. Mental processes cannot be explained without references to sense organs, muscles and nervous system.

Studies in psychology are not confined to human behaviour only. They also include the behaviour of all kinds of animals

Psychology deals with the different aspects of human behaviour at different stages of development starting from birth to old age.

Psychology deals with the normal as well as abnormal behaviour. It studies the individual behaviour and the collective behaviour.

Psychology studies the social customs and traditions, folklore and religion, myths and legends of different people. It deals with crowd and mob behaviour.

1.5 Branches of psychology

The domain of psychology is very wide. For the sake of convenience, it has been divided into different branches. Important branches of psychology are :

1.5.1 General psychol)gy

This branch of psychology deals with the fundamental principles of psychology related to normal persons.

1.5.2 Social psychology

This branch of psychology deals with social behaviour of people. It studies mores and customs, attitudes and prejudices, behaviour of crowd and mob. It studies the psychological principles of social organisation.

1.5.3 Abnormal psychology

This branch of psychology deals with various mental diseases, their causes, symptoms and treatment.

1.5.4 Physiological psychology

This branch of psychology deals with nervous system, sense organs, glandular systems, etc. These are intimately connected with the mental processes and behaviour of an individual.

1.5.5 Clinical psychology

This branch of psychology deals with the causes and treatment of mental diseases of patients coming to a clinic or hospital for treatment.

1.5.6 Experimental psychology

This branch of psychology deals with various kinds of psychological testing under controlled laboratory situations. It takes the help of scientific instruments for investigation into the behaviour of animals and human beings.

1.5.7 Industrial psychology

This branch of psychology applies psychological principles to investigate behaviour of an individual in industrial setting. Advertising and sale of products, selection and placement of personnel, labour problems, strengthening the morale of employees etc. are some of the topics which comprise the subject matter of Industrial psychology.

1.5.8 Educational psychology

In this branch of psychology, psychological principles and techniques are applied to study the teaching-learning process, evaluation of learning performance, guidance for exceptional children and various educational problems.

1.5.9 Para psychology

This new branch of psychology studies super-normal mental phenomena, such as : (a) Telepathy, (b) Clairevoyance, (c) Extra-sensory perception, (d) Psychokinesis or moving material objects by will-force, (e) Cases of rebirth and alleged super-natural phenomena.

1.6 Methods of psychology

There are three most important methods of psychology—Introspection, Observation and Experiment. Introspection is the subjective method. Observation and experiment are the objective methods.

1.6.1 Introspection

Introspection is the fundamental method of psychology. It means looking inward. It consists in trying to understand the nature of mental processes by looking within one's own mind. For instance, I want to know the nature of anger. When I am angry I look within myself and try to analyse the peculiarity of the emotion.

Our mental processes are always with us and we can introspect them whenever we desire. In this sense, introspection has a unique advantage. But it has disadvantages too.

Drawbacks : Following objections have been raised against this method:

1. Mental processes are vague. So it is difficult to introspect them. Only a few trained individuals can use introspection.
2. Mental processes are fleeting by nature. They tend to vanish when we try to introspect them. The act of introspection may also change the experience. As. William James puts it, "The attempt at introspective analysis is like seizing a top to catch its motion. So introspection becomes retrospection of the past events."
3. Introspection is purely subjective. For instance, two persons cannot have the same emotional experience during anger or fear.
4. In introspection, the same mind splits itself into two parts—the observer and the observed. But the same mind cannot thus cleave into two parts.

Those difficulties of introspection cannot be easily overcome. But in spite of its inadequacy, psychologists cannot dispense with it altogether. The difficulties of introspection are overcome by the collaboration of expert psychologists. Thus psychology becomes a science when introspection is supplemented by the observation of trained persons.

1.6.2 Observation

Observation is the most important method of psychology. By carefully observing the behaviour of a person, we can ascertain what is going on in his mind. For instance, when a person is angry, he frowns, howls and assumes a threatening posture. We cannot directly observe what is happening in the minds of other persons, but by observation of their external behaviour we can interpret the experience.

Drawbacks : However, the method of observation is not free from its defects. Hypocrisy of the individual whose behaviour is observed, is an obstacle to the correct diagnosis of his mental processes. A person may speak volumes of honesty yet be dishonest. However, this difficulty can be overcome by close observation of his activities in different occasions.

In spite of some drawbacks, the method of observation has proved of special significance in the field of psychology.

1.6.3 Experiment

An experiment is observation under controlled condition. The psychological experiment involves Experimenter and his subject. The experimenter gives a stimulus and the subject introspects his experience. The experimenter carefully observes the behaviour of his subject and immediately records his observation.

The experimental method has many advantages. We can multiply instances as often as we like and we can repeat the experiment under varied conditions to study a mental process.

Drawbacks : But one important limitation of the experimental method is that for various reasons we cannot control conditions adequately. Under artificial conditions the mental process of the subject may be totally modified.

1.6.4 Comparative method

Psychologists study human behaviour. They study animal behaviour also, because animal behaviour is much simpler than human behaviour, which is extremely complex. A study of animal behaviour throws much light on that of human beings. For instance, to understand the process of human learning, psychologists studied the learning process of animals like monkeys, cats, dogs, etc.

1.6.5 Case History method

This method is applied in case of abnormal behaviour. For example, a case history of a problem, or, delinquent child is prepared by the psychologist to find out the causes of the trouble and thereby suggest remedies.

1.6.6 Psycho-analysis

Psychologists use this method to study abnormal phenomena of the mental life of an individual. This method was first discovered by Freud to study the unconscious phase of mental life.

1.7 Scope of psychology

Psychology primarily deals with human experience. Human experience has three fundamental characteristics. These are cognition, affection and conation. Cognition includes sensation, perception, conception, imagination, memory, thinking, reasoning etc.

Affection includes feeling, sentiments, emotions, etc. Conation includes reflexes, instincts and general tendencies. Besides these, habits, character, personality and individual differences are the subject matter of psychology.

Formerly, psychology was concerned solely with the conscious phase of the human mind. But today it studies the conscious as well as unconscious process of our mental life.

1.8 Fields of psychology

Today the field of psychology has immensely widened. Its various branches are : General psychology, Child psychology, Animal psychology, Social psychology, Industrial psychology, Abnormal psychology, Physiological psychology, Psycho-analysis, Psychiatry or Medical psychology, Educational psychology, etc.

1.8.1 General psychology

General psychology studies the various mental processes of a normal individual. It uses introspection, observation and experiment as methods of investigation.

1.8.2 Child psychology

The purpose of this branch of psychology is to investigate the growth of the child mind. It deals with the genesis and growth of elementary processes of perception, imagination, memory, intelligence, instincts, etc. in a child. The important methods of child psychology are observation and experiment.

1.8.3 Animal psychology

Animal psychology studies the behaviour of animals in different situations. It is also called Comparative psychology because it compares the well-developed human mind with lower manifestations of animal life. The study of animal behaviour throws much light on the origin and development of certain tendencies, which are found in complicated form in man. We can investigate the animal mind by observation and experiment.

1.8.4 Social psychology

Social psychology deals with the group mind. It studies the behaviour of individuals in social context. Social psychology deals with social institutions, customs, traditions, fads and fashions. It studies the behaviour of the crowd and the mob. It is the meeting ground of psychology and sociology.

1.8.5 Industrial psychology

Industrial psychology applies the general principles of psychology to the practical problems of industry. It deals with fatigue, mental traits of the workers, their demands, prevention of accidents, growth and improvement of industry. It also deals with selection of workers, their training, publicity and marketing.

1.8.6 Abnormal psychology

It deals with mental diseases, their classification and their remedies. It offers psychological as well as physiological reasons of mental disorders.

1.8.7 Psycho-analysis

Psycho-analysis is an off-shoot of Abnormal psychology. It deals with unconscious motivation of abnormal and mental diseases. Sigmund Freud is the founder of the school of psychoanalysis. It deals with dreams, the sex or libido and other repressed unconscious wishes.

1.8.8 Medical psychology or psychiatry

It deals with causes of mental disorders and the psychical methods of curing them such as hypnotism, auto-suggestion, psychoanalysis, etc.

1.8.9 Physiological psychology

This school of psychology deals with the relations between mental processes and the nervous system. It deals only with those physiological processes which are connected with mental processes such as emotion, etc.

Summary

Psychology is the positive science of experience and purposive behaviour of living organisms.

Psychology studies mental processes, their expressions in behaviour, normal as well as abnormal behaviour, individual and collective behaviour.

Formerly psychology was defined as the science of the soul, science of the mind, science of consciousness. But today it is considered as science of behaviour of all living things.

At present the domain of psychology is very extensive. It has many branches and fields of study.

References

1. Guilford, J.B. : *Fields of Psychology,* New York : Van Nostrand, 1966.
2. James, W. : *Principles of Psychology,* New York : Henry Holt, 1890.
3. McDougall, W. : *Psychology—The Study of Behaviour.* New York : Henry Holt, 1912.
4. Munn, N.L. : *Introduction to Psychology,* Delhi, 1967.
5. Woodworth R.S. : *Psychology,* London : Methuen, 1948.

Questions and Assignments

1. Give a satisfactory definition of psychology.
2. Is psychology a natural science? If so, in what sense?
3. "Psychology is the science of behaviour."—Discuss.
4. It is said "the point of view of psychology is subjective." Is this view correct? Discuss.
5. Critically consider McDougall's definition of psychology as *The positive science of the behaviour of living things.*
6. Indicate various branches of psychology giving in detail the subject-matter of each branch.

Chapter 2

Educational Psychology—Meaning, Nature and Scope

2.1 What is Educational Psychology?

Educational Psychology applies the general principles of psychology to the art of education. It deals with memory, intelligence, attention, personality, instinct, motivation, learning processes, individual differences, heredity and environment. It also discusses educational and vocational guidance and mental hygiene. Educational psychology combines two fields—psychology and education. It provides the educators with a fund of knowledge that helps them to build an all-round development of the pupil's personality.

2.1.1 Definitions of Educational Psychology

Educational Psychology has been defined by psychologists in different ways. Skinner defines educational psychology as a branch of psychology that deals with teaching and learning process. According to Judd, it is a scientific study of the life stages in the development of an individual from the time he is born until he becomes an adult.

Kolesnik says, "Educational Psychology is the study of those facts and principles of psychology which help to explain and improve the process of education." E. A. Peel has described educational psychology as the Science of Education.

2.1.2 Relation between Psychology and Education

According to Kolesnik, educational psychology is the study of those facts and principles of psychology which help to explain and improve the process of education. Educational psychology applies the general principles of psychology to the practical needs of education. Thus psychology provides a sound and realistic foundation to education.

Today psychology is playing an important part in formulating educational theories and in improving the practice of teaching. The school has thus become in fact, the laboratory of the psychologists.

Formerly it was thought that the knowledge of psychology could not help a teacher in his profession. Teaching is essentially an art and the teacher is an artist. A teacher requires practical skill and not the power of analytical investigation of the mental processes. So, some people thought that psychology instead of being helpful to the educators, their indulgence in psychology is harmful and detrimental. It is not true. Educational psychology deals with the behaviour and experiences which are related to education of the child. It selects from general psychology those facts that are relevant to teaching learning process. Thus, educational psychology may be regarded as a specialised branch of general psychology.

2.1.3 Brief history of Educational Psychology

In 18th century Rousseau first applied psychological principles in the education of Emile. This has undoubtedly inspired the modern educationists. Besides, Rousseau, the contributions of Froebel, Montessori and Pestalozzi have accelerated the advancement of educational psychology. Pestalozzi rightly thought that we cannot solve the problems of education without taking the help of psychology. So he asserted, I want to psychologise education.

As a result of painstaking investigations of the psychologists like Wundt, James, Ebbinghaus, Kohler, Pavlov, Hull, Thorndike, Cattel and Skinner in the field of education, educational psychology has been raised to the status of positive science today.

2.1.4 Education is a bi-polar process

Education involves two agents, the teacher and the taught. The teacher should not only be a master of his subject. He should be thoroughly acquainted with the mind of the pupil and the method of communicating his knowledge to the pupil. He should be able to use the principles of psychology to develop the pupil's powers of observation, imagination, thinking and reasoning. As Sir John Adams said, "The verb of teaching governs two accusatives, one the person and another the thing the teacher taught John Latin. The teacher must know John as well as Latin." In fact, the more a teacher knows experimental psychology, the more he knows how to teach.

2.2 Contribution of psychology to education

Nowadays the results of psychological investigation have brought about a great change in the field of education. Traditional concepts of attention, memory, intelligence, learning, heredity, individual difference, character and personality have undergone dramatic change.

In fact, psychology has greatly influenced the aim, method and subject matter of education.

2.2.1 The aim of education

Psychology cannot help us in determining the aim of education. The aim of education is determined by Philosophy. But whether a particular aim is attainable or not is determined by psychology. If the ideal of education is not based on psychology, then all efforts to attain that goal through teaching shall fail.

2.2.2 Method of teaching

Success of education depends greatly on the method of teaching adopted by the teacher. In the actual practice of teaching, psychology proves very useful.

2.2.3 Subject matter of education

Psychology plays an important role in the selection of subject matter of education. Subject matters chosen for education may be ideal but they may not match the pupil's taste, interest and ability. The knowledge of psychology can be of immense value in determining the interest and capability of students.

Researches in psychology have contributed to education in the following manner :

2.2.4 Individual differences

The importance of psychology to education has increased due to the recognition of individual differences. Pupils differ from one another in physical, mental and emotional aspects.

Formerly individual differences received scant recognition. The educator used to give all attention to normal child only. But nowadays education has become Paedo-Centric. So judging pupil's intelligence, ability and interest, the subject matter as well as teaching methods are to be determined. Therefore, the educator must have sound knowledge of Child Psychology.

2.2.5 Development of personality

After birth the child passes through different phases—infancy, childhood, adolescence and maturity. The needs of the child are different in these stages. The teacher must adapt his teaching process according to their age, interest and ability. Thus, for proper development of personality of his pupil, the teacher must have ample knowledge of Psychology.

2.2.6 Method of teaching

Most of the modern methods of teaching have been developed on the knowledge of psychology. Herbart's lesson planning, Dalton plan, Project method, etc. are based on activity principle and individual difference.

2.2.7 Measurement of intelligence

Psychology has helped us to understand the nature of intelligence as well as how to measure intelligence. Nowadays a number of reliable psychological techniques of measuring intellect have been invented.

2.2.8 Instinct and emotion

Psychologists have conducted a number of experiments on instincts and emotion. The results of these experiments have greatly influenced the science of education.

2.2.9 Attention-memory and forgetting

Psychology has given us many important informations about the nature of attention and memory. It has shed much light on the causes of forgetting. These knowledge are of immense value to the teacher in his task of instruction.

2.2.10 Problem of Maladjustment

Children who cannot adjust themselves to their environment are said to be maladjusted. Teachers often find it difficult to handle them. Psychology can be of immense value to the teacher who deals with maladjusted and delinquent children.

2.2.11 Evaluation

Instead of traditional examination, nowadays a large number of psychological tests on interest, attention, attitude, intelligence, aptitude and personality are being successfully used in education. A teacher should be adept in handling these psychological apparatus for successful teaching and evaluation.

2.2.12 School administration

In the organisation and school administration, psychological knowledge is indispensable. In the preparation of time-table and institutional plan, knowledge of psychology is also essential. Above all, the Headmaster cannot maintain proper discipline without the knowledge of psychology. Psychology tells him how the group life influences the individual and how the corporate life of an institution influences the character of the pupils.

Psychology has helped education both in the theoretical as well as in the practical field. It is true that psychology cannot help the science of education in determining its aim. But it can determine the means of attaining the aim of education. It can be of immense help to the teacher in the method of teaching, curriculum construction, school administration and evaluation. Psychology studies mental process such as instinct, interest, motive, attitude, needs, emotions and sentiment of the child. Therefore, it can help the educator in moulding the personality and character of the pupils.

2.3 Nature of Educational Psychology

Nowadays psychology plays an important part in formulating the theory of education and in improving the practice of teaching. In fact, the results of experimental psychology have greatly influenced our educational practice. Educational psychology is defined as the study of those facts and principles of psychology which help to explain and improve the process of education (Kolesnik). The most important function of educational psychology is to deal in teaching-learning process and matters connected with it.

Educational psychology is a branch of Applied Psychology. The investigations of Applied Psychology helped education to progress at a spectacular speed. But it should be kept in mind that education has not flourished only through the contributions of psychology. E.A. Peel has described Educational Psychology as the Science of Education. But educational psychology is a science in its own right and, though it draws most of its material from general psychology, it has its own stand-point and scope (H.R. Bhatia). It possesses systematic body of reliable facts based on psychological laws and principles. It is constantly in search of truth and employs scientific methods. The educationists have taken help from other sciences such as, sociology, biology, physics, physiology, anthropology, medical science and statistics to enrich the science of educational psychology. Educational psychology has invented without depending on other sciences some methods of study of its own.

With the help of these methods, educational psychology has immense advancement and our traditional ideas about teaching-learning process have undergone a total change.

Nowadays to enhance the professional competence of the teacher, various techniques of teaching have been invented. To accelerate the learning process teaching machine has been invented. For teaching languages well-equipped language laboratory has been set up in educational institution.

One of the important functions of educational psychology is to investigate the problem behaviour of the children. Delinquency—its cause and remedy and other maladjustments are the subjects of investigation in education. The most important modern trend in education is to investigate scientifically the different complex problems arising in the field of education. Statistics are being used increasingly in educational research nowadays.

2.4 Scope of Educational Psychology

All kinds of human behaviour fall within the scope of general psychology. But educational psychology is primarily associated with the investigation of teaching-learning process. In this sense, the scope of educational psychology is more limited and specific than psychology. The scope of educational psychology may briefly be discussed as follows :

2.4.1 Mental processes

The teacher determines his method of teaching according to the pupil's ability, aptitude and other mental qualities. So, intelligence, memory, attention, instinct, interest, thinking, reasoning, imagination, sentiment, emotion, motive, need, work and fatigue, backwardness, delinquency and other problem behaviours come under the purview of educational psychology.

2.4.2 Stages of development

One of the most important function of educational psychology is to observe the physical, mental and emotional development of the children in different stages of their growth. The process of language development of a child after birth and psychological needs and urges of the adolescents are closely studied by the educator.

2.4.3 Development of personality

The educator should have knowledge about the traits of personality so that he can classify his subjects according to the needs. Therefore, development of personality comes under the purview of educational psychology.

2.4.4 Individual differences

The learning competence of all children are not equal. Therefore, determination of curriculum and technique of instruction depend on the knowledge of individual difference. Moreover, the knowledge of individual difference as well as the knowledge about its impact on vocational guidance, is essential for the educator.

2.4.5 Learning process

Educational psychology discusses theories of learning, problems in learning process, fatigue in learning, devices of effective learning and if transfer of learning is possible and so on.

2.4.6 Evaluation and measurement

The teacher needs to evaluate pupil's performance. One of the most important functions of educational psychology is to find out reliable and objective methods of examination system.

2.4.7 Statistics

Nowadays statistics is being used in every field of science. Students' progress cannot be determined without the help of statistics. In fact, all kinds of educational researches involve statistics. So, the educator should have elementary knowledge of this science.

2.4.8 Guidance

One of the important functions of educational psychology is to give pupils proper educational guidance as well as vocational guidance for future career. Therefore, vocational and educational guidance come under the purview of educational psychology.

2.4.9 Mental Hygiene

The teacher plays an important role in promoting the mental health of the pupils. Mental health is the full and harmonious functioning of the whole personality. Therefore, mental hygiene is an important subject and the teacher should have proper knowledge of it. Therefore, this subject should have prominent place in educational psychology.

While discussing the scope of educational psychology we should bear in mind that every day the educator has to face a number of problems related to teaching-learning process. He has to solve these problems intelligently. Thus experiments and constant research work are going on to enrich the science of educational psychology. In fact, educational psychology—like other natural sciences is extremely dynamic. Every day its scope is changing and expanding.

Summary

Educational psychology applies the general principles of psychology to the practical needs of education. It gives a sound psychological foundation to education.

Educational psychology is considered as the Science of education. It has a systematic body of facts. Though it draws materials from general psychology, physiology, biology and other natural sciences it has its own methods and field of work.

The scope of educational psychology is limited to some extent, because it is concerned only with the study of behaviour of the learner and teaching-learning process.

References

1. Cronbach, L.J. : *Educational Psychology,* New York : American Book Co., 1948.
2. Gates, A.I. : *Educational Psychology,* New York : Macmillan, 1948.
3. Sorenson, H. : *Psychology in Education,* New York : McGraw Hill, 1964.

Questions and Assignments

1. What is the subject-matter of psychology? Consider the place of Psychology in education.
2. Discuss the nature and scope of educational psychology. Why is it included in every teacher educational course?
3. Why should an educator study psychology? Indicate the relation between psychology and education.
4. Discuss the place of psychology in education.
5. What is educational psychology? Indicate the place of psychology in education.
6. *The verb of teaching governs two accusatives—one the person and another the thing.* Bring out the pedagogical significance of the statement.
7. Define educational psychology. Wherein lies the importance of educational psychology in a teacher training course? Cite any one problem of class-teaching and show how the study of educational psychology could help you in the matter of solving that problem.

Chapter 3

Methods of Educational Psychology

Introduction : The method of investigation of all sciences passes through three phases—observation, experiment and inference. Psychology investigates human behaviour by introspection, observation and experiment.

Educational psychology takes the help of psychological methods to investigate the behaviour of the learners. Besides those methods, educational psychology has got certain methods of its own.

The various objective methods of educational psychology are : observation, experiment, case study, genetic method, clinical method and statistical method. Introspection is the subjective method developed by structuralists in psychology.

3.1 Observation

The method of observation has achieved special significance in the field of educational psychology. In this method, pupils are carefully observed in their natural setting. How the pupils behave in the class-room or how they react with classmates are watched carefully and secretly. They should not know that they are being observed by somebody, otherwise their behaviour may become artificial. This is why screened glasses are used to keep the naturalness of behaviour of the children, who are allowed to stay in a room and to act as they please. They are observed by the psychologists without being conscious of the fact of observation.

Drawbacks : However, observation may be vitiated by the following defects :

1. There is a tendency in the human mind to read its own thoughts and feelings into other minds. An honest man may think that all men are

honest while a dishonest person has a tendency to think that every person is dishonest.

Thus it is not very easy to understand the mind of the so-called savages, the mind of the abnormals or the mind of the animals.

However, the difficulty can be overcome by long experience, constructive imagination and the power of inference.

2. Often bias and prejudice affect our interpretation of others' behaviour. For example, the mother cannot easily find fault in the conduct of her son. This defect of observation can be overcome if psychologist's mind is free from bias and prejudice.
3. Hypocrisy of the person whose mind is observed may be a barrier to the correct interpretation of his behaviour. A person may always smile and yet be a rogue.

This defect may be remedied by close observation of his behaviour in different life situations.

In fact, to increase the reliability of observation the investigator should be properly trained. He should be able to avoid the influence of bias and expectation. He should isolate as far as possible the events to be observed. He should state his results in quantitative terms whenever possible and should subject his data to rigid statistical treatment.

3.2 Experiment

An experiment is observation under known or prearranged conditions.

Experimental method involves the cooperation of the experimenter and his subject. The experimenter gives a stimulus which evokes an experience in the subject. The experimenter observes the reaction of his subject and the subject introspects his mental processes.

The method of experiment has played an important part in developing educational science.

By this method span of attention, onset of fatigue, rate of learning, remembering and forgetting, personality and several other mental processes are measured. This is the most reliable of all the methods.

3.2.1 Examples of laboratory experiment

Pavlov's experiment on dogs, Thorndike's experiment on cats, Skinner's experiment on monkeys and pigeons, Kohler and Koffka's experiment on monkeys are well-known examples of laboratory experiment. Similarly, educational problems on transfer of training, intelligence, emotion, memory, learning, etc. can be conveniently studied in laboratory.

Drawbacks : However, the experimental method has some limitations. Firstly, it is very difficult to control conditions adequately. Secondly, experiments under artificial condition of observation may change the mental processes of the subject. Hence great caution has to be exercised while we use this method.

3.3 Group technique

Often two parallel groups of children are used in this method. One group is called controlled group and the other group is called experimental group. The two groups are matched in age and intelligence.

Suppose, we want to know the effect of giving award to the pupils in their learning process. The controlled group is not given any incentive while learning a lesson. Whereas the experimental group, while learning the same lesson, is given award. Now the results of the two groups are compared. It is found that the experimental group which got incentive does better than the controlled group. This shows that giving incentive is favourable to the process of learning.

3.4 The genetic method

By this method the genesis or growth and development of the mind of an organism is traced. For instance, we may trace the growth of the human mind through early childhood, later childhood, adolescence and adulthood. Similarly, the development of thinking or imagination may be traced through different stages of growth of the child. This method involves well-planned and adequately controlled observation. To obtain correct knowledge of physical, emotional and intellectual development of the child, this method is applied in child psychology.

3.5 Case history or Case study

This method is used particularly to determine the causes of abnormal behaviour and delinquency. A case history of such a child is prepared by collecting informations from parents, teachers and his associates. This is a valuable method which suggests remedial measures for the rehabilitation of maladjusted children. This study is supplemented by the use of interview, questionnaire and free association.

3.6 Clinical method

Now a days some methods of psychiatry are being applied successfully in educational psychology. Techniques like free association, projective tests and questionnaire are applied to analyse problem behaviour of the child. This method aims at seeking the maximum adjustment and welfare of the maladjusted individual.

Following informations about the individual are to be collected for case study :

1. Preliminary information such as the name of the individual, his father's name, address, religion, caste, date of birth, nature of problem behaviour, etc.
2. Past history containing the history of the development of the individual.
3. Socio-economic status of the family.
4. Physical and mental conditions of the individual.
5. Emotional problems, if any.
6. Interests and special aptitudes.
7. Educational achievements, etc.

3.7 Comparative method

Often complex behaviour of human beings cannot be properly controlled. Hence the educational psychologists sometimes conduct experiments on animals. From the results of such experiments they infer by comparison the behaviour of human beings.

3.8 Psycho-physical method

Psychological experiences such as, sensation of weight or loudness are measured by this method. Of the psychophysical methods, the methods of limits, the method of mean errors and the method of right and wrong responses are generally used.

3.9 Statistical method

At present the science of statistics is playing a significant role in educational psychology. In many cases the findings of educational researches are being expressed in statistical terms. As a result a new science called Educational Statistics has come into existence.

3.10 Introspection

It means to look within. That is, it means systematic examination of one's own thought. The method of introspection is not available to other natural sciences. Introspection is attending to one's own experience and, hence, subjective. However, it is the fundamental method of psychology. It has a unique advantage as our mental processes are always with us and can be introspected at any time and in any situation. Inspite of certain limitations this method is still used in educational experiments.

Drawbacks : Introspection is beset with difficulties of various sorts. Mental processes are vague and fleeting. They may vanish completely when we try to introspect them. Attempt at introspection is like seizing a top to catch its motion. That is, introspection is really retrospection of the past incidents.

Moreover, introspection implies a cleavage in the observing mind. The same mind cannot divide itself into two parts—the knower and the known, subject and object.

Furthermore, introspection cannot be an effective method in the case of illiterate, infant or insane.

In fact, the data collected by introspection is highly subjective and reliability of the data cannot be proved.

However, defects of introspection can be overcome if supplemented by observation and experiment. In fact, we cannot do away completely with this method. We can get knowledge of joy, sorrow, anger and other emotions only by this method. Therefore, it is said to be the fundamental method of general psychology as well as educational psychology.

3.11 Educational psychology and teacher education

Educational psychology is of immense value to the educator in the task of instruction. It is included in every teacher education course for the following reasons :

1. Educational psychology deals with pupils' instinct, attention, emotion, interest, need, memory, learning, intelligence, aptitudes and so on. Teachers should know the nature of these mental processes and how to develop them in children.
2. Educational psychology discusses the physical, mental and emotional development of the children in different stages of their growth. The educator must have knowledge of these developments at different stages and adapt his technique of teaching accordingly.
3. Educational psychology investigates how children learn, what are the conditions of learning, how maturation is related to learning and why motivation is required in learning. The knowledge of these help teacher in the actual practice of instruction.
4. The science of educational psychology studies the role of heredity and environment in the life of a student. The knowledge of the influence of heredity and environment can be of immense value to the teacher in the educational and vocational guidance of the pupils.

5. Because of individual differences, modern education lays stress on child-centric education. Educational psychology investigates the nature of individual differences amongst children and helps the teacher in determining the proper method of teaching and guidance.

6. Educational psychology helps the teacher immensely in his teaching profession. It helps the teacher in drawing lesson plan, in organising both curricular and co-curricular activities, in maintaining discipline and in evaluation and measurement with the help of various educational tests.

7. Educational psychology imparts correct insight to the teachers about abnormal behaviour of the pupils. The knowledge of educational psychology helps the teacher to understand the problem behaviour of a delinquent child and suggests remedies for delinquent behaviour.

In fact, in addition to his knowledge of subjects, the teacher must know the nature of the taught. To quote Sir John Adams, The master taught John Latin. The verb of teaching governs two accusatives, one the person and another the thing. The teacher must know John as well as Latin. To know John, the teacher must turn to the science of educational psychology. Rousseau said that a child is a book, which the teacher is to learn from page to page. He advised the teacher, *Teach the child rather than the subject*. Educational psychology tells the educator how to teach a child with maximum efficiency and greater effectiveness. Hence teaching of educational psychology forms part and parcel of teacher-training program. To become an efficient teacher he has to know :

1. **The nature and mental processes of the pupil.** The teacher should know the best method of learning and memorization. He should know about pupil's nature of thinking and reasoning. We should be capable of measuring his intelligence and interests. He should have knowledge about the effect of habit on attention and so on and so forth.

2. **Subjects to be taught.** It is expected that the teacher should have a thorough knowledge of the contents of the subjects to be taught so that questions asked by the pupils may be answered correctly and thoroughly explained.

3. **Techniques and methods of teaching.** Traditional methods are defective. The teacher should be acquainted with such modern techniques of teaching such as, Activity method, Heuristic method, Programmed instruction, Micro-teaching, etc. He should also know the modern techniques of Evaluation.

   Educational psychology gives the teacher an insight and competence in these fields for attaining its desired objectives.

Summary

Educational psychology uses various methods to collect data about the learner's behaviour. These methods have been briefly discussed above. As because educational psychology is an applied branch of general psychology there is hardly any difference in the methods of educational psychology and general psychology. These methods have their own strengths as well as weaknesses.

Educational psychology studies behaviour primarily by observations, experiment and introspection. The observation method is important because it gives certain clues to the mental condition of the organism. But one of the limitations of this method is that from the overt behaviour we cannot get completely reliable information regarding the mental processes of hypocrite.

The experimental method is the most scientific method of studying behaviour. It attempts to make educational psychology an exact science by quantitative measurement. But the experimental method has its own limitations. Artificial situation of experiments often interfere and modifies the normal flow of mental processes of the subject.

Introspection is an important method of educational psychology, because it provides a simple and readily available method for studying one's behaviour. But as our mental processes are constantly changing the data colleted by this method are not always reliable. Furthermore, this method cannot be applied to animals, insanes or children.

For teaching to be successful the teacher should have intimate knowledge of the child's nature, the subjects to be taught, as well as the techniques of teaching.

References

1. Boring, E.G. : *A History of Experimental Psychology,* New York : Appleton Century Crofts, 1950.
2. Lawrence, E. Cole and William E. Bruce : *Educational Psychology,* The Times of India Press, Bombay, 1965.
3. Stephens, J.M. : *Educational Psychology,* Paloalto, 1969.
4. Stones, E. : *The Psychology of Education,* Methuen : London, 1984.

Questions and Assignments

1. How can we best study the mind of the child? Point out the difficulties of the observation method.

2. Discuss the peculiarities and chief difficulties of introspection. Is the experimental method an improvement on the introspective method?
3. What are the chief methods of educational psychology? Discuss their comparative advantages.
4. What are main contributions of educational psychology to education?
5. Explain the genetic method in psychological investigation.
6. Select one class-room problem where you can make use of the knowledge of educational psychology to solve it.
7. Discuss how the study of educational psychology can help a teacher in the education of a child.
8. Write notes on :
   (a) Psycho-physical method;
   (b) Statistical method;
   (c) Case study;
   (d) Genetic method.
9. How will you handle the following problems :
   (a) An inattentive boy;
   (b) A truant;
   (c) A boy who steals;
   (d) A habitual late-comer.

Chapter 4

Concept and Measurement of Personality

4.1 What is personality?

The word personality is derived from the Latin word persona. Persona was meant a mask which the ancient Greek actors used to enact the role of characters they portrayed on the stage. However, at present the term is explained in various ways.

4.2 Some definitions

J.P. Guilford (1952) defined personality as an integrated pattern of traits. It is the synthetic unity of all personal traits. All the mental traits such as emotions, intelligence, impulse should be organised and integrated into a unity. A sound personality comprises mental traits closely related and integrated. McDougall regards integration of personality as integration of intellect and integration of character.

According to Munn, personality is the whole individual considered as a whole. Personality may be defined as the most characteristic integration of an individual's structures, modes of interests, attitude, behaviour, capacities, abilities and aptitudes.

Watson (1930) on the basis of his behavioural studies defined personality as the sum of activities that can be discovered by actual observations over a long enough period of time to give reliable information. It is the reaction mass as a whole. This definition reflects a narrow meaning of the term personality.

Cattell (1970), Eysenck (1971) and Woodworth (1954) have emphasised the organisational aspect of behaviour. According to Cattell, personality is that which permits a prediction of what a person will do in a given situation. Eysenck stresses the stability of personality. According to him, Personality is more or less stable and euduring organisation of a person's character, temperament, intellect and physique. Woodworth defined personality as the total quality of an individual's behaviour.

Morton Prince (1929) stresses the importance of both hereditary and environmental factors to explain the term personality. According to him, Personality is the sum total of all the biological innate dispositions, impulses, tendencies, appetites and instincts of the individual and the dispositions and tendencies acquired by experience. But personality cannot be described through merely summing up the various traits of a person. This definition of Morton Prince has ignored the integrated and organisational aspect of personality.

However, Mark Sherman (1979) and Hartman while describing personality put emphasis on integration.

Mark Sherman : Personality is the characteristic pattern of behaviours, cognitions and emotions which may be experienced by the individual and/or manifest to others.

Harman : Personality is integrated organisation of all the pervasive characteristics of an individual as it manifests itself in focal distinctiveness to others.

Fredenburgh in his book, the Psychology of Personality and Adjustment defines personality as a stable system of complex characteristics by which the life pattern of the individual may be identified. Thus some psychologists while describing personality, stresses the social qualities of a person and adjustment to his environment. Again, while some stresses the importance of summative approach, the others on integrative approach. Thus we see that the concept of personality is difficult to explain.

However, Allport (1948) gives a definition which is comprehensive and includes all aspects of an individual's personality.

Allport (1948) : Personality is the dynamic organisation within the individual of those psychophysical systems that determine his unique adjustment to his environment.

This definition includes all conative, cognitive and affective behaviour patterns of an individual. Instead of a particular behaviour it stresses the organisation of behaviour that helps an individual to properly adjust to his environment. Allport's definition is significant because it is a synthesis of all definitions of personality.

4.3 Characteristics of personality

Some of the distinguishing features of personality are :

1. Personality is more than a summation of several traits. It is an organisation of psychological system.
2. Personality is more or less stable. But, with the change of environment, one's personality may undergo certain changes.
3. Acquisition of knowledge and experiences help growth of personality.
4. Personality is the joint product of heredity and environment.
5. The personality of an individual can be measured.

4.4 Theories of personality

Psychologists have developed several theories of personality, three of which may be discussed here :

1. Trait theory
2. Type theory and
3. Psychoanalytic theory.

4.4.1 Trait theory

Guilford defines personality as an integrated pattern of traits. According to him an individual is a bundle of traits. He defines trait as any common, relatively enduring way in which one person can differ from one another. Trait is relatively stable and consistent behaviour pattern of an individual.

Some characteristics of traits :

1. Traits are relatively stable. They are however, not entirely static in nature.
2. Traits are bipolar, for example, simplicity-sophistication, dominance-submission.
3. Certain traits are universal, for instance, nervousness, inferiority, etc.
4. Traits are learned. Traits like inferiority and nervousness are products of interaction with social environment.

Allport (1967), Cattell (1973), Guilford (1952) and Eysenck have tried to explore trait dimensions.

4.4.2 Allport's classification

Allport classified traits into three categories : 1. Cardinal traits; 2. Central traits and 3. Secondary traits.

Cardinal traits : These are dominant traits and limited in number. They pervade the whole life of an individual. For instance, if a person has simplicity as a cardinal trait, he will be simple in all thoughts and actions in every situation of life.

Central traits : These traits are generalised dispositions which may be used to describe a person, e.g., cooperation, agreeableness, honesty, etc.

Secondary traits : These traits are less dominant than central or cardinal traits. They are specific narrow traits and not integral parts of one's personality.

According to Allport personality is the dynamic organisation of all the traits that an individual possesses. To him traits have a real and vital existence.

To explain behaviour Allport gave a new dimension taking traits as the basic units of behaviour. However, his classification of traits into cardinal, central and secondary is greatly confusing.

4.4.3 Cattell's classification

Cattell, through factor analysis, found 16 basic traits :

1. Cyclothyma—*Schizothyma.*
2. General Intelligence—*Mental defects.*
3. Emotional stability—*Neuroticism.*
4. Dominance—*Submission.*
5. Surgency—*De surgency.*
6. Adventurism—*Introversion.*
7. Positive character—*Immature character.*
8. Emotional sensitivity—*Maturity.*
9. Paranoid schizothyma—*Trustful accessibility.*
10. Sophistication—*Simplicity.*
11. Suspiciousness—*Trustfulness.*
12. Self-sufficiency—*Lack of resolution.*
13. Radicalism—*Conservatism.*
14. Bohemianism—*Practical concernedness.*
15. Relaxed—*Tense.*
16. Controlled—*Uncontrolled.*

He classified traits into four categories :

1. **Common traits :** These traits are widely distributed in general population, e.g., honesty, cooperation and aggression.
2. **Unique traits :** These traits are unique to a person, e.g., emotional reactions, temperamental traits.
3. **Surface traits :** These traits are known from overt behaviour, e.g., curiosity, tactfulness.
4. **Source traits :** These are the underlying structures or sources which determine the behaviour of an individual, e.g., submission and dominance.

Cattell emphasised the importance of both hereditary and environmental factors in the development of individual traits. He made use of his 16 (sixteen) factors in the measurement of personality by devising a personality inventory.

4.4.4 Guilford's classification

According to Guilford a trait is any common, relatively enduring way in which one person can differ from another. By common way he meant a way of differing found among people at large and not an isolated peculiarity of one person only.

By factor analysis Guilford found 13 (thirteen) traits :

1. Social introversion.
2. Thinking introversion.
3. Depression.
4. Cycloid Tendency.
5. Rhathymia.
6. General activity.
7. Ascendance—*Submission.*
8. Masculinity—*Femineity.*
9. Inferiority.
10. Nervousness.
11. Objectivity.
12. Cooperation.
13. Agreeableness.

4.4.5 Eysenck's classification

Eysenck, a British psychologist, tried to synthesise the type and trait approaches. Like Cattell he adopted factor analysis technique and grouped traits into definite personality types. Eysenck found three basic dimensions of personality : 1. Introversion—*Extroversion;* 2. Normality—*Neuroticism* and 3. Psychoticism—*Realism.*

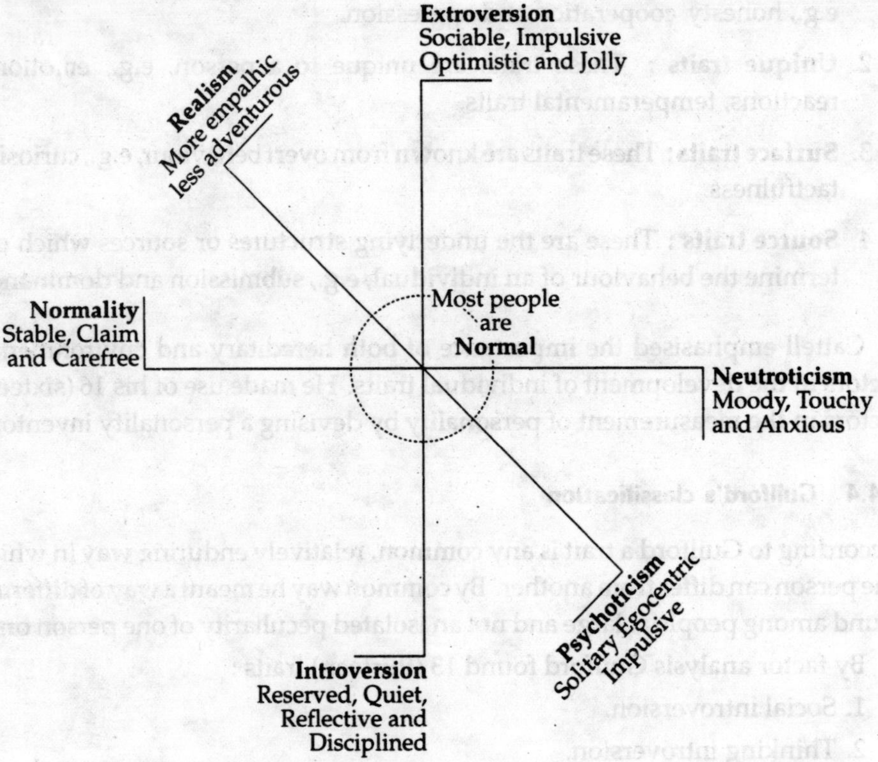

Fig. 4.1

Eysenck thought that, people are ambivert. Purely introvert or purely extrovert people are very rare. He, therefore, used a dimension or a scale.

Introversion Extroversion

1. On one end includes people who are highly extrovert. They are sociable, impulsive, optimistic and jolly. The other end of the dimension includes people who are quiet, introspective, reserved and disciplined.
2. Similarly at one end of the second dimension normality-neuroticism, are the persons who are stable, calm and carefree. At the other end are the people who are moody, touchy and anxious.
3. On one end of the third dimension psychoticism-realism are those people who are unrealistic, solitary, insensitive, egocentric, impulsive, etc., while the other end of the dimension includes people who are less adventurous and bold. They can concentrate on tasks well, has good memory and can communicate well.

Eysenck tried to strike a synthesis between type and traits approach. He showed through factor analysis that a number of traits may be grouped together to form a definite personality type. For example, how a definite type of personality (Introversion) is formed out of organisation of several traits is shown in the following illustration :

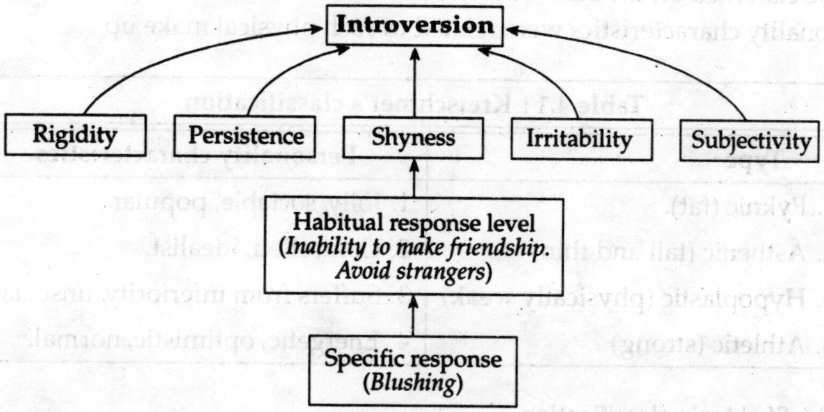

Fig. 4.2

In the opinion of Eysenck there are four levels of behaviour—at the lowest level is a specific response, say blushing. In the second level, some habitual responses are formed, for example, the individual is unable to make friendship or hesitant to talk to strangers. At the third level, the habitual responses give birth to a group of traits. In the fourth level, these traits are organised to give birth to a type called as introversion.

Criticism : Trait theory of personality has been criticised on the ground that psychologists do not agree as regards the number and use of the terms. Moreover, trait is not static, as individual is constantly changing through interaction with the environment and there is no valid and reliable tool for measuring traits. The classification of personality into two or three or any other number of traits are entirely arbitrary matter done merely for convenience in discussion (Gates).

4.5 Type theory

From ancient times philosophers and psychologists had attempted to classify human beings into clearly defined categories called types. As early as 1876 Lombroso demonstrated that criminals are by birth a distinct type and this type can be recognised by certain specific physical traits, such as a symmetrical cranium, protruding ears, sparse beard, broad cheekbones and so on. However, these studies of the relation of physique to human behaviour physiognomy have been attacked on the ground that they do not represent a normal sample of the total population.

4.5.1 Kretschmer's classification (Constitutional type)

According to the German psychiatrist earnest Kretschmer, all human beings can be classified on the basis of physical constitution. He thought that definite personality characteristics were related to each physical make up :

Table 4.1 : Kretschmer's classification

Type	Personality characteristics
1. Pyknic (fat).	1. Jolly, sociable, popular.
2. Asthenic (tall and thin)	2. Controlled, idealist.
3. Hypoplastic (physically weak)	3. Suffers from inferiority, unsocial.
4. Athletic (strong)	4. Energetic, optimistic, normal.

4.5.2 Sheldon's classification

Like Kretschmer, Sheldon recently classified human beings into types according to their physical structure and their corresponding temperamental characteristics:

Table 4.2 : Sheldon's classification

Physical characteristics	Temperament
1. Ectomorph (straight and slender).	1. Weak, fearful, introvert, restrained, pessimistic.
2. Mesomorph (strong and muscular)	2. Energetic, love risk and adventure.
3. Endomorph (Fat, soft and round)	3. Extrovert, affectionate, love physical comfort, easy going.

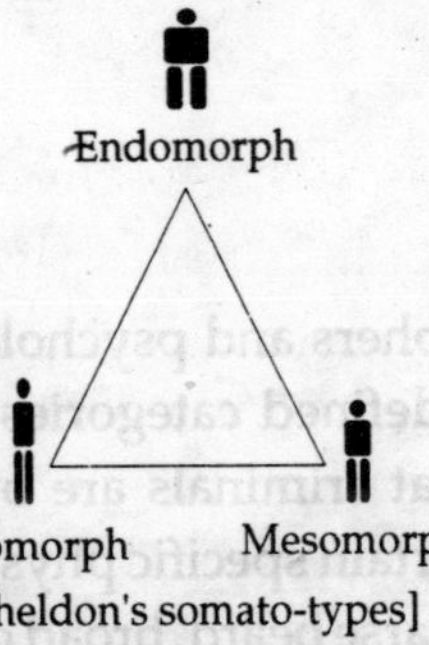

[Sheldon's somato-types]

Fig. 4.3

Criticism : Those classifications on the basis of physical structure cannot be accepted because of low correlation between the structure of the body and mental qualities. We cannot predict personality characteristics and behaviour of a person from somatotype ratings.

4.6 Psychoanalytic theory

The psychoanalytic theory was advocated by Sigmund Freud (1856–1939). C.G. Jung (1875–1961) was a close associate of Freud. He rejected Libido or sex as the only driving force in life and develop analytical psychology. Adler, who was a member of Freudian group, developed a system of thought which is known as individual-psychology. Adler opposed Freud's psychoanalytic approach of personality.

4.6.1 Freud's classification

Freud—on the basis of his theory of libidinal development, identified three types of personality : (i) Oral-erotic; (ii) Anal-erotic and (iii) Genital type.

4.6.2 Oral-Erotic type

At the oral stage of sex development, the child shows excessive pleasures associated with sucking, biting and other activities in infancy. Fixation at the oral stage results in two types of personality in adult life :

1. **Oral active type :** This type of person is pessimistic and jealous.
2. **Oral passive type :** This type of person is optimistic and immature.

4.6.3 Anal-erotic type

At the anal stage of sex development, the child obtains satisfaction through anal activities. Fixation at the anal stage results in two types of personality in later life :

1. **Sadistic type :** This type of person obtains pleasure by oppressing others.
2. **Passive type :** This type of person obtains pleasure from self-torturing.

4.6.4 Genital type

In the phallic stage, the child obtains satisfaction from touching, rubbing and exhibiting genital organ. This type of person shows exhibitionism and boasting.

4.7 Jung's classification

Jung classified human beings into two distinct types : (1) Introvert and (2) Extrovert.

1. **Introvert :** The introverts are people whose interests are turned inward upon themselves. Introvert people are shy, avoid people, like to be alone and are very much self-centered. Philosophers and scientists may be included in this category.

2. **Extrovert :** The libido of such people is oriented towards the external world. They are social and friendly. Politicians, salesmen and social workers may be termed as extroverts.

But in reality we do not find people belonging to such extreme types. In fact, they are ambivert or bi-vert. They can change and adjust their behaviour according to new situations.

Jung recognises four other functional types of personality : (1) Sensing type, (2) Intuitive type, (3) Feeling type and (4) Thinking type.

1. The sensing type depends on the evidence of their senses for their actions without exercising their reason upon it.

2. The intuitive type is also dominated by sense-perception, but he can discover the causes of the facts perceived and envisage what can be made of a situation. He is also irrational like the sensing type.

3. The feeling type is dominated by emotions. They have definite sentiments of right and wrong and they are governed by them in their behaviour.

4. The thinking type is dominated by reason and logic. This type initiates new ways of thought. Einstein, Newton, etc. be long to this type.

4.8 Adler's individual approach

According to Adler, human beings cannot be divided into distinct types. Every person is unique in himself. People strive towards gaining superiority and power. Different people have different styles of life. If we want to understand the nature of personality of a person, we have to study his specific life style.

Criticism of the type approach : Most theories of types have been criticised on the following grounds :

1. The idea of dividing human beings into distinct categories goes against the general laws of individual difference.

2. Types are discontinuous and non-measurable.

If we rate several hundred persons on a personality trait, we will find it to follow the law of normal distribution as shown in the Fig. 4.4.

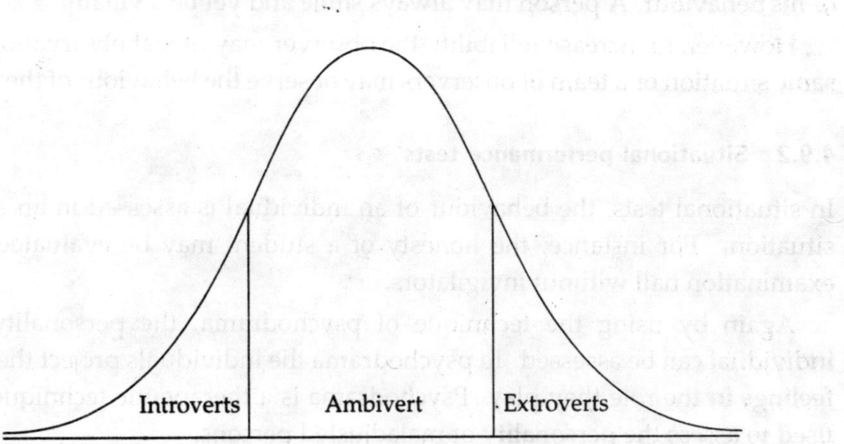

Fig. 4.4 According to the law of normal distribution.

According to type theory.

4.9 Assessment of personality

There are various methods for assessment of personality. Phrenology, physiognomy, palmistry and astrology are some of the pseudo-scientific methods which have been used to assess the personality of people since time immemorial. But these methods of personality assessment are not at all reliable. So they have been discarded and more reliable and scientific methods have been developed by psychologists. Some of the important methods may be discussed below :

4.9.1 Observation

Observation is the objective method of studying the behaviour of a person. There are two processes of observation. In open observation, the observer does not hide himself from the subject and in second method, he observes the behaviour of his subject from behind a screen. The data which are obtained from observation can be carefully analysed, classified and interpreted.

However, observation may be vitiated by certain defects. First, there is a tendency in the human mind to read its own thoughts, feelings and tendencies into other minds.

Secondly, bias and prejudice may vitiate our observation and affect our interpretation of others' behaviour. We do not usually find fault with our friends, but we always find fault with our enemies. Thirdly, hypocrisy of the person whose behaviour is observed, is a barrier to the correct interpretation of his behaviour. A person may always smile and yet be a villain.

However, to increase reliability the observer may repeat observation in the same situation or a team of observers may observe the behaviour of the subject.

4.9.2 Situational performance tests

In situational tests, the behaviour of an individual is assessed in an artificial situation. For instance, the honesty of a student may be evaluated in the examination hall without invigilators.

Again by using the technique of psychodrama, the personality of an individual can be assessed. In psychodrama the individuals project their inner feelings in the role they play. Psychodrama is a therapeutic technique and is used to assess the personality of maladjusted persons.

However, it is difficult to use situational test technique because it needs trained psychologists to observe and interpret behaviour of the subjects.

4.9.3 Interview

Interview is an important technique to elicit personal information from the subject in face-to-face contacts. On the basis of interview results most of the selections for different jobs and admission in various courses are made.

Interviews are of two types : Unstructured and structured. In unstructured interview, the interviewer is free to ask the candidate any question on any subject relevant to the situation. The primary condition of this type of interview is that a perfect rapport is to be established with the subjects so that they can freely express their feelings.

To reduce the unreliability and bias of the interviewer, structured interview technique has been evolved in recent years. In structured interview a systematic predetermined approach is adopted and all the subjects are uniformly asked similar questions. Usually a list of questions is prepared before-hand and all the subjects are to answer these pre-planned questions.

The limitations of the interview-method are : (a) it needs a well-trained competent interviewer, (b) it is not free from the subjective bias of the interviewer, (c) a hypocrat may hoodwink the interviewer by concealing his real thoughts and feelings. His response to questions may not tally with his intention.

4.9.4 The questionnaire method

This method is used to assess personality traits. The individual is asked a large number of crucial questions, which he has to answer by saying yes or no.

The following questions bring out extroversion or introversion of personality :

1. Do you like to talk before a group of people? Yes/No.
2. Are you ordinarily a carefree individual? Yes/No.
3. Are you inclined to rush from one activity to another without pausing for rest? Yes/No.
4. Are you at home among strangers? Yes/No.
5. Do you make friends easily? Yes/No.
6. Are you inclined to keep in the background on social occasions? Yes/No.
7. Do you worry over what people think of you? Yes/No.
8. Are you usually concerned about the future? Yes/No.
9. Do you suffer from a feeling of inferiority? Yes/No.
10. Are your feelings easily hurt? Yes/No.

The yes response to the first five of these questions is supposed to be the characteristics of the extrovert, while the last five indicate those of introvert. The score may simply be the number of answers yes or no.

This method has certain drawbacks. It lacks validity i.e., the test does not measure what they are supposed to measure. Again, the subject can slant his answers in either direction he wishes. Thus questionnaires are not good measure of personality.

4.9.5 Personality inventory

The questionnaire may be used for collecting informations not connected specifically with personality traits. But personality inventory is specifically developed to seek answers about the person and his personality.

R.S. Woodworth developed the first inventory consisting of 116 questions about common physical and mental traits.

Bernreuter devised personality inventory consisting of a set of items describing various aspects of introversion—Minnesota Multiphasic Personality Inventory (MMPI).

The Minnesota Multiphasic Personality Inventory (1943) was developed by J.C. Mckinby and S.R. Hathaway. The items of MMPI cover the total personality. The inventory consists of 550 items. Some of the items are as follows : My soul sometimes leaves my body.

I have never been in love with any one. I like to talk about sex.

There is something wrong with my sex organs etc.

The items are printed on separate cards. After reading the questions, the subject responds, yes, no or doubtful.

This inventory was devised to detect pathological cases.

4.9.6 Rating Scales

Rating scales are devised to evaluate a single trait. Teachers may use rating scales to classify their students on a particular trait like persistence, leadership or cooperation.

To make rating scales reliable three things are necessary :

1. The traits to be evaluated should be defined clearly.
2. The degree of possession of the trait has to be shown on a scale.
3. Judges for rating should be matured and experienced.

The divisions of the scale are indicated by numbers 1–3, 1–5 or 1–7, comprising a three-point, five-point or seven-point scale, respectively. The five point scale is of the following type :

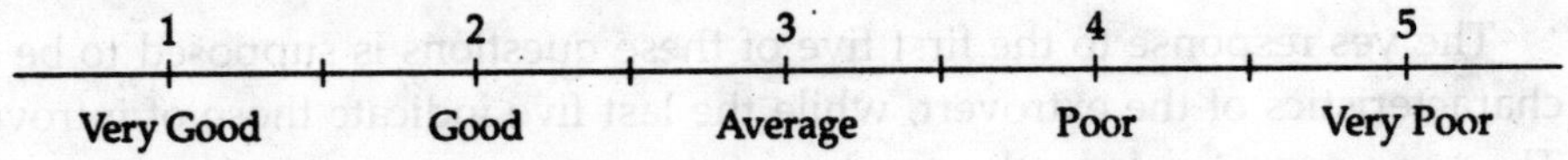

Fig. 4.5

Instruction : Place a check mark after the category that most closely describes the subject's behaviour.

The judges who rate the individuals, e.g., on persistence or leadership give scores ranging from 1–5 according to the degree of persistence or leadership they possess.

4.9.7 Some common errors in rating

Rating techniques suffer from some common errors :

The error of caution

Most raters place other people nearer the middle of the scale than giving very high or very low ratings.

The error of leniency

Most raters rate their friends in the direction of the favourable ends of the scales. They tend to overestimate the good qualities of their acquaintances and to underestimate their poor ones.

In case of self-ratings the error of leniency is most apparent.

The halo effect

The general impression about a person influences a judge who rates him on any particular trait. If the general impression of the judge is favourable, the person is rated high. The person is rated low if the general impression is low. Thus, ratings are distorted according to the level of the general impression of the judge.

To avoid these errors, the rating work should be assigned to a number of judges, who are matured and experienced. Final assessment is done by pooling the ratings of individual judges.

4.9.8 Case history

From the case history of an individual we can have some idea of his personality. The case history includes a brief account of a person's family and neighbourhood, his behaviour in childhood, his school experiences, his physical and mental development, etc. Previously, this method was used in the treatment of mental diseases. At present, it is, however, used in determining personality of a normal person.

4.9.9 Psycho-analysis

Free association and dream analysis: A psychoanalyst measures depth factors in personality by free association and analysis of a subject's dream. He asks his patient to recline comfortably on a sofa and directs his patient to talk out his troubles freely. Many such sittings may reveal sufficient factors of his personality.

The patient may relate his recurrent dreams. The psychoanalyst analyses them and brings out the motives that underlie them. Thus a correct knowledge of the unconscious motives of his personality is obtained.

4.9.10 Projective tests

The tests so far discussed evaluate the overt conscious behaviour of a person. But, projective tests attempt to reveal a person's unconscious repressed wishes. Frank (1939) defines projective technique as a kind of X-ray into those covert aspects of personality which subjects either cannot or will not openly reveal.

Characteristics of projective techniques : Projective tests generally have the following characteristics :

1. Projective tests attempt to study the totality of behaviour of a person. They try to evaluate the total personality of an individual rather than in fragments.

2. These tests use ambiguous material. The subject is free to interpret the test material in his own way revealing the unconscious phase of his mental life. The subject projects his inner thought in the test situations.
3. The purpose of the projective tests remain disguised. So the subject reacts freely without hiding his real feelings.

4.9.11 Some important projective tests

Some of the important projective tests are :

1. The word association test.
2. Sentence completion test.
3. Rorschach ink blot test.
4. Thematic apperception test (TAT).
5. Children's apperception test (CAT).
6. Psychodrama.
7. Socio drama.
8. Draw-a-man test.
9. Doll play.

Word association test

This test consists of a list of several unrelated words. The subject is asked a series of words from the list one by one. He is instructed to say immedrately the first word that comes to his mind.

The response to each word and the reaction time are noted. The reaction time and the nature of the response give clues for evaluating the individual's personality.

Jung for the first time devised such tests. Later on, Kent and Rosanoff developed similar type of tests and applied it in the treatment of mental diseases.

Sentence completion test

These tests comprise a list of incomplete sentences and the subject is directed to complete the sentences as quickly as possible without second thought. For instance, following incomplete sentences may be given :

I am easily disturbed by ...

My aim is ...

I am concerned about ...

I want to sit in the class with ...

The sentence completion tests are thought to be better than the **word association** tests, because the subject is free to react in more than one word. As a result, wider area of personality of the individual may be revealed.

The Rorschach Ink Blot test

Of the projective tests the best known is the Rorschach ink blot test. Herman Rorschach (1921), a Swiss psychiatrist, devised this ink blot test. In this test an individual projects himself into the test situation and reveals certain depth factors in his personality.

The subject is shown a series of 10 (ten) standardised bilaterally symmetrical ink blots one at a time. Five of the blots are black and white and five are multi-coloured. These ink blots are highly ambiguous and do not carry any specific meaning.

Fig. 4.6 An inkblot of the type used in the Rorschach test.

The subject is allowed to look at the ink blot from different angles. Different persons see different things in these ink blots. Some concentrate on the whole ink blot; other concentrate on its parts. Some see animals; some see plants; other see human beings. Some responses are prompted more by the colours and some more by the forms. Some tend to see objects as if moving. All these tendencies are presumed to have meaning concerning the examinee's personality.

Generally the interpretations of a Rorschach test are expressed in descriptive prose. It can be used individually as well as collectively of a group of individuals.

The Rorschach test stimulates the association of ideas in the personality of an individual. An individual gives free expression to his reaction on seeing these ink blots. Hence, these ambiguous ink blots are relatively free from cultural influences. However, it is obvious that the test demands a lot of training and skill in scoring and interpretation on the part of the examiner.

Validity and reliability of the test : According to the clinical psychologists the validity of the Rorschach test is very high. But, according to some, interpretation of Rorshach documents varies widely amongst the scorers. Moreover, the attitude and the personality of the tester may influence the responses of the subject. However, the clinicians who are experts in test administration and interpretation claim the Rorschach Test highly useful in determining the personality of mental patients.

Thematic apperception test (TAT)

This test (TAT) was devised by Murray and Morgan (1935). The test material comprises thirty pictures of human figures in some situations with definite outlines, but ambiguous enough to admit of a variety of interpretations. Ten of these pictures are meant for males, ten for females and ten are common to both sexes. Thus, the maximum number of pictures used on any one subject is twenty.

Fig. 4.7 A sample picture from TAT.

The pictures are presented one at a time. The subject is told to make up a story for each of the pictures presented to him and describe : (a) What is going on in the picture, (b) What has led to this scene and (c) What would likely happen in such a situation.

The subject identifies with one of the figures and indulges in a fantasy and interprets the pictures according to his dominant motives, complexes, sex-urge, frustrations, aspirations and outlook on life. Thus the interpretations given by the subject reveal his personality problems.

Children's apperception test (CAT)

Dr Leopold Bellak devised children's apperception test (CAT) for children between three and ten years of age.

This test consists of ten cards depicting animals in different life situations. Children are interested in animals and they can easily identify themselves with animal figures in the card. Children project their feelings and experiences on the animals of the card. The cards are shown one by one and the subject is asked to make up stories out of them.

The tester, while interpreting the stories reproduced by the subject, should note emotions of the child depicted in relation to parental figures, such as hatred, respect, aggression, fear, etc. He should note with whom in the family has the child identified himself, which figures has the child ignored, what kind of punishment has been prescribed and to whom. Besides these, overall contents of the stories, the reactions of the subject at the time of making up the story are also to be carefully noted.

Psychodrama

Psychodrama is one of the useful methods used in the assessment of personality. This method is generally used to determine the personality of maladjusted individuals.

In psychodrama individuals are asked to play certain roles in a particular situation. The observer carefully notes their behaviour. Those who participate in the drama project unknowingly their feelings and unconscious mental conflicts in the role they play.

Draw a man test

In this test the individual is asked to draw a human figure. The tester from the nature of the drawing can determine his inner feelings and mental conflicts, which he unconsciously project in the drawing. Good enough testers used this method to determine the intelligence of children.

Doll play

Psychologists use play therapy to uncover the unconscious wishes of maladjusted children. The child is asked to play with certain dolls. The nature of play with the dolls is carefully observed by a trained person. For instance, the child takes one of the dolls and strikes it. The doll symbolises his brother who deserves this treatment because the child does not like him. This reveals sibling rivalry and the mental conflicts within the child.

Weakness of personality tests

There are certain weaknesses of personality testing.

1. Psychologists do not agree upon the definitions of different traits. Unless we find a definite meaning of a trait, the effort to measure it becomes fruitless.

2. Most of the personality tests are superficial and they do not assess the depth of behaviour.
3. The personality traits are not stable. They change with age and vary from one situation to another. One may act as an introvert in one situation, he may act as extrovert in some other situation. Thus it becomes difficult to predict the behaviour of an individual on the basis of the results of personality tests.
4. Self-report inventories may be easily faked. The subject may hide his real motive while answering the questionnaire. Obviously, this vitiates the assessment of his personality.

4.10 Personality and the Endocrine system

The personality of an individual is to a great extent influenced by the hormones secreted by the ductless glands or endocrines. The adrenal glands, the thyroid glands, the pituitary gland, and the sex glands or gonads are the ductless glands.

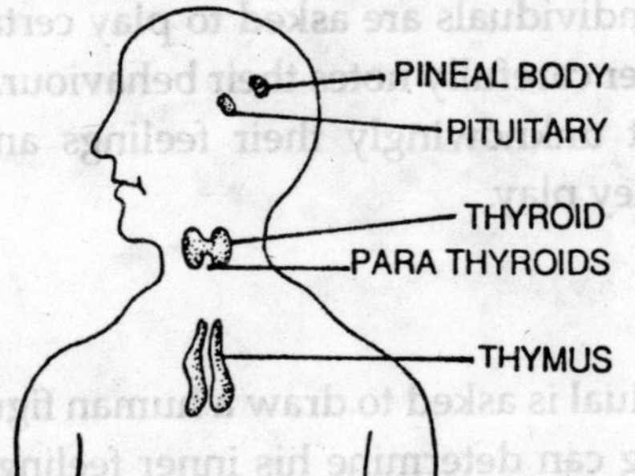

Fig. 4.8 The Endocrine Glands.

4.10.1 The adrenal gland

The adrenal gland is situated on top of the kidney—one on either side. It has two parts, the cortex and the medulla. The cortex produces the hormone called cortin. The medulla produces the hormone called adrenalin.

Cortin deficiency produces weakness, aversion to activity and loss of sex interest. Its overactivity produces increased virility, alertness and a feeling of general well-being.

Deficient secretion of adrenalin produces fatigability of muscles and dejected moods. Excessive secretion of adrenalin produces excessive muscular activity. With an overactive adrenal medulla, an individual becomes active, dynamic and optimistic.

4.10.2 The thyroid gland

The thyroid gland lies at the base of the neck in front of the wind pipe.

It secretes thyroxine, the main constituent of which is iodine. If the gland is defective, growth is stunted and intelligence is impaired with the result of slowness of thinking, memory, movement and depression. With an overactive thyroid, there is an overactive individual. He rarely takes rest, sleeps little, has high blood pressure and he loses weight.

4.10.3 The parathyroid glands

Marked changes in behaviour may occur when there is a deficiency of parathyroid hormone. Deficient parathyroid hormone produces muscular tenseness and quick, intense response to stimuli.

Excessive parathyroid hormone produces lassitude and lack of interest.

4.10.4 The pituitary gland

It is attached to the under side of the brain. It is called the master gland because its hormones affect most of the other glands. It has an anterior lobe and a posterior lobe.

The anterior part regulates the growth of bones and muscles and stimulates the growth of sexual functions. An individual with an underactive anterior pituitary may become a dwarf. Over activity of the anterior pituitary gland during childhood produces a giant.

When posterior pituitary is underactive, obesity may result. Mental consequences are submissiveness and a lack of sex interest. While when overactive, there are tendencies in the opposite direction.

4.10.5 The gonads or sex glands

The gonads are vitally connected with sex emotions. The lack of gonadal hormones tends to make a person of either sex neutral or devoid of sex characteristics.

Thus, glands determine traits of behaviour to a great extent. Often problem children are seen to misbehave because of disturbances of glandular function. Treatment with glandular extracts in many cases has resulted in remarkable improvement in behaviour.

4.11 Determinants of personality

The personality of an individual is conditioned by the two important factors : heredity and environment.

Heredity is of two types : (1) biological heredity and (2) social heredity or environment.

4.11.1 Physique and personality

In appearance, in bodily constitution, in stature, the son/daughter usually resembles his/her parents. Physique is an important factor of personality. We know that phrenology and physiognomy attempted to read personality traits from the individual's physical make-up.

The endocrine glands hold the key to personality. These glands produce differences in bodily build, as well as in behaviour traits. Glands determine personality traits. Glandular make-up is hereditary.

4.11.2 Family and personality

The family exerts great influence upon the personality traits of the child. The parents punish or reward him in hundreds of ways to mould the child's character in desired direction.

The number of siblings he has, his position among them, and the nature of their personalities, all contribute to his development. He seems to inherit their likes and dislikes, habits of thought and action, as well as character.

It is found that children coming from homes where good pattern of morality dominates are better adjusted and more satisfactorily related to their parents than the average adolescents of the group. On the other hand, those coming from homes showing family discord are poorly adjusted in their social environment. Quarreling parents and divorced parents produce situations in which the child often develop feelings of insecurity. Also unwanted child is likely to develop inferiority and feelings of insecurity.

4.11.3 Economic factor and personality

Poverty at home influences the development of personality. Communities, where there is poverty, are unfavourable for the development of desirable personality traits. It is found that children from poor home are more prone than normal children to inferiority feelings, nervousness, shyness, delinquency and lack of social initiative.

4.11.4 Social institutions and personality

School is a social institution where a significant part of a child's life is spent. Here the classmates and the teachers contribute their share in shaping personality of the child. The results of experiment conducted by Lewin, Lippit and White (1939) show that autocratic atmosphere in school tends to create aggression and hostility, whereas democratic set-up leads to constructive, thoughtful and cooperative behaviour. Thus, in developing good personality traits amongst children, democratic approach in all matters is better than autocratic approach.

The nature of curriculum and the present evaluation system in Indian schools are not conducive to the formation of healthy personality traits. Failure in examination results in frustration, suicide and other maladies.

Besides schools there are clubs and organised associations. As the child advances in age, he becomes the member of such institutions. These associations shape the personality of the child through games and other social activities. Thus the personality of the child grows out of the social fabric in which he lives.

4.11.5 Social roles

At different stages of life an individual has to play different roles such as son, student, brother, husband, officer, etc. Having been assigned to his role, he is encouraged to act the part and thus habitual traits are formed.

4.11.6 Culture and personality

Culture shapes the personality of an individual. E.B. Tyler defined culture as that complex whole which includes knowledge, beliefs, morals, law, custom and many other capabilities and habits acquired by man as a member of society. The personality of the individuals is moulded by the traditions, rituals, beliefs, customs of the country.

Thus considering the importance of social heritage and social forces—some may claim that a personality is entirely a product of its social environment. However, in reality, the individual is a product of his heredity and his environment.

Summary

Personality is the total quality of an individual's behaviour. It has been defined in many ways. Guilford defines personality as an integrated patterns of traits. Allport, instead of a particular behaviour, stresses the organisation of behaviour that helps an individual to adjust to his environment. Allport's definition is a synthesis of all definitions of personality.

There are various theories of personality of which trait theory, type theory and psychoanalytic theory are important. Allport, Cattel, Guilford, Eysenck and others tried to classify traits into different categories. However, some psychologists tried to classify human beings into clearly defined categories called *types*. Kretschmer and Sheldon classified human beings on the basis of physical constitution.

Freud on the basis of his theory of libidinal development—identified three types of personality : (a) Oral-erotic, (b) Anal-erotic and (c) Genital type. Jung classified human beings into two distinct types : (a) Introvert and (b) Extrovert. But we do not find people belonging to such extreme types. People are, in fact, ambivert. According to Adler human beings cannot be divided into distinct type. According to him if we want to understand the nature of personality of a person, we have to study his specific life-style.

There are various techniques of assessment of personality :

(a) Observation.

(b) Situational performance test.

(c) Interview.

(d) Rating scales.

(e) Case history.

(f) Psycho-analytic technique—free association and dream analysis.

(g) Projective tests, such as Rorschach ink blot test, Thematic apperception test (TAT), Children's apperception test (CAT), Psychodrama, etc.

The personality of an individual is greatly influenced by the hormones secreted by the endocrine glands.

For instance if the thyroid gland is defective physical growth is stunted and intelligence is impaired. Deficient secretion of adrenalin produces fatigability of muscles and dejected moods. With an overactive adrenal medulla, an individual becomes active, dynamic and optimistic. The pituitary or the master gland regulates the growth of bones and muscles and stimulates the growth of sexual functions.

The personality of an individual is conditioned by heredity as well as environment. The individual is a product of his heredity and his environment.

References

1. Anastasi, A. : *Psychological Testing*, New York : Macmillan, 1976.
2. Allport, G.W. : *Personality—A Psychological Interpretation*, New York : Holt, 1948.
3. Chauhan, S.S. : *Advanced Educational Psychology*, Vikas Publishing House Pvt. Ltd., 1997.
4. Eysenck, H.J. : *The Structure of Human Personality*, New York : Methuen, 1971.

5. Freud, S. : *An Outline of Psychoanalysis,* New York : 1939.

6. Guilford, J.P. : *General Psychology,* D.V. Nostrand Co. New York : London, 1952.

7. Murray, H.A. : *The Thematic Apperception Test,* Cambridge (Mass.) : Harvard univ. press, 1943.

8. Mangal, S.K. : *Advanced Educational Psychology,* Prentice Hall of India Pvt. Ltd. New Delhi, 1997.

9. Sheldon, W.H. : *The Varieties of Temperament,* A Psychology of Constitutional Differences. New York : Harper, 1942.

Questions and Assignments

1. What is meant by personality? Bring out the factors which influence the development of personality.
2. What is personality type? Discuss how personalities can be classified into different types and describe their characteristic features.
3. What is personality? How can it be measured?
4. Explain the meaning of personality and describe its factors.
5. How does psychology help you in everyday judgement of personality?
6. Mention the hormone provided by each of the endocrine glands, its physiological effects and the possible effects on personality of overactivity and of underactivity of the glands.
7. Discuss some of the important types of personality and indicate the limitations of the type-theories.
8. Write notes on:
   (a) Extrovert and Introvert.
   (b) Personality traits.
   (c) Rorschach ink blot test.
   (d) Situational tests.
9. What are the determinants of personality? Describe the importance of home on the personality of the child.
10. *Personality is the whole individual considered as a whole*—Discuss.
11. Can we measure personality? If yes, describe one of them.
12. What are projective tests? Describe any test of projection, you are familiar with.

Chapter 5

Stages of Development

Introduction : The study of the stages of development should be the basis of all planning of education. Each stage has its own characteristics. Therefore, adjustment of children to the school environment at every level of education is very important. In framing time-table, grading children, in compiling text-books, in organising cocurricular activities and in giving educational guidance due consideration should be made of different peculiarities of the stages of development.

Dr Earnest Jones divided the development of the child in four stages :

1. **Infancy :** Birth to 5 years.
2. **Later childhood :** 6 years to 12 years.
3. **Adolescence :** 12 years to 18 years.
4. **Maturity :** 18 years and above.

5.1 Infancy

Up to the age of three years after birth, the rate of physical growth of the child is very rapid. After three years the growth rate decreases. Generally, the height of the child at birth is 20.5 inches (51 cms). At the age of three the male child is about 33 pounds (15 kg.) and 38 inches (95 cms.) tall. By the age of five, the average height for boys is 43 inches and the average weight becomes 43 pounds (19 kg.). The rate of growth of boys and girls are not the same. In the beginning the rate of growth of the girls is more rapid than that of the boys.

At this stage the nervous system develops very rapidly. The child develops a variety of motor skills. Table 5.1 shows the motor development of the child.

Table 5.1

	2 years	3 years	4 and 5 years
Motor development	Walks without help, jumps and runs	Skips and hops	Free and active movement.
Fine motor coordination	Copying	Can match shapes, sees similarities and differences	Can name colours

5.1.1 Language development

The language development of the child starts from birth cry, which bears no purpose. We cannot distinguish between cry for hunger or cry for pain at this stage. But after six months the cry of the child becomes purposive. He cries when he feels pain. The babbling stage covers sixth to eighth months. Then from tenth to twelvth month the child starts using one or two meaningful words. Following table (Table 5.2) shows the development of vocabulary :

Table 5.2 : Development of vocabulary (*Smith*)

Age	No. of words
1 year	2
2 years	270
3 years	900
4 years	1,500
5 years	2,000

It has been reported by several studies that there is positive correlation between language development and intelligence. It also depends on environment and socio-economic condition. The child learns language from the adults by imitation.

5.1.2 Mental development

The special characteristic of this age is the inquisitiveness of the child. He starts asking questions about his environment. He begins to form concepts of physical and social reality. Fantasy is another characteristic at this age. With the development of language his powers of thinking and reasoning grow. At about the age of 5 years he is capable of abstract reasoning and logical thinking.

5.1.3 Emotional development

At this stage child's life is mostly guided by instincts, which clamour for immediate satisfaction. However, his emotions are temporary and fluctuating.

For instance, a child of four years who is crying, if given a toy, will become happy. At the age of five of his emotional expressions are controlled to some extent by social pressure. Children's emotion in the beginning centers round the personality of their mother. Gradually it extends from his family to outside environment.

5.1.4 Social development

At birth, the child does not exhibit any social behaviour. With age his social environment expands. In the beginning, the child remains egocentric. But with the expansion of social horizon, the child learns to cooperate with others and make friends. They actively take part in group games such as, hide and seek.

5.1.5 Development of Sexual life

Sex plays an important part in the life of a child. Four stages have been marked by the psychoanalysts in the evolution of sex-consciousness of an individual. These are :

1. Auto-erotic stage or the stage of self-love.
2. The Oedipus and the Electra complex stage or the stage of the love for parents.
3. The homosexual stage or the stage of loving an individual of the same sex.
4. The heterosexual stage when persons of opposite sexes are loved.

In early childhood, the individual goes through the first two stages of sexual development.

Infancy is an age of auto-erotism or self-love. This is called Narcissism, after the mythical Greek boy Narcissus, who fell in love with his own image seeing it in water.

5.1.6 Educational implications

Infancy is regarded as pre-school stage, hence it is considered a very significant period for education and training. Teachers and parents should be very careful so that good habits are formed at this stage. Proper environment should be provided at home and school. Children should be provided with opportunities for games and cultural activities. For the development of imagination proper stories, rhymes and games are to be chosen. Emotions of children should be properly trained. When they show emotional outbursts, they should be treated calmly. The elders should be very careful in showing their love towards their children. They should never show partiality to any child.

This is the age of curiosity. They should be given proper answers to their questions. Their individuality should be respected and they should be encouraged to express their feelings.

The education of the children at this stage rests mainly with the parents at home. But nowadays a number of nursery and kindergarten schools have been set up for their training. There are arrangements for senses training through music, drawing, painting, dancing, rhymes and various games.

5.2 Later childhood (6 years to 12 years)

Later childhood is an important period of life when proper guidance and counselling by parents and teachers are essential. It is a period of consolidation. We find remarkable stability—both physical and mental—at this stage. This period is also called latency period. In this period turbulent emotions of the early years are not active. They are latent and dormant.

5.2.1 Physical development

At this stage the brain of the child acquires nearly its adult size and weight. The child attains at the end of this stage pseudo-maturity. By this time he achieves a degree of adaptation to environment which enables him to live in harmony with others. This stage is marked with increased physical and motor strength and increased resistance to fatigue. Dearborn writes, Nine to eleven years old dash breathlessly from place to place, never walk when they can run, never run when they can jump or do something more strenuous.

5.2.2 Mental development

At this stage the child's thirst for knowledge shows a sudden increase. As the child enters formal schooling his capacity for learning and memorisation become more efficient. The child asks many questions which often seems to us silly. But they are significant as they show that the child has begun to think. At this stage capacity for logical thinking increases. The child can rationally analyse a problem. He shows interest in scientific and mathematical information.

They have genuine interest in collecting things like stones, tickets, cards, leaves, flowers and so on. Children between 7 and 8 years show interest in reading Animal stories, Fairy tales and Funny stories. While children between 9–11 years have dominating reading interest in Heroic and Adventure stories.

The child at this stage becomes more and more inventive rather than imitative. This is to be seen in his plays. He no longer plays beside another child, but plays with him. He does not mechanically imitate what other children do. He is now able to deal with the environment independently and in an efficient manner. ■

5.2.3 Emotional development

Emotions of the child change with age. At this stage early pattern of emotional outbursts in infancy become less diffuse and random. By the end of this period, the child learns to control his emotional expression. Love and joy, pleasure and grief appear in childhood.

5.2.4 Social development

The child at this stage achieves high sociability. He remains egocentric during infancy. But during later childhood social consciousness develop very rapidly. Gregariousness is one of the well-marked characteristics of this stage. He becomes a member of a gang. The members of the gang remain faithful to each other in all their difficulties. The gang or the peer group becomes important agent of socialisation. The groups of boys are more organised than the groups of girls. Boys and girls form their own groups. As group consciousness develops at this stage, the child becomes less self-centred but more cooperative. Both boys and girls take interest in group games. But boys love to play with boys and girls love to play with girls.

5.2.5 Development of sexual life

The child passes the stage of narcissism. Now his love is directed to persons other than himself. According to Earnest Jones the sex impulse lies dormant in later childhood. Boys and girls form their own group. Boys play with boys and girls play with girls. Girls seem to be more antagonistic towards boys.

5.2.6 Educational implications

Later childhood is the unique period of life when children enter into primary schools. Proper environment for security and freedom should be provided to the child at home and school. Children at late childhood stage should have ample opportunities to participate in group games and cultural activities.

This instinct of curiosity is at its best in this stage. The child asks many questions and these questions are required to be properly answered by the elders. The child whose instinct of curiosity is repressed at this stage will hardly show originality in later life. Reading habit should be formed at this stage. The wandering instinct of the child at this stage should be satisfied through picnic and excursions.

Gregariousness is another feature of this stage, when children form peer group of their own sex.

The child obeys the leader of the group whatever may befall. The parents and teachers may find it difficult to correct a child who belongs to an undesirable type of gang.

We have dealt with briefly the first two stages of development. We shall dwell at length on adolescence in the next chapter.

Summary

The major stages of development of a child are : Infancy (Birth–5 years), Late Childhood (6–12 years) and Adolescence (12–18 years).

The child in infancy is like a sprouting plant. He is tender-both in body and mind. He depends on others, both for the physical and emotional needs. His life is guided by instincts which clamour for immediate satisfaction. Child's emotion in the beginning centers round his mother. Gradually it extends from mother to outside environment. In the early stage, the child remains egocentric, but with the expansion of social horizon, he learns to cooperate with others and make friends. Formerly it was thought that the child had no sexual life. According to psychoanalysts, however, the sex life of the child is exceedingly rich and varied.

Later childhood (6–12 years) is marked with increased physical and motor strength. As the child enters formal schooling, his capacity for learning increases. He frequently asks questions which should be properly answered. By the end of this period the child learns to control his emotional expressions.

The child remains egocentric during infancy. But during later childhood, social consciousness develop rapidly. He loves to form peer groups. The members of the peer group remain faithful to each other. At this stage both boys and girls take interest in group games.

The sex impulse at this stage lies dormant. Boys play with boys and girls play with girls and often they seem to be antagonistic towards each other.

Infancy and childhood are very important periods of human life. They should be given proper training at these two periods. They should be encouraged to participate in games, manual activities, art and crafts, reading books etc.

References

1. Hurlock, E.B. : *Child Development*, 5th edition, McGraw Hill, New York.
2. Chauhan, S.S. : *Advanced Educational Psychology*, 6th edition, Vikash Publishing House Pvt. Ltd., 1997.
3. Bhatnagar, R.P. : Vishwavidyalaya Prakashan, Gorakhpur, 1959.
4. Mangal, S.K. : Prentice-Hall of India Pvt. Ltd., New Delhi, 1997.

Questions and Assignments

1. What are the stages of mental life of a child? What is the importance of recognising these stages?
2. Distinguish between the main features of infancy and later childhood. How does the education of each differ in essential features?
3. What are the characteristics of infancy? How should our education be in order to suit the needs of an infant?
4. Has the infant also a sex awareness? How does the evolution of sex consciousness affect the development of the child?
5. Write out your views on education of children at different stages of mental growth.
6. Throw light on Social and Intellectual development of the child during latency period.
7. What is the significance of the characteristics of various stages of development in Education?

Chapter 6

Adolescence

Introduction : The word adolescence is derived from the Greek word *adolescere*, which means to grow to maturity. During adolescence boys and girls move from childhood to adulthood—mentally, emotionally, socially and physically.

It is the most impressionable period of human life. As the child enters adolescence, there are marked changes both in its physical and mental life. Adolescence comes approximately in between the years 12 to 18. This is a period of recapitulation of infancy which no longer shows the stability of later childhood.

6.1 Physical development

Marked physical changes take place during adolescence. Both boys and girls show a sudden spurt in growth during this period. Girls become taller and heavier than boys at the age of 13, while by the age of 15 boys become taller and heavier than girls. During adolescence, the voice of boys becomes hoarse and girls' voice becomes shrill. The secondary sexual characteristics develop at this stage and sex-organs of both boys and girls acquire maturity. In case of both boys and girls the appearance of pubic hair and the growth of breasts in case of girls, have significant influence on the behaviour of adolescents. The average age of menstruation of girls varies from 12 to 14 years. On the whole, girls appear to mature earlier than boys in respect of physical growth.

6.2 Development of motor powers

As the body of the child grows and he gains balance, the motor powers also increase.

The boys are superior to girls in activities which involve speed and muscular strength.

6.3 Growth of sex-instinct

Sex is the most potent factor in the life of an adolescent. The awakening of sex instinct at this stage makes the adolescents restless and romantic in their behaviour. They are attracted towards the member of the opposite sex but they do not know the correct means of making friendship with members of the opposite sex. Children at this age may develop certain complexes due to premature indulgence in sex and due to sudden repression of the same. Repression of sex impulses may lead to phobia, anxiety-neurosis and melancholia.

6.4 Social development

During this period, social instincts develop most. The child becomes sensitive to public praise or blame. This tendency—if not properly cultured—may lead to over-self-consciousness, vanity and showing off.

One important development at this age is the increased influence of peer group. The peer group or the gang shapes the behaviour of the adolescents. His attitude, interests and moral values are guided by peers.

At this age the society and parents place certain responsibilities upon him. This often puzzles him because he fails to adjust successfully in the new role. He attempts to identify himself with adults and tries to play the role of adults.

6.5 Emotional development

Adolescence is a period of great excitability of emotion. Love is the dominant feeling of the adolescent child. But this love is of the most selfless kind. Most children at this period have their friends. The friends, at times, are so intensely loved that their separation is borne with pain. Love in the early period of adolescence is generally directed to a person of the same sex. But later it is directed to a person of opposite sex.

Adolescents at this age develop critical attitude towards religion and moral code dictated by elders. He becomes emotionally attached to a great religious leader, patriot or hero to whose ideals he wants to shape his life. The love impulse of the adolescent is easily directed towards the ideal person. Thus, adolescence is the period of hero-worship, which gives rise to religious sentiment and moral conduct.

Sudden changes in emotional aspect in adolescence completely bewilder the adolescent. As a result, many of them become introvert. Premature sex indulgence gives rise to inferiority complex and sense of guilt in them.

6.6 Mental development

Adolescence is a period of rapid mental growth. The adolescents can carry on abstract thinking. His ability to see relationship and to solve problems increase at this stage. His ability to generalise on conceptual level develops. He gains increasing confidence in his own opinion and he can take decisions on important matters. He has the ability to think about his future. The memory of adolescents develops greatly with the growth in vocabulary.

Adolescence is the period of imagination. It is a period of building castles in the air. Stanley Hall says, Puberty is the birth days of imagination. In this age every one is a poet and flies on the wings of rosy imagination. At this stage, the adolescents love to read novels and stories of adventure. Day dream and fantasy are the two special features of adolescent life. Urge for self-expression is very strong in adolescents which may result in writing, acting, painting, etc.

Boys and girls in adolescence are very much suggestible. At this period the personality of the adolescent is not well-organised. Whatever is suggested to them, they accept without any question. Hence the elders should send out only pious and character-building thought to them.

6.7 Development of interests

In adolescence boys and girls have a variety of interests. With the development of intellectual and social growth, their field of interests considerably expand. They start taking interest in international and national affairs. They discuss problems facing the nation or society from different angles.

In adolescence interest in reading reaches its climax. Adolescents love to read novels, adventure stories and biographies of great men.

Cinema, T.V. and radio have great impact on interests of adolescents in recent years. They have affected the behaviour of adolescents in both positive and negative directions.

Adolescents are interested in travelling. They aspire to gain some degree of freedom from the dull and monotonous home and have the joy of seeing new things. Therefore, going on travel is of very great importance at this stage. Besides travelling, adolescents take interest in adventurous activities, such as mountaineering and exploring unknown places.

Children at this age are interested in showing off their personal beauty. With multi-coloured clothes, styles of hair and facial beauty they want to attract the attention of others.

During adolescence, most boys and girls show a spurt in physical growth. They become conscious of their physical health and show interest in improving physical strength through games and other physical activities.

Another important characteristic of adolescence is their interest in vocation. When the adolescent reaches sixteen years of age, he begins to think about his future career. He wants to stand on his own feet.

6.8 Needs of adolescent

Adolescence is the unique period of life. G. Stanley Hall writes, It is a period of storm and stress. Sex asserts its mastery in field after field and works its havoc in the form of secret vices. The social instinct undergoes sudden unfoldment and new life of love awakens. Everything is plastic. Character and personality take form. Self-feeling and ambitions are increased. It is all marvellous new birth.

Thus, during adolescence, the child becomes somewhat perplexed due to sudden appearance of physical, mental and social needs. This period is considered by Stanley Hall and others as the period of strain and strife.

Based on the list of needs provided by Stanley Hall, we may discuss below the general patterns of needs of adolescents :

6.8.1 Sex need

In addition to basic physiological needs of hunger, thirst and oxygen the sex need is very much dominant in adolescence. With the maturity of sex-organ, sex urges increase and boys are attracted towards girls and girls are attracted towards boys. But sex urges cannot be satisfied due to social taboos in India and such other conservative countries and thus sex-life becomes a problem to them.

6.8.2 Need for freedom

During this age, adolescents want to work independently. They want to express their opinion freely and oppose control and restrictions imposed by others.

6.8.3 Need for self-expression

Children of this age intend to express themselves through study, games, dance, music, drama and other activities. They aspire for social status.

6.8.4 Need for adventure

At this age, adolescents love adventurous activities. Rashness and lack of proper thinking may invite reproof and censure from adults for such activities.

6.8.5 Need for philosophy of life

At this age, adolescents develop critical attitude towards established mores, customs and moral and religious values. They need satisfying answers to their enquiries.

6.8.6 Need for acquiring new knowledge

The adolescents with the growing intellectual capacities find a great interest in acquiring new knowledge. This spontaneous urge for knowledge should be properly guided.

6.8.7 Need for vocation

The adolescents at this age starts thinking about their future career. They want to stand on their own feet without seeking help from others. They need vocational guidance at this stage.

6.8.8 Need for security

Authoritarian attitude of the adults at home may produce a feeling of insecurity in the mind of adolescents. They fail to adjust with the home environment and may be a truant one day.

6.8.9 Need for moral values

Adolescents are anxious to know which is right or which is wrong. They form an idea of moral values. But when they see that the adults are not following the moral standards, they are perplexed. They need very much a satisfying philosophy of life.

6.8.10 Social needs

In adolescence the sphere of interests expands outside the family. The child now comes in contact with a variety of people. He loves to remain in association of his friends and passes most of the time outside family. In the peer group he discusses about the games, sports and matches and sometimes discusses about the problems facing the country. His interests and attitudes are mainly governed by peers. He becomes conscious of his place in the society and readily agrees to take active part in different fields of community life.

6.9 Problems of adolescence

Adolescence is a period of transition from childhood to maturity. Hall has called this period a period of storm and stress.

Adolescents have many problems and these mainly centre round the following : 1. Home; 2. School; 3. Society; 4. Vocation and 5. Sex.

6.9.1 Adjustment in home

In adolescence the child is reminded now and then about his duty and responsibility by the adult members of the family. They place upon him new demands. This confuses him and he fails to meet these demands. The parents have high expectation from the adolescents, but when they are not fulfilled, constant quarreling occurs among parents and adolescents. This may result in truancy from home or, in extreme case, suicide.

6.9.2 Adjustment in school

Most of the adolescents face a great problem to adjust with the rigid time-table and syllabus. There is hardly any scope for extracurricular activities in schools. Teachers are rigid and unsympathetic. Examination, pass-fail system and parents' aspiration are sources of worry to the adolescents. When the child fails to adjust with the rigid school system, either he becomes neurotic or becomes delinquent.

6.9.3 Adjustment in society

Adolescents are expected to behave like an adult in a society. They must learn social customs and manners. When they fail to obey the dictate of the adult members of the society, they are ridiculed. They have no freedom to act according to their conscience. All these result in severe mental conflicts in adolescents.

6.9.4 Vocational problem

The child starts thinking of his future career when he reaches adolescence. He needs money for various activities he follows. But he feels ashamed of begging money from the adults. Parents are not always willing to provide money for his frivolous pursuits. Under such circumstances, he craves for an occupation which will give him money. But how shall he get occupation when thousands of unemployed adolescents are roaming the street? This thought of uncertain future haunts the mind of the adolescents.

6.9.5 Problem of sex-impulse

The dawn of adolescence is marked by a special consciousness of sex. It is the awakening of this impulse that makes him so romantic in behaviour. The adolescent feels an attraction towards the member of opposite sex but he does not know how to make friendship with the member of opposite sex against the backdrop of social taboos. Thus the lack of proper guidance leads the young soul into great mental suffering. One whose sexual impulse has been altogether misdirected suffers from various mental diseases. Abnormal sexual activities of the adolescents give rise to melancholia in which he is haunted by a sense of sin, and thinks himself lost beyond redemption.

6.10 Educational measures

As the child enters adolescence there are marked changes both in his physical appearance and mental life. Physical energy in this age is at its climax. To utilise his physical energy, some kind of physical activity should be prescribed for adolescent boys and girls. Drill, gymnastics and manual training are of great help in developing physical and motor power of the adolescent. Various kinds of sports and games are to be encouraged among adolescents.

All kinds of outdoor activities should be provided to the adolescent boys and girls. This is good both for the development of their physical powers and for stopping them from idle brooding. Of all the extracurricular activities of a modern school, scouting is the most beneficial to the adolescent. It is a form of activity in which fullest scope is given for the development of these beneficial traits, which for lack of proper nurture, would have perished at the sprouting stage.

Dancing for adolescents is strongly advocated by some, because it is the most liberal of all forms of motor education. The adolescents love rhythm and like to sing. Dancing involves rhythmic movements and, hence, liked by the adolescents.

The new system of education in our country prescribes physical education and work education for school children to channelise their physical and mental energy. The adolescents should be encouraged to participate in these activities. In schools adolescents should be given physical and health education and there should be arrangement for regular medical check-up of the adolescent boys and girls.

For the expansion of knowledge, the school should have a good library and teachers should encourage the adolescents by giving reference of good books to be read by them.

The creative abilities of the adolescents should be developed through art and craft, drawing and painting, drama and recitation.

The adolescents should be encouraged to organise different functions in schools. They should celebrate Independence day, birthdays of patriots and saints, etc. They should organise picnics, educational excursions, debates and dramas. All these will provide adolescents the scope for self-expression and free-thinking. These will also help to resolve many problems of adolescents which are created because of communication gap among classmates.

Students at this age are very much suggestible. The teacher should hold out before them the ideals of great saints and patriots, so that they can follow their footsteps to make their own life sublime.

Adolescents should be taught to pass their leisure time through useful hobbies. They should be provided with proper environment for the expression of their pent-up feelings. They should be trained to control emotion.

In brief, proper and sympathetic guidance and counselling are necessary when adolescents are bewildered by a number of physical, social and emotional problems.

6.11 Sex education and adolescents

The dawn of adolescence is marked by consciousness of sex. Adolescents develop many complexes due to premature indulgence in sex. Sudden repression of sex impulses give rise to mental phobias and anxiety neurosis in which the adolescents are haunted by a sense of sin. They become victims of discouragement and utter despair.

The child comes to know about sex from the early stage of life. The important sources which provide sex knowledge to children are : companions, movies, T.V., reproduction in animals, literature, old people, etc. The insufficient, and often erroneous, knowledge thus gathered from these sources may prove injurious to mental and physical health of adolescents. Thus, the lack of proper sex education may lead the young soul into great mental agony.

6.11.1 How can this mental disturbance be prevented?

Our adolescent boys and girls feel ashamed to discuss freely their sex problems with their parents. In our country most of the parents are conservative in their outlook regarding sex problems. Thus they cannot be given the responsibility of providing sex-education to their sons and daughters. They need proper sex education in school.

Stanley Hall points out two kinds of causes that lead to sexual excitability—physical and mental. The physical causes are improper clothes, rich food, overwork, nervousness, habits of defective cleanliness, prolonged sitting or standing, monotonous walking, late rising, petting and indulgence and too much straining of the brain.

Prominent among the mental causes are erotic reading, attending adult movies and theatrical performances.

Certain drugs as cocaine and opium and intoxicating drinks have a stimulating effect. Certain perfumes, over-eating, fondling, fear and rocking chair predispose the mind to sex. Too soft beds predispose people to sensuous luxury and tempt them to remain in them long after awakening. This is, according to Stanley Hall, just the hour most dangerous of all.

Stanley Hall suggests moderate work and music as cures of the habit of self-abuse. Good music is a moral tonic.

Any talk that stimulates the sex impulse should be avoided. It is also advisable to give up companions who indulge in such talks.

According to some, coeducation improves sexual morality among boys and girls. In their opinion when boys and girls learn together and work together, they get habituated to the life of each other, and curiosity about opposite sex vanishes. However, coeducation has to be tried in this country cautiously.

Modern psychology does not believe in the ruthless repression of the undesirable instincts of the young—rather in their sublimation.

Sex-nuture is the only effective remedy against all evils. Sex nurture consists in the proper use of sex energy. It should be directed towards physical culture, athletic sports, manual labour, intellectual activity and all such work which require a considerable amount of physical power.

Sex education should form an integral part of curriculum. It should be imparted through the medium of the regular subjects of the curriculum. The attention of the adolescent needs not be specifically fixed on them, but while teaching natural science, literature, bio-science, home science, psychology, etc. teachers may incidentally lead the boys and girls to the understanding of the nature of sex phenomena also. According to some, if sex-education is introduced in our school curriculum, most of the sex problems of adolescents will be checked.

Summary

Adolescence is that span of years during which boys and girls move from childhood to adulthood, mentally, emotionally, socially and physically (Jersild). It comes approximately in between the years 12 to 18. Both boys and girls show a sudden spurt in growth during this period. Girls appear to mature earlier than boys in respect of physical growth.

Adolescents have many needs and problems : sex need, need for acquiring knowledge, need for vocation, need for security, need for freedom, need for self-expression, need for adventure, need for philosophy of life and so on. They have adjustment problems in family, in school and in society. They have vocational problems and problems related to sex. To solve these problems they need sympathetic guidance from parents and teachers. They should be given proper environment in home and school. They should be encouraged to participate in multifarious activities at home and school. Their interest in crafts and hobbies needs be developed. Games and sports—appropriate to the age and sex—should be organised in schools. Their emotional energy should be properly directed in socially approved channels.

Coeducational system is considered to be useful in improving sex morality. Sex education should form an integral part of the school curriculum. Scouting sublimates the basic instincts of the adolescents and provides a safety valve to the surplus energy.

References

1. Gates and Jersild : *Educational Psychology,* N.Y. : Macmillan, 1959.
2. Hurlock, E.B. : *Child Development*, McGraw Hill, New York.
3. Morgan, C.T. : *Introduction to Psychology,* New York : McGraw Hill, 1961.
4. Chauhan, S.S. : Vikash Publishing House Ltd. New Delhi, 1997.

Questions and Assignments

1. Discuss the physical and mental changes that occur during adolescence and their educational implications.
2. Identify the special needs of adolescents. How can they be satisfied?
3. Discuss the psychological needs and urges of the adolescents.
4. Adolescence is described as an ackward stage—a period of *storm and stress.* Do you agree? Give reasons for your answer.
5. State the characteristics of social and emotional development of adolescents and point out their educational implications.
6. What is meant by sex-education? Discuss the importance of sex-education for adolescents.
7. Discuss the problems of an adolescent and suggest measures to solve them.
8. Discuss briefly the interests of adolescents and their implications in school programs.

Chapter 7

Growth and Development

Introduction : Growth and development are not uniform at different ages. The life of the child consists of certain rhythmical periods of growth and development. As an educator has to deal with a large number of children at different age level, he must have the knowledge of basic principles of growth and development for effective guidance of the pupils.

7.1 Meaning of growth and development

Change is the most important characteristic of a living organism. Changes in the life of the child are brought about by the processes of growth and development. The two terms are considered synonymous and interchangeable. However, some psychologists think that there is some distinctions between the terms growth and development. Growth means quantitative change. For instance, a child increases in size, length and weight in a fixed period of time. Arnold Gessell used the word maturation to describe growth processes.

The term development implies qualitative change involving functional change. For example, with the increase in size, length and weight of the child, the function of these aspects also undergoes change.

But in reality there is hardly any distinction between growth and development. The quantitative change of growth and qualitative change of development are closely interrelated.

To some the term development includes both qualitative as well as quantitative aspects of change. So, the term development is more complex and comprehensive than the term growth. In fact, development is achieved through growth. Therefore, growth is a sub-system of developmental process.

Immediately after birth living organisms are capable of doing certain activities. For instance, just after birth, the ducklings can swim and peck at food. Whereas a human baby remains helpless at birth. His physical and mental ability remains in dormant stage. He depends totally on others for nourishment and physical comforts. Gradually he grows in length and weight. Not only his physical strength increases, his mental abilities like thinking, imagination, intelligence and interest increase. Thus the growth and development of a child depends on the interaction of environment, secretion of endocrinal hormones, maturation and learning.

The primary condition of growth in human being is his immaturity. Immaturity has two characteristics : (a) Dependence and (b) Plasticity.

Dependence : Dependence in case of human babies does not indicate complete reliance on others. Physically an infant may be helpless, but socially he is not. His faint cry at once attracts the attention of others who quickly extend their helping hands. Infants have immense capacity to attract the attention of others. Thus, though physically helpless, he is not helpless socially.

Plasticity : The growth and development of child are possible due to plasticity. On account of this quality, the child starts learning with attainment of maturity and thus his physical and mental development take place. Therefore, growth or development is a positive force that leads an individual to gradual improvement and harmonious development.

7.2 Principles of development

Development appears to follow a logical and sequential pattern from conception to maturity. Following are the important principles of development :

7.2.1 Development is a continuous process

Development of an individual is a continuous process. It starts with conception in the womb of the mother and continues till death. However, the development is not always gradual or smooth. There may be sudden spurts in physical and mental growth as in adolescence.

7.2.2 Principle of individual differences

Development is not uniform in all individuals. Though all individuals develop, there is difference in the rate of their development. Each child develops under the interaction of environment and heredity. No two children show same physical, mental and emotional growth in a particular age. Even at different ages they show different rate of development. Generally those who have high rate of growth in the beginning retain the rate of rapid growth in the later stage also. Those who have retarded growth in the early stage, have the same rate of slow growth in later life. There is also sex-difference in development.

Boys and girls differ in growth rate. Girls mature earlier in comparison to boys. During pre-adolescence girls are taller and heavier. But by the end of adolescence, boys surpass them.

7.2.3 Development is cumulative

The process of development is cumulative. Changes at certain period of life do not appear all of a sudden. Each stage of child's life is influenced by previous stage. Development of language does not take place in one day. In the beginning he starts babbling and gradually he learns to use meaningful words and complete sentences.

7.2.4 Each stage of development has speciality

Though development is a continuous process, yet each stage has certain special characteristics. According to Dr Earnest Jones these stages are :

1. **Infancy :** It lasts up to the age of five.
2. **Childhood :** It lasts up to the age of twelve.
3. **Adolescence :** It continues up to the age of eighteen.
4. **Maturity :** It is the final stage.

The physical and mental changes which occur during adolescence cannot be found in childhood. During adolescence sex organs of boys and girls mature and other secondary sex characters appear.

7.2.5 Development follows orderly sequence

Individuals differ in rate of growth and development, but it follows an orderly sequence. At first the child learns to crawl, then he stands and finally he learns to walk. Never do we see a child stand at first, and then crawl. Experiments of Gesell show that Patterns of behaviour in all species tend to follow an orderly sequence in their emergence.

7.2.6 Development proceeds from general to specific

Mental or physical, all types of development proceed from general to specific responses. For instance, after birth the baby exhibits mass action, that is, it reacts with whole body in response to external stimulus. Afterwards, these general motor responses change into specific responses like grasping or reaching out. With the physical development differentiation occurs, that is, different limbs of the child can function differently and coordination is established amongst the reactions.

7.2.7 Development is harmonious and coordinated

Physical, mental or social development of the child is not an abrupt and sudden phenomenon. Development in each field comprises a harmony and coordination of various dimensions of his personality.

7.2.8 Different aspects of development are interrelated

The various aspects of child's development are interrelated. A healthy child develops a healthy, emotionally stable mind, whereas a physically handicapped child becomes emotionally maladjusted.

7.2.9 Principle of cephalocaudal

According to the cephalocaudal principle development proceeds from head to foot. This is why the child in the beginning gains control over his head and then on his legs to stand.

7.2.10 Principle of proxi modistal

According to this principle, development starts from the near to the distant part of the body. The parts of the body near the central line develop before the extremities. The infant uses his arm and elbow before he learns to use his wrists and fingers.

7.2.11 Principle of spiral development

Development is a continuous process but it does not follow straight line. When the development attains a certain level, there is a period of consolidation, i.e., when apparently no progress takes place. Development turns back and again moves forward in a spiral way as shown in Fig. 7.1.

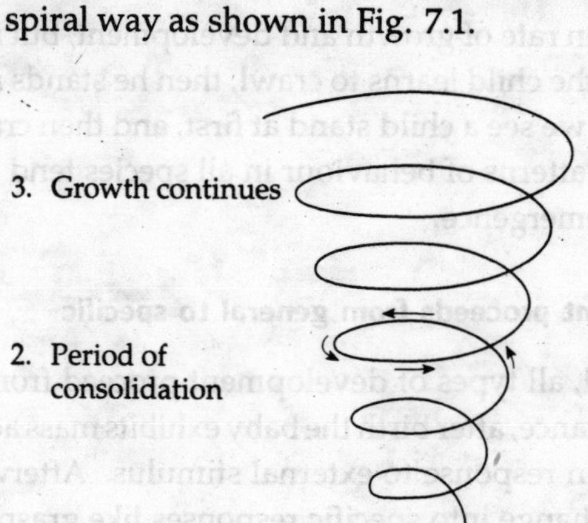

Fig. 7.1

7.2.12 Development is predictable

Development is a continuous process and it follows an orderly sequence. Moreover, the rate of development in case of each child remains more or less constant. Therefore, by observing the nature of growth and development of the early stage of the child, we can predict his future possibilities in adulthood stage.

7.2.13 Retardation of development

Development may be retarded by childhood diseases and emotional shocks at early stage of life.

Successful adjustments predispose the child to grow normally, but unhappy, early experiences tend to produce rebellion and thus prevent growth and development.

7.3 Theories of growth and development

There are many theories on how the child grows and develops. The major theories which explain child development from various angles may be classified as follows :

1. Psycho-analytic theory.
2. Erickson's theory of psychosocial development.
3. Kohlberg's theory of moral development.
4. Jean Piaget's theory of development.

7.3.1 Psycho-analytic theory

Freud, the father of psychoanalysis, believed that the developmental process consisted of a series of fixed stages through which every child passed in sequential order unless he became fixated. The stages are :

1. **The oral stage :** In this period the child's most organised source of gratification is sucking. The child in this period of life is primarily passive and dependent.
2. **The anal stage :** During the anal stage, the anal zone is of greatest importance in the child's development. The child takes interest in the activities related to anus. He draws pleasure in controlling his excretory functions. At this stage, traits related to orderliness, punctuality, and thrift are believed to develop.
3. **The phallic stage :** During this period the focus of pleasure shifts from anus to sex organs. The child becomes aware of genital differences. His love is directed to the parent of the opposite sex. This is referred to as

the Oedipus complex. For example, the boy develops a new form of love for his mother and takes the father as his rival. The child becomes afraid of being castrated by his father and develops castration complex. This complex is however resolved by identifying himself with his father. Similarly, the female child loves her father and hates her mother. This is Electra complex.

4. **The latency stage :** In this period, the child diverts some of his primary love interests to persons outside his family. He now becomes involved in education and social activities. This period is regarded as the period of calm before the storm of puberty.

5. **Genital stage :** Puberty starts at this stage. The focus of pleasure now shifts to the member of the opposite sex.

   Failure to be properly gratified at a particular stage may lead to fixation at that stage.

7.3.2 Adler's viewpoint

Instead of sex, Adler laid emphasis on human's motive to attain superiority and perfection. For the satisfaction of this motive, one develops a unique style of life. The style of life of a child is influenced by the order of birth, place and position of the child in the family. As the child grows and develops, the urge for gaining superiority also increases. If he succeeds in gaining power and superiority he becomes a properly adjusted normal person. But if he fails he develops inferiority complex and becomes maladjusted.

The Freudian view of psychosexual development was taken by Erikson and extended in a number of directions. To him states of human development is more of psychosocial than narrowly psychosexual.

Table 7.1: Stages of Psycho-social development.

Stage or Period	Psycho-social crises
1. Birth–1 year	Trust *vs* Mistrust.
2. 1–2 years	Autonomy *vs* Shame and doubt.
3. 3–5 years	Initiative *vs* Guilt.
4. 6–12 years	Industry *vs* Inferiority.
5. 12–20 years (*Adolescence*)	Identity *vs* Role confusion.
6. 20–45 years (*Early adulthood*)	Intimacy *vs* Isolation.
7. 45–65 years (*Middle adulthood*)	Generativity *vs* Stagnation.
8. 65 years and above (*Late adulthood*)	Integrity *vs* Despair.

7.3.3 Erikson's theory of psychosocial development

According to Erikson, the development of a child is the result of his interaction with social environment. At each stage of his development, the child has to face a new crisis.

Enikson classified eight stages of development linked with corresponding psycho social crises.

A brief description of the eight psychosocial stages of development is given below :

Stage 1 : Period of trust vs. mistrust : This period ranges from birth to eighteen months of age. At this stage, the infant completely depends on mother and relatives for the satisfaction of its needs. The sense of trust or faith towards environment is thus laid down during this period. But if the child's needs are not satisfied, then he loses his sense of trust and security in the surroundings.

Stage 2 : Period of autonomy vs. shame and doubt : This period ranges from eighteen months to three years. Having gained a sense of faith and security and with the newly developed motor and physical skills, the child develops a sense of autonomy. He does not ask any help from others. He wants to do all things by himself independently. A child who is denied the freedom to explore his environment begins to doubt his ability and feels ashamed in the presence of others.

Stage 3 : Period of initiative vs. guilt : This stage covers the period from three years to six years. During this stage a child has rapid growth in mental and physical ability. His social boundaries also expand beyond family environment. He begins to take initiative in interacting with his environment. If the child is discouraged from taking such initiative, he may develop a sense of guilt.

Stage 4 : Period of industry vs. inferiority : This stage covers the period between six years to twelve years. At this age children learn various skills and tasks in school. They are full of energy and try to produce new things. Praise motivates them to work and a sense of industry grow in them. But if their performance is poor and they are criticised, they develop a sense of inferiority.

Stage 5 : Period of identity vs. role confusion : This period ranges from twelve years to nineteen years. This is the period of adolescence, when there is a sudden spurt in physical and mental growth. At this stage, the adolescent tries to search for his new role in society. The adolescent is bewildered when he fails to resolve the crises.

Stage 6 : Period of intimacy vs. isolation : This period covers the ages between twenty to forty-five. During this period, the individual seeks to form close intimacy with another person. But failure to develop such intimacy may lead one to develop a sense of isolation.

Stage 7 : Period of generativity vs. stagnation : This stage ranges from forty-five to sixty-five. At this age a person is established in a professional career. Now he finds time to engage himself in creative, productive and socially beneficial activity. But instead of generativity some individuals may become egoistic and selfish. This leads to personal stagnation.

Stage 8 : Period of integrity vs. despair : This period covers old age, about sixty-five onwards. This is the last phase of psychosocial development. The successful resolution of all the seven previous crises provides a person with a sense of satisfaction. He develops a positive outlook about himself and the outside world. But an individual who has failed to resolve successfully the previous crises of the developmental stages develops a deep sense of despair and depression.

Erikson has brought a shift in emphasis from psychosexual development to the social conditions and organisation in which the ego must be rooted in order to develop normally.

7.3.4 Kohlberg's theory of moral development

Lawrence Kohlberg, a psychologist of the Harvard University, emphasises that moral development of an individual proceeds in sequential stages right from early childhood. The stages may be described briefly as follows :

Stage 1 : Pre-moral level (Age 4–10 years) : During early infancy, the child's morality is mainly guided by the fear of physical punishment. He obeys his elders only to avoid punishment. In true sense, the child has no moral understanding of which is right or which is wrong.

At this stage, the child is very much egocentric. He obeys those orders of the elders which satisfy their interests and needs.

Stage 2 : Conventional morality level (Age 10–13 years) : At this stage, the child conforms to the standards of society. Theft, for example, is judged wrong because the society considers it as wrong. He does not decide himself what is right or wrong. His moral judgement is controlled by the conventions, rules and regulations of the society.

Stage 3 : Self-accepted moral principles levels (Age 13 to adulthood) : At this stage, moral judgement rests with the individual himself. He declines to conform to an idea merely because of consideration of the views of others. He scrutinises and recognises different views of different people. At this stage, he starts thinking in rational terms.

At the advanced stage of moral development the individual develops a true moral consciousness. The decisions of the individual are now guided mostly by his conscience and universal principles.

Moral development :	**Pre-moral level** (4–10 *years*) No moral sense, Guided by Pleasure-Pain principle	⇒	**Conventional Morality level** (10–13 *years*) Guided by rules and conventions of society.	⇒	**Self-accepted moral principles level** (13 *years to adulthood*) Guided by conscience and universal view-point

Kohlberg's concept of moral development

Kohlberg is of opinion that most of the adults do not cross the second level and very few can reach the third level when people venture to base their moral judgement on the dictates of their conscience only.

7.3.5 Jean Piaget's theory of development

Piaget identifies four stages of child's intellectual development : Sensory-motor, pre-operational, concrete operational and formal operational (A detailed account of this theoy has been given in the next chapter).

Summary

Changes in the organism are brought about by the processes of growth and development. Growth means quantitative change. The term development however, includes both qualitative as well as quantitative aspects of change. The term development is more comprehensive than the term growth. It is related to the overall changes of one's personality.

Development follows a sequential pattern from conception to maturity. It follows some basic rules. Development is continuous process and each stage of development has speciality. Development is harmonious and coordinated.

There are various theories on how the child grows and develops. *Freud's psychoanalytic* theory points out five distinct stages of development : *oral, anal, phallic, latent* and *genital.*

Instead of sex, Adler laid stress on human's urge to attain superiority and perfection. For satisfaction of this urge, one develops a unique style of life. As the child grows, the urge for gaining superiority increases. If he succeeds in gaining power and superiority, he becomes properly adjusted person. But if he fails, he develops inferiority complex and becomes maladjusted.

Erikson's theory of psychosocial development brings out eight stages of development linked with corresponding social crises. These are trust vs mistrust (birth–1 year), Autonomy vs. Shame and Doubt (1–2 years), Initiative vs. Guilt (3–5 years), Industry vs Inferiority (6–12 years), Identity vs. Role confusion (12–20 years), Intimacy vs. Isolation (20–45 years), Generativity vs. Stagnation (45–65 years), Integrity vs. Despair (65 years and above).

Kohlberg's theory emphasises that moral development of an individual proceeds through three stages : *Premoral* (4–10 years), *Conventional morality* (10–13 years) and *self-accepted moral principles* (13–adulthood). Kohlberg is of opinion that most of us cannot cross the second level of moral development.

Piaget's theory of cognitive development identifies four distinct stages of a child's intellectual development (to be discussed in the next chapter).

References

1. Erickson, E. : *Identity : Youth and Crises,* New York : Norton, 1968.
2. Freud, S. : *An Outline of Psychoanalysis,* London : Hogarth Press, 1953.
3. Kohlberg, L. : *Moral Stage and Moralisation,* The Cognitive Developmental Approach, In: T. Lickona (Edn), Moral Development and Behaviour. New York : Holt, Rinehart and Winston, 1976.
4. Hurlock, E.B. : *Child Physiology,* Tokyo : McGraw Hill, 1959.
5. Mangal, S.K. : *Advanced Educational Psychology,* Prentice Hall of India Pvt. Ltd. New Delhi, 1997.

Questions and Assignments

1. Distinguish between growth and development.
2. Describe briefly the principles of development.
3. Discuss Erikson's theory of psychosocial development.
4. Discuss briefly Kohlberg's theory of moral development.
5. Write notes on :
   (a) Development is a product of the Interaction of an organism and his environment.
   (b) Development proceeds from the general to the specific.

Chapter 8

Piaget's developmental psychology

Introduction : Credit goes to Jean Piaget, a Swiss biologist, for devising the concept of cognitive development. According to Piaget, cognitive development of a person takes place by constant interaction with his physical and social environment. The process of cognitive development proceeds through an orderly sequence of stages. At first, the child has to acquire and exercise the strategies of the earlier stages. Then he can master the strategies of the later stages.

According to Piaget, the human baby is born with certain fundamental instincts and reflexes such as sucking and grasping. With the process of natural growth, the cognitive structure of a child develops. The process of development is brought about by the processes of assimilation and accommodation. Assimilation means incorporating old ideas with new ideas. Accommodation indicates adjustment to new situation. Through the processes of assimilation and accommodation, the child ceaselessly tries to adjust to his changing environment. Thus he maintains equilibrium between him and his environment. However, in the interaction of the individual with his environment, the processes of assimilation and accommodation get out of balance, forcing the individual into the next stage of development to restore the balance.

There may be certain individual differences among children of the same age in mental abilities, the pattern of their development in different stages, however, remains more or less constant.

8.1 Stages of cognitive development

Piaget has recognised following stages in the cognitive development of children :

8.1.1 Sensori-motor phase (Birth to 2 years)

At birth, the human baby shows a few reflexes such as sucking and looking. During the next four months, the reflexes are coordinated and the child can perform certain activities. For instance, he tries to suck anything that is put into his mouth or grasps whatever is put into his hands.

At this stage, his view of environmental objects is quite transitory. To the child, the objects exist only when they are physically present before him. For instance, if we take a doll out of his hand and conceal it under the bed, the infant will at once forget it.

In the first year of life, the infant begins to realise that the objects in the environment are separate from his own body and they have permanent existence. So, he will now search for the doll that has been kept hidden under the bed. This shows that the child is now able to form mental images of the external objects. At this stage, perception of space, time, imitation, and causality develop.

8.1.2 Symbolic and pre-conceptual phase (2 to 4 years)

This is the stage of rudimentary concept formation. At the end of sensori-motor stage, the child begins to think by symbolic representations. The learning of language provides him with tool for thinking. Children belonging to this age group, generally use such concepts as are neither complete concepts nor representation of an object. They now use notions which lie between the concept of an object and the concept of a class of object. They can identify an object by its name. But often they fail to make correct identification. For instance, to them all men are daddy and all women are mummy.

At this stage, children are found to be egocentric in nature. They are unable to take a proper perspective of another person. They see the world only from their own standpoint.

The other major characteristic of the mental structure of the child at this stage is animism. They tend to attribute life to all inanimate objects. For them, like a living being, their dolls are capable of crying or smiling.

8.1.3 Intuitive phase (4 to 8 years)

The child's thinking at this stage is not logical and is based on intuition. It is often illogical and full of contradictions.

The child cannot think in terms of quantity. He thinks in terms of static configuration and neglects transformation. This can be illustrated by the following experiments :

1. The child is shown first two balls of clay equal in size. He is asked to flatten one of them and then he is asked to tell which of the two objects

have more clay. The child would say the flattened one, which is bigger in size, has greater amount of clay in it.

Piaget found that most of five to six years old children believed that a change in form produced a change in amount also.

2. Two glass vessels A and B are taken. They are of equal shape and size. The vessels are filled with water. At first, the child agrees that the amount of water in the two vessels A and B is equal. But when one of the vessels B is replaced by a taller but narrower vessel C and filled with same amount of water, the child may say that C has more water because the level of water is higher in this vessel.

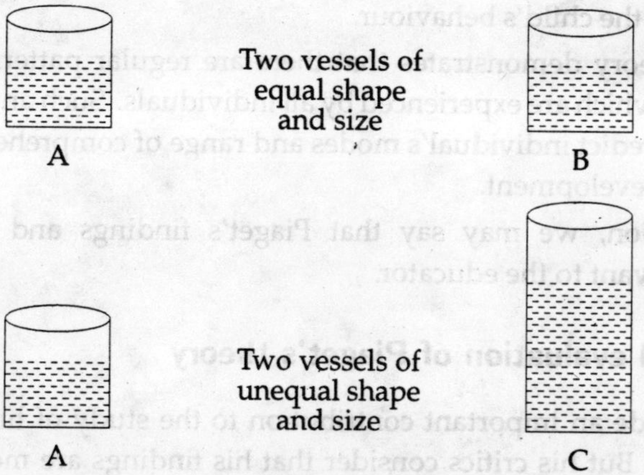

Fig. 8.1

8.1.4 Concrete operational phase (8 to 11 years)

By concrete operation is meant that the child is able to develop concepts pertaining to the size and shape of objects. During concrete operations, the child is able to understand that a change in the form of an object does not necessarily lead to change in its content.

At this stage, the child can reason well and his thinking becomes more logical and systematic. He is no longer egocentric in his thinking. He learns to appreciate the views and ideas of others which may differ from his own.

During this stage, the child can arrange objects into classes and subclasses. He can tackle concrete problems and carry out complex operations.

However, the child at this stage is unable to think in abstract terms. In the cognitive development, concrete operations are followed by formal operations.

8.1.5 Formal operational phase (11 to 15 years)

The period of formal operations, according to Piaget, is between 11 to 15 years, that is, it covers the period of adolescence, when the thought-process of the child becomes logical, systematic and well-integrated. He now learns to deal with obstruction. Gradually he learns logical rules. He can generalise and arrive at abstract rules in specific situations. While tackling a problem, he attempts to explore various solutions in a systematic way. At this stage, the child shows interest in dealing with things that often do not exist in reality. At this stage, the development of formal operations enables the child to transfer understanding from one situation to another situation.

After the expiry of this stage, the child is expected to reach full intellectual potential of the advanced stage of his cognitive system.

Conclusion : Piaget studied the child's cognitive structure and mental development, his language, reasoning and moral judgement through careful observation of the child's behaviour.

Piaget's theory demonstrates that there are regular patterns in cognitive development which are experienced by all individuals. Such an understanding allows us to predict individual's modes and range of comprehension all along his course of development.

In conclusion, we may say that Piaget's findings and postulates are extremely relevant to the educator.

8.2 Critical evaluation of Piaget's theory

Piaget has made an important contribution to the study of human cognitive development. But his critics consider that his findings are mostly subjective and lack sufficient evidence. In fact, the pattern of cognitive development, as stated by Piaget, is not so uniform and universal as he claimed.

Again, according to Piaget, a child before attaining concrete operational age (8–11) cannot think logically. But this has been refused by modern psychologists. Moreover, his claim that children below this age are egocentric has been also disproved by modern researches.

However, all these criticism levelled against Piaget's theory are mostly biased and one-sided. We cannot underrate Piaget's theory, because he has studied the child's language, reasoning, moral judgement and intellectual development through careful observation of the child's spontaneous behaviour.

In conclusion, we may assert that the substance of Jean Piaget's findings on cognitive development of the child is highly relevant and useful to the teacher.

8.3 Contribution to education

According to Piaget's theory, there are regular patterns in cognitive development of the child. This understanding helps us to predict the child's intellectual level and range of comprehension and power of thinking all along his course of development.

Piaget's theory gives us valuable information as regards planning and framing school curriculum. It advises which subject is to be introduced at a particular level and which is to be excluded. For instance, world history should not be introduced at early primary stage, because at this stage, the students have not yet attained desired maturity. Similarly, it is not advisable to introduce algebra to the students of third or fourth standard since the children have not yet developed capacity for abstract thinking. The children of nursery and elementary classes cannot think in abstract terms. So, while teaching them mathematics and science, concrete materials should be used for better understanding.

Thus, Piaget's theory makes the teacher aware of the nature of thought processes of the child at a particular stage of development. This knowledge helps an educator to plan his lesson and method of teaching.

Piaget's theory introduces the concept of assimilation, accommodation and equilibration in the process of learning and development. The teacher should know the technique of linking new experiences of the child with the old knowledge, so that they may be easily assimilated by the learner.

Piaget's theory highlights the importance of physical and social environment for the intellectual development of the child. Therefore, the family as well as school should attempt to provide conducive environment for the proper development of their intellectual abilities.

Piaget's theory emphasises the importance of motivation in the learning process. Teaching should not be limited to passive verbal instruction. The pupils should be encouraged to discover things by themselves. This will develop their cognitive abilities.

Piaget has thrown enough light on the significance of moral development. According to him, children during later childhood begin to develop moral and social values. Therefore, teachers should make an effort to guide children in developing desirable moral and social values.

Summary

Jean Piaget has made a significant contribution to the study of human cognitive development. According to him, the child is born with a few practical instincts and reflexes. In the course of the child's mental growth, important changes occur in his cognitive structure by the processes of assimilation and accommodation.

Piaget has recognised clear-cut stages in the cognitive development of children, which are : *The sensori-motor stage* (birth to 2 years), *pre-conceptual stage* (2 to 4 years), *intuitive stage* (4 to 8 years), *concrete operational stage* (8 to 11 years) and *formal operational stage* (11 to 15 years).

Piaget has acquainted us with the thought processes of children at different levels of maturity or chronological age. He has laid emphasis on the organisation of optimal conditions for an individual's development. In brief, Piaget's findings on cognitive development of the child is highly useful to the educator.

References

1. Piaget, J. : *Judgement and Reasoning in the Child,* New York : Harcourt & Brace, 1926.
2. — *The Moral Judgement of the Child,* New York : Harcourt & Brace, 1932.
3. Dinkmeyer, D.C. : *Child Development*, Prentice-Hall India Pvt. Ltd. New Delhi, 1967.
4. Mangal, S.K. : *Advanced Educational Psychology,* Prentice-Hall of India Pvt. Ltd. New Delhi, 1997.

Questions and Assignments

1. Briefly describe the cognitive development idea of Piaget.
2. What are the special characteristics of concrete operational phase?
3. Describe the special features of formal operational phase. in the cognitive development of a child.
4. Evaluate Piaget's theory of cognitive development and its contribution to education.

Chapter 9

Heredity and environment

Introduction : The development of the child is conditioned by the two important factors : heredity and environment or nature and nurture. It is important to know what exactly is the part played by these two factors in the growth and development of the child.

9.1 What is Heredity?

Heredity, according to Oxford dictionary, is the property by virtue of which offspring inherits the nature and characteristics of parents and ancestors.

Heredity is the innate characteristics of a child with which he is born. The child receives many of his physical and mental traits from his parents. In physical appearance, the child usually resembles his parents. He also appears to inherit their attitude and aptitude, belief and interest, habit and character. There is a common proverb : 'Like tends to beget like.' It is also popularly believed that children of honest and intelligent parents are honest and intelligent, whereas those of the dishonest and stupid parents often become wicked and intellectually defective. It is a common belief that just as we inherit our bodies from our parents, so also we inherit their intelligence, temperament and character.

Every trait that an individual exhibits after birth is potential. In other words, his heredity is fixed, nothing can possibly be added to it. You cannot make a silk purse out of a sow's ear—goes a proverb. Therefore, Sandiford has defined heredity as the sum total of the traits potentially present in the fertilised ovum.

G. Mendel (1865) postulated that chromosomes contain the hereditary characters. Subsequently, it was learnt that genes are DNA particles present inside the chromosomes, which are carried from one generation to other, carrying the hereditary characters along with it.

9.2 Theories of Heredity

Does a person pass on to his son both innate as well as acquired traits or pass on those traits only which he received from his ancestors? There are several theories as to the transmission of physical and mental traits from one generation to the other.

9.2.1 Continuity of Germ plasm

August Weismann (1834–1914) propounded the theory of the continuity of the germ-plasm. According to this theory, the body grows by the multiplication of germ cell. In this process, some cells are set apart to form reproductive cells in the new individual. These reproductive cells do not take part in the development of the body; these cells are continued down from generation to generation. Thus the parent is rather the trustee of the germ-plasm than the producer of the child.

Weismann argued that any variation imposed on the somatic cells by environment could not affect the germ cells, and, therefore, could not be transmitted to the next generation. He performed experiments with rats. For successive generations, he cut off their tails, but each new generation had a tail at birth. This shows that the rats did not inherit the modification in the bodily structure of the previous generation. They continued to resemble their remotest ancestors. There was no transmission of the acquired traits. The theory of Weismann is supported to some extent by the experiments of Mendel.

9.2.2 Mendel's Laws of Heredity

George Mendel (1822–1884) performed his epoch-making experiments on different varieties of garden peas. He experimented in cross-fertilisation of peas.

As the result of extensive experiments spread over many years, Mendel formulated two laws : (1) The Law of Segregation and (2) The Law of Independent Assortment.

1. **The Law of Segregation :** Whatever factor may come to the zygote, they never lose their individual identity. The allelomorphs (T_c) separate out at meiosis.
2. **The Law of Independent assortment :** The pairs of factors coming together in the F_1 generation separate out from the pure forms and combines in various ways forming hybrids in succeeding generations. Each pair of unit character is inherited independently of the other.

Mendel's experiment : Mendel's law is well-illustrated by some plant species like peas, maize, rice, etc., in which there exist two distinct varieties.

Mendel crossed a plant of pure tall race with a plant of pure dwarf race. All the plants in the first hybrid generation (F_1) were tall. When these tall hybrid were self-fertilised, it was found that the second filial generation (F_2) contained tall and dwarf plants in the relative proportion 3 : 1, that is, out of every hundred plants, 25 were dwarf and 75 were tall.

He further found that the dwarf plants of the F_2 generation when self-fertilised, produced pure dwarf plants. Similarly, the tall plants of the F_2 generation when self-fertilised produced only pure tall plants. But the remaining tall plants produced hybrid talls when self-fertilised. They produced tall and dwarf plants in the ratio of 3 : 1.

The results may be presented in the tabular form as follows :

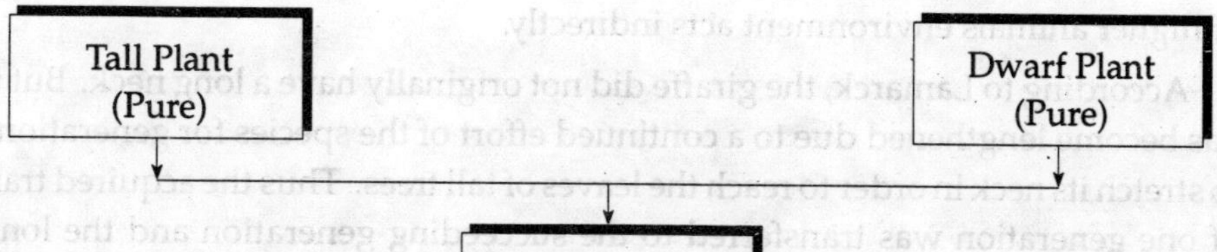

Fig. 9.1: Tall variety : Dwarf variefy : : 3 : 1.

9.2.3 The law of variation (Evolution theory)

If heredity worked so rigidly as never to allow an acquired t.ait to be transmitted to the progeny, the evolution of the species would have been impossible. From the evolutionary point of view variation is of the utmost importance as it forms the raw material of evolution.

Evolution is explained usually in two ways : through an inner urge of the species to adjust itself to changed environment and through chance variation and natural selection. There are three main theories of organic evolution :

1. Lamarck's theory of inheritance.
2. Charles Darwin's theory of natural selection.
3. Hugo deVries' mutation theory.

9.2.4 Lamarck's theory

According to Lamarck (1744–1829), in case of plants and lower animals environment acts directly on the organisms and modifies them. In the case of higher animals environment acts indirectly.

According to Lamarck, the giraffe did not originally have a long neck. But it has become lengthened due to a continued effort of the species for generations to stretch its neck in order to reach the leaves of tall trees. Thus the acquired trait of one generation was transferred to the succeeding generation and the long neck of the animal has become a permanent feature of its physical structure.

During the last few years, experimental evidence has gradually accumulated which seems to prove that acquired variations can be inherited. This revival of Lamarckism is known as Neo-Lamarckism.

The Neo-Lamarckians believe that the germ cells are not always immune from the effects of environment. In some cases, an acquired variation may be transmitted as such to the offspring through the germ cells, while in others environment seems to have some direct effects on its germ cells.

9.2.5 Darwin's natural selection theory

According to Charles Darwin (1809–82), variations are not due to some inward urge but are accidental. They are retained by the species by the process of natural selection and survival of the fittest. In the struggle for existence, those only survive who have favourable variations.

9.2.6 Hugo deVries' mutation theory

This theory postulates that new species arise suddenly at a single step from previous species without any intergrading forms. Evolution, according to this theory, is not a gradual but a jerky process. In fruit fly, Dorsophila melanogaster, numerous mutations occur, and these are definitely inheritable.

9.2.7 View of genetics

According to the modern theory of heredity, a given character may be represented in the chromosomes by a gene. At the time of conception, the genes of the father pair with the genes of the mother, and thus, they determine the qualities of the children. We call the result of the union of these genes as Heredity.

9.3 Importance of Heredity

It is of prime importance to the educator to determine what exactly is the part played by heredity or environment in the development of the child. Some educators believe that heredity is the only factor to be considered and the influence of environment is insignificant in the child's development. The child receives his physical and mental traits from his father or the mother.

9.4 Experimental studies

Various techniques, such as correlation method, co-twin control method, family study and foster-children method have been used to study the factor of heredity. Following experiments prove the importance of heredity in the life of an individual.

9.4.1 Weismann's experiment

Weismann (1834–1914) cut off tails of rats for several successive generations. He observed that each new generation got a tail at birth and they continued to resemble their remotest ancestors. It has been also observed that any physical deformity of a person due to accident or disease is not inherited by the child. Thus, Weismann concluded that, there is no transmission of the acquired traits. His theory shows that man comes out of man and not the horse, due to the continuity of germ-plasm.

9.4.2 Family study

Galton's experiment (1869) : Francis Galton studied the family history of 977 eminent persons and found that 536 of them were well-settled in life. He studied family history of another 977 persons of an ordinary average family and found that only 4 persons of them were eminent. This experiment of Galton shows the influence of heredity.

Goddard's experiment : Goddard studied the family history of Kallikok, who had two wives—one normal and the other feeble-minded. The offsprings from the normal and intelligent wife were all intelligent and social. But the offsprings from the feeble-minded wife were mostly antisocial and mentally defective.

Dugdale's experiment : Dugdale studied the family history of Yukes, who was a criminal. Dugdale found that most of the people of this generation are murderers, thieves, alcoholics and antisocials.

Karl Pearson's experiment : Karl Pearson traced the family tree of Wedgegood-Darwin-Galton family for over thousand years. It shows that the members of the family have been for five successive generations fellows of the Royal Society of England. There have been many eminent persons in that family.

9.5 Study of twins

Newman's experiment : Newman studied two identical twins, Fred and Edwin. They were brought up in two different families. Newman found them when both were 26 years of age. He found marked similarities between them. They resembled each other in physical appearance, colour of eyes and hair, height, weight, shape of the ears, etc. Both of them married two girls of the same age and similar nature.

Newman concluded that despite difference in environment, this resemblance between the twins was due to heredity.

Lauterback's experiment : Lauterback's study shows that environment is inadequate to account for the resemblances of twins : the older and younger twins are alike in their mental resemblances and training does not materially affect the resemblance.

Thorndike's experiment : Thorndike applied statistical device of correlation to determine the resemblance between twins and siblings. His findings show :

1. There is greater resemblance among the twins (correlation 0.78) than among the siblings (correlation 0.30).
2. The younger the twins, the greater the resemblance among them. Those between the ages of 9 and 11 showed a correlation of 0.89 and those between the ages of 12 to 14 shows 0.70.

Thorndike concluded that similarity and differences in the original nature of men are due to the nature of the germ cells. The influence of environment in the creation of likeness and differences is slight.

Merriman's experiment : Merriman used intelligence tests to determine the coefficient of correlation between younger and older twins. His findings indicate that the older twins are less alike than younger twins. This means environment has played its part in increasing the differences. The results are given in the next page :

Stanford Binet I.Q.s		
Pairs compared	No. of pairs	Coefficient of correlation
All pairs 5–7 years	47	0.81
All pairs 10–16 years	58	0.76

National intelligence tests		
All pairs 5–9 years	54	0.80
All pairs 11–18 years	48	0.87

Fig. 9.2

From the above facts we may conclude that the limits of growth and development of an individual are to a great extent determined at birth by his heredity.

9.6 Importance of Environment

Environment comprises all factors acting on an organism, such as temperature, light, air, the nature of the medium, nutrition, etc.

According to some psychologists environment plays an important role in the development of the child and heredity plays a negligible part.

Watson, the famous behaviourist, asserted : Give me a dozen healthy infants and my own specific world to bring them up in and I will guarantee to take any one at random and train him to become any type of specialist.

Following experiments by eminent scientists illustrate the importance of environment in the growth and development of the child :

9.6.1 Harrison's experiment

Harrison observed that in industrial area, the colour of the moth is generally black. He fed a few moths on metallic salt and produced black moths.

9.6.2 Cunningham's experiment

A flat-fish is white on the lower surface and pigmented on the upper surface. Cunningham by arranging mirrors in an aquarium allowed light to pass into the water from below with the result that the upper surface became white and the lower pigmented.

It has also been possible to change the pigmentation of many birds, mammals and butterflies by lowering the temperature.

9.6.3 Gudernatsch's experiment

Gudernatsch fed the tadpole of a single frog on different types of food. Those fed on the thyroids of mammals passed through all stages of metamorphosis rapidly. But those fed on ordinary food took much longer time to metamorphose.

9.6.4 Candolle's experiment

Candolle of France studied the lives of 552 members of the distinguished academies of Europe. He found that most of them belonged to well-off family and they had ample facilities for higher education.

9.6.5 Easter Brook's experiment

Easter Brook conducted further research on family history of Yukes previously studied by Dugdale and he concluded that with the improvement of environment personality improves. Easter Brook showed that with the improvement of environment, many of the members of Yuke family improved intellectually.

9.6.6 McDougall's experiment

McDougall placed some rats in a tank of water from which they could escape by two paths—the one was lighted and the other was dark. The rats naturally followed the lighted path, but here they received electric shock.

The first generations of rats committed on an average 165 errors before they learnt to change the route. When the experiment was repeated with the progeny, the number of errors diminished till in the twenty-third generation they committed only 25 errors.

This shows that useful habits acquired in one generation may be transmitted in subsequent generations.

9.6.7 Pavlov's experiment

According to Pavlov conditioned reflexes can be inherited. Some white mice were trained to run to the feeding place on the ringing of an electric bell, 300 lessons being required. Succeeding generations required in turn 100, 30, 10 and five lessons.

9.6.8 Cattell's experiment

Like Galton, Cattell also studied the family history of some American Scientists. From the research Cattell found that mental development of an individual depends upon his economic condition, opportunities and social environment. In fact, this study of Cattell contradicts the views of Galton on heredity.

9.6.9 Barbara Burk's study

Barbara Burk first measured the intelligence of 204 foster children. Then the intelligence of their real parents and their foster parents were measured. From the comparative studies of these three groups, it was found that I.Q. of the children changed from 7 to 20 points. This change in intelligence was due to the influence of foster parents who were better educated than their real parents.

9.6.10 Otto Klien Burg's study

Otto Klien Burg found that the Negro children, who came from village to the town were more intelligent than the rural Negro children.

In this connection a few instances may be cited. The Murray Islanders had no words in their language to count beyond six, but after receiving training at the hands of the Scots, who occupied the island, they developed as good a mathematical ability as the one possessed by any civilised people.

The life history of Gladys and Helen also illustrates the influence of environment. Gladys and Helen, who were twins, got separated at the age of 18 months and were brought up in two different families. Gladys had to give up studies at an early age and to earn his livelihood she had to work in a factory, whereas—Helen became a graduate with the help, care and effort of her foster mother. She was then married to a businessman. After thirty-five years when they were discovered, it was found that they had a gulf of difference in behaviour and every respect. Helen became superior to Gladies in intelligence, beauty, conviction, conduct and mental abilities.

The life history of Ramala and Kamala also points to the effect of training. The two daughters were brought up by tigress in the forest of Sunderban in Bengal and behaved like animals. They were trained in human habits. Ramala did not live long, but Kamala learnt a number of human habits as a result of training.

9.6.11 Wellman's study

Influence of environment on intelligence has been studied by Wellman. He found marked increase in I.Q. on repeated tests and greatest gains were made by children of the lower levels of I.Q. Thus, Wellman concluded that, Within certain limits intelligence is modifiable by environmental conditions.

Prof. S.D. Scruggs has also proved that improved education results in an increase of intelligence. Freeman, Bayley, Sherman, Skodak all have expressed similar view.

9.7 Relative importance of Heredity and Environment

A great controversy has appeared in the field of education as regards the influence of heredity and environment on the development of the child. Those who believe in heredity say that heredity is everything and education can not make the child superior if he is born inferior. The believers of the continuity of germ plasm theory state that no amount of education can change the individual from what he is. Thus education to them is futile.

On the other hand, environmentalists believe that heredity is an illusion. Environment makes or destroys the man. Education through controlled environment can change the man in any way it likes. To the environmentalists, education is a great force.

Behaviourists ignore the factor of heredity and lay a great stress on environment. To them, environment is all and all.

However, we cannot accept any of the extreme view. The results of investigations on heredity and environment by different scientists do not confirm the superiority of one over the other. In fact, both heredity and environment play equally important role in the physical and mental development of an individual. Thus mathematically, Personality = Heredity × Environment and not Personality = Heredity + Environment.

9.8 Role of heredity and environment in education

The quality of an individual and his progress depend both on heredity and on environment. Sandiford said, "Child is born with a biological heritage, he is born into a social heritage."

The social heritage of an individual consists of all the knowledge, beliefs, customs, laws, language, traditions, folkways, art, literature and science and so on.

Just as the biological heredity determines our heredity, structure and our instinctive patterns of action, in the same way social heredity moulds our habits from childhood, determines our social behaviour and then transmits them to the next generation.

Weismann's germ plasm theory makes the improvement of the human race almost impossible. But social heredity, good education and improved environment show bright silver linings of racial improvement.

The child inherits not only structural changes and biological traits from his ancestors, but also inherits social heredity. Man is truly the heir of all the ages.

The child's development is conditioned by biological heredity and social heredity, both of which are correlated factors.

Intelligence may be hereditary. But this much is definite that poor environment may retard the development. So, the duty of the educator is to provide the best kind of environment to the children. If I.Q. cannot be increased vertically, it may be expanded horizontally. Even for the gifted child with high I.Q. proper environment is needed, otherwise it will remain dormant. So we cannot lose sight of the environment.

Like intelligence, the teacher can develop moral and sense of beauty in the child through proper education.

But education is not all-powerful. There are certain limits to the educable capacity of each child and these limitations are provided by heredity. The feeble-minded child cannot be educated to the same extent as the normal child can be. The teacher has no control over the hereditary factor. He does not know with what hereditary factors the child has born. He can only provide the child with optimum environment, best opportunities and best education.

The teacher can improve the child through determining his social heredity. The social heritage has to be acquired a fresh by each generation. The educational efforts of any generation therefore, should not be allowed to relax.

9.9 Role of the teacher

Accepting the reality that the child's development is the joint product of heredity and environment, the teacher's role may be discussed as follows:

1. The results of intelligence tests confirm the view that there are congenital differences in the aptitudes and abilities of children. Therefore, the syllabus should be framed keeping in view of individual difference among the learners. Also special classes should be organised by teachers for backward students and there should be provision for remedial teaching in schools.
2. The school should have educational and vocational guidance centres for counselling. The teacher should maintain cumulative Record Card for each and every student.
3. The school should be situated in an ideal environment away from din and bustle of the town. The classrooms should be well-ventilated.
4. The school should have a good library. The students should be encouraged to read books of knowledge and biographies of great men.
5. Prof. Nunn believes in Lamarckism and he holds that the principal factor in the process of development is the child himself. So, an urge for improvement should be created in the child. He should be motivated to use the educational opportunities provided by the school. He should be encouraged to actively participate in various functions organised by the school.

6. The method of teaching should be scientific. Teaching aids should be used profusely when needed.
7. Child clinic should be set up in school for the treatment of the mal-adjusted and handicapped pupils.

Summary

Heredity is the transmission of parental characters to the progeny. It is the innate characteristics of a child. Environment comprises all factors acting on an organism, such as temperature, light, air, the nature of the medium, nutrition, etc. The development of the child depends both on heredity and environment.

The theories of heredity prove that heredity is the tremendously important factor in the development of the child. Mendel's laws show that the type of growth and quality of development of the child depend upon the blend of certain characteristics from male and female side and that what the child would be is predetermined at the time of conception. Similarly, the theory of evolution and *its survival of the fittest* tenet lead us to think that life has no higher purpose to fulfil and education is all useless. Continuity of the germ plasm and the theory of genes also assert the same fact. When genes are so powerful to determine the lines of growth and development, how can education be effective? But all such thinking is erroneous as education and training both are great factors in the development.

A number of experiments conducted by eminent scientists illustrate the importance of education and training. The results of these experiments show that useful habits acquired through training may be transmitted in subsequent generations.

The educator can improve the child through determining his social heredity. But the social heritage has to be acquired afresh by each generation. Therefore, the educational efforts of any generation should not be allowed to relax.

References

1. Nunn, T.P. : *Education, Its Data and First Principles,* (E. Arnold).
2. Skinner, C.E. : *Essentials of Educational Psychology,* Englewood Cliffs, New Jersey : Prentice-Hall, 1958.
3. Sorenson, H. : *Psychology in Education.* New York : McGraw Hill, 1964.

4. Ross, J.S. : *Ground Work of Educational Psychology,* London : George G. Harrup & Co., 1951.

Questions and Assignments

1. Examine the roles of heredity and environment in the development of a child and show their relation to each other.
2. What do you understand by heredity? Discuss in brief some of the important theories that explain the functioning of heredity.
3. What is social heredity? Discuss the significance of the concept in the field of education.
4. Discuss the relative importance of heredity and environment in the development of the child.
5. Children are born with biological heritage, they are born into a social heritage. —Discuss.
6. Describe Mendel's laws of heredity and explain their significance.
7. Give an account of experimental studies that have been made to know the extent of influence of heredity and environment on the growth and development of the child.
8. What is meant by social heredity? How can one improve the social heredity of the child?
9. What is meant by nature and nuture? Develop the idea that nature is a greater factor which moulds human lives.
10. *Intelligence is inherited and character is formed*—discuss the implication of the statement.
11. What do you understand by Evolution theory and what is its significance?
12. Write notes on :

    (a) Mendel's Law of Heredity.

    (b) Darwin's Natural Selection Theory.

    (c) Study of twins.

    (d) Importance of Environment.

Chapter 10

Schools of psychology and their relation to education

Introduction : Psychology may be considered as a nursery of various schools of thought. Formerly, psychology was more philosophical than psychological in nature. Now it is regarded as a natural or positive science.

The efforts of psychologists to provide an objective base to the study of human behaviour gave birth to a number of schools of psychology. The tenets of these schools have greatly affected the teaching-learning process.

It is, therefore, imperative for a student of educational psychology to know how far these schools of psychology have contributed towards the growth of education.

There are several important schools or systems of psychology which have become popular. Some of them are briefly discussed here.

10.1 Faculty psychology

The term faculty is derived from the Latin word *facultas* meaning a capacity to act.

Faculty psychology assumes that our mind is made up of a large number of independent faculties such as sensation, perception, imagination, memory, thinking, feeling, reasoning and so on. Faculty psychology does not recognise the causal interaction of mental processes. But modern psychology regards the mind as an organic unity of interdependent processes.

This school of psychology has now lost its importance and has become obsolete.

10.2 Structuralism

Wilhelm Wundt (1832–1920) established the first psychological laboratory at Leipzig in 1879 with a view to study the mind systematically. He studied the structure of consciousness and analysed it into its elements and their relations. This approach to psychology is known as structuralism.

Wundt and his associates conducted experiments by using the method of introspection. Introspection means to look within. It means systematic process of self-observation. According to this method, the psychologists look within the mind to discover how the subject thinks, reasons and imagines and then they suppose that the process of thinking, reasoning and imagination is the same in case of others too. Therefore, they ask other individuals to report what is going in their minds. Introspection is the fundamental method of psychology. The other natural sciences have no such method.

Titchener (1867–1927) a pupil of Wundt, was an exponent of structuralism in America. According to Titchener, psychology is the science of consciousness or the study of experience. Consciousness or experience can be analysed into three basic elements : sensations, feelings and images. Titchener proposed that the human mind was made up of more than 30,000 sensations, feelings and images. Like Wundt, he also believed in mental chemistry. The combination of the three mental elements in varying proportions accounts for different compound mental processes, in which the qualities of the separate mental elements are lost.

Titchener considered mental processes more or less persistent entities with fixed qualities and other attributes. He carried structural psychology to perfection in which every problem of general psychology finds its place.

10.2.1 Critical estimate

As a system of psychology, structuralism does not cover all aspects of human behaviour. It does not deal with children, mentally defective and insane persons, who cannot introspect.

The behaviourists find fault with structuralism both with respect to its introspectionism as well as the results arrived at on its basis.

Other opponents of structural psychology are Gestalt psychologists and William James. Wertheimer, one of the founders of Gestalt psychology, demonstrated through the phi-phenomenon that the whole precedes the parts.

The introspection method used by the structural psychologists for studying behaviour is unreliable because mental processes change so rapidly that introspection fails to record them. William James observed, "The attempt at introspective analysis is like seizing a top to catch its motion."

In conclusion, it may be pointed out that in spite of all that can be said against structural psychology, its contribution to psychology is immense. It raises subjective introspection method to an experimental method applied under controlled conditions. Lastly, Titchener's great work experimental psychology remains a classic text as regards the methodology of experimentalism.

10.2.2 Contribution of structuralism to education

Structuralism provides introspection as a technique of investigating human behaviour. It is one of the important techniques by which we can understand the process of thinking, feeling, reasoning and imagination of an individual. The educator may use this method to study the mental process of his pupils.

It is structuralism, which first established psychological laboratory to investigate the activities of the mind. This is a positive contribution of structuralism to educational psychology.

Researches in sensation, perception, feeling, memory and attention have been conducted by the structural psychologists and the findings have been utilised in educational psychology.

10.3 Functionalism (1842–1910)

William James (1842–1910) was the founder of functional psychology in America. William James (1842–1910), John Dewey (1859–1952) and J.R. Angell (1869–1962) are advocates of functional psychology.

Like structural psychology, functional psychology defines psychology as the science of consciousness. But functional psychology seeks to show the part different kinds of consciousness play in the life of the individual. It attempts to discover the functions of sensation, perception, memory, emotion, imagination, reasoning, etc. in the life of an individual.

According to the functional psychologists, understanding the structure of the mind is not as significant as knowing its functions. Prof. William James did not split up the mind into self-contained entities as the structural psychologists did. To him, all mental processes are but phases of the continuous whole of experience without sharp break.

William James adopted the evolutionary point of view and tried to show that higher and complex mental processes emerged to meet the pressing needs of the organism for a wider control of the environment. Thus functional psychology takes biology as its basis.

In addition to the study of consciousness, functionalism also deals with automatic and habitual responses which are not attended with consciousness.

10.3.1 Critical estimate

Functional psychology is concerned more with mental operations as against the structure of the operating parts. But it is doubtful whether functions can be explained without explaining structures.

The physiological and biological basis of functional psychology renders the method of introspection inappropriate. But the functional psychologists are reluctant to give up introspection because all mental functions involve consciousness or experience which is amenable to introspective study only.

Thus, functionalism may be regarded as a necessary complement of structuralism.

10.3.2 Contribution to Education

Functionalism is a more practical system of psychology than structuralism. It had a positive impact on educational psychology. Functionalism initiated applied research to solve various educational problems.

Functional psychology stressed the importance of making curriculum and school syllabus functional and useful. Instead of memorising certain theories, the system of education should be practical and useful in everyday life of the students. This is why Prof. Dewey, an advocate of functionalism, stressed the importance of making the system of education as useful and pragmatic as possible.

In framing curriculum the needs of the pupils should receive first attention. This paedo centric approach has lead to the invention of new techniques in teaching-learning process.

The school of functional psychology—which is a more scientific and more practical system of psychology than structuralism widened the scope of educational psychology by providing a variety of new methods other than introspection. Some of these methods are : the method of observation, the experimental method, the case-study method and the biographical method.

Functionalism has also enriched the measurement and evaluation system by introducing the technique of questionnaire, rating scales and other mental tests.

In brief, it may be said that the system of functional psychology paved the way for applied research in the field of education and completely revolutionised modern system of education.

10.4 Associationism

The history of associationism goes back to Aristotle, who anticipated the principal laws of association by contiguity, similarity and contrast. Locke,

Hume, Berkeley, Bain and James Mill were advocates of associationism. They reduced mental life to sensations, ideas and reflex actions according to the laws of association. Sensations are elementary units of cognition. Ideas are faint copies of sensation. These are combined in various ways according to the laws of association and give rise to complex cognitions. Reflex actions are elementary units of action. They are combined into complex voluntary actions according to the laws of association.

John Stuart Mill, the illustrious son of James Mill, regarded the mind not as a passive product of association. He substituted association by mental chemistry. Mental chemistry is the fusion of sensory elements in a new compound which is more than the mere sum of the constituent parts.

10.4.1 Reaction against Associationism

The main criticism of associationism is that it fails to account for the unity and continuity of mental life. James Ward emphasised the unity of human experience and behaviour.

According to McDougall, the founder of hormic psychology, associationism is mechanistic and non-purposive psychology.

Gestalt psychology emphasises the conception of Gestalt whole, pattern, or configuration. It looks upon mental processes as whole as distinguished from mere aggregates.

Associationism wrongly denies the unity and activity of the mind. Sensations are not elementary units of experience. Sensations are not retained in the subject as isolated items unrelated to one another. They are retained as interrelated to one another in systems of knowledge.

Associationism wrongly regards perception as an aggregate of sensations and memory images. Gestalt psychologists rightly regards perception as an experience of a whole, which cannot be broken up into elementary units. McDougall rightly calls associationism atomistic psychology or mosaic psychology.

Thus associationism has been rejected by contemporary schools of psychology.

10.5 Behaviourism

Behaviourism arises as a revolt against the introspective structural and functional psychology of Wundt, Titchener and William James. As a rebel, behaviourism may be regarded as the most vigorous and aggressive of the modern schools of psychology.

John Broadus Watson (1878–1950), the father of the behaviourist school, defined psychology as a science of behaviour. He thought that the whole idea of consciousness or experience is absurd. Mental processes are invisible and intangible. They are elusive and do not serve any useful propose.

In his work entitled Behaviour (1914) Watson made his behaviouristic position very clear. Psychology is a purely objective experimental branch of natural science. Its goal is the prediction and control of behaviour. Introspection is a deceptive method and not at all necessary for psychological investigation. Its methods are observation and experiment, which are the methods of physical science.

Psychology is the science of behaviour in terms of stimulus and response. Watson regards a reflex action as the simplest type of activity.

He denies the existence of sensations. He uses such expressions as response to light, olfactory response, auditory response, etc. Watson seeks to explain all mental processes in terms of sensori-motor or stimulus-response behaviour (S–R). He rejects sensation because it is not sensori-motor behaviour. He does not mention perception because it involves interpretation of meanings of sensory signs, and because it is difficult to explain meanings in terms of sensori-motor behaviour.

Watson never uses the term memory. He reduces it to neural habit. He believes in habit-memory only and rejects pure memory. The feeling of familiarity involved in memory simply means the revival of old viscelaral responses.

Watson reduces thinking to subvocal talking. It consists in implicit speech movements. In the beginning, the young child says aloud what he is doing. At the next stage, he whispers to himself instead of talking aloud. Then he makes lip movements only instead of whispering. Finally, he talks to himself without making any audible movement. Thus, the young child learns to think through the movement of vocal organs.

Watson regards the feeling, of pleasantness and unpleasantness as partly sensory impulses from the sex organs or other erogenous zones.

According to Watson, emotion consists of profound changes of the bodily mechanism as a whole, but particularly of the visceral and glandular systems. Watson credits a very young child with fear, rage and love. Fear is aroused in him by the loss of support by falling, or by hearing a loud sound. Anger is excited by obstructing his freedom of movements. Love is aroused by gently patting him. All other emotions are induced in him by conditioning.

Watson regards instict as a system of chained reflexes. He rejects instincts as hereditary predisposition to perceive specific objects. Watson believes in environmentalism. He stated that children of the least intelligent as those of gifted parents stood an equal chance of success in life. He asserted that he can make any healthy, normal child into a scholar, an engineer, a poet, or a philosopher by placing him in the proper environment.

Consistent with his behavioural standpoint, Watson explains learning by the law of exercise, the law of use, the law of disuse, the law of frequency and the law of recency. He rejects the law of effect of Thorndike because it refers to pleasure and pain and because they are mental processes.

Adopting Pavlov's nomenclature, Watson asserted that all learning is conditioning.

The important tenets of behaviourism may thus be summarised as :

1. Psychology is a purely biological science. It is a natural science of behaviour. It is the science of stimulus response or S–R unit.
2. The method of psychology is objective. Experience of the subject can be studied through verbal report method.
3. The mentalistic concepts such consciousness, sensation, perception, memory, feeling, emotion, thinking, etc. have no place in psychology. They are only sensori-motor reflexes.
4. An instinct is a system of chained reflexes. It is not innate or hereditary.
5. Habit is a complex pattern of reflexes learned or acquired by the individual. It is purely neuro-muscular in nature.
6. Learning is due to the Law of Exercise only, involving the factors of frequency and recency. Or, it can be explained by conditioned reflex.
7. Behaviourism is another name for environmentalism. Environment, and not innate or hereditary endowment, determines the personality of an individual.

10.5.1 Criticism of Behaviourism

Behaviourism has been criticised on the following grounds :

1. Behaviourism regards conscious as a byproduct of the brain. This is absurd because consciousness is a fact of experience.
2. Psychology is a science of experience and behaviour. Experience is known by introspection. The behaviourists rely on verbal report. But what does the subject report? Obviously, he reports his experience of the reaction of the stimulus upon his mind. In fact, verbal report cannot do away with introspection. Thus, Watson introduces introspection and mental concepts in his behaviouristic approach.
3. Behaviourism explains sensation and perception purely in sensori-motor terms. It does not recognise sensation as experience. It does not mention perception because it involves interpretation of meanings of sensori signs. The behaviourists ignore the bare awareness, which is the nature of sensation and determinate awareness or consciousness.

4. Behaviourism does not recognise pure memory, image and imagination. It wrongly reduces memory and imagination to neural habit. Images are considered as implicit kinesthetic impulses and verbal responses. Behaviourism does not take account of recognition, which is essential in these processes.

5. Behaviourism wrongly identifies thinking with subvocal talking. The equation, thought = speech may be expressed also as speech = thought. But this is absurd because thoughtless or meaningless speech is quite possible.

6. Behaviourism wrongly considers that learning is possible only by trial and error. So it brushes Thorndike's Law of Effect aside. But incentive, motivation and interest play an important part in the process of learning. So, mental element cannot be totally banished from the system of learning. Besides, human learning is mostly intelligent, rational or by insight. According to Gestaltists, even chimpanzees learn by insight.

7. Feeling and emotion are also wrongly explained by the behaviourist in sensori-motor terms. Watson regards the feelings of pleasantness and unpleasantness as sensori impulses from the sex organs or other erogenous zones. Emotions are regarded as pattern reactions of the visceral and glandular systems. But such a peripheral account of emotion and feeling goes against the findings of Cannon and Sherrington which confirm that the loss of visceral sensations does not affect the animal's emotional behaviour.

8. Behaviourists explain habit as neuro-muscular integration or organisation of reflexes. But they cannot explain why one act is repeated, while another is not. In fact, motivation plays an important part behind an act repeated. Thus, the account given of habit as nervous integration is not satisfactory.

9. Behaviourists highlighted the role of environment in moulding the personality of an individual. They totally denied the role of heredity. But an individual cannot be completely moulded and determined by the environment. He determines his own actions freely with the limits of the physical and social environment. Environmentalism reduces man to an automation. Behaviourism is mechanistic and deterministic. Bengelski rightly remarked, 'No one ever offered Watson the control of the children he wanted and his claim was never brought to a test.'

10.5.2 Merits of Behaviourism and its contribution to education

The merit of behaviourism lies in its recognition of the importance of behaviour in the study of psychology. Behaviourists attempted to make traditional psychology a progressive and dynamic science. They replaced introspective measures with the scientific and objective methods.

Behaviourism helped to extend the scope of educational psychology by including the study of animals as a method to understand human nature. It also advocated the inclusion of abnormals, maladjusted, backward and delinquents in educational psychology.

Behaviourism denied the role of heredity and stressed the role of environment in shaping the behaviour of an individual. This held a rosy picture of the chances of rapid social improvement through better education. It stressed the need to provide pupils with the best educational environment.

The school of behaviourism has influenced educational psychology mainly in the area of teaching and learning. It highlighted the importance of motivation and the use of reinforcement in the process of learning and shaping of behaviour of the pupils.

The experimental findings of the behaviourists have considerably helped to deal with retarded, maladjusted, delinquent and problem children.

Lastly, behaviourism gave birth to new innovations and modern techniques of learning through programmed text-books, teaching-machines and computer-assisted instruction.

10.6 Gestalt psychology

Wolfgang Kohler (1887–1967), Kurt Koffka (1886–1941) and Max Wartheimer (1880–1943), are the three champions of Gestalt psychology. In Germany, Gestalt psychology began as a revolt against functionalism and associationism.

10.6.1 Meaning of Gestalt psychology

Gestalt is a German word, which means configuration, pattern, form, shape or structure.

10.6.2 Tenets of Gestalt psychology

1. Gestalt psychology regards mind, consciousness, behaviour or other mental processes as an integrated whole rather than a conglomeration or summation of parts.

   Gestalt psychology began in Germany as a revolt against the psychology of associationism. According to Gestalt doctrine organism acts as a whole, and its behaviour does not consist of a sum of reflexes.

   Gestalt psychology rejected the notion of association altogether, and regarded every kind of experience or behaviour as a whole. Experience is indivisible and unanalysable whole. The whole is different from the sum of its parts or elements. For instance, musical melody cannot be found in the individual notes composing it.

2. Sherrington demonstrated the integrative action of the nervous system. Lashley showed that the brain functioned as a whole in all kinds of learning. Gestalt psychology stresses the organised wholeness of behaviour.

3. Gestalt psychology rejected sensations as well as reflex actions because they are elements of experience and behaviour.

4. According to Gestalt psychology perception, not sensation, is the unit of immediate experience. We perceive an object as a Gestalt or a whole. Gestalt psychology rejected sensations because they are elements or atoms of experience.

5. Gestalt psychologists distinguish between figure and ground in perception. We always perceive a figure in a background. We have a natural tendency to close-up gaps. The Gestaltists believe that when an irregular figure with gaps is seen, there are unbalanced tensions in the brain. But it receives a closed figure with tensions restored to equilibrium. The brain responds to a figure as a whole.

6. The phi-phenomenon illustrates the perceptual Gestalt as a whole experience. Wertheimer showed that if two points are illuminated at an interval of .06 second, a single light is perceived as moving from one point to the other. Thus objects lying in the perceptual field tend to be perceived as a whole rather than as separate entities.

7. According to the Gestalt psychologists learning is not a trial and error process. They regard learning as an insight into its object as a whole. Insight is not a slow process of development, but a sort of sudden flash.

   Kohler conducted a number of experiments on chimpanzees to ascertain the method of the animal's learning. One of the experiments show how Sultan, a chimpanzee, combines two bamboo sticks into one useful tools to get at the suspended bananas. The animals learn by insight. They have the power of seeing the point. They see key to a situation. Perceptual reorganisation of the situation is necessary for learning a new movement to master a novel situation.

8. Gestaltists regard the character of a person as an organised, whole, a Gestalt, and not as a mere sum of traits. It cannot be estimated by measuring each trait separately. Thus, character and personality are not mere sum total of isolated traits but pattern or configuration.

   Thus, Gestalt psychology opposed traditional psychology comprising structuralism, functionalism and behaviourism. It rejected the brick and mortar concept of structuralism. It is anti-analytical and it revolted against mosaic or atomistic psychology.

10.6.3 Critical estimate

Gestalt psychology seems to be right when it rejects atomistic psychology and lays stress on experience as wholes. But it does not explain the nature of wholes or Gestalten. The Gestalt school condemns analysis too much. It is not justified in discarding analysis altogether. Psychology is a science and it should use both analytic and synthetic methods. By refusing analytical method, the Gestalt doctrine opens the gate to unanalysed conception and arbitrary interpretation of mental phenomena. Gestalt psychology keeps itself confined mainly to problems of perception and learning. It has paid little attention to the detailed study of feeling, emotion, instincts, interests and conation. The Gestaltists fail to understand that the meanings are achieved through our interests and desires out of sensations. They ignore the role of affective and connative tendencies in perceiving things.

Organisation of wholes cannot be explained without the conative impulse or striving of the subject. Interest determines the nature of the field of organisation. Thus Gestalt school does not probe deep into the nature of Gestalten or patterns.

Lastly, it is difficult to explain what is meant by insightful learning. Insight seems to be vague as a scientific concept. Trial and error and Conditioned reflex theories of learning seems to be more precise from the scientific point of view. However, the Gestalt theory of learning and Trial and Error theory of Thorndike are not very much antagonistic. Insight does not occur like a flash of lightning. It evolves through trial and error process.

10.6.4 Contribution to Education

The unique contribution of Gestalt psychology lie in their experiments in perception, learning, motivation and other problems related to education :

1. Gestalt psychology stresses organised wholes. It holds that learning consists in organisation of perceptual activity and organisation of behaviour. It is never a complex of mechanical reflex actions. This doctrine of wholeness or principle of integration has been introduced in methodology of teaching and in framing modern curriculum and syllabus. Modern educationists lay much stress on inter-disciplinary approach and integrated teaching. They present the subject matter of teaching as a whole in the class.
2. The Gestalt approach makes learning and problem solving an intelligent activity rather than a mere stimulus-response process. The Gestaltists

stress that improvement of child's intelligence depends not on mechanical drilling but on insight into the whole situation to be learnt.

3. According to the Gestalt psychologists, motivation plays an important role in the teaching-learning process. Kurt Lewin has made a Gestalt study of the general field of motivation and established its important role in the field of education. Goals and purposes have an important place in learning. Goal creates tension which activates the learners.

10.7 Hormic psychology

William McDougall is the propounder of the hormic psychology. The Greek word *horme* means an urge or impulse to action.

Purpose is the central concept of hormic psychology. McDougall asserts that every action of animal or human being is purposive or strongly teleological.

Psychology is defined by McDougall as the science of behaviour. Behaviour, according to him, is not mechanical response to stimulus. It is biologically purposive. Purposive behaviour is goal-seeking. Even instinctive actions are purposive.

McDougall regards instincts as the primary motives or springs of action in individual as well as social behaviour. He holds that behaviour cannot be explained without purpose.

10.7.1 Criteria of purposive behaviour

McDougall mentions the marks of purposive behaviour as :

1. Purposive behaviour involves spontaneity of movement.
2. Purposive behaviour persists even when the stimulus has ceased and continues till the goal is reached.
3. It is indefinitely variable.
4. It terminates when the goal is reached.
5. The repetition of a behaviour response to a given situation under similar circumstances shows some degree of improved efficiency in dealing with that situation.
6. In purposive behaviour there occurs the totality of reaction of the animal. The animal does not react to the behavioural situation in a piecemeal fashion but as a whole.

10.7.2 Theory of Instinct

McDougall defines instincts as certain specific innate modes of behaviour in certain specific situations which do not have to be learnt and which are common to all members of the species.

10.7.3 Chief characteristics

Instincts are innate. They are common to all living organisms. They are goal-directed. They are the mainsprings of human action. McDougall gives a list of 14 important instincts. With each of them is connected a specific emotion as follows :

Table 10.1

Name of instinct	Emotions connected with the instincts
Instinct of escape	Fear
Instinct of combat	Anger
Repulsion	Disgust
Parental instinct	Tender emotion, love
Appeal	Distress
Sex (mating)	Lust
Curiosity	Wonder
Submission	Negative self-feeling
Assertion	Positive self-feeling, elation
Social (gregarious)	Feeling of loneliness
Food seeking	Appetite
Acquisitive	Feeling of ownership
Construction	Feeling of creativeness
Laughter	Amusement

According to McDougall, though instincts are hereditary, they are modifiable through learning and experience.

McDougall agrees with the Gestaltists that higher animals learn by insight. But he asserts that foresight is also necessary for learning. Learning involves foresight as well as insight. McDougall recognises two forms of learning: (1) Intelligent learning through insight and foresight. (2) Quasi-mechanical learning through trial and error. However, all kinds of learning—intelligent learning through insight and foresight and unintelligent learning through mere repetition—are purposive.

10.7.4 Critical estimate

Hormic psychology rightly rejects the concept of mind as a mosaic of discrete sensations and ideas. It rightly emphasises the purposive nature of experience and behaviour. Its emphasis on the integral nature of personality allies it with Gestalt psychology. Moreover, the stress laid by hormic psychology upon objective methods of psychological investigation, side by side with introspection, is also justifiable.

However, McDougall makes too much of instincts and wrongly regards intelligence as subservient to instincts. Intelligence guides and regulates the instincts, and redirects them into rational and social channels.

McDougall revives the faculty psychology by regarding instincts as mental entities. Many instinctive actions, such as mating, self-assertion, etc. which are acquired by the individual through his contact with the social environment, are learned actions.

Instincts play an important part in social behaviour. But reason plays an important part in social conduct. It is also determined, to a certain extent, by thought and reflection. McDougall emphasised the role of instincts too much in social behaviour.

McDougall revised his list of instincts many times. He started with a list of twelve instincts in 1908 (Introduction to Social Psychology) and raised it to eighteen in 1932 (Energies of Men). Some other psychologists recognised as many as forty instincts. Different psychologists define instinct in different ways. Thus, instinct is a vague and mysterious entity incapable of experimental verification. This is why many psychologists want to abolish the term instinct from the subject of psychology.

10.7.5 Contribution to Education

The hormic or purposive psychology helped educational theory and practice by its emphasis on purpose. Education must have a goal and it should be purposive.

Modern education is said to be paedocentric. The education of a child should be based on his natural tendencies or instincts.

All animals have instincts. But instincts are much more modifiable in the case of man than in the case of other animals. Man's superiority lies in the greater plasticity of his instincts. The child is born with instincts but those are very plastic. The young puppy or kitten, within a few days of its birth, learns all that it requires to carry on its existence. But a human child is absolutely helpless at birth. It takes years to become self-supporting. The long period of infancy enables the child to learn more from experience than is possible for the animals. The very educability of the child depends upon the fact that at birth it is fully helpless and has no highly finished mental structure. It is due to the plasticity of the child's native tendencies that development of higher life is possible. Thus instincts have great importance in education.

Instincts are the moving forces of human behaviour. The function of the educator is to guide the expression of this urge in the desirable direction. The natural ways of satisfaction of the instincts may not always socially be desirable. It is the duty of the educator to work with these instincts which are the bricks out of which the child's character is fashioned. The educator meets them in their crude form and his function is to modify and purify them.

It is the duty of the educator to know the time when an instinct comes in full vigour and to direct his effort in such a way as to modify it properly to enrich the child's character. According to William James, there is a period in a child's life when certain of his instincts show themselves in full vigour and if they are not properly handled at this time, great harm may be caused to the personality of the child.

Again, there are delayed instincts which appear late in child's life. Educators should not thrust upon the child the studies for which his mind is not prepared. Rousseau rightly said that nothing should be taught to the child today that can be postponed till tomorrow.

Every teacher in his class daily faces the problem of discipline and other undesirable behaviours. There must be certain instinctive force behind such problematic behaviour. For instance, in young children, instinct of self-assertion may be responsible for various activities of indiscipline. To draw attention of the teacher towards himself they may raise hands a gain and again or make noise. So, the educator must find out the root cause of such behaviour and try to remove it.

Thus, the doctrine of instinct has a great influence upon the method of teaching and curriculum construction. Project method, play-way method or activity method, etc. have been devised on the consideration of importance of the instincts.

Instincts determine the interests of the pupils. This helps a teacher to prepare suitable text-books at different age-levels. The materials of the text-books are made attractive and interesting to the pupils of tender age.

Finally, the educator should know how to control and guide instinctive energy of the pupils so that maximum benefit occurs to them. There may be three possible ways of controlling instincts :

1. Complete repression of instincts.
2. Modification or sublimation of instincts.
3. Encouraging useful instincts.

Repression : If an evil tendency is checked for a given period of time, it may disappear because of disuse. But this does not always happen. If an instinct is repressed for a long time, it breaks out into violent eruption when opportunity occurs. Strong instincts like pugnacity and sex, when repressed, usually manifest themselves in undesirable ways.

However, repression is not identical with self-restraint. Self-restraint includes conscious repression, which is sometimes socially desirable and a necessity.

Sublimation : The process of redirecting instinct from its primitive biological goal to worthy ends is known as sublimation of instinct. An instinct is said to be sublimated when the energy behind it is utilised in activities that are socially valuable.

To take an example, the instinct of combat or pugnacity, which normally manifests itself in anti-social activities, may be redirected to games, to solving difficult problems in mathematics or beating classmates in studies. Similarly, the acquisitive instinct of the child may be sublimated to collecting things that are educationally valuable. The child may be directed to collect stamps, pictures and different kinds of specimen.

The constructive instinct of the child may be utilised by providing him with materials for constructing models of houses, boats, ships, etc. In the Montessori and Froebelian systems useful lessons are learnt by the children through handling objects of different size and shape.

Similarly, the instinct of sex may be sublimated through engaging children in music and art, poetry and other aesthetic pursuits. Such activities should form the normal part of the school-work.

Encouraging useful instincts : Those instincts which are socially and individually uplifting should be strengthened. For example, instinct of construction should always be reinforced.

Thus an educator cannot remain ignorant of this system of psychology.

10.8 Psychoanalysis

Psychoanalysis literally means the analysis of the psyche. Sigmund Freud (1856–1939), a Viennese physician, formulated the theory and technique of psychoanalysis.

Here we shall discuss some of the major concepts of psychoanalytic theory.

10.8.1 Topographical concept of the mind

While explaining the structure of the human mind, Freud divided it into three layers : the conscious, the subconscious and the unconscious. The conscious mind is compared to the tip of an iceberg occupying only one tenth of our total mental life. The mind follows the social code of morality in conscious life and represses the natural desires which come into conflict with it. The desires which are repressed become unconscious wishes. According to Freud, following facts prove the existence of unconscious :

1. Slips of tongue and pen.
2. Forgetfulness.
3. Solution of problems during sleep.
4. Dreams.

5. Somnambulism.
6. Post-hypnotic suggestions.
7. Psychoses and neuroses.

The unconscious is the deepest structure of our psyche. It contains all the repressed wishes, drives and motives. Many of them relate to sexual impulse (libido). Freud regards the unconscious and irrational part of mind as more important than our conscious mind. The unconscious is responsible for most of our behaviour. In fact, Freud asserts that our conscious behaviour is always determined by the forces residing in unconscious.

Freud conceives the mind as dynamic. The repressed wishes in the unconscious always strive to come up to the conscious level; sometimes in disguised and indirect forms as in our dreams, phantasies and the like. The repressed unconscious desires cannot be directly brought back to consciousness. Whereas, informations dormant in subconscious can be easily brought to the level of consciousness whenever required.

10.8.2 Concept of Id, Ego and Super-ego

Freud further devised a theory which recognised three layers of the mind—the Id, the Ego, and the Super-ego.

Id is the most primitive part of the psyche. It remains unconscious and represents the animal in man. It contains all the unethical instinctive driving forces of the individual's life and is dominated by the pleasure principle. It considers only the satisfaction of its own selfish needs.

The ego develops out of the Id, and serves us a connecting link between the Id and the outside world. It is an intermediate principle between the Id and the Super-ego. Ego follows the reality principle. It follows the code of morality prevalent in society.

The Super-ego corresponds to what is called our conscience. It represents the ethical and moral aspect of the psyche. It is the introjected parent who punishes the Ego for discharging psychic energy in irresponsible ways.

Thus, Id is the primitive rebellious instincts, ego corresponds to prudence and the Super-ego corresponds to conscience or judgement from within.

10.8.3 Libido and its stages of growth

Libido or the driving force of the life instinct is synonymous with the sex urge or sexuality. It also means love—sexual love, love for friends, filial love, love for parents, etc. It also means all kinds of physical pleasures arising from any of the organs. It includes the pleasure of thumb-sucking, the pleasure of urination or defecation, etc. Freud regards sex urge as the dynamic force behind all human behaviour at all stages.

10.8.4 Infantile sexuality

Sexuality is not only the characteristic of the adults, the child has sexual urges also. The libido of a child cannot often be fulfilled owing to the ban of the society during infancy. So it is repressed and becomes an unconscious wish.

The psychosexual development of a child passes through the following stages :

1. **The oral stage :** At this stage, the mouth provides pleasure to the child. The child derives pleasure by putting his thumb or anything in his mouth. His love object is his mother's breast which he sucks to satisfy his hunger.

2. **The anal stage :** At this stage, the libido shifts from the mouth of the child to another erogenous zone, namely the anus. The child derives pleasure by holding back waste material through the anus. He derives pleasure from urinating and defecating. This stage normally ranges from two to three years.

3. **Phallic stage :** At this stage, the focus of pleasure shift from anus to the genitals. This stage may give rise to a number of complex like Electra complex in girls and Oedipus complex in boys.

   The Electra complex is the sexual attraction of a female child to her father and her hatred for her mother. The girls may have a feeling that they have been deprived of the male organs by their mothers.

   The Oedipus complex is the sexual attraction of a male child to his mother and his hatred towards his father. The male child feels his father as a powerful rival and is afraid of being harmed by castrating him. This fear is called Castration Complex. These complexes are formed long before puberty—around the age of four to six.

4. **The latency stage :** During this stage, boys and girls prefer to be in the company of their own sex. This period starts from six years and extends up to the on-set of puberty.

5. **Genital stage :** The focus of attraction at this stage shifts towards the members of the opposite sex.

   Thus there are different stages of libido or sexuality : Narcissism or auto-erotism, homosexuality and heterosexuality. The infant is auto-erotic and he loves his own body, and derives pleasure from the satisfaction of his hunger and thirst, urination and defecation. This stage is called Narcissism. As he grows older, he becomes homosexual and when he grows into an adult, he becomes heterosexual.

10.9 Polarity of life instinct and death instinct

Freud includes life instinct (Eros) and death instinct (Thanatos) in the concept of libido or sex urge. The life instinct is opposed to death instinct. Most people wish to live while some individuals have suicidal tendency.

Masochism and Sadism are two other manifestations of the libido. Masochism is a tendency to self-torture and sadism is a tendency to torment the object of love. Masochism and sadism are regarded by Freud as the joint effects of sex instinct and the death instinct. Thus Freud recognises the polarity of the life instinct and the death instinct.

10.9.1 Criticism of Freud's system of psychoanalysis

Freud's system of psychoanalysis has been criticised on the following grounds :

1. Freud over-emphasises the role of sexuality. It is true that the sex instinct is a very dominant urge of human life. But it is not the only instinct that motivates human conduct. The instinct of hunger for food, self-assertion and will-to-live are also more fundamental than the sex urge. In fact, human nature is too complex to be explained by one sex instinct only.

2. There is a great deal of confusion in Freud's theory of libido. Libido is considered as genital sex gratification. Libido is regarded as bodily pleasure, for example, pleasure of thumb sucking, of urination, of defecation, etc. Again, libido is said to be parental love. To Freud, all these kinds of love are expressions of libido. He has lumped wrongly all these urges together under sex instinct. This shows that Freud is not sure of the nature of libido.

3. Freud investigated abnormal persons who suffered from sexual maladjustments. He thus hastily devised his theory that repressed sexual urge was the cause of all personality disorders. He is not justified in proceeding from the abnormal to the normal. He should have started from the normal to the abnormal to evaluate human behaviour.

4. Freud's stand on Oedipus and Electra complex is erroneus. Most normal persons do not find a trace of them in their minds.

5. Freud attaches too much importance to the role of the unconscious. It is true that repressed desires become unconscious, but they may also remain in the margin of consciousness and colour the focus of consciousness. Again, the unconscious need not be considered as a dumping ground of repressed unsocial wishes. It also harbours useful thoughts and higher ideals.

6. Freud makes too much of childhood experiences in determining our overall personality and behaviour. The experiences of adult life also shape one's character and personality. In fact, experiences in the adulthood are no less important than infantile experiences.

7. Lastly, the effect of psychoanalytical doctrine on moral values is disastrous. It has led to the belief that fulfilment of a natural desire is a must and that repression of it is a wrongful act. Thus psychoanalysis leads to hedonism and tends to destroy the moral fabric of society.

   According to Freud, religion is an illusion and infantile. But Freud cannot explain the creative dynamism of the saints and prophets.

10.9.2 Contribution to Education

Freud had great insight into the workings of human behaviour and his doctrine opened a new vista in psychology. It has influenced modern system of education to a great extent:

1. Freud's doctrine of unconscious and subconscious behaviour has widened the scope and method of educational psychology. Before Freud, the concept of human behaviour was limited to conscious behaviour only.

2. By stressing the importance of inner nature of man and highlighting the role of repressed wishes and inner urges, the doctrine of psychoanalysis has greatly influenced the present system of child-centric education.

3. The repression of an instinct brings about the formation of complexes in the unconscious. The presence of a complex in child's personality leads to many undesirable consequences. The system of psychoanalysis has highlighted the importance of sublimation of child's instincts through games and useful social activities.

4. The knowledge of psychoanalysis helps a teacher in framing school curriculum. Nowadays, the teacher provides cocurricular activities along with the curricular activities in school programs for releasing pent-up emotions and repressed wishes of the child.

5. Freud's system of psychoanalysis has highlighted the bad effects of unnecessary restrictions imposed on the children and advocated giving maximum freedom to them for expression of their natural urges. It has stressed the importance of providing education for mental health.

6. Freud's theory of unconscious has enabled the teacher to understand the causes of delinquency and maladjusted behaviour of the children. It has immensely helped the educator to take necessary measures for prevention of such behavioural deviations.

7. Last, but not least, psychoanalysis has highlighted the importance of imparting proper sex education to school children.

10.10 Adler's Individual psychology

Alfred Adler (1870), a disciple of Freud, replaced sex instinct advocated by Freud with two important concepts : (1) Will to power and (2) Style of life.

10.10.1 Will to power

Every individual has a strong innate urge to dominate, to gain superiority and to achieve perfection in some field of life. For gaining superiority, an individual strives hard but he may succeed or fail depending upon circumstances. If he succeeds, he remains satisfied and normal. But if he fails, he may develop mental illness. Adler stresses the importance of Ego and ignores the Freudian sexuality.

10.10.2 Style of life

The style of life of an individual depends on the field in which he chooses to gain superiority. One's style of life is influenced by one's order of birth in the family. If the child is unwanted in the family, he may develop neurotic behaviour or become a delinquent.

In some cases, an individual's style of life may be fashioned according to his physical appearance. He may develop feeling of inferiority because of certain physical deformities.

Often the creative power of an individual may change one's lifestyle. This power of creativity may be innate or this may be gained through environmental experiences.

Again, social interests and aspiration also determine our style of life. Accordingly, we may strive to become a political leader, an orator, a writer, or a musician.

10.10.3 Contribution to education

Adler was interested in the problems of children, their proper education and upbringing. He started an institute of pedagogy at Vienna to provide guidance and counselling to students. His system of analytical psychology has great educational values.

Adler opposed Freud's concept of sex urge as the only motive behind our behaviour. He rather stressed the importance of the urge of self-assertion. Therefore, while educating children, the teacher should take into consideration this inner urge of children. In the name of maintaining discipline, this inner craving of children should not be thwarted. Every child should be given freedom and opportunity to express themselves. Thus, Adler's system provided an impetus to individualised instruction and paedocentric education.

According to Adler, parents and teachers should be very careful not to do anything that may develop inferiority complex in children. They should not feel neglected or unwanted in the family or in the school.

Often rivalry and unhealthy competition encouraged in the school may give rise to the feelings of insecurity and other serious problems of behaviour. Rather, group activities should be encouraged in schools, so that each and every boy can participate. Instead of unhealthy rivalry, cooperation should be the motive force behind all school activities.

Adler's doctrine has proved its value in teaching of mental hygiene. It helps children to overcome their maladjustment.

10.11 Jung's Analytical psychology

Carl Gustav Jung, (1875) was a staunch supporter and follower of Freud. He established a school of thought called analytical psychology.

10.11.1 Structure of the psyche

According to Jung one's psyche can be divided into three parts : (1) Conscious mind, (2) Personal unconscious and (3) Collective unconscious.

Conscious mind consists of the memories, thoughts and feelings. It is the seat of one's ego. It is the upper layer of the mind and below it is the vast unconscious. The unconscious part may be divided into the personal unconscious and the collective unconscious.

Personal unconscious is highly individualistic and it is the abode of repressed desires, fears, anxieties, guilts, dreams, etc. experienced in the lifetime of an individual.

Below the layer of the personal unconscious lies the racial or collective unconscious, which is universal in nature.

The primary elements of the collective unconscious are termed *archetypes*, which are the common heritage of the whole mankind. They are found in old myths, folklores, fairy tales, religious rituals, magic and various arts.

10.11.2 Libido and Personality development

Jung equated libido with the life urge, which is responsible for every type of human activity. The persons in whom libido flows inward are known as Introverts. The philosophers, writers and scientists belong to this category. While persons in whom the libido flows outward are known as Extroverts.

Politicians, Salesman, Lawyers, etc. belong to this category. However, nobody is purely introvert or extrovert. Usually people are Ambivert or bi-vert.

10.11.3 Dreams

According to Jung, dreams predict future events. These are not merely wish fulfilment mechanisms as Freud suggested. A person may have two types of dreams, originating from the *personal unconscious* and the *collective or racial unconscious.*

10.11.4 Religion and motive of self-actualisation

According to Jung, man is not merely a biological entity seeking always for his sexual satisfaction. Rather he has some higher aims in life. Morality and religion are deep-seated in his collective unconscious. Thus he has a strong urge for self-expression. Self-actualisation is the ultimate aim of human life.

10.11.5 Contribution to Education

Jung's system of analytical psychology has important educational bearings. According to this system, the educational activities of the children should be so designed as to maximise actualisation of their potentialities. So, ample opportunities should be provided to them in school for actualising their innate aptitudes and abilities.

Jung considered that Religion has a great influence on one's personality. It gives inner peace by resolving mental conflicts. Therefore, religious and moral education should form a part of school curriculum.

According to Jung, man inherits vast stores of valuable social, cultural and moral qualities from his ancestors. So, the system of education should be planned in such a manner that basic tenets of our culture and racial heritage find a prominent place in school curriculum.

Jung divided personality into two types : Extrovert and Introvert. The Word Association Test has been devised to discover the personality type of an individual.

The teacher should see that the pupils do not drift towards the extreme type of introversion of extroversion and thus develop unbalanced personality. The teacher should guide the extroverts to devote some time to introspection and meditation. While the introverts should be encouraged to take part in games, sports and other extracurricular activities of the school.

Conclusion : We have discussed above the tenets of different schools of psychology along with their merits and demerits. However, the recent trend is towards eclectic approach in dealing with human behaviour. Eclectic approach is accepting the best of many systems, as opposed to exclusive—one-system approach. In reality, the various viewpoints of different systems of psychology help in the investigation of the complex human behaviour by focusing light on its different aspects.

Summary

Different schools of psychology have greatly influenced the system of our education. The structural psychologists emphasised the structural aspect of mind. This school of psychology adopted introspection as the main technique to study the structure of consciousness.

Functionalism laid emphasis on the function or activity of mind. It is a more practical system of psychology than structuralism. It advocated the necessity of making the curriculum life-centric.

Behaviourism considered unit of behaviour as stimulus-response (S–R) connection. It emphasised the role of environment and its impact on child's growth and development. Behaviourism helped in revolutionising all the programs and method related to education.

Gestalt psychology began as a revolt against structuralism and functionalism. This school emphasised the importance of organised wholes. It has emphasised the need of scientific approach to problem solving and learning.

Hormic psychology asserts that behaviour of an organism cannot be explained without a purpose. In fact, all behaviour is teleological. It has helped educational theory and practice by its emphasis on purpose. According to this school instincts are the prime movers of all human activity. Hormic psychology emphasise that the educator should have a clear idea of child's instinct to utilise it for child's education.

Psychoanalysis has revolutionised the theory and practice of education. It has highlighted the role of earlier experiences and the need for proper education to the child in early stages of its growth.

References

1. B.R. Bugeski. : *An Introduction to the Principles of Psychology,* Holt, Rinehart and Winston, New York, 1961.
2. Freud, S. : *A General Introduction to Psychoanalysis,* New York : Live Right, 1935.

3. Murphy, G. : *An Historical Introduction to Modern Psychology,* 4th ed. New York : Harcourt, Brace & Jovanovich, 1975.

4. Wertheimer, M. : *A Brief History of Psychology,* New York : Holt, Rinehart & Winston, 1970.

5. Woodworth, R.S. and Sheehan, Mary R. : *Contemporary Schools of Psychology,* Ronald Press, 1964.

Questions and Assignments

1. Give a critical estimate of structuralism and functionalism and their contribution to education.
2. *There is no psychology without introspection*—Explain.
3. Give a critical exposition of Wundt's contributions in psychology.
4. Bring out the main features of functional psychology. Can functional psychology dispense with introspection? Make a critical estimate of functional psychology.
5. What is behaviourism? Expound the behaviouristic psychology of Watson. Describe its contribution to education.
6. What is meant by Gestalt? Explain how Gestalt psychology stands related to other schools of psychology. Explain its contribution to education.
7. Explain the Gestalt view of perception. Distinguish between figure and ground.
8. What is the Gestalt theory of learning as distinguished from that of Thorndike? How does it have its support in experimental evidences?
9. Why is psychoanalysis called depth psychology? Explain the topographical aspects of mind.
10. Explain the fundamental concepts of individual psychology.
11. Explain the main points of comparison between Jung, Freud and Adler.
12. Give a brief analysis of Jung's psychological types. Explain Jung's concept of the unconscious.
13. Give a critical estimate of Jung's analytical psychology.
14. What is meant by hormic psychology? Bring out its distinctive character.

15. Write notes on :
    (a) Imageless thought.
    (b) Apperception.
    (c) Horme.
    (d) The phi phenomenon.
    (e) Sublimation.
16. How does Gestalt psychology account for learning in higher animals?
17. *The distinction of figure and ground is regarded by the Gestalt psychologist as absolutely fundamental in the process of seeing.*—Explain the statement.
18. Examine the following statements :
    (a) Psychology can dispense with introspections as a method of investigation.
    (b) Thinking is subvocal speech.
19. How does hormic psychology differ from behaviourism?
20. Give a critical estimate of Freud's theory of psychoanalysis.
21. *Behaviourism and Gestalt psychology both revolted against the established view of psychology, but they revolted differently*—(Woodworth). Explain the statement.
22. Write short notes on :
    (a) Libido.
    (b) Functionalism.
    (c) Faculty psychology.
    (d) Repression.
    (e) Associationism.

Chapter 11

Motivation

Introduction : In all phases of education motivation is highly significant. In fact, the problem of education is the problem of motivating the child. Motivation gives rise to interest and interest is short-cut to all learning. A well-motivated student takes to his work whole heartedly and achieves maximum success in his task. Thus psychology of motivation has great importance for the teacher.

11.1 Meaning and nature

Every activity has a driving force behind it. This may be called motive-force of our behaviour. Without motivation no activity is possible.

The word motivation is derived from the Latin root movēre, mōtum, that is, to move. Thus, motivation means the process of arousing movement in the organism.

Atkinson defined motivation as, the arousal of tendency to act to produce one or more effects. To Bentham and Mill, motivation is a feeling which incites or urges us to action. Motive is that state of organism which makes it perform certain act or duty. The organism goes into action under some form of inner pressure. Thus, motivation may be considered as that force which compels us to act, to behave in a particular direction. The Oxford dictionary defines a motive as, That which moves or induces a person to act in a certain way. Thus, in brief, motive is an aroused feeling generated through basic needs which compels an organism to respond by developing a kind of tension. It is goal-oriented activity.

Motives are attached to specific goals. Motives are not mere passive impulses. They are active impulses to achieve a goal. It has the elements of cognition, feeling and connation. The activating forces behind motivation are needs and drives. Feeling of want for something is called need. Need gives rise to drive. Drive arouses the individual to activity. When goal or purpose is achieved, need is satisfied and tension is reduced. For example, hunger is a need of the child. Hunger gives rise to drive and the child cries and searches for food. This arousal of purposeful activity is motivation. On getting the food, his need and drive get satisfied and the child starts playing.

Thus, the different stages of motivation are :

Need (Feeling of want)	⇒	Drive (Activating force)	⇒	Motive (Purposeful activity)	⇒	Goal (Need reduction)

11.2 Needs, drives and incentives

Needs

General wants or desires are called needs. Every man strives for the satisfaction of his basic needs. Needs may be of two types : (a) Organic and (b) Psycho-sociological.

Organic needs are : Need for food, water and oxygen; need for rest and sleep. Need for satisfaction of sex urge. Need for protection from natural calamities and wild animals etc.

Socio-psychological needs are : Need for freedom. Need for social recognition. Need for company. Need for love and affection. Need for social and economic security. Need for fame and reputation etc.

Drive

Drive is internal stimulus which moves the body. According to Dashiell, drive is an original source of energy—that activates the organism.

Drive means aroused awareness. A need gives rise to drive. Drives are of two types : (a) Biological drive and (b) Psycho-sociological drive. Biological drive includes : hunger, thirst, sex, etc. Psycho-sociological drive includes : desire for social approval, desire for independence, etc. These drives move an organism to act in a particular way.

Incentives

An incentive acts as a reinforcing agent. It adds force to a drive. Rewards, praise, appreciation, achievement of the desired goal are a few instances of incentives, e.g., a piece of bread may act as an incentive for a hungry boy. There is some distinction between incentives and motives. Incentive refers to the objective appeal, whereas motive to the subjective striving.

11.3 Classification

There are numerous motives based on the basic needs. For better understanding of the nature and role of these motives we may classify them into two categories: (a) Primary motives and (b) Secondary motives.

11.3.1 Primary motives

Most important of these are : (a) Biological motives, (b) Social motives and (c) Personal motives.

11.3.2 Biological motives

Biological motives originate from organic needs, such as hunger, thirst and sex. Want of food gives rise to hunger drive and the individual searches for food. Thirst motive comes from the sensation of dryness in the mouth and throat.

The source of all kinds of behaviour according to Freud is sex motive. Of course, sex motive in human organism is mainly controlled by social influence. Although not so indispensable like food, air and water, sex motive is a highly powerful factor. It is a complex blend of psychophysiological factors.

11.3.3 Social motives

The social motives develops from social-interaction. Social motives include gregariousness, acquisitiveness, aggression, self-assertion and tendency to seek social approval. All animals have strong motivation to live in company of others. When an individual is separated from the group, he feels a strong urge to go back to his group.

Acquisitive motive is also very strong in human beings. People earn money and love to deposit it in the banks.

Aggression motive is expressed in violent activities intended to inflict physical or psychological harm on others. To some, aggression is an essential reaction to frustration.

Self-assertion is another powerful social motive. Showing of excessive desire for attention, status and prestige can be explained in terms of self-assertion. The impulse to make ourselves the master of the environment is dominant in all of us.

The desire to seek social approval and earn prestige is one of the important strong social motives. Craving for recognition, fame, power and leadership is the result of achievement or status motive.

All these social motives are influenced by experiences and cultural heritage. During childhood, these motives remain within the limits of the family. But as the child grows up, his social field also expands and his social needs change.

11.3.4 Personal motives

Esteem motive, self-actualisation motive, achievement motive, etc. are included in personal or egomotive. Egomotive drives an individual to strive to gain mastery over challenging situations. Every individual desires to unfold his skills and capacities for earning fame and prestige from the members of the society. This egomotive becomes very strong in adolescence.

11.3.5 Secondary motives

Motives are modified as a result of learning and experience. Such modified motives are attached to different goals or stimuli. These stimuli become learned motives of secondary motives. They are merely reinforcing conditions of motives.

Rats have been experimentally led to learn a completely new maze on the basis of secondary reinforcement. Through imitation, learning by conditioning and suggestion, human beings acquire a number of secondary motives.

Punishment, rewards, praise, knowledge of results, interest, etc. work as incentives. Rewards and punishment play a very great role in the motivation of school work. Reward is a positive motive. It takes the form of praise, promotion, badges, honorary degree etc. While punishment is a negative motive and based on fear.

11.4 Determinants of motivation

Motivation is the source of energy that activates the human organism. Psychologists have tried to determine the ultimate cause of motivation. Some of the important views may be described :

11.4.1 Hedonism

Thomas Hobbes held that all our actions are motivated by the desire for gaining pleasure and avoiding pain. Our likes and dislikes, habits and attitudes are all guided by the desire to gain happiness. Motivation is a wish for pleasure and avoidance of pain.

11.4.2 Instinct

McDougall held that the instincts are the spring boards of all our actions. The instincts are innate tendencies that lead to some purposive actions. McDougall provided a list of 14 instincts and explained that all our activities are determined by these instincts.

11.4.3 Ideals

Every man has an ideal in life, which motivates him to act. He may not reach the ideal, but there is an incessant effort to reach that goal.

11.4.4 Sense of values

Every person has some sense of moral and religious values. He judges his organic needs and social needs against his own standard of values and behave accordingly.

11.4.5 Participation

Participation is another strong incentive. When a student gets opportunity to take part in the activities of the school, he is enthused. Thus, a child should be given a voice as well as a place in the social as well as in the school life. Modern scientific methods of teaching encourage pupils' participation in the teaching-learning process.

11.4.6 Role of unconscious

Freud proposed unconscious motivation as an explanation of behaviour. Repressed desires form complexes in our unconscious and influence our activities. Freud identified two basic instincts : Eros—the life instinct and Thanatos—the death instinct. Eros was the Greek love-god and thanatos in Greek meant death. According to Freud, these two instincts are the ultimate sources of motivation. To Freud, sex-motive is an important motive that activates an individual's behaviour.

11.5 Function of motives

Motives may be fully or partially realised. They may be inhibited. They may be disguised through rationalisation. They may be reinforced or substituted for the original ones.

Men are always in need of satisfying their wants. But they do not always get what they want. This results in dissatisfaction and frustration. Frustration may result in aggression or suicidal tendency.

Again, when two or more motives act in different directions, the individual becomes the victim of conflicts. Conflicts retard the normal process of life.

11.5.1 Imitation

The child imitates his parents, pupils imitate their teachers and the young imitates their leaders. Ordinary people imitate the dress and behaviour of great men. Thus the tendency of imitation is regarded as a determinant of motive.

11.5.2 Habit

Habit is an important determinant of motivation. It is formed when a voluntary action is repeated. Habit, once formed, becomes functionally autonomous.

11.5.3 Incentive

Motives are greatly influenced and guided by incentives. Incentives may be concrete or abstract. It may be material, social or spiritual. It may be food, praise, promotion, badges or honorary degree.

11.5.4 Level of aspiration

The level of aspiration often determines our behaviour. If the level of aspiration is very high, an individual has to strive hard to attain that goal. A learner, who intends to rank first in the class, has to strive very hard.

11.5.5 Success

Often success acts as strong motive. The student who stood first in the examination last year strives hard this year also to occupy the first rank in the class.

11.6 Theories of motivation

What compells one to act is not a simple question to answer. Psychologists have tried to describe the process of motivation in various ways. Some of the important views are :

1. Behaviourists' learning based theory.
2. McDougall's theory of instinct.
3. Freud's psychoanalytic theory.
4. Maslow's theory of self-actualisation.
5. Theory of intrinsic motivation.
6. Theory of achievement motivation.

11.6.1 Behaviourists' learning based theory

According to the behaviourists, behaviour is a mechanical response to a stimulus (S–R). The organism lives only through making proper responses to the stimulus that excites it to activity. Sandiford says, An organism is no self-starting mechanism; its reactions are always started by stimulus outside of itself.

According to S–R theory, motivational force flow out of biological drives, autonomic acts and reflexes. The lower organism acts mainly through the help of the inherited mechanism, reflexes and instincts. But man acts through experience and learning.

The S–R theories of learning may be divided into two types : (a) S–R theories of non-reinforcement and (b) S–R theories with reinforcement. Under the category of non-reinforcement theories of learning come Thorndike, Pavlov and Watson who laid emphasis on repetition, recency and contiguity between S–R bond for learning to take place.

Thorndike conducted an experiment in the learning process of animals and formulated the law of exercise on frequency. With this law are associated two factors—intensity and recency. The more intense the stimulus, the deeper is its impression. Hence, to make such an impression lasting, constant repetition is required. Again, what has been recently learned is remembered, because the nervous connections are fresh and time has not played its part in wiping out these connections.

Pavlov found that a conditioned response is established by connecting the natural stimulus with an artificial stimulus. Any artificial stimulus (substitute stimulus)—such as the ringing of the bell, the shining of an electric light connected with the natural stimulus, such as giving food to a hungry dog a number of times—evoked the same response, e.g., the excretion of saliva.

The role of reinforcement as a major factor for the motivation of behaviour was emphasised by Thorndike, Hull and Skinner. Thorndike's Law of Effect states that satisfaction tends to fix a learned pattern of behaviour, and dissatisfaction tends to root it out. In his opinion, mere trial and error working blindly will not result in learning. It is satisfaction that guides the whole learning activity.

Thus, for good conduct, honesty, industry, punctuality, etc. the child is praised. He gets satisfaction thère by, and these patterns of behaviour become fixed.

C.L. Hull (1943) developed Thorndike's law of effect into a systematic theory of motivation called drive-reduction theory of reinforcement. He replaced satisfaction of Thorndike by drive-reduction. According to this theory, biological drives such as hunger, sex, etc. produce internal tension in an individual. The individual then tries to reduce the tension by doing such activities as would reduce the drive. The important role of reinforcement has been emphasised in B.F. Skinner's Operant conditioning, Skinner developed various schedules of reinforcement which can be used in shaping the behaviour of an individual. According to him, primary reinforcers are food, water, etc. and primary negative reinforcers are pain and punishment. While secondary reinforcers are money, degree, social approval etc. and secondary negative reinforcers are social disapproval and teachers' rebuke etc.

Following Skinner, Albert Bandura (1977) maintained that human motivation depends largely on social rewards and social approval. According to Bandura, parental approval or fear of punishment in early childhood, affect the moral and social development of the child. Another important factor according to Bandura is imitation by which a child learns moral and social behaviour from his parents and his peers.

11.7 McDougall's theory of instinct

Instincts are the main springs of human action. McDougall defines instincts as certain specific innate modes of behaviour in certain specific situations which do not have to be learnt and which are common to all members of species.

Every living organism is born with Hormē, an inner urge to act. This urge to act is not random. It is goal-oriented. According to McDougall, all human behaviour can be explained on the basis of instincts.

McDougall gives a list of 14 important instincts which are appeal, acquisition, curiosity, combat, construction, sex, submission, self-assertion, parental, escape, repulsion, laughter, hunger and gregarious instinct. He proposed that each instinct is accompanied by a specific emotional disposition. The instinct of escape, for example, at the sight of a dangerous object, has the emotion of fear in its core.

The theory of instincts is not free from criticism. Psychologists have failed to find a limited number of instincts to account for all human behaviour. Again human behaviour cannot be termed innate because most human activities are learned and acquired. Human behaviour is shaped by the forces of his social and cultural environment. Moreover, instincts are not blind. They are modified by experience, habit and the new environment.

11.8 Freud's psychoanalytic theory

Freud proposed that causes of behaviour can be determined by exploring the unconscious mind of an individual. He recognised three layers of the mind, namely, the Id, the Ego, and the Super ego. The Id is unconscious and it follows the pleasure principle. It contains all the motivating forces of the individual's life. Id is mostly sexual. Freud maintains that the sex instinct (libido) is a very dominant urge of human life. Thus according to Freud, sex motive is the most important motive that activates human behaviour.

Freud's psychoanalytic theory is not free from criticism. He makes too much of libido or sexuality. Although sex instinct is a very dominant urge of human life, it is not the only instinct that motivates human conduct.

Alfred Adler, a disciple of Freud maintained that human beings are motivated primarily by social urges. Adler points out that the instinct of self-assertion or the will to power is more dominant than sex instinct.

Jung rightly points out that the sex urge cannot be the only motive of human behaviour. To him the will to live is more fundamental than the sex urge. In fact, the only one instinct sex cannot be a sole motivating factor in human life.

11.9 Maslow's Self-actualisation theory

To understand the nature of human motivation Abraham Maslow (1954) advocated the hierarchy of five sets of basic needs. The highest need in the hierarchical order is self-actualisation and the lowest need in the system is physiological needs, such as hunger, thirst etc. An individual can be motivated towards self-actualisation only when his lower order needs such as physiological needs, safety needs etc. have been fulfilled. A hungry boy can be motivated to solve a problem in arithmetic only when his hunger has been satisfied. He cannot be motivated to concentrate his attention on study when hungry.

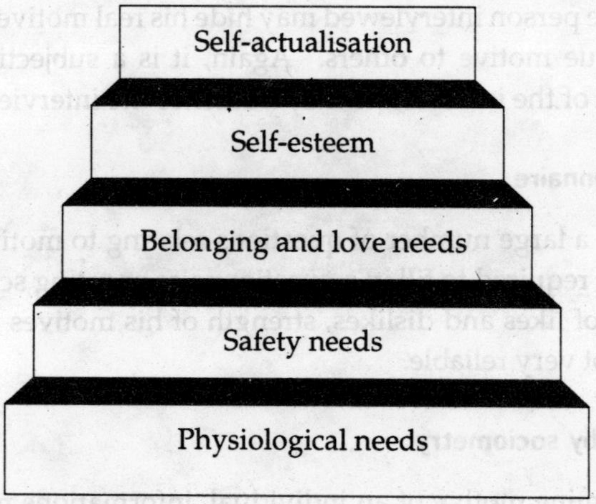

Fig. 11.1: Maslow's hierarchy of needs.

11.10 Theory of Intrinsic Motivation

Man does not always act according to his biological needs such as hunger, thirst, sex or social motives such as prestige and money. Often curiosity drive may motivate a person to act for considerable period of time. Harlow (1950) and others conducted experiments on animals and found that those animals learned to solve problems without external incentives.

11.11 Theory of Achievement motivation

The theory of achievement motivation was first proposed by McClelland (1951). According to this theory people differ from one another in their strength of achievement motive. McClelland proposed that economic growth of nations, primarily depends on this strength of motivation to achieve.

School and family play a significant role in moulding attitudes and motives of children. Parents' expectation about his child develop the need for higher achievement in life. The teacher can also arouse achievement motive in children by proper instruction and guidance.

11.12 Techniques of measuring motives

Measuring the strength of human motive is not a simple task. However, psychologists have attempted to measure human motives and developed certain methods. Some of the methods may be described as follows :

11.12.1 Interview

The oldest method of measuring motives is interview. But the defect of this method is that the person interviewed may hide his real motive and may refuse to divulge his true motive to others. Again, it is a subjective method and personal opinion of the interviewer may influence the interview result.

11.12.2 Questionnaire

In questionnaire, a large number of questions relating to motives are asked to the subject. He is required to fill in a questionnaire or rating scale. On analysis of his responses of likes and dislikes, strength of his motives is assessed. But this method is not very reliable.

11.12.3 Rating by sociometry

In order to determine motive of an individual, informations may be collected from his friends and relatives. From the analysis of the sociogram, the motives of the individual can be successfully determined.

11.12.4 Projective tests

Projective tests are indirect methods of determining motives of an individual. Murray and Morgan devised the technique called Thematic Apperception Test (TAT), which consists of a number of vague and unstructured pictures. The subject is required to make a story out of them. The subject projects his unconscious motives in the story. Recently Childrens' Apperception Test (CAT) have been devised to measure different motives of children.

Rorschach Ink Blot Test consists of ten meaning less ink blots and the subject is shown these ink blots one by one. He is asked to describe what he is seeing in these figures. From the analysis of the description, his imagination need and motive can be determined.

All the projective methods like TAT, CAT, Rorschach, Word Association, Role Play, etc. are indirect methods of assessing motive.

11.13 Educational significance of motivation

Motivation is very important in every phase of education. The success of teaching-learning process depends upon encouragement, incentives and all those forces that set the child to learning activity. In other words, the problem of education is the problem of motivating the pupils. When the pupils are motivated, half the work of the teacher is done.

Motivation is the act of stimulating interest in the pupil. In fact, motivation gives rise to interest and interest is short-cut to all learning. A well-motivated pupil is highly attentive. He takes to his work whole heartedly and achieves maximum success in the activity.

The problem of discipline in the class disappears when the pupils are rightly motivated in the desired channels. Formation of character depends upon right type of guidance in motivation. In fact, all our methods of teaching go in vain without motivating that child.

Thus, the knowledge of techniques of motivation is of great importance to the teacher.

11.14 Techniques of motivation

Motivation is an essential condition of learning. The stronger the motivation, the more efficient will be the learning.

Some common techniques which the teacher may use to motivate the students are :

11.14.1 Rewards and punishment

Rewards for good performance create interest in the students. Rewards may take the form of praise or grades. Reward has a positive effect in motivating pupils for learning. However, physical punishment should be sparingly used. The teacher should give warmth and support to the learning process.

11.14.2 Cooperation and competition

Cooperation is a strong incentive for motivating pupils. The teacher should encourage participation of all students in learning activities. He should make use of gregarious impulse and the desire for prestige and status. Interpersonal competition among peers and group competition often generate motivation. But the teacher should be careful to use competition, as because it tends to breed antagonism amongst the pupils.

11.14.3 Novelty

Teaching should not be monotonous. Students' attention fluctuate when the teacher uses purely lecture method in the class. The subject matter of teaching should be presented in a variety of novel ways so that curiosity of students may be maintained.

11.14.4 Feed-back

It has been observed that knowledge of the result or feedback tend to increase the frequency of the response. In programmed learning, the learner immediately gets the knowledge of his performance and this acts as a motivating force in the learning process. Therefore, the educator should provide immediate knowledge of their performance to the students to motivate them in learning activities. The teacher should keep charts of progress on individual learners.

11.14.5 Setting of goal

Motives have goals. The more clearly the goal is perceived, the more strongly the act is motivated. Therefore, the teacher should make every effort to make the goal more vivid both for individuals and the class. However, the setting of goal should be in keeping with the aspiration level of the students. The aspiration level of the students is correlated with their intelligence and socio-economic status. Thus, if setting of goal is too high to achieve, then it may not motivate the students.

11.14.6 Providing models

Students learn through observation and imitation. The teacher should set the proper example. He can influence the behaviour of his students by his ideal living. The teacher should keep in mind that example is better than precept. He should create confidence in learners. He should try to create conducive environment in the classroom.

11.14.7 Use of modern techniques

Instead of traditional lecture method the teacher should use computers, audiovisual and other technological aids in course of his teaching. Programmed books may be used for the students of large classes. The techniques of team teaching and group discussion, where feasible, may be adopted to motivate the students.

Summary

Motive is the tendency which induces a person to act in a certain way. It is the active impulse to achieve a goal. Motives energise, sustain and regulate our behaviour.

Motives may be classified into two categories : *Primary motives* and *Secondary motives.* Important primary motives ard biological, social and personal. Motives are modified as a result of learning and experience. Such modified motives are called *secondary motives.* Through imitation, learning by conditioning and suggestion, human beings acquire a number of secondary motives.

Psychologists have proposed a number of theories of motivation of which Behaviourists' Learning based Theory, McDougall's Instinct Theory, Freud's Psychoanalytic Theory, Maslow's Theory of self-actualisation ard Theory of Achievement Motivation and Important.

It is difficult to measure human motives. Psychologists have attempted to measure motives by a number of techniques, such as : interview, questionnaire, rating by sociometry and projective tests.

Motivation is needed in every field of education. The success of teaching-learning process depends upon incentives, encouragement and all those forces that set the child to learning activity. Motivation gives rise to interest and interest is short-cut to all learning. The problem of discipline disappears when the pupils are rightly motivated. Formation of character of pupils depend upon right type of guidance in motivation.

Some of the common techniques which the teacher may use to motivate pupils are : Judicious use of rewards and punishment, encouraging cooperation and competition, introducing novelty in teaching, providing feedback, setting of goal in keeping with the aspiration level of the students and providing models.

The use of modern techniques of teaching, such as the use of audiovisual and other technological aids and use of programmed books will go a long way in motivating pupils. The techniques of team teaching and group discussion may be adopted wherever feasible to motivate the students.

References

1. Atkinson, J.W. : *An Introduction to Motivation,* Princeton Van Strand, 1964.
2. Brown, J.S. : *The Motivation of Behaviour,* McGraw Hill. New York, 1961.
3. Freud, S. : *An Outline of Psychoanalysis,* London : Hogarth Press, 1953.
4. Hall, J.F. : *Psychology of Motivation,* Lippincot : Chicago, 1961.
5. McDougall, W. : *Social Psychology,* Boston : John Luce, 1921.

6. Young, P.T. : *Motivation and Emotion,* John Wiley and Sons. New York, 1961.

7. Maslow, A. : *Motivation and Personality,* New York : Harper & Row, 1954.

8. Korman, A. : *The Psychology of Motivation,* Prentice Hall. New Jersey, 1974.

9. Weiner, B. : *Human Motivation,* New York : Holt Rinehart & Winston, 1980.

10. Valley, F.P. : *Motivation—Theories and Issues,* California, Brooks Cole, 1975.

Questions and Assignments

1. What is motivation? Classify motives.
2. Define motivation. What are the motives behind human behaviour?
3. Mention various determinants of motivation.
4. Give in brief the theory of self-actualisation.
5. What do you understand by motivation? What is their sources?
6. Discuss how you can motivate students in school learning.
7. How will you motivate children in classroom teaching? Illustrate your answer with examples.
8. Describe the nature of motivation and their functioning.
9. What is the significance of motivation in education?
10. What are the most important motives that may find a place in our school?
11. Write notes on :
    (a) Drives.
    (b) Needs.
    (c) Incentives.
    (d) Social Motives.

Chapter 12

Physiological basis of mental life

Importance of the study : Body and mind are closely related. The child whom we are to teach possesses body as well as mind. In fact, the child is a psychophysical organism. It is difficult to teach a diseased or a physically-handicapped child. The purpose of education is to form sound mind in a sound body (mens sana in corpore sano—Juvenal). It becomes easier for a teacher to teach a healthy normal child than a diseased one. In fact, the teacher is concerned both with the child's body and mind.

12.1 Relation of body and mind

Education of a child is intimately connected with central nervous system, senses like eyes and ears, reflex action, synapse and endocrine glands. If we want to have knowledge about educational processes, we must know the intimate link between body and mind.

Often, head injury causes mental abnormality. During emotion, many kinds of physical changes occur, e.g., during anger, eyes of an individual become red, breathing and blood circulation get disturbed. Some physical causes may give rise to mental conflicts in children too. Fear, anxiety and sorrows often influence our normal organic processes and drug affects our mind severely. Thus, a teacher must have proper knowledge of the intimate relationship between body and mind.

In ancient times, educationists observed the close relation between body and mind and stressed the need of proper physical development of the child. The countries like Athens, Rome and Sparta in Greece made physical education compulsory for children. In ancient India, Pranayam (breathing control) and Hatayoga formed an important part of education. The ideal educators like John

Locke and Rousseau laid much emphasis on physical education of the child. Froebel asked to give education to the child through plays.

Thus the study of physiological processes forms a significant part in educational psychology. Moreover, the Behaviourists of present day try to explain all our behaviour without the assumption of mind or consciousness. These psychologists are more concerned with the objectively verifiable forms of behaviour. Because of this hypothesis, the importance of the study of nervous system and endocrine glands has greatly increased.

12.2 The structure and functions of the nervous system

The nervous system is composed of 15–20 billion of neurons. It consists of : (1) The cerebro spinal system and (2) The autonomic system.

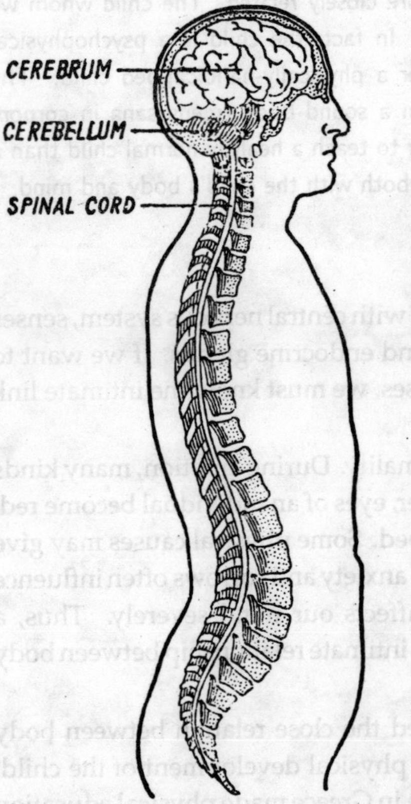

Fig. 12.1: The Cerebro-spinal axis.

12.2.1 The cerebro-spinal system

It consists of : (a) The central nervous system and (b) The peripheral nervous system.

The central nervous system comprises : (a) The brain and (b) The spinal cord.

The peripheral nervous system consists of : (a) The afferent or sensory nerves and (b) The efferent or motor nerves.

The cerebro-spinal system consists of the following parts : (a) spinal cord and (b) the brain.

Spinal Cord

The spinal cord is a cord-like substance running through the spinal column. It is composed of the grey matter and the white matter. The grey matter consisting of nerve cells lies inside and the white matter consisting of nerve fibres, lies outside covering the grey matter.

The spinal cord is the centre of reflex actions. It converts sensory impulses into motor impulses. The spinal cord is the channel of communication from the brain and to the brain. It not only connects the brain with several parts of the body but it also controls reflex actions.

Thus the function of the spinal cord is principally two :

1. It acts as an organ for conduction of nerve impulses.
2. It acts as an organ for reflex actions.

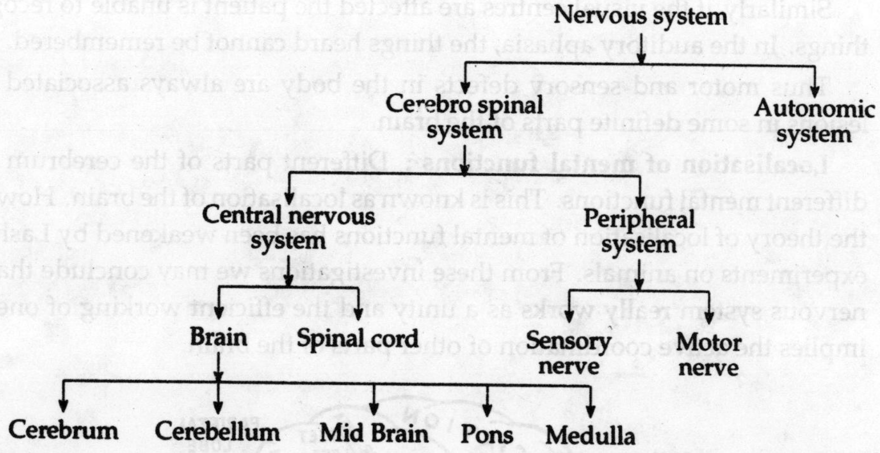

The Brain

The brain : (a) Cerebrum, (b) Cerebellum, (c) Mid-brain, (d) Pons varolii and (e) Medulla oblangata.

Cerebrum : The brain is divided into two hemispheres. The right hemisphere controls the movements of the limbs on the left side of the body and the left hemisphere controls those on the right side. There are convolutions and fissures in the brain. The greater the number of convolutions in the cerebrum, the greater is the intelligence. The fissures of Rolando and Sylvius divide each cerebral hemisphere into four lobes : (a) Frontal lobe, (b) Parietal lobe, (c) Occiptal lobe and (d) Temporal lobe.

The grey matter in the brain is called the cortex and comprises nerve cells or neurons. There are about 14,000,000,000 nerve cells in the brain. The nerve cells are connected with one another by the synapses.

Function of the cerebrum : The cerebrum is the sovereign of the whole nervous system. It controls the sensory and motor nerves. It is the seat of sensation, perception, thought, memory, emotion and volition. It helps us to think, judge, learn and remember. It is the seat of intelligence.

Some of the portions of the cerebrum are sensory areas which receives sensory impulses from the sense-organs. The motor areas of cerebrum send out motor impulses to the muscles.

There are some areas in the cerebrum which are called association areas. They are concerned with higher mental processes. Great disturbances in speech may take place due to some injury received in some portions of the brain concerned with speech. In case of aphasia, the patient can express his thoughts through gestures or writing but not through speech.

Thus if any motor area is disturbed, the person loses the capacity to perform corresponding functions.

Similarly, if the visual centres are affected the patient is unable to recognise things. In the auditory aphasia, the things heard cannot be remembered.

Thus motor and sensory defects in the body are always associated with lesions in some definite parts of the brain.

Localisation of mental functions : Different parts of the cerebrum have different mental functions. This is known as localisation of the brain. However, the theory of localisation of mental functions has been weakened by Lashley's experiments on animals. From these investigations we may conclude that our nervous system really works as a unity and the efficient working of one part implies the active coordination of other parts of the brain.

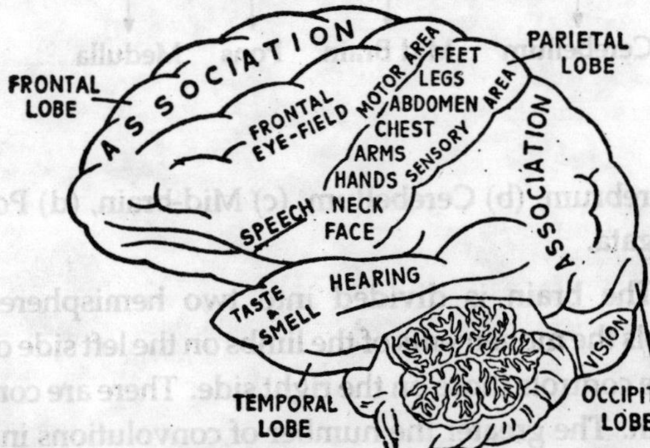

Fig. 12.2: Localisation of mental functions in the Brain.

Cerebellum : Cerebellum is situated below the cerebrum. Like the cerebrum it is also divided in two hemispheres. They are connected by a bundle of nerves called the pons. This is connected with the medulla, oblangata and the mid-brain.

The chief function of cerebellum is to coordinate impulses and maintain bodily balance. It controls movements such as walking, sitting, standing, etc. and preserves bodily equilibrium.

Mid-brain : It is above the cerebellum and forms the base of the brain. It contains the thalamus and the hypothalamus. The thalamus controls bodily functions involved in metabolism. The hypothalamus controls emotions.

In lower animals, the thalamus is the highest sensory centre. But in man, the functions of thalamus is taken over by it. While thalamus remains as a center for recognition of some crude sensations, their finer discrimination lies with cortex.

Pons varolli : It is a bridge-like band of nervous substance above the medulla oblangata. It connects the two lobes of the cerebellum. Nerve fibres from the cerebrum pass through it to the lower parts of the body. Pons controls mastication, movements of the eye and also influences salivary secretion. It acts as a sensory relay station of hearing.

Medulla oblangata : It is the upward enlarged prolongation of the spinal cord. It is also called spinal bulb or the stem. It acts as a conductor between the brain and the spinal cord. It controls heart rate, respiration, circulation, etc.

The peripheral nervous system : This system is composed of two main groups :

1. **The efferent nerves** (motor nerves) which carry impulses from the central nervous system outward to the peripheral tissues (skin, sense organs, etc.)
2. **The afferent nerves** (sensory nerves) which carry impulses from the peripheral tissues inward to the nerve centres.

Motor nerves are nerves of action. Sensory nerves are nerves of knowledge. The motor nerves start from the brain and end at the muscles. The sensory nerves starts from the skin and end in the brain.

12.2.1 The autonomic nervous system

The autonomic or involuntary nervous system consists of a series of ganglia or groups of nerve cells. It is an off-shoot of the central nervous system. The nerves of the autonomic system run to the heart, lungs, stomach and intestines. The central nervous system controls the skeletal muscles. But autonomic nervous system controls the involuntary muscles and glands.

The autonomic nervous system is divided into :

1. **Cranial section** which connects the brain stem with the iris muscle and salivary glands.
2. **Sympathetic section** which is connected with the central part of the spinal cord.
3. **Sacral section** which connects the spinal cord with the genital system.

The cranial and sacral autonomic sections are collectively known as para-sympathetic system. The sympathetic nervous system and the para-sympathetic system work in opposite directions. For example, while the cranial section accelerates digestive activities, the sympathetic section inhibits them.

The action of sympathetic system depends on production of adrenaline and of para-sympathetic on acetyl choline.

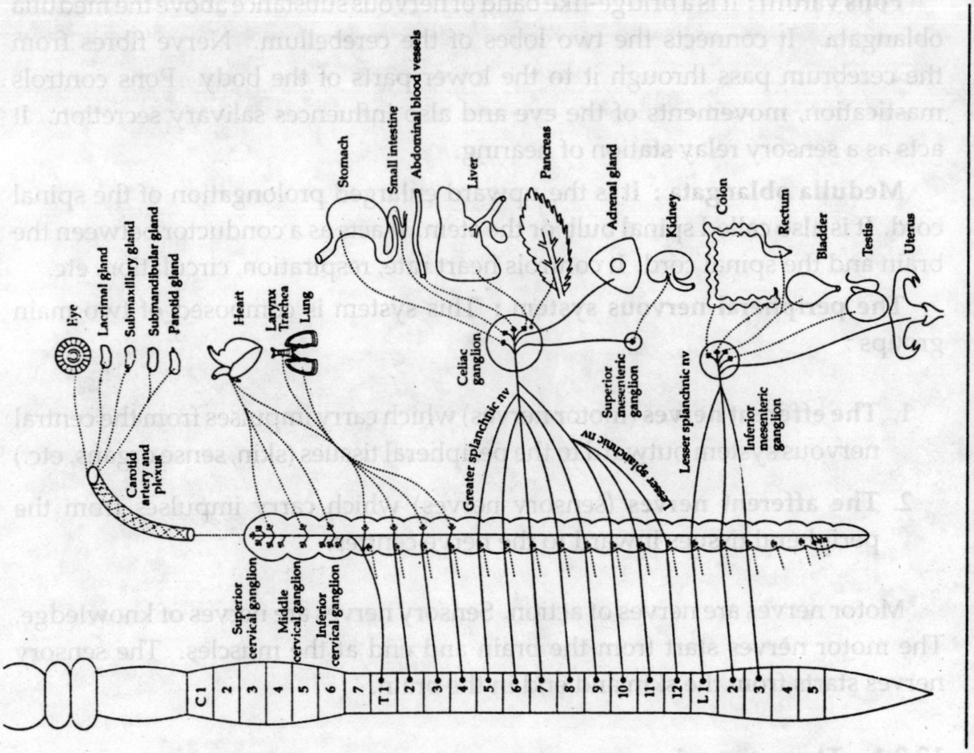

Sympathetic nervous system (Courtesy : Dr. Asim K. Ghosh)

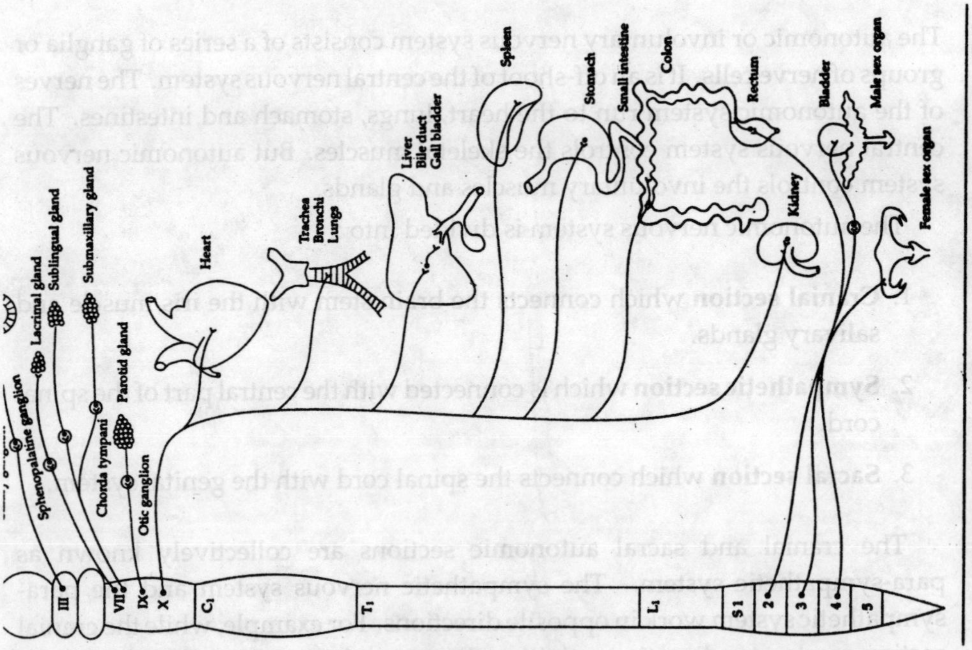

Parasympathetic Nervous System

These two systems establish a delicately balanced cooperation for maintaining a uniformity of conditions for body tissues.

The sympathetic section is connected with emotions like anger and fear, while the cranial and part of the sacral section are connected with mild pleasant states.

Part of the sacral section is connected with sex excitement.

Thus the health of the body and the arousal of emotions depend on the action of autonomic system. Hence the knowledge of the autonomic nervous system is very important to the teacher.

12.2.2 Disorders concerning Nervous System

All our behaviour and activities are influenced by our Nervous system. Brain is the central organ of this system. Disorders of nervous system including brain give rise to various mental disorders—like epilepsy, hysteria, neuroses and psychoses. Various types of speech defects such as Motor aphasia, Cortical aphasia, Verbal aphasia, Agra phia etc. are the resultant of defective nervous system.

12.3 The Neuron

The nervous system consists of series of units known as neurons. A typical neuron is a nerve cell having :

1. Short branching processes, the dendrites or dendrons.
2. A single long process, the axis cylinder or axon.

It is the function of the dendrites to receive an impulse. The axons pass the nerve impulse to the dendrites of the next neuron. An axon has a myelin or medullary sheath which insulates it. The outer thin covering of axon is known as neurolemma.

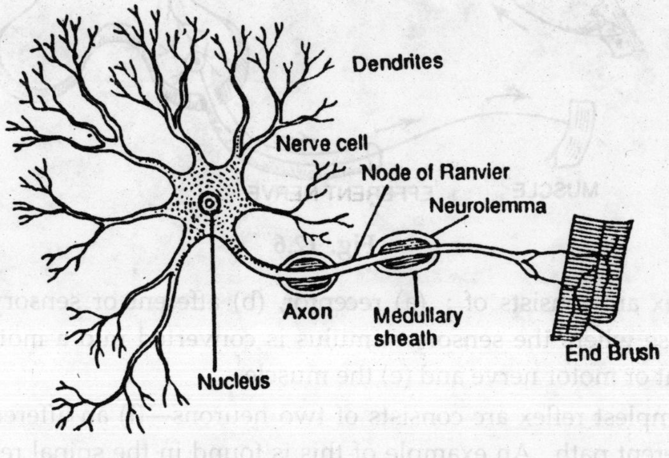

Fig. 12.4

Synapse : The junction of two neurons is called the synapse. At the synapse, the axon end-brush of one neuron stimulates the dendrites of another neuron. But there is no continuity between the two processes. The nervous current can pass only through axons to the dendrites. The synapse is a one-way valve. There is inhibition of nerve impulse in the synapse. Synaptic transmissions are brought about either by chemical or by electrical or by both processes.

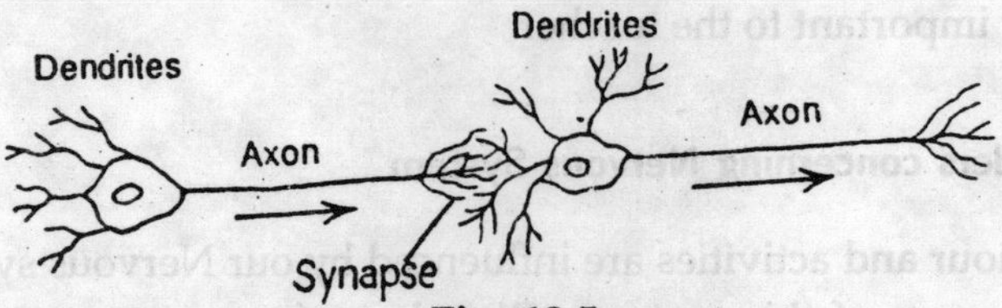

Fig. 12.5

12.4 Reflex action

The reflex action is an involuntary activity produced in a tissue in response to an afferent impulse. A sense organ is stimulated by a stimulus. A sensory neuron carries the nerve impulse from the sense-organ to a sensory centre or nerve-cell in the spinal cord or the brain stem. There is a synaptic connection between a sensory neuron and a motor neuron. The motor neuron carries the nerve current from the central switching station to a muscle or a gland. This combination of a sensory neuron with a motor neuron through a synaptic junction is called the reflex arc.

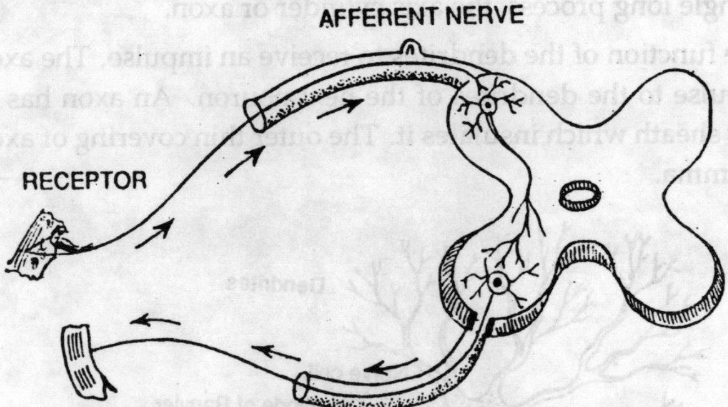

Fig. 12.6

A reflex arc consists of : (a) receptor, (b) afferent or sensory nerve, (c) the synapse where the sensory stimulus is converted into a motor impulse, (d) efferent or motor nerve and (e) the muscle.

The simplest reflex arc consists of two neurons—(i) an afferent path and (ii) an efferent path. An example of this is found in the spinal reflex of knee jerk.

A reflex action is the simplest form of the behaviour of an organism. In such action there is no mediation of the brain. For example, we see a flash of light. At once our eyes are closed. Complex activities of human beings also involve the use of such a mechanism. However, this is achieved through the mediation of the brain.

12.4.1 Varieties of reflexes

There are mainly two types of reflexes :

1. **Unconditioned reflexes or Inborn reflexes :** These are inherent, fixed and cannot be altered normally, e.g., knee jerk, coughing, sneezing, vomiting, constriction of pupil, sexual reflexes, etc.

2. **Conditioned reflexes :** These are acquired. They can be established and abolished.

12.5 Muscles

The muscles, with their property of contraction in response to the impulse produce the important function of movements in the higher animals.

There are two kinds of muscles—(1) voluntary muscles and (2) Involuntary muscles.

Voluntary muscles are under the control of the volition or will. The muscles of the limbs, trunk and face are voluntary.

Involuntary muscles are not under the control of the will. The muscles of the stomach, viscera and the blood vessels are involuntary.

The voluntary muscles are long drawn out and striated. The involuntary muscles are shorter and taper at both ends and are smooth.

The heart muscle is intermediate between those two. Though striated in structure like the voluntary muscles, they are shorter than ordinary striated muscle fibre.

The striated muscles are generally attached to the bony skeleton of the body. So they are called skeletal muscles. They are found also in other places for example, in the external muscles of the eyeball, in the tongue and in the middle and external ear.

Smooth muscles are known as visceral muscles. They are attached to the internal organs.

Normally, a muscle (smooth or striated) in the body contracts by a stimulus from the central nervous system through its motor nerve. An isolated muscle can be made to contract by artificial stimuli, the mechanical, thermal or electrical, when applied directly to it.

12.6 The Endocrine glands

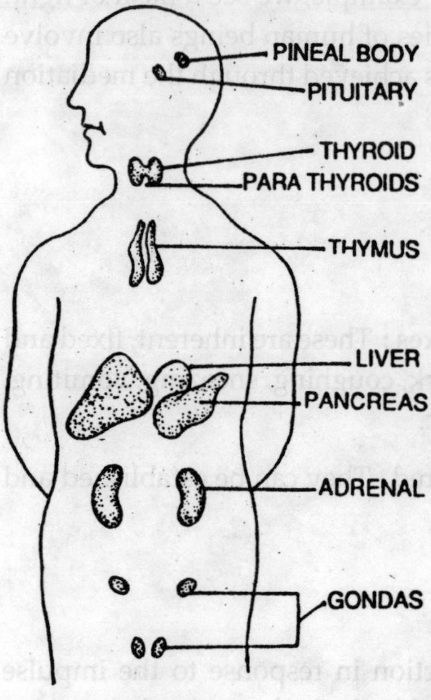

Fig. 12.7

Glands are situated at different centres of the body. They may be divided into :

1. **Endocrine glands**—the glands of internal secretion and

2. **Exocrine glands**—the glands of external secretion.

Examples of exocrine glands are the sweat, salivary, liver, pancreas and mammary glands which pass their secretion along ducts to the external surface of the body.

The endocrine glands (ductless glands do not possess any duct or opening to the exterior. The endocrine (Greek, endon = within; crinein = to set apart) system consists of a number of ductless glands, which manufacture certain chemical substances known as hormones.

Hormones are secreted directly into the blood stream by the ductless glands. The hormones guide and control the metabolic activities of the body. Thus, throughout the whole life—from the early stage of foetal development right up to the moment of death—the endocrine glands exert a profound influence on various bodily activities including the mental and behavioural patterns.

The important ductless glands are : (a) Pituitary gland, (b) The Thyroid, (c) The Parathyroid, (d) The Adrenals, (e) Thymus gland, (f) The Gonads and (g) Pineal.

12.6.1 The Pituitary gland

The pituitary gland is a small oval-shaped structure situated at the base of the brain. It is called the master gland because its hormones affect most of the other glands.

The pituitary body has two parts :

(a) The anterior lobe and

(b) The posterior lobe.

The anterior lobe produces hormones that stimulate the thyroid, the adrenal and the sex glands. It has great influence on the growth of bones. Before adolescence, its overactivity produces a giant (gigantism), while its underactivity produces a dwarf (dwarfism).

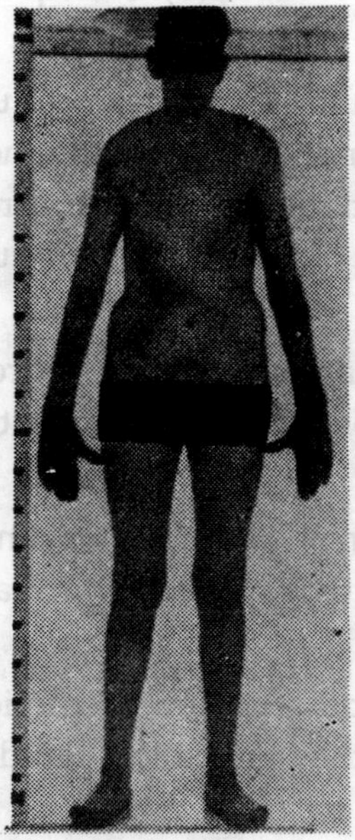

Giantism

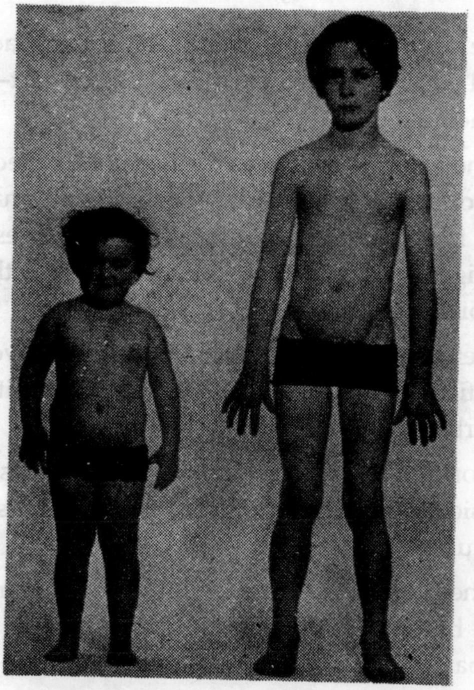

A 9-year old pituitary dwarf compared with age and sex matched control

Fig. 12.8

12.6.2 The Thyroid gland

The Thyroid gland is situated at the base of the neck above the wind pipe. The gland secretes a chemical known as thyroxin in which the important ingredient is Iodine. It speeds up metabolism and stimulates the growth of the body and mind. The gland controls the supply of energy needed for vital life activities. If the gland is defective, the physical and mental growth of a child is retarded. His growth is stunned and intelligence is impaired. Feeble-mindedness and retardation arises in children due to the improper functioning of the Thyroid gland. The disease is to some extent curable through an artificial supply of thyroxin.

12.6.3 The Parathyroid

The Parathyroids are four small oval-shaped bodies situated in the posterior surface of the thyroid. Parathyroids secrete parathormone. They are essential for life, as they help growth of bone. The absence of parathormone causes neuromuscular irritability, twitchings or convulsions.

12.6.4 The Adrenal glands

There are two adrenal glands on the surface of the kidney. Each adrenal gland consists of two parts : (a) Outer part—the cortex and (b) Inner part—the medulla.

The medulla produces the hormone called adrenalin. The cortex produces the hormone called cortin. The adrenalin hastens and strengthens the heart beat, increases the blood pressure, removes the fatigue of muscles, arrests the digestive function of stomach, expands the pupil of the eye and produces perspiration.

Deficient section of adrenalin produces weakness and prostration. Chronic insufficiency of adrenal secretion causes vomiting, anorexia and gastrointestinal disturbance.

Cortin acts as a general stimulant. Its deficiency produces weakness, aversion to activity and loss of sex interest. Its over-activity produces increased masculinity in both sexes.

The study of adrenal glands is important from the point of view of emotions. They become very active during emotion. Hence they are called glands of combat, emergency and preparedness.

12.6.5 Thymus gland

The Thymus is located in the anterior of the thorax. It consists of two elongated and flask-shaped lobes. The Thymus secretes hormone called thymosin or thymin. Animals lacking this organ seem to be abnormally sensitive to environmental stress.

12.6.6 The Gonads

The gonads or sex glands are connected with sex emotions. They are situated near the sex organs. The lack of gonadal hormones tends to make a man devoid of sex characteristics.

12.6.7 The Pineal gland

It lies at the brain. It controls the brain and sex development.

The functions of the different Endocrine glands are interrelated to each other. A disorder in the function of one gland may cause disorders in the functions of others. Though the functions of the Endocrine glands are not yet properly understood our personality is influenced to a great extent by the hormones secreted by the ductless glands.

12.6.8 Disorder concerning Glandular System

From the early stage of foetal development right up to the movement of death, endocrine glands exert a profound influence on various bodily activities including the mental and behavioural pattern. Our personality is to a great extent influenced by the hormones secreted by the ductless glands. If the thyroid gland is defective both physical and mental growth of an individual become stunted. Failure of secretion of adrenal hormone gives rise to Addision's disease. The under activity of Pituitary Gland produces a giant. The lack of sexual hormones tends to make an individual of either sex neutral or devoid of sex characteristics. Thus an individual's personality is greatly affected by disorder of glandular system.

Summary

Body and mind are intimately connected. Education of a child depends upon healthy physiological processes. His central nervous system, sense organs and glandular system must be sound and perfect. Otherwise all attempts to teach him will fail.

The nervous system is composed of an infinite number of neurons. It consists of : (a) the cerebro-spinal system and (b) the autonomic system. The central nervous system comprises : (a) the brain and (b) the spinal cord. The brain includes : (a) cerebrum, (b) cerebellum, (c) mid-brain, (d) pons varolii and (e) medulla oblangata.

The cerebrum controls the sensory and motor nerves. It is the seat of intelligence.

Glands are of two types—Endocrine glands and Exocrine glands. The Pituitary gland is called the master gland. Its hormones affect most of the other glands. The Thyroid gland controls the supply of energy needed for vital life activities. Feeble-mindedness arises in children because of malfunctioning of the thyroid gland. The study of Adrenal glands is important from the point of view of emotions. They become active during emotion and are called glands of combat.

References

1. Morgan Clifford T. : *Physiological Psychology,* 3rd ed. McGraw Hill. Koga Kusha Ltd., 1965.

2. — : *Introduction to Psychology,* McGraw Hill, New York, 1956.

3. Das, A.K. : *Medical Physiology* (Vol. I & II), Books & Allied (P) Ltd., Calcutta 700 009, 2000.

4. Chaudhuri, S.K. : *Medical Physiology,* New Central Book Agency (P) Ltd., Calcutta 700 009, 2000.

Questions and Assignments

1. Write a short essay on the physiological basis of mental life.
2. Mention some of the relevant facts which show the intimate relation of body and mind.
3. Describe in outline the structure and functions of the nervous system.
4. Give a general idea of the central nervous system.
5. Describe with the help of a diagram the different parts of the human brain and briefly state their functions.
6. Write notes on :

   (a) Neuron;

   (b) Synapse;

   (c) Reflex action.
7. Draw a labelled diagram of the human brain. Mention the names of the different parts of the brain and state in short the functions of each part.
8. Write notes on endocrine glands.
9. Write short notes on :

   (a) Pituitary gland;

   (b) Cerebrum;

   (c) Adrenal gland;

   (d) Thalamus.
10. Write notes on Endocrime Glands. Describe the functions of Thyroid Gland.
11. What are the relation between the central and the autonomic nervous system? How are emotions aroused?
12. What is the value of the study of Nervous system to a student of Educational Psychology? Describe the main parts of the central nervous system.

Chapter 13

Sensation and Perception

Introduction : Sensations are the first impression that the child receives from the external world. Perception is considered as an integration of sense-impressions into a meaningful pattern. It is the foundation of all higher forms of knowledge. Psychology of perception helps the teacher most in the task of improving power of observation and reading skill of his pupils.

A. Sensation

13.1 Nature of sensation

A sensation is an inner experience aroused by the respective stimulus through sense organs.

It is the elementary rawmaterial of our knowledge. It is the simplest form of cognition. The bare awareness of a sensory quality like sound, colour, odour or taste is a sensation.

Everything we experience comes to us through our sense organs. For instance, a ray of light acts upon the eye and produces the sensation of colour.

A sensation is the simplest form of mental activity.

Sensations originate from the sense organs. Sensations may be classified according to sense organs :

Sense organs	Sensations
Eye	**Visual** Light Colour Shape Distance
Ear	**Auditory** Pitch Intensity Quality Localisation
Nose	**Olfactory** Various kinds of odours.
Tongue	**Gustatory** Acid Sweet Bitter Salt Alkaline
Skin	**Tactual** Pressure Pain Temperature

13.2 Kinds of sensations

There are three types of sensations :

1. **Organic sensations :** Hunger, thirst, etc. are examples of organic sensations. Organic sensations are produced by internal organs.

2. **Motor sensations (Kinaesthetic sensations) :** These are produced by changes in the organs of movement viz., muscles, tendons and joints.

3. **Special sensations :** Sensations of colours, sounds, tastes, smells, pressures, heat, cold etc. are special sensations. They originate from eye (visual), ear (auditory), skin (tactual), nose (olfactory) and tongue (gustatory). They are produced by special kinds of stimuli like light waves, air waves and so on.

4. **Attributes of sensations :** Sensations have following attributes : (a) Quality, (b) Intensity, (c) Extensity, (d) Duration and (e) Localisation.

Quality : Sensations differ in quality. Sensation of colours, sounds, tastes, smells, heat and cold differ from one another in quality. They are produced by different kinds of stimuli and they have different sense organs. For example, sensations of colours are produced by light on the retina, whereas sensations of sounds are produced by air on the ear.

Intensity : All sensations differ in intensity and vary from weak to very intensive nature. For example, a loud sound produces an intense sensation of sound, white a faint sound produces a faint sensation of light.

Extensity : Extensity is the attribute of a sensation which depends upon the area of the sensitive surface stimulated by a stimulus. For example, touch a book with a finger tip and then with your palm. You have two tactual sensations. The first tactual sensation has greater extensity than the second one.

Duration : Every sensation has a sensible duration. A sensation may linger in the mind for a shorter or longer duration. Again, a sensation may last longer than its stimulus, causing after sensations. This is specially noticable in case of vision.

13.3 Localisation

It is an attribute of sensation which distinguishes a sensation of one part of a sense organ from an identical sensation of another part. For example, if you close your eyes and a person touches your forehead and finger successively with the same pencil point and with the same degree of pressure, your tactual sensations will differ from one another. You will be able to state clearly which parts of the body have been touched.

Some organic sensations cannot be localised, e.g., sensations of comfort or discomfort. These sensations mingle into one total sensation. But some organic sensations can be definitely localised, e.g., cuts or burns in the injured muscle.

13.4 Sense of sight

How we see : The eyes are the sense organs of sight. Light waves from an object enter the eye through the pupil and pass through the lens. They focus on the retina. The optic nerve attached to the retina carries the visual impulses to the nervous system.

The retina has two kinds of receiving cells—rods and cones. Cones enable us to see colours and rods while light. In the very centre of the retina is a small depression which is known as fovea centralis. It is the area of sharpest vision in daylight.

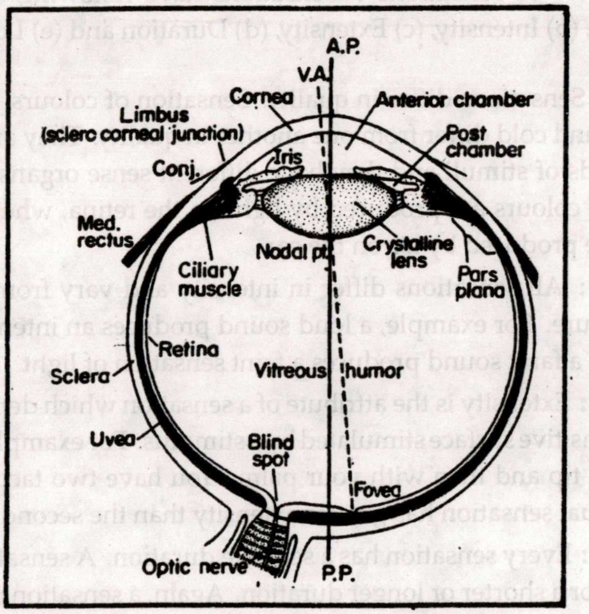

Fig 13.1 Structure of the eye.

13.4.1 Colour blindness

Some people cannot distinguish certain colours. It is believed that the colour-blindness is due to defect in the fovea centralis where the cones are concentrated.

13.4.2 The blind spot

This point of retina is not sensitive to any light stimulation. At this point, the optic nerve enters the eye-ball. It is devoid of rods and cones.

13.5 After image

After image is the visual sensory experience which persists after the external stimulus has been removed. If you stare at a bright object intently and remove your eyes suddenly, you will continue to see the image of the object. This is termed after image. We experience positive after images and negative after images.

In the positive after image, the same kind of brightness and colour of the original impression is experienced. But in the negative after image complementary colour or pattern to that of the original image is seen.

13.6 Sense of hearing

How we hear : The ear is the sense organ for sounds. When the sound waves strike the tympanic membrane of the human ear, we experience sound.

The hammer, anvil and stirrup are involved when younger persons are hard of hearing. Their difficulty may be due to a reduction in the flexibility of the joints between the bones. In some cases, the joints become fixed resulting in otosclerosis.

Within the cochlea is a section called the organ of corti containing minutely sensitive hair cells. These hair cells are fundamental units of the auditory receptors.

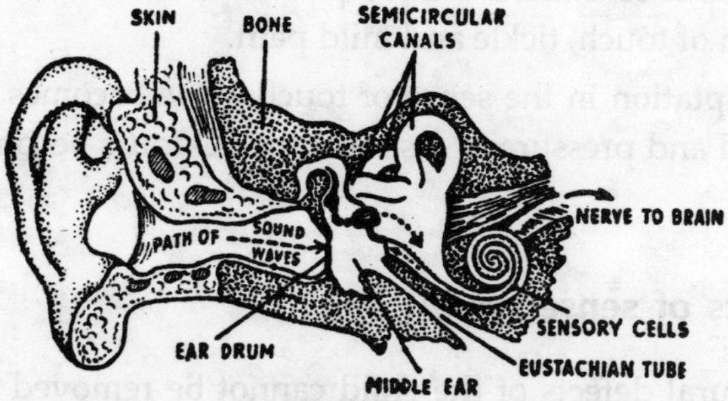

Fig. 13.2

13.7 Our sense of taste and smell

Taste : Taste is a chemical sense. Taste buds on the surface of the tongue are the organs of taste sensations. There are five basic taste sensations—sweet, sour, bitter and salty, plus the taste of metallic substances.

In most cases, the sense of smell supplements our taste associations. In an experiment, a subject was blind-folded and his nostrils were plugged with cotton wool. Then he was asked to distinguish between the taste of an onion and an apple. In general, the responses were no more accurate than a 50–50 guess.

Smell : Smell or olfaction is a chemical sense. Our sense of smell is activated when gaseous particles of a substance reach the nasal fluids. The receptors for smell are spindle-shaped cells embeded in the olfactory tissues, which are connected to the olfactory nerve.

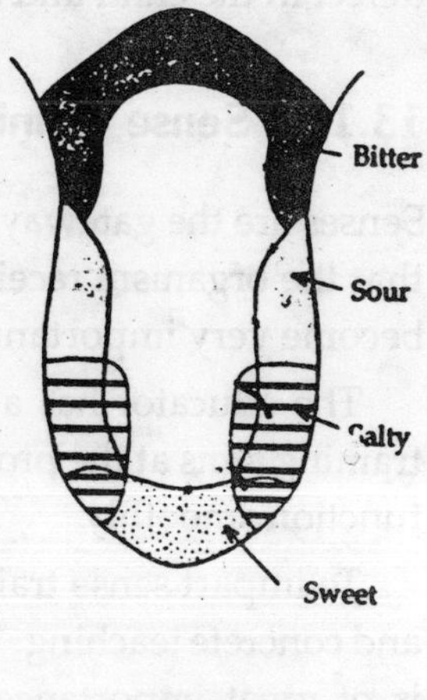

Fig. 13.3

Smell adaptability : If you come into the presence of a bad odour, although unbearable at first, the unpleasantness will not disturb you as much after several minutes. Thus, adaptability is an important characteristic of our sense of smell.

13.8 Cutaneous sensations

The skin is the organ of tactual sensation. There are four distinct organs called cold spots, warmth spots, pain spots and pressure spots in the skin.

Many cutaneous sensations are compound sensations. For instance, Itch is the combination of touch, tickle and mild pain.

There is adaptation in the sense of touch. One becomes quite insensitive to warmth, cold and pressure in a short time. Odours become weak through adaptation.

13.9 Defects of sense organs

The inborn natural defects of the child cannot be removed by training. But early detection of sense organ defects is very important for remedial measures. Therefore, the teacher should be acquainted with the nature of some sense defects.

The number of defective eyes among school children is very high. Some children are colour-blind.

Myopia or short-sightedness and Hypermetropia or long-sightedness are common defects of eyes. These may be corrected by using lenses. But colour blindness is a congenital defect which cannot be corrected.

Defects of the ear are not uncommon in children. These defects retard mental growth. Therefore, it shall be the duty of the teacher to note symptoms of this defect in the child and seek medical advice as early as possible.

13.10 Sense training

Senses are the gateways of knowledge and sensations are the first impressions that the organism receives from the environment. The training of senses thus become very important.

The educator has a primary duty to train the senses of his pupils. Sense training aims at the proper growth and perfection of the senses so that they can function smoothly.

To impart sense training, the educator should go ahead with object lessons and concrete teaching. They should avoid abstract teaching. Learning by doing is of great importance. Montessori method, Kindergarten method, Project method, Excursions, etc. are important processes of sense training.

Madam Montessori invented a new method of training the senses of the child by didactic apparatus.

In the kindergarten system of Froebel three kinds of materials are used for sense development : (i) gifts and occupations, (ii) mother play and (iii) nursery songs.

In the project method, emphasis is laid on the principle of learning by doing.

B. Perception

13.11 Nature of perception

Sensations are simple impressions of sensory qualities. But their meanings are not known. As soon as their meanings are interpreted, they become perception. For instance, I hear a sound from a distant place. This is sensation. But when I know it to be a sound of bell from a distant church, it becomes perception. Meaningful sensation is perception.

Instances of pure sensation in human experiences are rare. We never have pure sensation. According to James Ward, a pure sensation is a psychological myth. It is possible to have pure sensation only in case of a baby just born.

A baby just born will have pure sensations. But adults can never have absolutely pure sensations, because they interpret the meanings of sensations and know them to be sensations of qualities of certain objects. They do not see the red colour but see a thing coloured red. It is only possible for a just born baby to have pure sensation because it has no previous knowledge to interpret it. The bare awareness of a sensory quality is a sensation, but the knowledge of an object together with sensory qualities is known as perception.

Often perception is accompanied by feeling. We perceive a rose, and have a feeling of pleasure. But when we perceive a loud noise we feel pain. This feeling of pleasure or pain depends on our past experiences.

In sensation our mind remains passive. But in perception our mind becomes active. Perception may be accompanied by an action or followed by an action. When we climb a hill we perceive its steepness through our muscular actions. Here perception is accompanied by action. On the other hand, we may hear a knock on the door and then open the door. Obviously, here perception is followed by an action.

Perception is determined by mental readiness. For example, a person may continue to sleep while his wife wakes up at her baby's cry. This is because she is set to hear her baby's cry.

Perception depends on habit formed by past training. For example, an astronomer perceives much more in the sky than an ordinary people.

According to Pillsbury, perception is a synthesis of sensation and memory, i.e., perception = sensation + memory.

Differences between Sensation and Perception

Sensation	Perception
1. Sensations are the simple awareness of qualities, e.g., colour, sound, etc.	1. Perception is the interpretation of the meanings of sensations in the light of past experience.
2. Sensation is the simple form of cognition.	2. Perception is more complex than sensation. It is a fusion of sensation with ideas.
3. Sensation does not involve selection and combination of stimuli.	3. Perception involves selection and combination of stimuli into a pattern.
4. Sensation is the first response of the brain. It is the response of the sensory area of the cerebrum.	4. Perception is the second response of the brain. Perception is the response of the association area as well as the sensory area.

13.12 Attributes of perception

Perception has four attributes : (a) Quality, (b) Intensity, (c) Extensity and (d) Duration.

Quality : There are differences in our visual, auditory, tactual and olfactory perceptions. Perception of colours, tastes, sounds, smells, heat and cold differ from each other in quality. They are produced by different kinds of stimuli.

Intensity : By intensity we mean the intensity of quality. For example, a sound may be faint or loud or a pressure may be light or heavy. Perceptions of these two qualities will differ from one another.

Extensity : Extensity of perception depends on the area of the surface occupied by the object. Put a coin on your skin and then put a book. The two perceptions will not be the same.

Duration : Perception may be of shorter duration or of longer duration. The sound of a bell may last for a longer or shorter duration. Perceptions alike in quality and intensity may differ in duration.

Besides those four attributes perception has certain special features :

1. Perception requires attention. Without attention, the interpretation of a sensation is not possible.

2. Perception is entirely personal or subjective. There are individual differences in perception of a thing or an incident. Our perception is influenced by our physical or mental condition. It may be affected by our expectation and past experiences.

3. Perception involves affective processes, e.g., a beautiful flower is pleasant but an ugly object is unpleasant.

4. Perception is selective activity. Numerous stimuli assail our sense organs at a moment. We select some of them and interpret the meaning of the sensations produced by them.

5. Perception is determined by a context. For example, the same person appears tall by the side of a dwarf, but appears short by the side of a very tall person.

6. In perception, there is a fusion of present and past experiences.

7. Perception is linked with association. In the past, you have seen and touched ice. Now if you see a piece of ice, you at once perceive it as a cold object.

8. We perceive an object as a figure in a ground. We perceive a star in the sky. The star is a figure and the sky is its ground. The figure is compact while the ground spreads out behind the figure. This aspect of figure-ground relations has been stressed by the Gestalt psychologists.

Stout considers perception as a bundle of separate sensations. But the Gestalt psychologists oppose this view. According to them, perception is not a part but whole experience. We perceive a house as a unit, and not as an aggregate of the doors, windows, pillars, etc.

13.13 Gestalt view of perception

Perception is not a bundle of some separate sensations. It is a single unitary experience. We perceive an object as a whole or pattern and not as a mosaic of elementary experiences. Perceptual knowledge is always organised. By arranging some dots you can form a circle. But when the dots are quite separate, the property of a circle is lost.

The reasons behind organisation are discussed below :

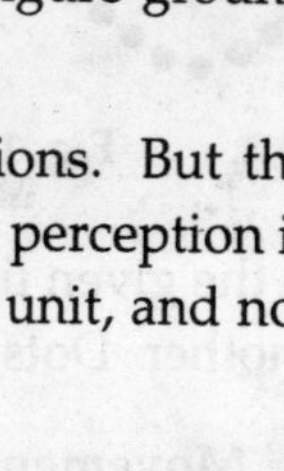

Proximity : Proximity of elements favour grouping of them into a pattern. Things which are in close contact with each other form a unit. For example, four lines in the given figure do not appear as four discrete lines. They are perceived as two pairs of lines.

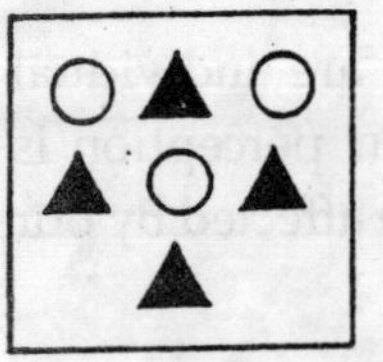

Similarity : Similar objects form a group. In the given figure, the triangles form a group and the circles form another group and they are perceived as two different groups of circle and triangle.

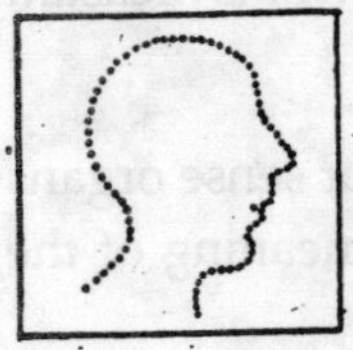

Familiarity : Previous knowledge of a thing favours our perception. In the given figure, several dots have been arranged to give the shape of a human face. Previous knowledge of human face helps us to perceive the figure of dots as a human face. Similarly, we can readily perceive a familiar voice from among a mass of unknown voices.

Principle of closure : There are gaps in each of the given figures. But they are perceived as complete figures having no gaps in them. This filling in gaps in stimulation is termed closure.

Figure ground relation : In order to have a knowledge about organisation, we should understand the figure ground relation. The figure seems to have some sort of shape, while the ground tends to be formless. The figure appears to be in front and the ground behind. The figure is always more organised than the field or ground. The given figure appears as either a flower-vase or two profiles.

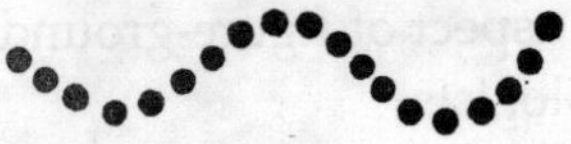

Fig. 13.4

Continuity : Continuity of patterns is favourable to grouping elements into regular wholes. The dots in the given figure appear to be continuous though they are separate from one another. Dots scattered about irregularly are not easily perceived.

Movement : In film shows, a series of still pictures is rapidly exposed to our vision. We perceive motion in the still pictures.

Again, we are familiar with the electric advertising signs in which arrows seem to move back and forth. They do not move in the physical sense. They simply create an illusion of movement by turning lights off and on in sequence. This illusion of movement is termed as the phi-phenomenon.

Set or readiness : The set of readiness at a particular moment determines what shall be perceived at that moment. If a person is ready to see certain pattern in a figure, he can easily perceive it.

Visual perception of depth of distance or space : When we see an object, an image of the object is formed at the retina. This image is bi-dimensional. But we perceive it as tri-dimensional. How does it happen?

13.14 Berkeley's theory

According to Berkeley, we perceive distance by active touch, movement or tactuo-muscular experience. When we see objects at different distances from us and gradually approach them, we get certain visual signs of objects, which are associated with our tactuo-muscular experiences, so that when later their visual signs are perceived, their distances from us are suggested.

Berkeley's theory is corroborated by the fact that babies unacquainted with distance stretch out their hands to catch the moon. They had at first no idea of distance and perceived objects at different distances on the same plane like pictures in a screen. They gradually acquire knowledge of distance through movements, and then acquire visual perception of depth or distance.

But Helmholtz held that due to the movement of our eyeball, certain sensation is produced in the external muscles of the eyes and the ciliary muscle. As a result, we perceive depth and distance.

However, the causes of distance, depth and tri-dimensional perception may be classified into : (a) physiological and (b) psychological.

13.15 Physiological factors

Convergence : The nearer the distance of the object from the eye, the smaller is the convergence. Whereas, the greater is the distance of the object, the greater is the convergence of the lines (see the figure). This results in different kinds of sensation in the muscles of the eye and accordingly distance is perceived.

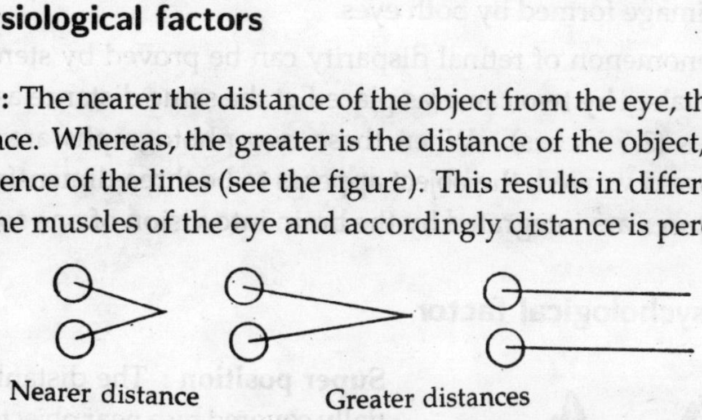

Fig. 13.5

Accommodation : It is done by the ciliary muscles of the eye. The nearer is the distance, the greater is the convexity of the lens. The greater is the distance, the less is the convexity of it. The different degrees of tension of the ciliary muscle and processes suggest different distances.

Retinal disparity : The left eye and the right eye get somewhat different retinal images of the same object. The right eye gets the retinal image of the right side of the object, whereas the left eye gets the retinal image of its left side. The two retinal images are slightly different. This phenomenon is called retinal disparity. The nearer the object, the greater is the disparity of the retinal images and the greater the strain infusing them into one.

The phenomenon of retinal disparity can be explained by the given figure of the backside of a book :

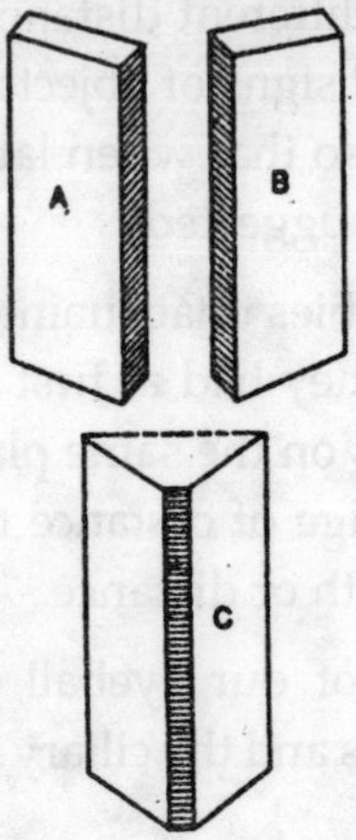

Stereoscope

Fig. 13.6

A : The image on the left eye.

B : The image on the right eye.

C : The image formed by both eyes.

This phenomenon of retinal disparity can be proved by stereoscope. Two pictures are taken by two cameras placed at the same distance as that between the two eyes (2.5 inches). When these two photographs are placed in the stereoscope and viewed, the object appears to be three-dimensional. Here the two flat pictures are integrated by the brain into vision of one solid object.

13.16 Psychological factor

Fig. 13.7

Super position : The distant object is partially covered by a near object. When we see the outline of an object being overlapped by another, we judge the former to be farther, and the latter to be nearer. If there are two mountains, one behind the other, the outline of the distant mountain is partially hidden by the nearer mountain. In the given figure B appears to the farther than A.

Light and Shade : The lighted portion of a picture, appears nearer and the shaded portion appears further. If a picture is shaded and lighted, we see the objects at different distances.

Clearness of outline : If the outlines of an object are clear and distinct, it is near. But if the outlines are vague and hazy, it is distant.

Apparent convergence of parallel lincs : The greater is the distance, the greater is the apparent convergence of the lines which are known to be parallel. As the distance become greater, the parallel railway lines appear to converge. Thus the apparent convergence of parallel lines is a visual cue to distance perception.

Fig. 13.8

Size of the object : From our experience we know that distant object appears to be shorter than the near object. This helps our perception of distance.

Filled and empty space : Filled space appears to be farther from empty space. According to the Gestalt psychologists figure and ground, closure and law of pregnance play an important part in the perception of distance.

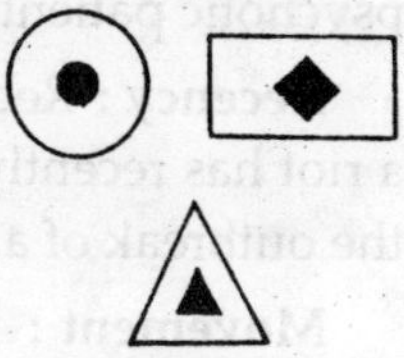

Fig. 13.9

Parallax : If you move your head, you can observe that the objects in your visual field appear to move. If you observe closely, you will find that the objects that are nearest to you, appear to move in the opposite direction. But the distant objects appear to move in the same direction as your head.

When we travel in a train we see that the trees nearby move in opposite direction, but the trees at distance appear to move slowly in the direction we move. This apparent movement of the observed objects due to variation of distance is known as parallax. This helps or misprint as misprint of distance.

13.17 Perception and illusion

Perception is the right interpretation of sensations. Illusion is the wrong interpretation of sensation. It is a false perception.

For instance, when we perceive a rope as a rope, we have perception. But when we perceive a rope as a snake, we have an illusion.

If you put a pencil into a glass of water, the pencil will appear bent. Your perception of the pencil as bent is a false one—an illusion.

13.17.1 Causes of illusions

Habit and familiarity : Some illusions are due to habit and familiarity. Proofreaders are apt to read the word "preception" as "perception" due to habit.

Expectation and set : Sometimes expectation and set cause illusion. You have invited a friend to join a dinner in your house. You are greatly expecting him. At this time if any other person comes to your home you are apt to mistake and address him as your friend.

Anxiety or fear : Anxiety or fear is the cause of some illusions. A timid person hears the sound of house-breaking by a burglar at night when the sound is caused by rustling of the air outside.

Suggestion : Suggestion causes errors of perception. Suggestion may cause some persons to experience feelings of nausea.

In hypnotism our senses are deceived by what the mind is directed to see, feel or hear in an extreme state of suggestibility.

Disorders in sense organs : Disorders in some of our sense organs may give rise to illusions. A white cat appears yellow to a man whose eyes are affected by jaundice.

Suspicion and jealousy : Suspicion and jealousy may cause illusion. A psychotic patient misinterprets crow's caw as his enemy's voice.

Recency : Recency of a similar experience is the cause of some illusions. If a riot has recently broken out in a town, any disturbance will be mistaken for the outbreak of a riot.

Movement : Movement causes illusions. When we travel in a train, the nearby trees appear to move in the opposite direction.

In a cinema show still pictures are exposed to our vision in rapid succession, which produce in us illusion of movement.

Contrast : Contrast is the cause of many illusions, e.g., a tall man appears to be taller by the side of a short man.

Similarity : Similarity between two objects may cause illusion. For instance, we mistake a rope for a snake or rays of the sun for water in a desert.

Geometrical illusion : Geometrical drawings may cause illusion. A few geometrical illusions are illustrated below :

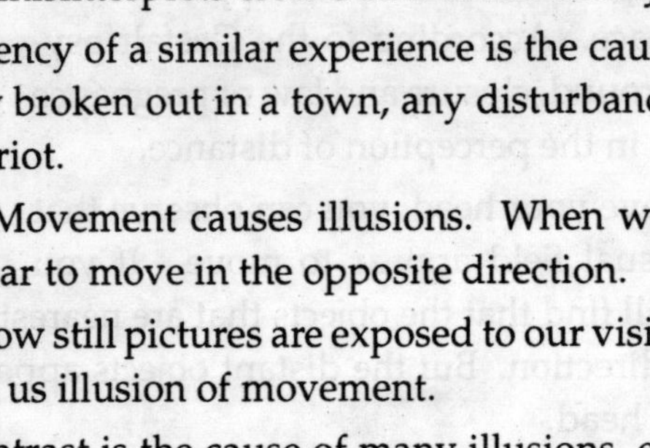

Fig. 13.10 : The straight lines A, B, C, D, E, F are parallel. But they appear as non-parallel lines due to small bent lines.

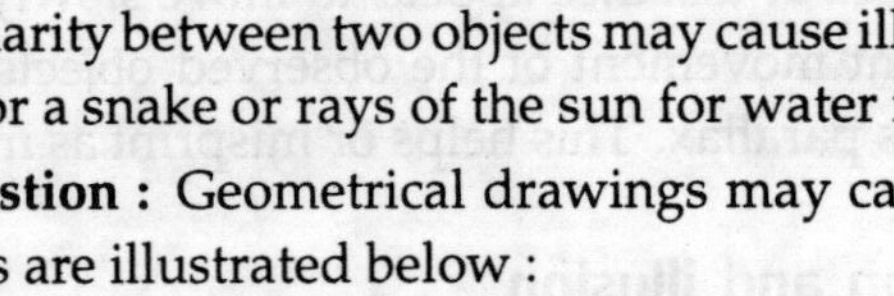

Fig. 13.11 : Though AB, CD are two parallel lines, they appear to be two bent lines due to other lines.

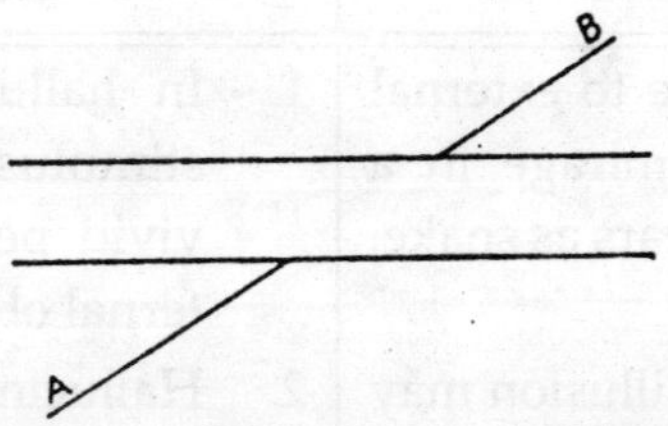

Fig. 13.12 : The straight line AB which cuts two parallel lines, appears to be two separate lines.

Muller Lyer illusion : In this figure BB′ appear to be bigger than AA′. But AA′ = BB′. This geometrical illusion is known as Muller-Lyer illusion.

Fig. 13.13

13.18 Tactual perception

We perceive solidity, weight and movement of objects directly by active touch. Weight of an object is perceived through motor sensation when the object is lifted.

The movement of an object is perceived by passive and active touch. For instance, if a blind person touches a moving object without moving his hand, he will have a succession of tactual sensations and he perceives that it is due to the movement of the object.

13.19 Synesthesia

Coloured hearing is a typical example of syneshesia. Sounds are heard by some normal persons as if they possessed colours. A loud sound may be heard as dark blue while, a trumpet as bright red.

13.20 Abnormalities of perception

Illusion, Hallucination, Agnosia and Super perception are examples of Abnormal perception. Illusion and hallucination are two types of unusual perceptions. Illusions are false perceptions due to external causes. But hallusination are false subjective perception.

Illustion	Hallucination
1. Illusions occur due to external stimulus, e.g., a mirage in a desert, a rope appears as snake.	1. In hallucination, no external stimulus is present. They are vivid perceptions without external objects.
2. In normal person, illusion may sometime occur.	2. Hallucinations are found in delirium and insanity. Visual and auditory hallucinations are more common.

Agnosia or Imperception is lack of perception due to defect in association areas of the brain. In agnosia the patient cannot name the objects seen or identify sounds heard. Super perception is highly developed perception of an expert in his field, for example, a botanist quickly perceives and identifies the different kinds of plants and flowers in a garden.

13.21 Training in perception

In modern paedo-centric education, children are to be taught through practical experiences. This means that children should earn knowledge of the external world through their senses. By reading books only they cannot acquire perfect perception of their environment. Through different senses, children want to have knowledge. This is why the great educators like Rousseau, Pestalozzi, Froebel and Montessori laid so much stress on sense training. At present teachers teach the young students with various kinds of audio-visual aids to make their perception clear and make their lessons meaningful. Incomplete and defective perception may generate false ideas in them. Therefore, the teacher should help them to form true perception of an object, so that the children can have correct ideas and their power of observation develops. The teacher must train their students proper methods of observation. They should learn to observe the relevant items amongst innumerable stimuli. The teacher should give the students correct perception of space, time, depth, distance, movement, colour, three-dimensional object, etc.

Modern educators have discovered a large number of methods for correct perception and sense training. Pestalozzi, who wanted to psychologize education, stressed on object lesson. The children will learn through the observation of concrete objects. Observation and sense perception, according to Pestalozzi, should be the foundation of all education. Froebel's kindergarten system, Montessori method and Dewey's project method also laid stress on sense perception and learning through experiences.

Summary

Sensations are the staff out of which perceptions are made. Sensations are received passively, but perceptions require selective activity of the consciousness. We have discussed sensation and perception separately, but for the purpose of education, we need not study one in abstraction from the other. Perception is sensation plus meaning.

Senses are the gateways of knowledge. The educator, therefore, has a supreme duty to train the senses of his pupils. He also must be aware about the defects of sense organs so that early medical advice may be sought.

References

1. Donald, M. Jhonson : *Essentials of Psychology,* McGraw Hill. New York, 1948.
2. Gill, H.S. : *Psychology Made Simple,* W.H. Allen. London, 1957.
3. Guilford, J.P. : *General Psychology,* D. Van Nostrand Co. New York.
4. Sinha, J.N. : *A Manual of Psychology,* New Central Book Agency, Calcutta 700 009, 1984.
5. Bhatnagar, R.P. : *A Study of Educational Psychology,* Vishwavidyalaya Prakashan, Gorakhpur, 1954.

Questions and Assignments

1. What is sensation? Explain the general characteristics of sensation.
2. What is perception? Discuss the contribution of Gestalt Psychologists toards perception.
3. *In the adult mind there is no such thing as pure sensation.*—Explain.
4. Explain the characteristics of perception. Distinguish a perception from sensation.
5. Describe how we perceive solid objects and distant objects visually.
6. Explain how we can visually perceive the distance of an object.
7. What is perception according to Gestalt Psychology? Discuss its importance in education.

8. Write notes on :

   (a) Local signs.

   (b) Illusions.

   (c) Hallucination.

   (d) Training in perception.

   (e) Depth perception.

Chapter 14

Intelligence

Nature of intelligence : Man as well as animal cannot learn without intelligence. But man is superior to animals in intelligence, because man can make proper use of his past experiences. He can adapt himself to a new situation more easily than a dog. This capacity to master a new situation is a mark of intelligence. It is an innate ability quite distinct from thinking or remembering or other mental processes.

14.1 Definitions of intelligence

It is not easy to define intelligence. A number of psychologists have tried to define it. But none of their definitions are complete.

Johnson : Intelligence is the ability to solve the general run of human problems, to adjust to new situations and in short, the ability to think.

Stern : Intelligence is general mental adaptability to new problems and conditions of life.

Terman : Intelligence is the ability to think in terms of abstract ideas. An individual is intelligent in the proportion that he is able to carry on abstract thinking.

Buckingham : Intelligence is the learning ability.

Boring : Intelligence is what intelligence tests.

Jean piaget : Intelligence is the ability to adapt to one's surroundings.

Weschler : Intelligence is the aggregate or global capacity of the individual to act purposefully, to think rationally and to deal effectively with his environment.

Woodrow : Intelligence is a capacity to acquire capacity.

In fact, no one knows what intelligence is. It is so vague and ambiguous. However, we can divide the definitions given by different psychologists into five broad categories :

1. Biological definition.
2. Physiological definition.
3. Educational definition.
4. Sociological definition.
5. Faculty definition.

14.1.1 Biological definitions

The biological definitions lay stress on the capacity for adjustment of the human beings. For example, William Stern defines intelligence as general adaptability to new problems and conditions of life. McDougall defines it essentially as the capacity for making new adjustment. Wells defines it as the power of recombining our behaviour patterns so as to act better in novel situations.

But biological concept of intelligence is criticised on the ground that many great men of exceptional intelligence have been found to be ill-adapted in their social environment.

14.1.2 Physiological definitions

Some psychologists consider intelligence as the function of physiological process. Sandiford defines intelligence as the function of nervous system. The behaviourists do not accept intelligence as a mental process. Intelligence depends upon the cerebral cortex. It depends upon the greater complexity of brain cells in the cortex.

14.1.3 Educational definitions

In educational definitions, the ability to learn has been emphasised :

Buckingham thinks that intelligence is the learning ability.

Dearborn defines intelligence as capacity to learn.

Bridges defines it as the capacity to learn or acquire ideas, sentiments, and skills.

14.1.4 Sociological definitions

According to Boynton, the best indication of intelligence is the behaviour of individual in his group.

14.1.5 Faculty definition

Terman defines intelligence as the ability to carry on abstract thinking. Rex Knight defines intelligence as capacity for relational constructive thinking. Binet defines intelligence as the power of attention, of adaptation, and of self-criticism. Thorndike defines it as the sum of average of all specific abilities. Ebbinghaus defines intelligence as synthetic or combining ability.

From the above discussion it is clear that there is much overlapping among the characteristics of intelligence stressed by different psychologists and no single definition is perfect. In fact, there are as many definitions of intelligence as there are psychologists who have tried to define it.

14.1.6 Comprehensive definition

However, the definition of intelligence given by Woodworth is much more comprehensive. According to him, intelligence is an innate ability which helps us :

1. To learn by past experience.
2. To adapt to a novel situation.
3. To find out the essentials of a problem.
4. To see the whole situation as a pattern of interrelated parts.

Man is more intelligent than an animal because man can utilise past experience to seek a goal. He can adjust himself to a novel situation more easily than an animal. He possesses insight to find out the essentials of a problem. He has foresight in seeing the whole situation as a pattern of interrelated parts. Man reacts to the whole situation rather than to some striking part of it.

However, the different kinds of definition of intelligence are not exclusive of each other. In fact, they are inter-dependent.

14.2 Types of intelligence

Intelligence may be broadly classified into two categories : (i) Abstract intelligence and (ii) Concrete intelligence.

Abstract intelligence : All intelligence tests which require handling of symbols are tests of abstract intelligence. For example, abstract intelligence is required in solving mathematical problems.

Concrete intelligence : Concrete intelligence is required in doing various activities of our daily life.

The performance tests of different types measure concrete intelligence.

14.3 Theories of intelligences

It is difficult to find out the true nature of intelligence. Some psychologists consider it to be a single mental ability. Whereas, some others consider intelligence as a sum of many abilities. These views may be classified as : (1) Monarchic theory; (2) Oligarchic theory and (3) Anarchic theory.

14.3.1 Monarchic theory

According to this theory, intelligence is one all—pervading mental ability. According to Burt, intelligence is inborn all-round mental efficiency. To Stern it is general adaptability to the new problem and conditions of life. Intelligence is a central intellectual ability which dominates all mental activities.

If this unifactor theory of intelligence is accepted, we may think that if a man performs one intellectual task well, he will do others also equally well. But this is contrary to facts. Moreover, if this view is accepted as true, no intelligence test can be constructed. In order to measure intelligence in practice we split it up. In fact, this theory constitutes an uncertain intellectual basis for mental testing.

14.3.2 Oligarchic theory

According to oligarchic theory, intelligence is not a single faculty. It comprises a few major faculties, functioning independently of one another. Each of them requires separate measurement. For instance, Binet holds that intelligence is a sum of different faculties such as the comprehension of a problem, ability of directing attention to it, power of adaptation to a new situation, and the ability for self-criticism.

The oligarchic theory believes in faculty psychology which is not true. It contradicts the unity of the mind.

14.3.3 Anarchic theory

According to this theory, intelligence is a sum of many abilities which are independent of one another and they function separately. Thorndike holds that intelligence is the sum of average of all specific mental abilities, Thompson opines that the mind of each person is a sample groups of qualities. The theories of Thompson and Thorndike are multifactor theories of intelligence.

This doctrine holds that a person may show his skill in performing a particular task. But there is no guarantee that in doing some other task he will show equal efficiency. Therefore, one mental test is not enough to measure the intelligence of a person. Thus a number of tests, varying in character, is required for the measurement of intelligence.

But Thompson's sampling theory is not without defects. We cannot determine which abilities should comprise the sample.

Further we cannot be certain that in our sample we have no abilities overlapping each other. Moreover, if the abilities are independent of one another, an average has no meaning. We cannot take an average for a person's height and weight which are quite different from each other.

14.3.4 Spearman's two-factor theory

Spearman propounded two-factor theory of intelligence in 1904. This theory has greatly influenced the measurement of intelligence. According to Spearman, the frank adoption of two-factor theory would seem to supply an adequate basis for a unified science of all human ability (The Ability of Man).

According to two-factor theory, intelligence consists of two factors— a general ability (g) and a special ability (s). The general ability or g comes into play in all kinds of activities. A special ability or s comes into play in any particular activity. There are many special abilities such as verbal ability, ability to deal with numbers, ability to deal with spatial relations, ability in music, ability to deal with mechanical relations and so on. All these specific abilities presuppose a general ability (g) without which they cannot function.

The general factor, g, varies from one individual to another, but is constant for any one individual in all his scores. The specific factor s varies from one individual to another. Any mental test, then, measures g, and s, some measuring 'g' prominently, others 's' predominantly. Thus, in working out certain problem in mathematics, a student will need G_m+S_m. In case of learning language, he will need G_L+S_L and so on.

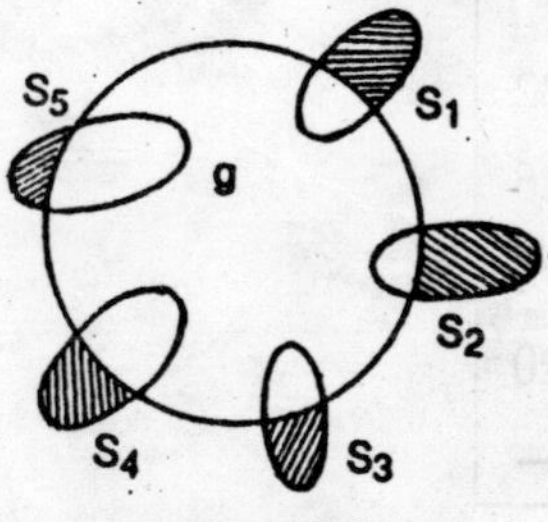

Fig. 14.1

Spearman's theory can be explained by the adjoining diagram. It will be clear from the diagram that for different mental works some amount of 'g' and 's' are needed. According to Spearman if there is a positive correlation between two intelligence tests, it may be supposed that there is one common factor 'g' and two separate specific factors 's' in the two tests.

Suppose there are two tests a and b and their common factor 'g' and two specific factors S_a, S_b.

Suppose there are other two tests p and q and their common factor g and specific factors S_p, S_q. Then it was shown by Spearman that

$$\gamma_{gg'} = \frac{\sqrt{\gamma_{ap}\gamma_{aq}\gamma_{bp}\gamma_{bq}}}{\sqrt{\gamma_{ab}\gamma_{pq}}}$$

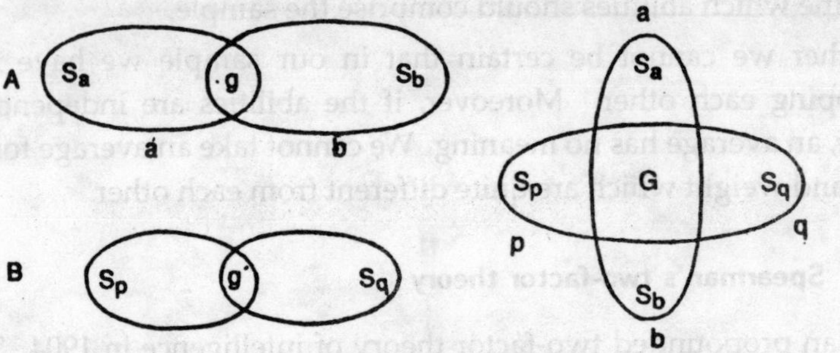

Fig. 14.2

In the above equation $\gamma_{gg'} = 1$ and g and g' are equivalent, and in all intelligence tests they are identical. Further it was shown that

$$\frac{\gamma_{ap}}{\gamma_{aq}} = \frac{\gamma_{bp}}{\gamma_{bq}}$$

$$\text{or,}\quad \gamma_{ap} \times \gamma_{bq} = \gamma_{bp} \times \gamma_{aq}$$

$$\text{or,}\quad \gamma_{ap} \times \gamma_{bq} - \gamma_{bp} \times \gamma_{aq} = 0.$$

This difference is known as Tetrad difference.

It may further be clarified by an example. Suppose we have measured five mental abilities and prepared their correlation matrix :

Correlation matrix

	a	b	c	d	e
	(.8)	(.7)	(.6)	(.5)	(.4)
a	—	.56	.48	.40	.32
b	.56	—	.42	.35	.28
c	.48	.42	—	.30	.24
d	.40	.35	.30	—	.20
e	.32	.28	.24	.20	—

Now, taking correlation coefficient of any four abilities, it may be shown that the tetrad equation becomes zero.

For example,

$$.40 \times .42 = .48 \times .35$$

$$\text{or,}\quad .40 \times .42 - .48 \times .35 = 0$$

According to Spearman, the tetrad equation holds good for the inter-correlations of all kinds of abilities.

Spearman's theory seems to incorporate the truths of other theories. The monarchic theory is true, if the central intellective factor is regarded as g.

The anarchic theory holds good if the specific factors are independent of one another. The oligarchic theory is true to the extent that faculties distinct from the universal factor, and fairly distinct from the specific factors, are revealed in the broad group factors.

Criticism : But Spearman's two-factor theory is not free from criticism. Instead of considering the general factor of intelligence, we can explain the nature of correlation also by assuming a group factor. The correlation is not always determined by g only. For example, in case of performances of a and b without assuming g we can say that there is some correlation between S_a and S_b (see the figure). This overlapping of factors is known as Group factor.

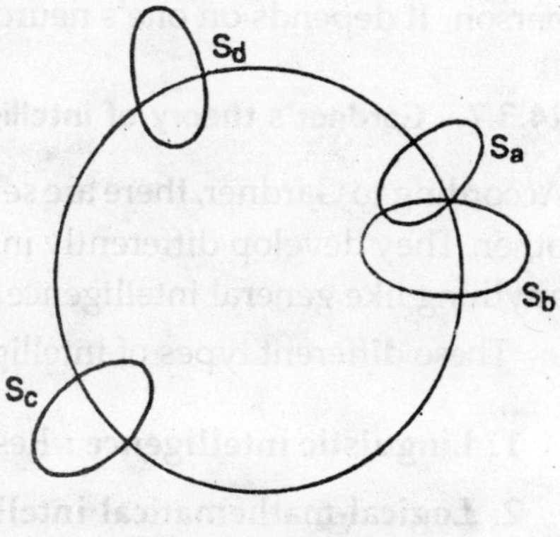

Fig. 14.3

Spearman also has admitted such group factors as verbal, numerical and mechanical group factors. In the opinion of Thorndike, Thompson and others, there is no general factor in intelligence. Instead, intelligence is a sum of many abilities which are independent of one another.

14.3.5 Thompson's sampling theory

Prof. G.H. Thompson thinks that our mind is composed of a number of independent abilities or factors. When we perform a mental task, several factors combine together to complete the work. But how many factors will be needed and which factors will be required depend on the principle of sampling.

Thompson's sampling theory may be explained by a diagram. In the adjoining figure, the dots indicate innumerable factors. The factors which are needed for performing the tasks A, B, C, D are encircled. From the diagram it is clear that there is no correlation between A and B, C, D. But correlation exists between B, C, D.

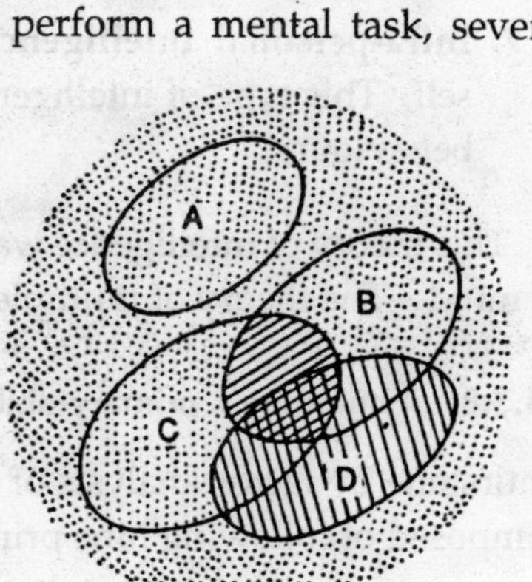

Fig. 14.4

In this doctrine of Sampling theory, it is assumed that mind is composed of a large number of factors and hence it is called multifactor theory.

14.3.6 Cattell and Horn's theory of intelligence

According to Cattell and Horn, there are two types of intelligence—Crystallised intelligence and Fluid intelligence.

Crystallised intelligence is acquired and it depends on education and culture. Fluid intelligence, on the other hand, is innate mental ability of a person. It depends on one's neurological development.

14.3.7 Gardner's theory of intelligence

According to Gardner, there are seven types of intelligence independent of each other. They develop differently in different people. They are not influenced by anything like general intelligence.

These different types of intelligence are :

1. **Linguistic intelligence :** Responsible for all kinds of linguistic abilities.
2. **Logical-mathematical intelligence :** Responsible for abilities related to logic and mathematics.
3. **Spatial intelligence :** Responsible for abilities concerning spatial relationship.
4. **Musical intelligence :** Responsible for talents and skills concerned with the musical field.
5. **Bodily kinaesthetic intelligence :** Concerned with the abilities required in using one's body or limbs to do skilful movements.
6. **Inter-personal intelligence :** Consists of the abilities to understand others, which is needed for social interactions.
7. **Intra-personal intelligence :** Consists of the abilities to know one's self. This type of intelligence provides insight into an individual's total behaviour.

This theory of intelligence was published in Gardner's book (1983), Frames of mind—The theory of multiple intelligence.

14.3.8 Thurstone's primary ability theory

Thurstone by factor-analysis of mental tests results found that intelligence is composed of following nine primary abilities :

1. Visual or Spatial ability (S).
2. Perceptual ability (P).
3. Numerical ability (N).
4. Verbal ability (V).
5. Memory (M).
6. Induction (RI).
7. Deduction (RD).
8. Word Fluency (W).
9. Problem-solving ability (PS).

According to Thurstone, any intellectual work depends on these nine primary abilities. In some activities, some of these factors are needed or, in other cases, all the factors may be needed. For example, if you want to be come an engineer, you will need spatial ability (S), numerical ability (N), abilities of Induction (RI) and Deduction (RD).

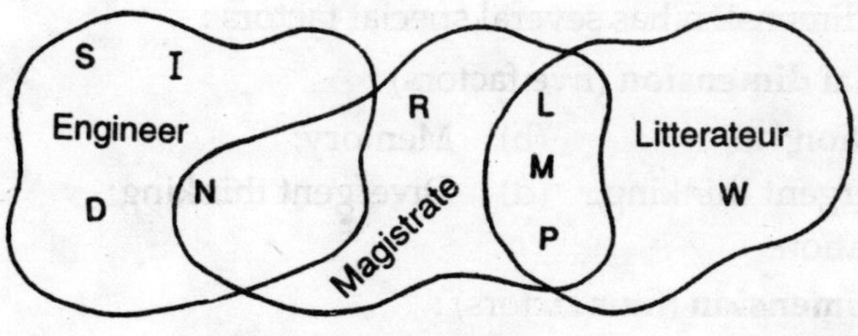

Fig. 14.5

If you want to become a litterateur, you will need verbal ability (V), Word Fluency (W), Perceptual ability (P) and Memory (M). But if you want to become a District Magistrate, you must need Verbal ability (V), Numerical ability (N), Perceptual ability, Memory and Problem solving ability (PS).

The defect of this theory is that it discarded the concept of the general factor.

14.3.9 Vernon's hierarchical theory

Vernon's hierarchical theory may be explained by the following diagram :

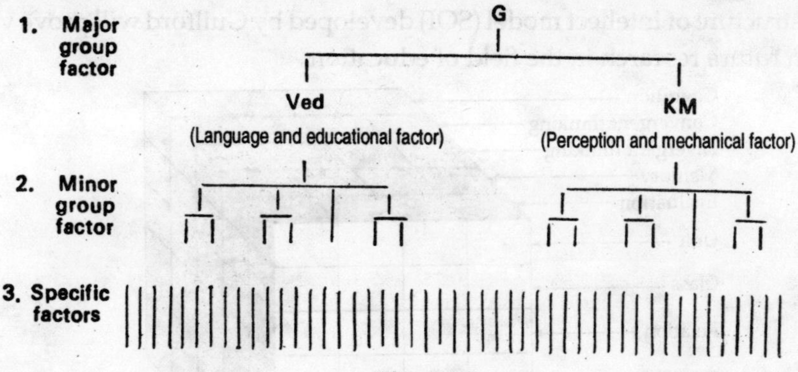

Fig. 14.6

According to P.E. Vernon, G is such a mental ability that can be measured by intelligence test. It has two major group factors, Ved and KM. Ved comprises language and educational factor while KM comprises perception and mechanical factors. These two factors again may be divided into minor group factors. Finally, these minor group factors may be analysed into a number of specific factors. These are again associated with several minor mental abilities. By different tests, these abilities can be measured.

14.3.10 Guilford's theory of intellect

Structure of intellect (SOI) was developed by Guilford in 1966.

By factor-analysis Guilford, has given a model of intelligence. According to him any intellectual work has three dimensions : 1. Operational dimension. 2. Content dimension. 3. Dimension of product.

Again, each dimension has several special factors :

1. **Operational dimension** (five factors) :
   (a) Cognition; (b) Memory;
   (c) Convergent thinking; (d) Divergent thinking;
   (e) Evaluation.
2. **Content dimension** (four factors) :
   (a) Concrete or Figural; (b) Symbolic;
   (c) Semantic; (d) Behavioural.
3. **Dimension of product** (six factors) :
   (a) Concept of unit; (b) Concept of classes;
   (c) Concept of relation; (d) Concept of system;
   (e) Concept of transformation; (f) Concept of implication.

Guilford's theory of intelligence may be explained by means of a figure of solid model of a cube.

According to this model, total number of factors of human intelligence are $4 \times 5 \times 6 = 120$. Out of these Guilford and his associates have found out eighty factors through analysis.

The structure of intellect model (SOI) developed by Guilford will prove very useful in future research in the field of education.

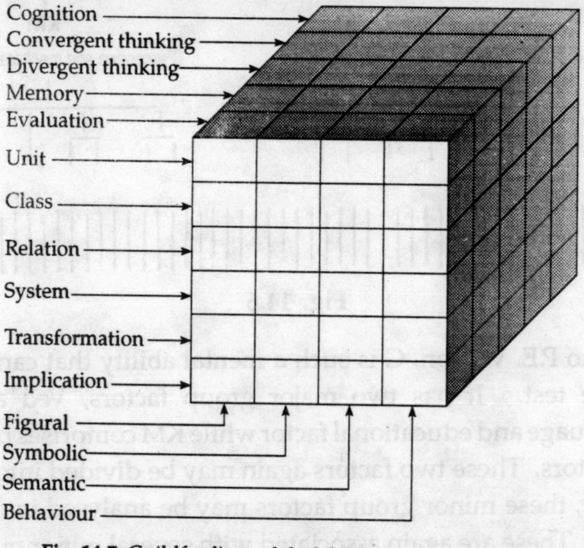

Fig. 14.7: Guildford's model of the structure of intellect.

14.4 Measuring intelligence

Previously it was thought that intelligence is closely associated with our physiological structure. Based on this idea, different theories of phrenology, physiognomy, etc. had come into existence, mainly in the second-half of the nineteenth century. Those scientists measured skull with brass instruments and observed facial structure of a person to ascertain his intelligence. Some other scientists tried to determine intelligence by mesuring sensory discrimination power of an individual. But the products of such efforts with costly instruments were not uniform and contradicted each other.

Alfred Binet and Simon first discovered a reliable method of measuring intelligence in 1905. In 1904, the French Government appointed a Commission to determine the cause of feeble-mindedness amongst school-going children. As a result, Binet-Simon Scale, came to light in 1905. The scale consisted of thirty tests arranged in order of difficulty from the easiest to the most difficult. According to this scale, it was thought that an Idiot could not answer more than six tests and an Imbecile not more than fifteen.

In 1908, the scale was modified and each test was classified under a particular age. Thus the concept of Age-scale and Mental age were introduced for the first time.

Further revisions of the scale were made in 1911 and the total number of tests increased to 54. The Binet Scale was improved by Goddard, Terman, Yerke and Burt. The most important revisions of the Binet's scale were :

1. The Vineland Revision of Goddard (1911).
2. Yerke's Point Scale (1915).
3. Terman's Standford Revision (1916).
4. Cyril Burt's London Revision (1921).
5. Standford Revision (1960).

14.4.1 Standford revision

The Standford revision of Binet scale at present is most widely used. In 1916, Prof. Terman introduced the idea of Intelligence Quotient (I.Q.) :

$$\text{I.Q.} = \frac{\text{M.A.}}{\text{C.A.}} \times 100$$

where M.A. denotes the mental age of the subject,

C.A. the chronological age.

Some items of 1916 Standford scale are :

Age 3 years :

1. Pointing out nose, eyes and mouth.
2. Enumerating the objects in pictures.
3. Repeating two numbers.
4. Repeating six to seven syllables.
5. Giving surname.

Age 8 years :

1. Finding omissions in pictures.
2. Counting backwards from 20 to 1.
3. Repeating 5 digits.
4. Giving months and year.
5. Giving differences from memory.

14.4.2 Mental age

If a 5-year old boy could answer all the items meant for this age, he was considered as a boy of normal intelligence. If he failed to answer these tests fully, but could answer all the questions for age 4, he was supposed to have the mental age (M.A.) of 4 years.

Then his I.Q. will be : $\text{I.Q.} = \frac{\text{M.A.}}{\text{C.A.}} \times 100 = \frac{4}{5} \times 100 = 80.$

Concept of mental age was first developed by Binet. Stern introduced the term intelligence quotient (I.Q.) and Terman multiplied it by hundred to avoid decimal fractions.

Prof. Terman classifies human intelligence in terms of intelligence quotients, in the following way :

Class	I.Q.
Genius	Above 140
Very superior	121–140
Superior	111–120
Normal	91–110
Dull	81–90
Border-line deficiency	71–80
Moron	51–70
Imbecile	26–50
Idiot	0–25

Fig. 14.8

The lower three groups are designated as Feeble-minded.

In 1937, Terman and Merrill published a Revised Standford-Binet scale. There are two parallel forms—L-form and M-form. These two tests are of equal difficulty and any one of them may be used for measuring intelligence. In the 1916 revision, there were 90 items but in 1937 the number of items rose to 129 in each form.

In 1960, another revision of the test was published (1960, Standford Revision). In this revision one test was constructed instead of L-form and M-form. Here I.Q. is found out in Standard score. However, Terman Merrill's Test of 1937 is the most popular tests and widely used in different countries.

14.4.3 Intelligence test in India

Construction of intelligence test in India is a difficult task. The difficulties may be enumerated as :

1. India is a multilingual country and a large section of people are illiterate. So, such tests can only be administered to the students of educated higher classes. Thus a standardised test covering all sections of the population is difficult to construct.
2. There is a lack of due encouragement on the part of the government. No funds are provided to promote intelligence testing in this country.
3. There is dearth of trained personnel who are capable of construction of intelligence tests.
4. Moreover, it is difficult to determine the correct age of the examinees. The entries of their age in the school records are not reliable. Often, even the parents cannot tell the exact age of their wards.

However, in spite of the above difficulties, some psycologists in India have tried to prepare suitable intelligence test and obtained tentative norms. These works may be mentioned here :

1. The psychology department of Calcutta university has translated and published two parallel forms of Terman-Merrill's Test in Bengali. But these could not be standardised.
2. Herbert Rice's Test : His scale is an adaptation of Binet scale in Urdu. His scale comprises thirty-five tests out of which nine are performance tests. This is a standardised test.
3. State Bureau of educational and vocational guidance, Gwalior (M.P.), prepared a test, Samanya buddhi pariksha, an adaptation of W. Stephenson's Test.

4. Jha's Group Tests : Pandit Lajja Shankar Jha of Benares Teachers' Training College, devised tests in Hindi and Urdu. It is a standardised group test. He has also made a revision of Terman's Test.

5. Kamat's Age Scale Revision : Dr. V.V. Kamat of Belgaun Training College adapted Standford Revision in the age scale in Kanarese and Marathi languages.

6. Jhingran's Revision of Otis Tests : Prof. Jhingran of Benares Teachers' Training College brought forth a revision of the Otis Self-administering Test. The revision consists of 75 questions to be answered within half an hour. The test is in Urdu and Hindi and administered to about 4000 children.

Besides the above tests, Prof. M.V. Gopalswami of Mysore University prepared test in Kanarese. These tests are adaptation of Binet Test.

Prof. S. Jalota of D.A.V. College, Lahore, prepared Urdu Tests and standardised it.

Prof. H.P. Maity adapted Binet Tests in Bengali, Calcutta.

Department of Education, Gorakhpur University, Gorakhpur has prepared general mental ability test.

Prof. C.M. Bhatia has prepared battery of performance tests of intelligence for students of 11 to 15 years of age. Bhatia's battery contains Koh's Block Design Test, Alexander's Pass-along Test, Pattern Drawing Test, Picture Construction Test and Memory Test for Digits.

14.5 Group tests of intelligence

Individual tests have certain defects. The administration of these tests take quite a long time. Out of necessity, Group tests were introduced first in America. During First World War (1914–1918), large number of soldiers were to be recruited within a short period in the army. It was felt that the Traditional Individual Intelligence Tests are not suitable for such quick recruitment and hence Group Intelligence Tests were devised. Thus two sets of Army Alpha and Beta Tests were constructed. These tests were standardised and were given to the new recruits in the army. The Alpha tests were given to those who could understand English language. But those who were illiterate or could not understand English were given the Beta tests. In the Army Alpha Tests 212 questions were given and had to be answered in 23 minutes and 15 seconds only. These tests contained arithmetical problems and the items of informations mainly. The Beta tests consist of a variety of diagrams and pictures involving no language.

Besides the Army Alpha and Beta tests, there are several other group tests such as, Terman's Group Intelligence Tests and Otis Self-administering Tests of mental ability.

Terman's group tests : These tests were devised for school children. The number of items in these tests were 185 to be answered in 27 minutes.

Otis self-administering tests : These tests comprises 75 questions to be answered in 30 minutes. The examiners are free to regulate the time and he can spend more time for difficult questions and less time for easy ones.

Dear born intelligence scale : This scale has been devised for grades IV to XII. It comprises 7 sub-tests.

Raven progressive matrices tests : This test consists of geometric figures and designs. It was devised in England and is widely used.

The Cattell culture-free test : These group scales are free from cultural effect and may be used universally.

14.5.1 Advantages of group tests

Group tests are mostly verbal and written. Within a limited time, the examiner can classify a large number of students according to their intelligence.

Again, though the number of test items in a group test are too many, the examinees are to give short answers. So, scoring becomes easier for the examiner. Moreover, the group tests are made fool-proof by admitting only one correct answer.

The standardised group tests are very handy. The instruction for the examiner and the subjects are clearly written in the booklet. So, the examiner's duty is simply to inform the examinees the time-limit for the test.

Comparison of group test with individual test of intelligence.

Group test	Individual test
1. It can be administered to a number of individuals at a time.	1. It can be administered to one individual at a time.
2. Untrained persons can administer the test.	2. Trained persons are required to administer the test.
3. These tests are mostly verbal or written. It is suitable for those who can read or write.	3. It is suitable for a child who cannot read or write.
4. In terms of administration and time it is not costly.	4. In terms of administration it is costly and time consuming.
5. Results may be affected by speed and reading ability of the individual. It is less reliable.	5. It is more reliable.

14.6 Classification of intelligence tests

Intelligence tests may be broadly classified as :

1. Individual tests.
2. Group tests.

Individual tests may be divided into verbal tests and non-verbal tests. Similarly, group tests may be divided into verbal tests and non-verbal or performance tests :

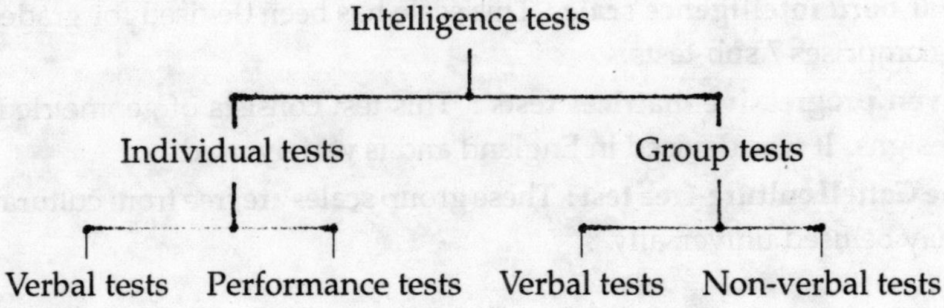

14.6.1 Verbal tests

These tests include varieties of verbal material and the examinees respond in language verbal or written. A few examples of such tests are :

1. **Comparison :**
   (a) Of the two things which is heavier?
   (b) Where lies the difference between a triangle and a square?
2. **Memory :** The subject is told several digits 8 3 9 2 7 5 and he has to repeat them correctly and in correct order.
3. Association tests :
   Which of the items is the odd one?
   (a) Geometrical figures Δ □ ○ *?
   (b) Gold, iron, silver, tomato?
4. **Similarity tests :**
   (a) Fish swims, birds ... ... ?
   (b) Ice is cold, fire ... ... ?
5. **Completion tests :**
   Complete the series :
   (a) 2, 4, 8, 16, ? ?
   (b) 4, 6, 8, 10, ? ?

6. **Sentence making :**
   (a) Make sentences with—Book, Bird, Head.
   (b) Arrange to make a meaningful sentence—Ram to went Calcutta train by.

14.6.2 Non-verbal tests

In these tests, use of language is not necessary. Performance tests are a typical example of such tests. Following are some of the important performance tests :

1. Koh's Block Design Test.
2. Alexander's Pass-along Test.
3. Healy's Puzzle Test.
4. Porteus Maze Test.
5. Good Enough's Man Drawing Test.
6. Terman's Ball and Field Test.
7. Knox's Cube Construction Test.
8. Dearborn's Form Board Test.
9. Army Beta Test.

These tests are used to ascertain intelligence of the illiterate, deaf and dumb, feeble-minded and foreigners.

14.7 Some characteristics of intelligence

Normal distribution of intelligence : All men are not equally intelligent. Some are gifted, some are feeble-minded. Terman, on the basis of mental tests, found that human intelligence is normally distributed.

The following normal distribution curve shows that the majority of people are at the average. Only a few people are very bright, and a few are very dull.

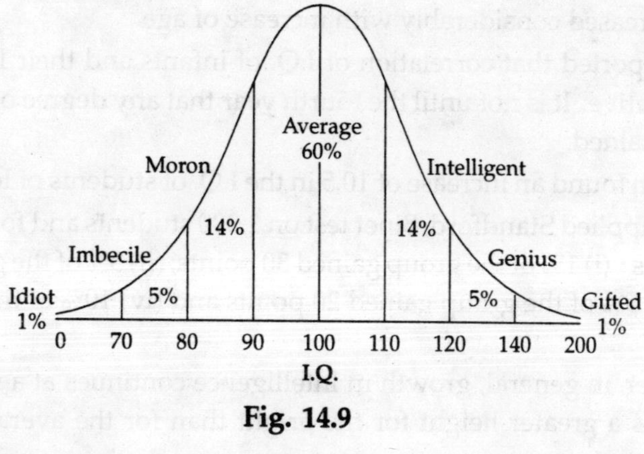

Fig. 14.9

Constancy of I.Q. : Some psychologists hold that as the child grows in age, his intelligence also grows. It tends to stabilise during adolescence period (Age 16–18 years). However, Terman set 16 years as the limit of mental growth. The I.Q. of a person remains relatively constant throughout his life and declines in old age. However, horizontal growth of intelligence in terms of experience may continue throughout an individual's life.

Some other psychologists think that I.Q. does not remain constant over years. Fluctuation may occur due to unreliability of the tests. This is why psychologists like Bayley, Jones, Wellman, Cattell expressed doubts about the constancy of I.Q.

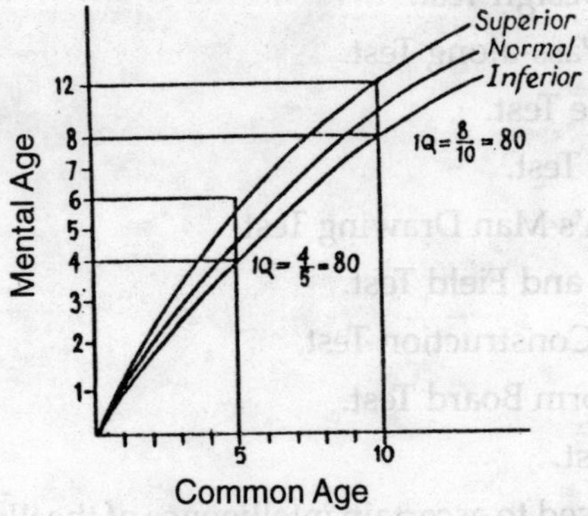

Fig. 14.10

Bayley, by applying Standford Binet test, found that I.Q. of two boys, Mark and Gerald, underwent a considerable change :

Name	Age→	9	10	11
Mark	I.Q.	117	122	130
Gerald	I.Q.	85	84	76

Fig. 14.11

I.Q. of Mark increased with increase of his age. On the other hand, I.Q. of Gerald decreased considerably with increase of age.

Jones reported that correlation of I.Q. of infants and their I.Q. a few years later is negative. It is not until the fourth year that any degree of stability in the I.Q. was attained.

Wellman found an increase of 10.5 in the I.Q. of students of Iowa University.

Cattell applied Standford-Binet test on 1,300 students and found an increase in the I.Q. as : (i) 1% of the group gained 30 points; (ii) 3% of the group gained 40 points; (iii) 5% of the group gained 20 points and (iv) 10% of the group gained 15 points.

However, in general, growth in intelligence continues at a more rapid rate and reaches a greater height for the bright than for the average individuals.

On the other hand, the growth rate of the retarded progresses more slowly and reaches its limit sooner and at a lower level than the normal individuals.

Conclusion : From the above discussion, following conclusion may be drawn :

1. The I.Q. does not remain constant. The change of environment may bring out a change in I.Q.
2. The I.Q. is the product of native endowment and training.
3. No test is completely reliable. Repetition of same test on same subjects may not give the same I.Q.
4. Fluctuation occurring in the I.Q. stems from fatigue, lack of motivation and other personal factors of the testes and personal equation of the examiner.
5. I.Q. fluctuates in case of infants. But it relatively remains constant between the ages 4 and 15.

14.8 Intelligence and racial differences

The results of modern studies reveal that no race can claim to be superior in intelligence to other races. In every race dull and bright people can be found. The apparent differences which are found in race or cultural group are really the product of environmental influences.

14.9 Intelligence and the sexes

There is no significant difference in intelligence between man and woman.

14.10 Intelligence and occupation

Different occupational groups have been found to possess different degrees of intelligence within certain limits. Teachers, accountants and persons of professional occupation have been found to possess the highest average intelligence. On the other hand, farmers and labourers have been found to have the lowest average intelligence, of course with a few exceptions.

14.11 Intelligence and heredity

Intelligence is an innate ability. Generally we believe that children of intelligent persons are always intelligent, whereas those of feeble-minded are always stupid. But such a belief is not justified.

The development of intelligence depends both on heredity and environment. But how much development is due to heredity or to environment—or to their interaction—the psychologists could not definitely determine. In fact, the two are so closely interwoven that it is difficult to separate the effect of one from that of the other. The influence of both heredity and environment on the growth of the individual's intelligence is really inseparable.

14.12 Standardisation of the tests

The standardisation of intelligence tests is a very laborious process. A standardised test must be valid, reliable and objective. The construction of standardised tests involves certain steps. They are as follows :

Selection of test items : The validity of a test score depends upon the care with which the items in the test have been selected. The test items should be chosen initially by competent persons. The ˙tems should be graded in difficulty from easy to hard. (A test made up of items all of which are passed by approximately 50% would be the most discriminating test.)

The test should be administered very cautiously. The direction both for the examiner and the examinees are written on the booklet. This should be strictly followed.

Try out : Thus constructed, the test is administered on a small representative sample. This process is known as try out.

Item analysis : Then the items are analysed and their difficulty value and discriminating value are determined. A test made up of items all of which are passed by approximately 50% would be the most discriminating test. Unsuitable items are rejected.

Final application : The remaining test items are arranged according to difficulty level and administered over a bigger sample.

Determination of norms : The scores of the test are then arranged in groups and a norm is prepared by Statistical methods.

Determination of validity and reliability : At the final stage, the validity and reliability of the test is determined by Statistical methods.

14.13 Criteria of a Good Intelligence Test

Following are the criteria of a good intelligence test :

1. **Objectivity :** It means that the test score should be free from the whims and attitude of the examiner.
2. **Validity :** This means that the list should truly measure those qualities for which it is constructed.
3. **Reliability :** A good test must have a high degree of reliability. When a test is reliable, scores made by an individual upon retest with the same test, will not differ from the original scores.

4. **Scorability :** Scoring should be simple and easy. It should be rapid and bring about correct result.

5. **A good intelligence test should not be expensive.**

14.14 Uses of intelligence tests

Intelligence tests are useful for educational guidance. They can be used to supplement traditional examination. Following are the uses of a good intelligence test :

Predictability : Intelligence tests help in forecasting the intellectual and vocational possibilities of young children. There is a positive correlation between the child's I.Q. and his ability to succeed in school. The I.Q. of a child remains constant throughout his life. Thus, by intelligence tests we can predict the intellectual and vocational future of a child at any stage.

Classification into ability groups : Intelligence tests help us in having homogeneous groups of pupils. Teachers find great difficulties to teach pupils who are widely different in their learning abilities. In traditional classroom, pupils with higher I.Q.s progress faster than those with lower. Consequently, difficulty arises in their teaching and bright and dullard suffer.

So it has been proposed that pupils may be classified into three groups in each grade, according to their I.Q.s :

1. Group A containing the bright pupils (I.Q. above 110).
2. Group B containing the average pupils (I.Q. 90–110).
3. Group C containing slow pupils (I.Q. below 90).

Thus classified through Intelligence testing, enrichment program for the bright and remedial education for the backward can be arranged. This will go a long way towards reducing wastage and stagnation.

Educational guidance : The results of intelligence tests may be used in providing educational guidance to students. Problems like what special subject a child should study or what course a student take up may be solved on the basis of the results of intelligence testing.

Vocational guidance : Results of intelligence tests can be used for vocational guidance. Vocational guidance means finding the proper man for the proper job. There are certain professions which demand greater general intellectual capacity than do certain vocational courses of lower category. Hence, proper vocational guidance is required for job satisfaction of an individual.

Unfortunately, in India we have not been able yet to develop a sound system of vocational guidance services.

Judging teacher's work : We may use intelligence tests to assess the work of any teacher in a subject. If the I.Q. of the students in a class does not correspond to their E.Q., it may be supposed that the subject has not been properly taught in the class.

Selection for admission in schools : Intelligence tests can be used for admission of suitable students to special courses of education in our schools and colleges.

Though, in India, the number of schools and colleges have considerably increased, the opportunity of admission to special courses is still limited.

Staff selection : Nowadays, intelligence tests are used in army and big mercantile firms to select office staff.

Identification of gifted children : Teacher's identification of gifted children is not always accurate. Therefore, for proper identification of gifted students and offer of scholarships to such students, intelligence tests are often used.

Ascertaining mental retardation : Intelligence tests have been used to find out accurately the levels of mental retardation.

Using the intelligence tests, we may assess the level of mental retardation.

Level	I.Q.
Dull	81–90
Border-line deficiency	71–80
Moron	51–70
Imbecile	26–50
Idiot	0–25

Fig. 14.12

Diagnosis of problem behaviour and mental diseases : Intelligence tests are used to diagnose problem behaviour, delinquency and mental diseases. The results of the test may suggest possible remedial measures.

Ascertaining mental growth : Mental abilities of a child develop in a consistent process up to 18 years of age. Intelligence tests have thrown much light on the intellectual growth of a child at different stages of development.

Use in research work : Intelligence tests are used for conducting research in different fields of Psychology, Sociology and Education, for instance, whether delinquency or other problem behaviour is related to inferior intelligence of an individual or how mental abilities grow with age or experience and so on.

14.15 Limitations of Intelligence Tests

Though Intelligence Tests are today widely used, they have following draw-backs :

1. Intelligence test is not free from the effect of culture. An individual brought up in a healthy family, who most probably, have done such tests previously, will do better than an individual reared in a slum who has never done or heard of such tests. Intelligence tests are influenced by socio-economic conditions.
2. Intelligence test results are often affected by practice and training.
3. Physical condition like fatigue, ailments, anxiety of the subject at the time of administration of tests may vitiate the result of Intelligence Tests.
4. Test and Retest of intelligence do not give the same result. Jensen found that a retest on a different form of the same test yielded an I.Q. of 8 to 10 points higher.
5. Speed is an important factor in intelligence tests. An individual with higher speed may score higher than the person who is slow in response.
6. Intelligence tests cannot measure the most important aspects of intellectual ability—original thinking, artistic abilities, abstract thought or inventiveness.

In fact, intelligence tests can illuminate some areas of a child's development but they cannot give a total picture of the abilities of a child. We cannot rely too much on the results of intelligence testing. It cannot predict wholly success in school achievements profession and future life of an individual. There are some other factors such as motivation, effort, perseverance, resolution and will which contribute to success.

Along with the results of intelligence test, those of achievement tests, interest inventory, tests of attitude, teacher's rating etc. should also be considered for reliable prediction of future life of the subject.

14.16 Achievement tests

Achievement tests measure the result of school education. They show how much knowledge the pupil has acquired in school subjects. By giving achievement tests to a certain class, the teacher can determine the progress of students in different subjects. He can accordingly guide them in those subjects the students are weak.

Achievement tests are constructed with care just like an intelligence test. The questions of the test cover the whole syllabus. Usually the number of questions is large but the answers are short.

The achievement quotient (A.Q.) of a pupil is determined by the following formula :

$$\text{A.Q.} = \frac{\text{E.Q.}}{\text{I.Q.}} \times 100$$

$$A.Q. = \frac{\frac{E.A.}{C.A.} \times 100}{\frac{M.A.}{C.A.} \times 100} = \frac{E.A.}{M.A.} \times 100$$

$[\because E.Q. = \frac{E.A.}{C.A.} \times 100 \text{ and } I.Q. = \frac{M.A.}{C.A.} \times 100]$

E.Q. = Educational quotient.

I.Q. = Intelligence quotient.

E.A. = Educational age.

C.A. = Chronological age.

M.A. = Mental age.

Limitations of Achievement Test : Achievement tests are limited to school-work only. They do not test the general knowledge from the environment outside of school.

Achievement tests give an undue advantage to the bookish child.

Achievement tests cannot serve the purpose of intelligence tests. They are quite different in nature. Intelligence is the innate ability of a person to comprehend and master a novel situation. Intelligence tests measure the general knowledge of the child acquired from the environment. Thompson says, Just as the intelligence tests measure the innate intelligence, an Achievement test measure the result of intelligence plus application. This is why to measure acquired knowledge of a pupil both Achievement tests as well as Intelligence tests should be applied.

14.17 Performance tests

Whether individual or group, most of the intelligence tests are chiefly linguistic in character and most of them are written tests. But performance tests do not make any use of language. They test the ability to perform certain tasks.

Examples of performance tests : Some of the important performance tests are : Army beta test, Dearborn's Form Board test, Good enough's Man drawing test, Healey's Construction test, Porteus Maze test, Alexander's Pass Along test, Koh's Block Design test and Knox's Cube Construction test.

The Army Beta tests : In these tests, the subject is asked to perform certain tasks. It is noted how quickly he does a task and how many mistakes are committed by him to complete it.

The Form Board test : It consists of a board with openings of various shapes cut out of it. Blocks of different shapes are to be fitted into the appropriate holes in the board as per four model diagrams placed before the subject. The time of completion is noted, and the errors committed by the subject are counted.

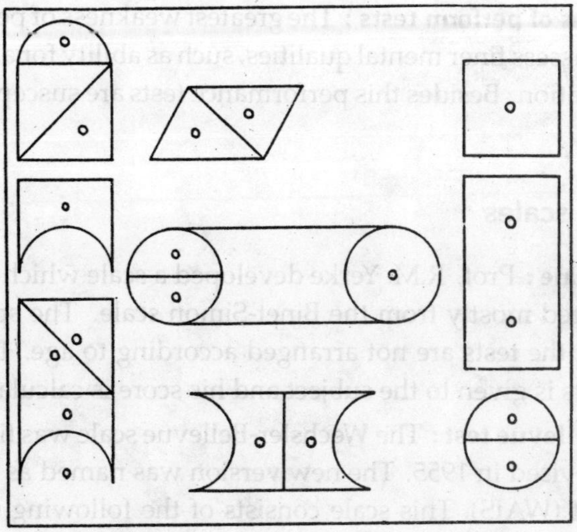

Fig. 14.13: Dear born Form Board.

Good enough's drawing test : In this test, children are asked to draw a human figure with pencil on paper. The test is scored for the completeness and coherence of the drawing. It is used to measure the intelligence of children from 3.5 to 13 years.

Healey's construction test : The test is divided into two sets—A and B. Healey's test A consists of rectangular pieces of wood from which an inner rectangle has been cut out and divided into five pieces of different size. The subject is required to fit them in appropriate places.

The test B consists of wood cut out and divided into eleven pieces of various size which are to be correctly fitted. The tests are meant for children above the age of ten. It is noted whether the subject performs the task with foresight or follows trial and error method. The subject who follows trial and error method, naturally takes longer time and commits serious mistakes.

Proteus maze test : A maze is drawn on paper with a number of blind alleys. The shortest path has to be traced with a pencil without straying into a blind alley.

Terman's Ball and Field test : In the Ball and Field test of Terman, a circle is drawn about two and a half inches (6.25 cms) diameter with a small gap. The subject is told to imagine that his ball has been lost somewhere in the field. He is then asked to mark out with a pencil the path he would take in his search for the ball. The subject is to start from the gap. The test is meant for children of ten years of age.

Advantages of perform tests : Performance tests are most useful with children who had not the good fortune to attend regularly some school or to come in contact with cultured society. They are suitable for illiterate persons and those who have language difficulty.

Disadvantages of perform tests : The greatest weakness of performance tests is that it cannot assess finer mental qualities, such as ability for abstract thinking or concept formation. Besides this performance tests are susceptible to practise effect.

14.18 Point scales

Yerke's point scale : Prof. R.M. Yerke developed a scale which consists of a set of 20 tests selected mostly from the Binet-Simon scale. The special feature of this scale is that the tests are not arranged according to age. In this scale, the whole set of tests is given to the subject and his score is calculated.

Wechsler-Bellevue test : The Wechsler-Bellevue scale was first published in 1939 and was revised in 1955. The new version was named as Wechsler Adult Intelligence Test (WAIS). This scale consists of the following sub-tests which may be divided broadly in two types : (A) Non-verbal performance tests and (B) Verbal tests.

(A) The non-verbal tests include : 1. Block design; 2. Picture arrangement; 3. Picture completion; 4. Object assembly and 5. Mazes.

(B) The verbal tests include : 1. Vocabulary; 2. Information; 3. Comprehension; 4. Similarities; 5. Arithmetic and 6. Digit span.

In the Wechsler-Bellevue scale, the items are not grouped in terms of mental age. This is a point scale and points are given for correct answers. In this test, instead of I.Q., **the coefficient of intelligence** (C.I.) is calculated. Thus,

$$\text{C.I.} = \frac{\text{Point score}}{\text{Mean point score}} \times 100.$$

Comparison of point scale with age scale.

Point scale	Age scale (Binet test)
1. In this scale test items are not grouped in terms of age. Test items are varied and unrelated.	1. In this scale tests are grouped in terms of age.
2. The test is standardised and flexible.	2. The test is standardised but inflexible.
3. The test scores are wholly amenable to statistical analysis.	3. The test is partially amenable to statistical treatment.
4. Measurement for different ages comparable.	4. Measurement for different ages relatively incomparable.
5. Coefficient of intelligence is determined by the formula : $\text{C.I.} = \frac{\text{Point score}}{\text{Meanpointscore}} \times 100.$	5. Intelligence quotient is determined by the formula : $\text{I.Q.} = \frac{\text{M.A.}}{\text{C.A.}} \times 100.$

Summary

Different psychologists have defined intelligence in different ways. These definitions are not exclusive of each other. In fact, they are interdependent.

There are various theories of intelligence. The representative theories are: Spearman's two-factor theory, Thompson's sampling theory, Thurstone's group factor theory, Vernon's hierarchical theory and Guilford's structure of intellect model. These theories are based on factor analysis techniques to find common abilities which constitute our intelligence. These factors may be arranged in hierarchical order or in the form of some model.

Alfred Binet and Simon first discovered a reliable method of measuring intelligence in 1905. The Binet scale was revised by Goddard, Terman, Yerke and Burt. In 1916, Prof. Terman introduced the idea of Intelligence Quotient. In spite of various revisions of Binet Scale, the revised Standford-Binet scale of Terman and Merrill are widely used.

The two sets of group tests, the Army alpha and beta tests were constructed during the World War I (1914–1918) to measure the intelligence of would be soldiers. After the World war, a number of psychologists devoted themselves to construct group tests. Group tests are advantageous because it can be administered to a number of individuals at a time.

Performance tests are used to measure the ability to perform certain tasks. Some of the important performance tests are: Dearborn's form board test, Alexander's pass-along test, Koh's block design test, Healy's construction test, Porteus maze test, Goodenough's drawing test. These tests are useful in case of individuals who have language difficulty such as illiterate and deaf and dumb.

In point scale, test items are not grouped in terms of age. In this case, coefficient of intelligence is determined instead of intelligence quotient.

The construction and standardisation of intelligence test in India is a difficult task for, India is a multilingual country and a vast section of her people are illiterate.

References

1. Anastasi, Anne : *Psychological Testing,* Macmillan Publishing Co. New York, 1982.
2. Binet, A. and Simon, T. : *The Development of Intelligence in Children,* Baltimore : Williams & Wilkins, 1916.
3. Crow, L.D. and Crow, A. : *Educational Psychology,* New Delhi : Eurasia Publishing House, 1973.
4. Freeman, F.S. : *Psychological Testing,* Holt, Rinehart, New York, 1962.

5. Gardner, H. : *Frames of Mind : The Theory of Multiple Intelligence,* New York, 1983.

6. Guilford, J.P. : *The Nature of Human Intelligence,* New York : McGraw Hill, 1967.

7. Piaget, J. : *The Origins of Intelligence in Children,* New York : International Univ. Press, 1952.

8. Spearman. : *The Abilities of Man,* New York : Macmillan, 1927.

9. Terman, L.M. and Merrill, M.A. : *Measuring Intelligence,* Boston : Houghton Mifflin, 1937.

10. Thompson, G.H. : *The Factorial Analysis of Human Ability,* London : London Univ. Press, 1939.

11. Thurston, L.L. : *Primary Mental Abilities,* Chicago : Univ. of Chicago Press, 1938.

12. Vernon, P.E. : *The Structure of Human Abilities,* London : Methuen, 1950.

13. Wechsler, D. : *Wechsler Scale of Intelligence,* New York : Psychological Corporation, 1939.

14. Woodworth, R.S. : *Psychology : A study of Mental Life.* New York : Century, 1932.

Questions and Assignments

1. Write a brief note on the concept of intelligence. Discuss how far intelligence depends on hereditary and environmental factors.

2. How are intelligence tests standardised?

3. What is intelligence and what is its nature?

4. Explain the nature of intelligence and discuss the validity and reliability of intelligence tests.

5. What are the uses of intelligence tests? Explain the relation of intelligence to achievement in schools.

6. Discuss the merits and demerits of group test of intelligence.

7. Is I.Q. constant? Give reasons for your answer.

8. Write notes on :
   (a) Mental age.
   (b) Moron.
   (c) Binet-Simon tests.
   (d) I.Q.
   (e) Performance tests.
9. What are performance tests? Fully describe one test by which intelligence is measured.
10. Give a short history of intelligence testing movement. What do you know of the development of intelligence test in India.
11. Distinguish between intelligence tests and attainment tests.
12. How is scholastic learning is related to intelligence.
13. Define intelligence. Bring out the mean of G factor and S factor. Describe the present form of Standford-Binet scale of intelligence.
14. Discuss Spearman's Two-factor theory. What are g- and s-factors of intelligence?
15. Discuss advantages and disadvantages of group tests of intelligence.
16. What are various factors of intelligence as given by Thurstone? What is the latest position with regard to the nature of intelligence?
17. What are the criteria of a good intelligence test? Discuss the uses of intelligence test.

Chapter 15

Nature and Theories of Learning

15.1 Nature of learning

Learning is the process of changes which enables an organism to adjust itself to the environment. It is, therefore, a process of development and growth. it is characterised by flexibility because the individual has to adapt itself constantly to the circumstances of the environment.

Learning is an activity aroused by the personal and social needs. But the individual may learn both desirable and undesirable things. Education and training enable the individual to learn the desirable and avoid the undesirable. Thus, learning is the process of improvement. According to Gates, "Learning is the modification of behaviour through experience and learning." Learning benefits an individual by the experience of the past. It involves all those training and experiences acquired right from birth.

Learning involves problem solving. It helps one to understand and discover relations between different contents in a situation. According to Gestaltists, "Learning is an apprehension of meaning and relationship with or without reference to previous experiences."

Learning is always concerned with satisfying motives or attaining goals. According to Garret, "Learning is a function of motive incentive condition. That is, Learning = f (Motive × Incentive).

15.2 Theories of learning

We may discuss theories of learning under two broad categories : (1) S–R theories and (2) Cognitive field theories.

1. **S–R theories includes :**
   - (a) Throndike's theory.
   - (b) Watson's theory.
   - (c) Guthrie's theory.
   - (d) Skinner's operant conditioning.
   - (e) Hull's theory.
   - (f) Pavlov's classical conditioning.
2. **Cognitive field theory includes :**
   - (a) Tolman's sign learning theory.
   - (b) Gestalt theory.
   - (c) Lewin's field theory.

15.2.1 Experimental studies by Thorndike

Thorndike made experiments on animals, like cats, dogs, rats and monkeys. He confined a hungry cat in a cage closed by a door which could be opened by turning a latch or a button and food was put near by. The cat made a large number of random movements. She clawed bit and scratched at the walls of the cage. Sooner or later, by pure chance she pressed the button, opened the

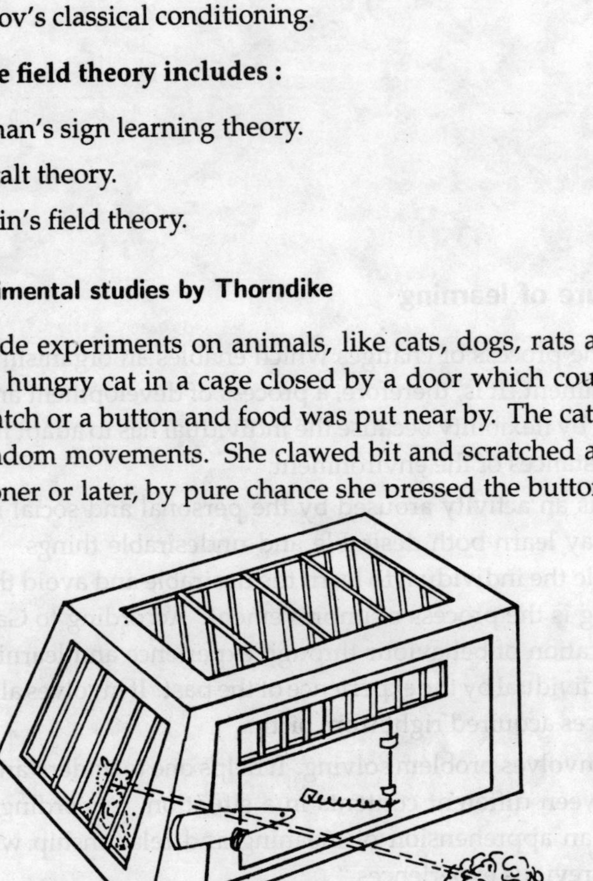

Fig. 15.1: An illustration showing Thorndike's cat trying to come out.

door and excaped. When put in the cage again she went through a series of random movements a second time and again hit upon the correct response by chance each trial, on the average required less time than the preceding one. After a number of repetitions, the cat would perform the successful movement at once every time that it was put into the cage. A time-curve of trial and error learning of the cat is shown (Fig. 15.1).

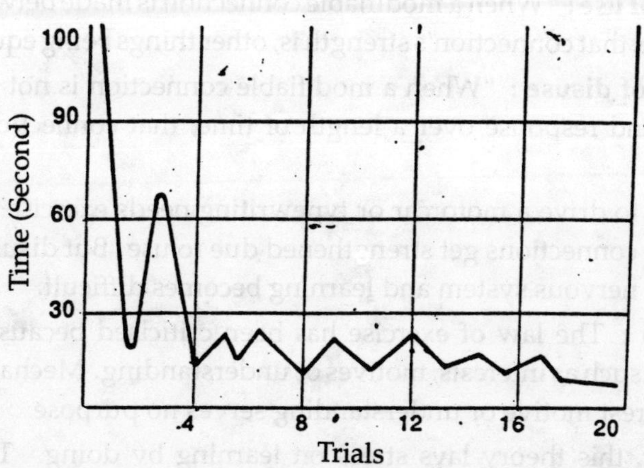

Fig. 15.2

Thorndike's laws of learning : According to Thorndike, "Learning is due to the formation of bond between Stimulus and Response." He has formulated three laws of learning on the basis of his experimental data :

The law of effect

This law runs as follows : "When a modifiable connection is made between a situation and response and is accompanied or followed by a satisfying state of affairs, that connection's strength is increased, and when such a connection is made and accompanied or followed by an annoying state of affairs its strength is decreased."

A successful reaction gives satisfaction to the individual, tends to be repeated and stamped in as a habit. An unsuccessful reaction gives annoyance to the individual, tends to be inhibited and stamped out. Thus pleasure and pain have their effects on learning reactions.

Significance in education : According to the law of effect if the responses satisfy the individual they are learnt and selected. While those which are not satisfying are eliminated. Thus for honesty, punctuality and industry if the child is praised or given prizes, he gets satisfaction and those patterns of behaviour becomes fixed. But when the child is rebuked for laziness, dishonesty and irregularity, the child does not get satisfaction and they tend to be eliminated.

So, the teacher should not associated anything useful to the child with something annoying. For instance, school tasks should never be given as a punishment.

The law of exercise or frequency

This law has two parts : (i) Use and (ii) Disuse.

The law of use : "When a modifiable connection is made between a situation and response, that connection's strength is, other things being equal, increased."

The law of disuse : "When a modifiable connection is not made between a situation and response over a length of time, that connection's strength is decreased."

Learning to drive a motorcar or typewriting needs exercise and repetition. The nervous connections get strengthened due to use. But disuse weakens the bonds of the nervous system and learning becomes difficult.

Criticism : The law of exercise has been criticised because it disregards other factors such as interests, motives or understanding. Mechanical repetition without interest motive or understanding serves no purpose.

However, this theory lays stress on learning by doing. The old saying, "Practice makes one pefrect" is true. Various scientific inventions have been made by repeated trials and errors.

Moreover, repetition sometimes helps eradication of bad habits. Dunlop found that a particular mistake of typing may be corrected if it is consciously repeated. A bad habit may be broken if it is repeated keeping in mind its bad effect.

The law of readiness

The law states : "When any conduction unit is not in readiness to conduct, for it to conduct is annoying. When any conduction unit is in readiness to conduct for it not to do so is annoying."

This means a state of readiness or inner drive to learn. The learner must be made ready to learn. Unless the learner is ready to learn nothing can be taught. The boy who is not allowed to answer the question which he can answer feels annoyed. He also feels annoyed when he is asked a question for which he is not prepared to answer.

The above laws of Thorndike covers several other subordinate principles, such as recency, frequency and intensity. Recency means what has ben learned recently is remembered well. The principle of frequency emphasizes that an act of learning to be effective should be repeated again and again. Intensity means that the more intense the stimulus, the deeper is its impression. Interest strengthens the intensity of the experience.

15.2.2 Watson's theory of learning

John B. Watson (1878–1958) is widely known as the chief-spokesman of Behaviourism. He rejected the consciousness and introspection as methods of study of human behaviour. According to Watson, the study of mind belongs to the province of Philosophy. It has no place in Psychology. The science of psychology must be based on objective phenomena and the ultimate explanation of behaviour must be found in the nervous system. Watson reduced all mental events to physiological processes. It is he who popularised theory of conditioning in America.

Watson's experiment : Watson described a number of methods of studying animal learning. He trained rats to dig through sand to get into a goal-box. They were required to wait for the delivery of food. On the basis of the experiment, he formulated certain laws of learning.

Watson's first law of learning states that learning consists of strengthening S–R connections. But the strength of learning depends not upon the effect of the response and nor on reinforcement. The strength of S–R connection depends on frequency of response. Watson emphasised the importance of exercise on frequency in learning. The basis of learning is S–R connection and all types of learning may be reduced to S–R bondage.

Watson's second Law of Recency states that the most recent response is strengthened more by its frequent occurrence than is an earlier response. Watson rejected thorndike's law of effect.

Watson's famous experiment was conditioning fear in a child called Albert. The conditioned stimulus was a white rat. Little Albert looked at it and reached out to touch the rat. Just at this moment, an awful sound was made. After the pairing of the rat and the frightening sound, the very sight of the rat elicited fear. The process may be represented as follows :

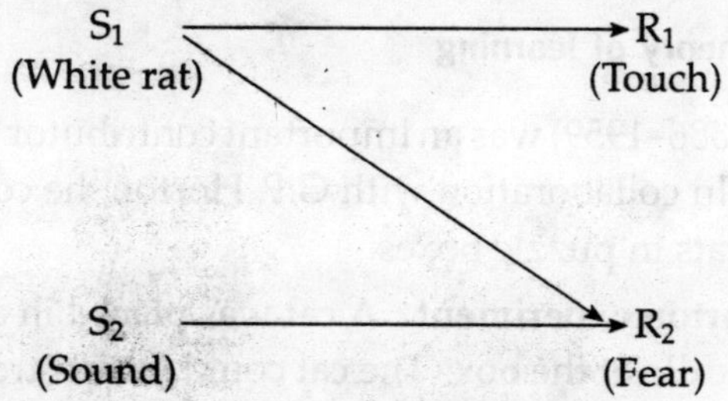

Fig. 15.3

Watson, unlike Pavlov, demonstrated that sometimes a single trial was sufficient to produce a strong and permanent connection of stimulus to response. Watson conditioned fear reaction by only one trial.

Watson agreed with Pavlov and Thorndike that learning is to be analysed in terms of S–R connections. But his position, according to Bolles was simpler than Pavlov's and much more systematic than Thorndike.

Watson's contribution : Watson brought psychology out from mentalistic concept. He laid stress on the objective study of behaviour. He claimed that all human behaviour can be explained in terms of S–R connections in the brain. Watson did not mention perception because it involves interpretation of meanings of sensory signs.

Watson never used the term memory. He reduced it to neural habit. He reduced thinking to subvocal talking.

Watson regarded a reflex action as the simplest type of activity and instinct as a system of chained reflexes.

Watson explained the process of learning by the law of exercise, the law of use, the law of disuse, the law of frequency, and the law of recency. He rejected Thorndike's law of effect because it refers to mental processes of pleasure and pain. He regarded all learning as conditioning.

Watson believed in environmentalism or complete determination of the individual by the environment. He asserted that he could make any healthy child into a scholar, a lawyer, an engineer, a poet or a philosopher by putting him in the proper environment.

Criticism : Watson wrongly regarded all learning as conditioning and by trial and error. Human learning is mostly intelligent or by insight. Watson wrongly reduced memory to habit and did not recognise pure-memory.

Environmentalism reduces man to an automaton. An individual cannot be entirely moulded and determined by the environment. He is free to determine his own actions within the limits of the physical and social environment. Therefore, Watson's mechanistic and deterministic view of environmentalism cannot be totally accepted.

15.2.3 Guthrie's theory of learning

Edwin R. Guthrie (1886–1959) was an important contributor to the development of learning-theory. In collaboration with G.P. Horton, he conducted a number of experiments on cats in puzzle boxes.

The Guthrie-Horton experiment : A cat was placed in a puzzle box with a small pole in the middle of the box. The cat could escape from the box through a door by touching the pole. Outside the box food was kept for the cat. A number of cats were used in the experiment and it was observed that the cats learned to escape from the box in their own way. The specific response learned by a particular cat was the one that the cat had hit upon just before it escaped from the puzzle box. The cat did not try new ways of release. It was also observed that the cat escaping from the box, would very often ignore the food kept outside the box.

On the basis of his experiments, Guthrie developed the following fundamental theories of learning.

One trial learning : Thorndike and other behaviourists laid stress on gradualness of learning-process. But according to Guthrie, in only one trial a response is connected with a stimulus and there is no need for repetition of the S–R bond. He rejected Thorndike's law of frequency. Guthrie said, "A stimulus pattern gains its full associative strength on the occasion of its first pairing with a response." Guthrie believed that conditioning occurs after a single trial.

Law of contiguity : According to Guthrie, the principle of association by contiguity is most important. Contiguity implies the coming together of the stimulus and a response. Guthrie rejected Watson's law of frequency and emphasised that only the last response in the series which was connected to the stimulus is important. In fact, contiguity theory was simplest because it gave no place to effect in learning.

The recency principle : The principle of recency states that what was being done in the past in the presence of a set of stimuli will tend to be done next when that stimulus combination occurs.

According to Guthrie, learning does not depend on reinforcement or reward. The law of contiguity accompanied by the recency principle can easily explain the learning behaviour of the organism.

Movement-produced stimuli : Movement-produced stimuli are responsible for conditioning the responses to elicit the desired behaviour. Guthrie emphasised that the organism responds to various stimuli by contraction of muscles and secretion of glands. These specific responses were termed movement-produced stimuli (different from external stimuli). The movement, once started, maintains itself by the stimuli it furnishes. One movement starts another, then a third, the third a fourth and so on. These movements and their movement-produced stimuli make possible a far-reaching extension of association or conditioning.

Role of reinforcement : Guthrie disagreed with Thorndike on the role of reinforcement in the learning-process. According to him, learning does not depend on reinforcement of behaviour. Guthrie observed that the cats escaping from the puzzle box often ignored the food kept outside. In fact, the food did not affect their proficiency in coming out of the box. Thus, regardless of any reinforcement, the cat tried to repeat the last response to obtain their release.

Forgetting and extinction of behaviour : According to Guthrie, forgetting and extinction of behaviour do not take place due to lack of reinforcement but due to interference. We do not forget by disuse but by *retroactive inhibition.*

Role of punishment : Guthrie studied the effect of punishment in learning. He emphasised that it is not the feeling of pain caused by punishment, but the specific action caused by punishment that determines what will be learned. He further added that in training a dog to jump through a hoop, the effectiveness of punishment depends on where it is applied—front or rear.

Motivation : According to Guthrie motives play a significant role in the field of learning, because they keep the organism active until a goal is reached. Any source of stimulation which is capable of maintaining stimuli can be called a useful motive. Motive accelerates the movement of the organism to reach a goal.

Transfer of training : Guthrie rejected the formal discipline theory. But he found some truth in Thorndike's identical element theory of transfer. Guthrie was hopeful of the possibility of transfer knowledge from one situation to another if there were similarity between two situations.

Contribution of Guthrie : Guthrie's theory of learning is based on the principles of Pavlov and Watson. Guthrie explained behaviour in terms of S–R connections, but he rejected the concept of reward or reinforcement. His theory has considerable impact in the field of education.

Guthrie laid stress on the importance of drill and exercise in the process of learning. For, this generates a number of stimuli for eliciting the desired behaviour. For instance, to teach addition, subtraction, multiplication or division to a child, the teacher should use various method involving concrete objects in the school.

Guthrie believed that the most important cause of forgetting is retroactive inhibition. So, we should always try to avoid interference caused to the past learning by the present learning.

Guthrie emphasised the law of contiguity and the recency principle in the learning-process. It we want to elicit a learned response, we should arrange for the occurrence of conditions similar to the situation in which the behaviour has been learned.

According to Guthrie, motives occupy an important place in the process of learning. So, motives, rewards and punishment should be used for evoking and intensifying the response.

Guthrie's theory provided certain techniques for breaking bad habits. In fatigue technique an individual is allowed to repeat the task concerning the bad habit till he becomes tired and develop an attitude of avoidance. In correcting wrong behaviour, behaviour theraputists often use Guthrie's technique.

15.2.4 Skinner's operant conditioning

B.F. Skinner (1904) put forward his theory of operant conditioning of behaviour which arose out of observations of animal performances. Skinner coined the term operant, which stresses the fact that the behaviour operates upon the environment to generate consequences. These consequence are getting of food or other reward. His theory of operant conditioning is a development along the lines of Thorndike's trial and error learning. His theories were expounded in his two books Behaviour of Organisms (1938) and Science and Human behaviour (1953).

Two types of response : Skinner proposes two kinds of responses : (a) Elicited response and (b) Emitted response.

Responses which re-elicited by known stimuli are known as respondents, e.g., pupillary constriction to light. Respondent behaviour includes all reflex actions. The emitted responses are called operants, which need not be correlated with any known stimuli. Almost all of the human behaviours are operant in character. Chickns peck at grain, squirrels dig for nuts and men drive a car or write a letter are all examples of operant behaviour. Operant behaviour is controlled by the strength of its consequences.

Two types of conditioning : Related to the two types of response, there are two types of conditioning :

1. **'S'-type** or respondent conditioning where reinforcement is correlated with stimuli. In Pavlovian conditioning, the conditioned stimulus (bell) is presented together with the unconditioned stimulus (e.g., food) to elicit the response (e.g., salivation).

2. **'R'-type** or operant conditioning in which a response occurs spontaneously in the absence of any stimulus with which it may be correlated. In this case, it is a response which is correlated with reinforcement. The law of conditioning of Type R is similar to Thorndike's law of effect : If the occurrence of an operant is followed by presentation of a reinforcing stimulus, the strength is increased. It may, however, be noted that nothing is said here about satisfying state of affair or about drive reduction.

Skinner does not attribute much importance to respondent conditioning (S-type). He believes operant conditioning (R-type) to be more important.

Thus there are two effective experimental methods for producing learning :

1. Pavlovian conditioning, Classical Conditioning or Respondent Conditioning (S-type).
2. Trial and error learning, Instrumental learning, Reinforcement learning or Operant conditioning (R-type).

Comparison between classical and operant conditioning

Operant conditioning	Classical conditioning
1. It was developed by B.F. Skinner and is called R-type conditioning.	1. It was developed by Ivan Pavlov and is called S-type conditioning.

Operant conditioning	Classical conditioning
2. Operant conditioning helps in learning operant behaviour. It is correlated with operant behaviour.	2 Classical conditioning helps in learning of respondent behaviour. It deals with responses that follow a specific stimulus.
3. It is response-oriented.	3 It is stimulus-oriented.
4. Response occurs spontaneously in absence of stimulus with which it may be correlated.	4. Conditioned stimulus is presented together with unconditioned stimulus to elicit response.
5. S–R connection is on the basis of law of effect.	5. S–R connection is on the basis of law of contiguity.

The Experiment of Skinner : Skinner developed an apparatus to study operant conditioning. This apparatus is known as Skinner box, which contains a device that presents a rat with a pellet of food whenever it depresses a lever. Every push of the rat is recorded by an electrical device.

The rat was kept hungry for 24 hours and placed in the box. After a period of initial hesitation, it started exploring the box. Eventually, the rat, by chance depressed the lever. A pellet of food was released, but the rat failed to notice it. The process was repeated for the second and third time though the rat failed to see the pellet of food. However, on the fourth lever response, the rat seized the pellet of food and ate it. The process was repeated and the rat learned to press the lever.

The above experiment shows that the organism in the beginning is motivated by a need (hunger). The need produces general exploratory activity. Eventually, a response is accidentally made that is instrumental in achieving the appropriate goal. This response is learned.

Skinner also used pigeon box to conduct experiments on pigeons to study the simple processes of learning-like pressing the lever as well as the complex process of learning of the animal.

Concept of reinforcement : Reinforcement is a common term used to represent the reward in operant conditioning. The term refers to the effect of attaining an object or state that satisfies a motive (need or want) on the establishment of a response. It is the attainment of a goal that can satisfy a need, e.g., the hungry rat in the Skinner box, reinforcement is securing food.

Reinforcements may be divided into following types : 1. Positive reinforcement. 2. Negative reinforcement. 3. Punishment.

Positive reinforcement : Positive reinforcements are of two types : (1) Primary reinforcement and (2) Secondary reinforcement.

1. In primary reinforcement, a response results in the reduction of a need. For instance, food is a primary reinforcing agent for the hunger drive of the rat in the Skinner box.
2. Now if we reinforce it with a green light that had been paired with eating food, the green light works as well as a reinforcer. The green light in this case is called secondary reinforcement. The clicking sound and the lighting of a bulb in Skinner's experiment act as secondary reinforcement when they are paired with the appearance of a pellet of food.

The positive primary reinforcement, are based on biological need, such as food and water which are essential for survival of the organism. Money, for man, can be a reinforcing agent although it does not reduce primary drive like hunger. But as money is associated with the securing of food we call it secondary reinforcement. Secondary reinforcement is important, particularly in human learning.

Negative reinforcement : The effect of reinforcement is always to increase the probability of response. A positive reinforcer, when added to a situation, strengthens the probability of an operant response. Food, water, sex may be classified as positive reinforcers. But a negative reinforcer is one which, when removed from a situation, strengthens the probability of an operant response. A loud noise or an electric shock may be considered as negative reinforcer. In negative reinforcement an organism reacts to avoid unpleasant and annoying stimuli.

Punishment : The effect of reinforcement is to increase the probability of response.

Reinforcers, positive or negative, strengthen behaviour. But punishment weakens it. Punishment reduces behaviour by imposing unwelcome consequences.

However, the permanent effects of punishment are much smaller than expected. Skinner's experiment with rats to study the effects of punishment on extinction shows that punishment has a negligible effect upon the total reserve of responses emitted during extinction. However, it has been observed that if punishment is delivered every time the response is made, the rate of responding is seriously depressed. While it is not depressed as much if punishment is given only occasionally. The effects of punishment persist longer in the latter case.

Mechanism of operant conditioning : Several important mechanisms are involved in the process of operant conditioning. These may be described in brief :

Shaping : It is a technique for bringing about certain desirable changes in the behaviour of an individual by proper use of selective reinforcement. Shaping is done by building a chain of responses through a step-by-step process. For effective shaping, control of the reinforcing mechanism is necessary.

Chaining: When the required task or behaviour is difficult, it may be broken down into small steps to facilitate learning. Chaining refers to the process of linking one step with the other step in its proximity. For shaping behaviour of an organism, cues produced by one response need to be linked with the next response. Chaining takes place when one response brings the individual into contact with stimuli that reward the last response and cause the next response.

Discrimination and cuing : Cues or signals indicate whether operant behaviour should be omitted or performed, that is, they determine which behaviour is to be punished and which behaviour is to be reinforced.

Generalisation : Generalisation refers to the ability of an organism to provide similar operant responses, to stimuli similar to the training stimulus. Thus, if a C–S is obtained to one tone, another tone of slightly different frequency will also produce a C–R. If the two stimuli are sufficiently distinguishable, the organism can be taught to respond to one of them. Such a discrimination is possible by the method of contrast.

Extinction : It consists of withholding reinforcement when the appropriate response occurs. When the rat in the Skinner box presses the bar several times, but fails to get food, the behaviour of bar pressing will be extinguished.

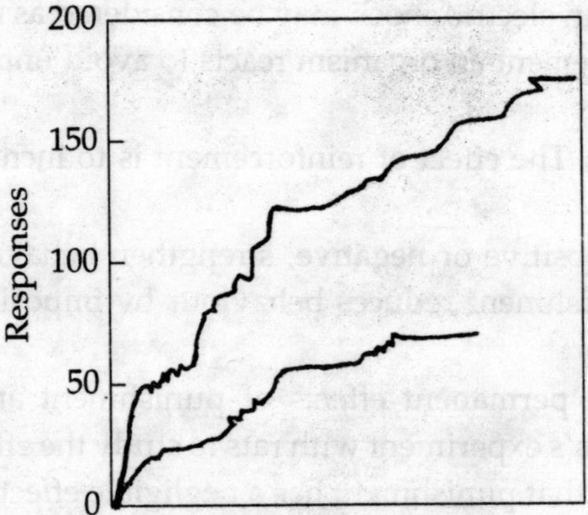

Fig. 15.4: Time (One Hour)

Extinction of level-pressing by rats following a single reinforcement and following 250 reinforcements.
(From E.R. Hillgard's Theory of Learning).

It has been shown that a single reinforcement is sufficient to produce a number of conditioned operant responses in extinction. After receiving a single pellet of food following one pressing of the bar, a rat responds 50 or more times, yielding a typical extinction curve. An extinction curve following a single reinforcement and one following 250 reinforcements are represented in the Fig. 15.4. As the curve levels off it means that responses have stopped.

Spontaneous recovery : Extinction refers to the gradual decline in a conditioned response (C–R) as a result of presenting the conditioned stimulus (C–S) alone, over and over again. Extinction is not unlearning but involves an inhibition of the CR. The CR regains some of its original strength when C–S is repeated without intervening reinforcement. This recurrence in strength is called spontaneous recovery.

Schedules of Reinforcement : In everyday life, most of our behaviour is reinforced intermittently rather than continuously. For example, a fisherman does not hook a fish with every cast of the line. Skinner spoke of two types of intermittent reinforcement : (i) Interval Reinforcement and (ii) Ratio Reinforcement.

Interval Reinforcement: Interval reinforcement means reinforcement given at fixed intervals of time, say every ten minutes, at the discretion of the experimenter.

Ratio Reinforcement: In Ratio Reinforcement, instead of delivering a pellet of food at fixed intervals of time, a pellet is delivered after a fixed number of responses. For example, in the Skinner box, the rat gets a pellet of food after pressing the bar 20 times. A learner may be given a chocolate after he answers a fixed number of questions, say 4.

Variable Reinforcement : In variable reinforcement schedule, reinforcement is provided randomly. The learner does not know when he is going to be rewarded. Hence he remains motivated throughout the learning-process expecting reinforcement at any moment. In gambling, rewards are unpredictable and thus the players remain well-motivated through occasional gains.

Continuous Reinforcement : In this case, reinforcement is provided after every correct response. For instance, a learner may be rewarded for his every correct answer to the questions asked by his teacher.

Educational implications of Skinner's theory : Skinner's theory of operant conditioning has wide implications in the field of education. The mechanism of operant conditioning provides valuable techniques for training individuals to learn complex behaviour and difficult skills. It has been successfully applied in modification of behaviour of the learner.

The theory of operant conditioning stresses the role of secondary reinforcers such as prizes, high scores, verbal praise, etc. in motivating a student. It also stresses the importance of reinforcement schedules in the acquisition of a learning.

According to Skinner's theory, reward increases operant strength. So in any learning-process reward has an important role to play. But reinforcement should be intermittent rather than continuous. Similarly, intermittent punishment is more effective than punishment delivered everytime the response is made. However, delayed punishment often proves ineffective.

Operant conditioning is a practical approach to learning-process and can be successfully used in classroom teaching. Based on the principles of operant conditioning, a number of devices have been evolved in modern times, e.g., programed learning, computer of assisted instruction, teaching machine, etc. The principles of operant conditioning also provides valuable techniques for psychotherapy.

In Skinner's teaching machine, carefully prepared sets of frames are presented to the learner serially. He makes a response to the first frame. Positive reinforcement comes when he finds that his response is correct. The machine—like a good private tutor—reinforces the student for every correct response. It provides feedback and shapes his behaviour efficiently.

15.2.5 Hull's theory

Clark L. Hull (1884–1952) presented his systematic behaviour theory in his books Principles of Behaviour (1943) and A Behaviour System (1952). His theory had great impact on contemporary psychologists.

Hull synthesised different theories of his predecessors into a unified and scientific theory of human behaviour. Like Watson's his theory is also .mechanistic. But while Watson discarded Thorndike's law of effect, Hull accepted it with certain modifications. Hull tried to explain purpose, insight and other conscious experiences which the behaviour psychologists had totally rejected. His basic concepts about human behaviour and learning are :

Change in S–R formula : Hull rejected Thorndike's S–R formula and replaced it by the formula S–O–R, as suggested by Woodworth incorporating organism's interest, drives, needs, etc.

Hull elaborated S–O–R formula. According to him, when a stimulus S impinges on an organism, it results in a neural impulse (s). The stimulus trace cause a motor neural response (r) which results in an overt response (R). Thus, instead of the simple S–R, we get the formula S–s–r–R.

Habit formation : Hull treated habit as a function of the number of reinforcements. According to Hull, when a stimulus accompanied by a reinforcer emits a response, the S–R bond is strengthened. Repetition of the reinforcement strengthens the bond and, finally, it brings about an organisation in the nervous system called habit, which may be represented as sHr. Thus Hull reduced learning to habit formation.

Hull asserted that habit is built up as a result of drive reduction. Relief from hunger and pain are also examples of reinforcement by drive reduction. Hull's experiment with dogs show that drive reduction produces learning of the new response.

Reinforcement : Hull's concept of reinforcement is not the same as that of Skinner or Thorndike. To Skinner, reinforcement is that which increases the probability of the reoccurrence of a response. Thorndike's concept of reinforcement may be explained through his law of effect. Hull, on the other hand, viewed reinforcement in terms of the reduction of one's biological need or drive. According to him, need produces behaviour and that behaviour which reduces the need of the organism is gradually learned.

According to Hull, there are two types of reinforcement—Primary and Secondary. Primary reinforcement tends to strengthen behaviour through satisfaction of biological needs. But secondary reinforcement is brought about by a neutral stimulus in association with a primary reinforcer. For instance, a sugar candy is a primary reinforcement but a coin becomes a secondary reinforcement to a child because he knows that sugar candy can be purchased by the coin.

Stimulus generalisation : It means that when there are two or more similar stimuli, they can evoke the same response from the organism as was elicited by the original stimulus. For instance, a child who is afraid of a snake also fears a rope or a thing similar to it with this type of generalisation. Hull, tried to explain the case of transfer of training by stressing that learning under similar conditions is likely to be transferred to the new learning situation.

Habit strength and learning : Hull's theory of learning is based on reinforcement. He treated habit as a function of the number of reinforcements. He used the symbol **sHr** to indicate habit strength. According to Hull, habit strength is the strength of the S–R bond which increases with the number of trials provided there is a reinforcement in every trial. Hull reduces learning to habit formation.

Hull explained habit formation with the help of the following formula :

$$sHr = 1 - 10^{-aN}$$

where N = number of trials to form a habit;

a = empirical constant (equal to .03).

Habit strength (sHr) is a function of reinforcement.

Reaction potential : According to Hull, reaction potential is the potential of an organism to react or respond. He explained its meaning with the help of the following formula :

$$\text{Reaction Potential} = sHr \times D \times V \times K$$

where sHr = habit strength

D = strength of drive

V = stimulus intensity

K = incentive reinforcement

It is clear that if any of the above factors had a value equal to zero, reaction potential would be zero. For instance, if the strength of drive (D) is zero, a learned response will not occur. However, reaction potential varies from individual to individual. Hull postulated the existence of factors that inhibit behaviour.

Inhibition : Inhibition has a regressive effect on reaction potential. There are two types of inhibition : (a) Reactive inhibition (I_R) and (b) Conditional inhibition (s|r).

Reactive inhibition occurs due to prolonged work and the fatigue associated with muscular activity. Such inhibition due to fatigue disappears if some rest is provided.

Conditional inhibition results from psychological and environmental factors instead of physiologal factors.

When a child refuses to learn further, it may be due to physical fatigue or because of some psychological factors, such as dislike for the subject.

Reactive inhibition and conditional inhibition may work together to reduce or eliminate the probability of the reoccurance of a learned response.

Educational implications : Hull's system of learning was acclaimed for putting forward a scientific theory of learning-process. He related learning to the needs of the individual. Need produces behaviour and the behaviour that reduces the need is gradually learned. Hull's theory stresses the importance of needs, drives, incentives and adequate motivation for having satisfactory results in the learning-process. When the needs of the child is properly satisfied, learning becomes meaningful. Therefore, the aim of education should not be merely to collect theoretical knowledge. It should be pragmatic and need-based. Similarly, we should provide need-based curricula to our school children. Our method of teaching also should be interesting and motivate students to learn.

Hull's theory extends the concept of reinforcement. Reinforcement not only includes reward and satisfaction but, according to Hull, it includes reduction of need and elimination of punishment also.

Hull reduced the art of learning to mere habit formation and laid stress on adequate exercise and practice. He advocated continuous and gradual introduction of small doses of reinforcement.

Fatigue reduces reaction potential of an individual. So, Hull emphasised the need for proper rest and other measures to eliminate fatigue in the act of learning.

Hull's theory opposed all kinds of inhibition in the path of learning-process. To obtain desired result in the teaching-learning-process, it stressed the importance of removing both internal and external inhibitions by introducing change in subject matter and teaching methods.

15.2.6 Tolman's sign learning theory

Edward C. Tolman (1886–1959) developed a theory of learning which is known as sign-Gestalt theory or sign learning-theory. He published his major systematic work purposive behaviour in animals and men in 1932. As the name indicates the sign learning-theory is based on the assumption that learning follows certain cues or signs leading to the performance of the task.

Tolman's system is known as purposive behaviourism. He rejected the S–R unit as a means of explaining behaviour. Tolman strongly opposed S–R associationism and tried to replace it with a system emphasising the adaptive, creative and intelligent aspects of behaviour. In fact, Tolman was a different kind of behaviourist who rejected the mechanistic approach of behaviourism. However, his sign learning-theory has close connection with McDougall's hormic psychology, Gestalt psychology and Watson's behaviourism.

Tolman's main tenets are briefly :

1. For psychological science introspection and verbal report has no place as a method.
2. The system is a molar rather than a molecular behaviourism. Watson's behaviourism is molecular.
3. The system is a purposivism because it recognises that behaviour is regulated by ends or goals. Watsonian behaviourism rejects the problem of goal-seeking behaviour.

Main concepts of sign learning-theory

Molar approach: Tolman adopted the molar approach in the study of behaviour instead of the molecular approach of Thorndike, Watson, Guthrie, Skinner and Hull. Tolman's theory emphasises that the study of behaviour involves a complete purposeful exercise.

The chief characteristics of molar behaviour are :

1. Molar-behaviour is goal-directed. It is purposive and cognitive.
2. It is not stereotyped like a reflex action.
3. There is a selective preference for easy means-activities as against difficult ones called the principle of least effort.
4. It is a Gestalt or complete whole instead of the parts of which it is supposed to be composed of.
5. The molar behaviour makes use of environmental supports as means-objects toward the goal.

Intervening variables : Tolman highlighted the role of intervening variables in the complete act of behaviour. According to him, there are five strong determinants of behaviour. The behaviour of an organism is the function of all these variables, which may be represented thus :

$$B = F(S, P, H, T, A)$$

where, S = environmental stimuli

P = physiological drives

H = heredity

T = previous training

A = age.

Now, which type of intervening variable will prove more effective depends upon physiological and psychological conditions of the individual. For instance, sometimes drug or curiosity may prove stronger than drives like hunger.

Tolman revised his list of intervening variables in 1951. These are :

1. **The need system :** The need system is similar to the drive theories and depends on physiological deprivation or drive situation.
2. **The behaviour space :** The behaviour space is a space of objects in various places, with distance and direction as perceived by the actor at a given point. The behaviour space is similar to Lewin's life space.
3. **The belief-value matrix :** It indicates the preference of certain goals and their relative value in gratification of needs.

Sign learning : In a learning situation, the learner follows signs to a goal, learns his way about and follows a sort of map. Tolman found that the rats in a puzzle box were able to find new routes when their initial routes were blocked by constructing a mental picture or map of their environment.

Like animals we also make use of such mental mapping to solve problems of our daily life.

Tolman's theory of sign learning is supported by experiments on : (a) Place learning, (b) Reward expectancy and (c) Latent learning.

Place learning : Tolman and his associates conducted experiments to show the place-learning ability of the rats. In one of the experiments, a T-maze was used. The response-learning group starting randomly from either P_1 or P_2 always found food by turning to the right. But the place-learning group always went to the same place for food. This group was more successful than the response-learning group. This shows that the animals learn places and not the fixed sequence of movements like turning left or right. They act according to some sort of map of the situation, and not according to blind habit.

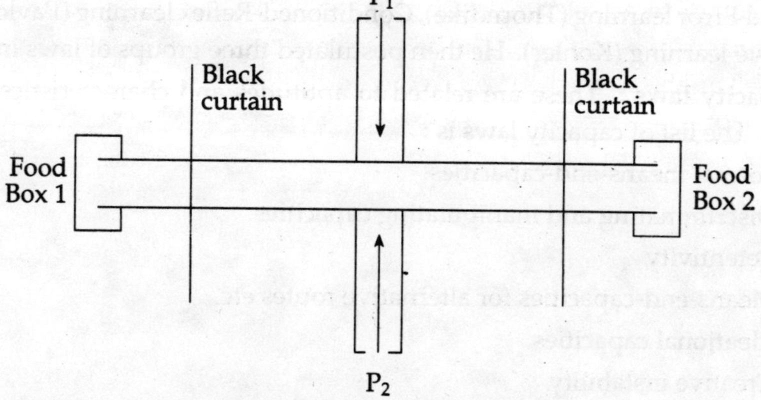

Fig. 15.5 Tolman's Experiment.

Reward expectancy : Our learning behaviour is goal-oriented and purposive. If we perform certain act, we expect some reward in exchange. If we do not get it or get less than our expectation, we get frustrated and behave abnormally.

In an experiment, a banana was kept hidden from a monkey in one of the two containers. The monkey picked up the right container and got the banana. The experimenter then substituted banana for a lettuce leaf, which is a less preferred food. The monkey rejected the lettuce leaf and exhibited signs of disruptive behaviour. This shows that animals have some sort of expectancy of specific goal objects and other goal objects naturally produce signs of behaviour disruption. Such behaviour of the animal indicates that the theory of sign-learning is quite appropriate.

Latent learning : Tolman and Honzik (1930) performed an experiment to demonstrate the nature of latent learning. Three groups of rats were allowed to run through the mazes without giving food :

1. The first group was rewarded throughout.
2. The second group was non-rewarded throughout.
3. The third group (experimental group) was non-rewarded until the eleventh trial.

But as soon as the food was introduced on the twelfth day, the rats of the experimental group improved their performance rapidly and caught up with the first group that received food continuously. Tolman argued that since this gain did not reveal in performance, the learning taking place is latent.

According to reinforcement theory, habits are strengthened by reinforcement. Experiments on latent learning demonstrate that reinforcement is not an essential principle of learning.

Types of learning and their laws : Tolman reviewed three kinds of learning : Trial and Error learning (Thorndike), Conditioned-Reflex learning (Pavlov) and Inventive learning (Kohler). He then postulated three groups of laws in 1932 :

Capacity laws : These are related to aptitudes and characteristics of the learner. The list of capacity laws is :

1. Formal means-end-capacities.
2. Discriminating and manipulating capacities.
3. Retentivity.
4. Means-end-capacities for alternative routes etc.
5. Ideational capacities.
6. Creative instability.

Laws relating to the nature of the material : These laws deal with conditions inherent in the material itself :

1. Togetherness.
2. Fusibility.
3. Other Gestalt-like laws.
4. Inter-relations among the spatial, temporal and other characters of the alternatives.
5. Characters in the material favouring new closures and expansions of the field.

Laws relating to the manner of presentation : These laws are based largely on association psychology. The list is :

1. Frequency, recency.
2. Revival after extinction etc.
3. Motivation.
4. Not effect but emphasis.
5. Temporal orders and sequences in the presentation of alternatives.
6. Temporal relations between the presentation of certain alternatives and the true solution.

In 1949, Tolman proposed six types of learning :

Cathexes : A cathexis is an association between certain objects and certain drives. Cathexis may be positive or negative. For example, if a hungry child wants bread, it is positive cathexis. Whereas, if a burned child dreads a burning candle, the cathexis is negative, for he shuns the candle.

Equivalence beliefs : This is similar to secondary reinforcement whereby a sub-goal provides the same motivation as provided by the main goal. In psychological clinics, evidences of faulty equivalence beliefs are seen.

Field expectancies : In this case, learning takes place on account of expectation of some signs in the environment. These expectations allow the organism to take shortcuts or round-about routes. This is not S–R connections but S–S connection or sign-sign learning.

Field cognition modes : A field cognition mode represents a readiness to acquire field-expectancies. This type of learning involves the learning of a strategy by arranging the perceptual field in a specific way.

Drive discrimination : In this type of learning, the learner tries to identify and determine his own drive state and respond accordingly. In the experiments of Hull (1933) and Leeper (1935), the animal learned to go one way when thirsty, another way when hungry.

Motor patterns : In this type of learning, the motor patterns are conditioned by behaviour as explained by Guthrie.

Tolman's contribution : Tolman's theory is an eclectic approach towards learning. His catholicity towards new ideas have probably prevented him from developing an independent well-defined system of learning.

However, in spite of this, he is not less prominent than other theorists of learning. His main contribution is purposive behaviourism against mechanistic Watsonian behaviourism. He considered behaviour as purposeful and docile rather than mere stimulus-response connection. His emphasis on the cognitive processes makes learning an intelligent task. Tolman asserted that all learning is purposeful and goal-oriented rather than response-oriented. The essence of learning process, according to him, is understanding and map making rather than conditioning or building-up S–R connections.

According to reinforcement theory, habits are strengthened by reward. Tolman's experiments on latent learning shows that reinforcement is not an essential principle of learning. Latent learning shows its existence in terms of good performance shortly after reward was introduced.

Educational implications : Tolman stresses the importance of purpose in learning. According to him, molar behaviour is purposive and goal-directed. Therefore, education should be need-based and goal-oriented. Teaching should be purposeful and it should have clear cut objectives.

According to Tolman, reinforcement is not an essential principle of learning. A reward is not, therefore, always necessary for every step of learning. Rather, the intrinsic value of learning should be stressed instead of some external reward.

Tolman's experiments on latent-learning demonstrate that no learning is a wastage. Although immediate purpose may not be served, attempts at learning never goes in vain.

Moreover, Tolman emphasised the adaptive, creative and intelligent aspect of learning. Therefore, children, while learning, should not be forced to follow a stereotyped routine but they should be motivated to explore all possible means for solving the problems.

Lastly, Tolman highlighted the role of intervening variables such as drives, previous training, age, etc. in a learning-process. To derive, therefore, the maximum benefit, the educator should take proper note of those variables and make necessary changes in teaching-technique.

15.2.7 Gestalt theory of learning

The approach of the behaviourists to learning did not satisfy those who wanted to study human behaviour as a whole. Dissatisfied with the behaviourists' approach the Gestalt psychologists considered learning as a more conscious effort of the organism rather than a S–R mechanism. They were opposed to the molecular and mechanistic approach to behaviour. They tried to interpret learning as a purposive, exploratory and creative enterprise.

Meaning of Gestalt : Gestalt is a German word which means pattern, configuration or organised whole. Three German psychologists, Max Wertheimer, Kurt Koffka and Wolfgang Kohler were the advocates of Gestalt theory.

Gestalt psychology is mainly concerned with the nature of perception. According to it, we perceive an object as a Gestalt, whole or pattern. We do not perceive it as an aggregate of parts. Proximity of elements help them in being grouped into a pattern. Also similarity of elements is favourable to their being combined into a pattern. Perception always involves a problem of organisation. The Gestalt psychologists do not separate sensation of an object from its meaning. According to them, everything we perceive stands against a background. There is a close relationship between figure and ground.

Kohler's experiment : Kohler conducted a number of experiments on chimpanzees during the period 1913–1917 and recorded his findings in his book, Mentality of Apes (1925). These experiments demonstrated that chimpanzees do not learn by trial and error but by insight, provided the path is clearly visible to the animal. Some of Kohler's experiments are :

Experiment 1 : A chimpanzee, called Sultan, was put in a cage. Outside the cage some bananas were placed. On seeing the bananas, Sultan showed restlessness and tried to reach the bananas outside but failed. All of a sudden he saw a stick inside the cage and pulled the bananas inside by means of the stick.

Experiment 2 : In the second experiment, the chimpanzee was given two sticks, one of which could be fitted into the other end and made a long stick. The chimpanzee first tried to get the bananas with the help of a single stick but he failed. He gave up the job and began playing with the two sticks. By chance, he succeeded in fitting both the sticks and pulled in the bananas. Next day, Sultan made a few useless movements, but in a few seconds joined the sticks and got the bananas. This shows the animal learned the movement through insight.

Experiment 3 : A banana was hung from the ceiling of a cage. A box was put in the corner of the cage. The animal could not reach the fruit by stretching his hands. He suddenly dragged the box under the banana, climbed on it and got the banana.

Fig. 15.6: Köhler's chimpanzee learns to assemble a long stick from two shorter ones.

Experiment 4 : In another experiment, Kohler made the problem more difficult and a few boxes were put on the floor. The animal tried to reach the banana by jumping but failed. Suddenly he got an idea and put two or three boxes one on top of the other in order to reach it. He learned the trick by insight.

These experiments demonstrate the role of intelligence or insight in higher learning. The learning through insight is fundamentally different from trial and error process. According to the Gestaltists, the perception of the field and gradual restructuring of it is insight. But Thorndike considers insight as a case of rapid learning. He says, Insight is an unanalysed form of learning and one in which trial and error still plays an important, though hidden part.

According to the Gestalt psychologists, Sultan learned to solve the problem by insight. The time curve, according to Kohler, does not show a gradual downward movement during the learning-process. Rather, the sudden sharp change in the learning curve indicates the animal's intelligence and insight.

Foresight and hindsight : In fact, insight involves foresight as well as hindsight. In trial and error learning there is hindsight. The cat in a cage does not see the way to the goal before reaching it. The button is hidden from her sight. After a series of trials, she finds out the right lead. This is hindsight.

Foresight is seeing the way to the goal before reaching it. When the whole situation is presented, there may be foresight, but when the essential characteristics of the situation are concealed, there may be hindsight. The Gestaltists discard the role of hindsight or experience and stress the role of the present situational factors.

Characteristics of insight : Learning by insight has the following characteristics :

1. The individual reacts to a situation as a whole.
2. It reacts to certain relationships within the situation as a whole.
3. The individual reconstructs the field and perceives it.
4. At the initial stage, insightful learning passes through the process of trial and error. But this stage does not last long.
5. Finally, there is a sudden change in its total behaviour. The suddenness indicates insight in learning.
6. **Generalisation :** The insightful solution found in a particular situation helps the individual to react insightfully in other identical situations.

Implications of the Gestalt theory of learning : Gestalt theory of learning has greatly influenced our modern education. Some of its contributions are :

1. An individual does not learn by blind and mechanical trial and error process but by insight, provided the goal is clearly visible. The teacher therefore, should discourage application of mechanical process by learners while solving a problem.

2. The learner reacts to a situation as a whole, not merely to a part of it. The teacher should therefore present a topic before the students not by parts, but by whole. This will help comprehension. One of the important maxims of modern education is from the whole to the parts. If an individual wishes to learn a poem, it should be presented to him as a whole. On being understood as a whole, the poem may be broken into parts for effective memorisation.
3. The important contribution of the Gestalt theory is that it has made learning purposeful. Thus the learner needs to be motivated by arousing his interest. He has to be well-acquainted with the specific aims and purposes of the learning.
4. The learner should have clear idea about the aims and objectives of learning.
5. The learner learns through insight. For the development of insight two process—differentiation and generalisation—are essential. So, while teaching, irrelevant elements should be rejected and the essential elements should be focussed for generalisation.

Comparison between T–E learning and insightful learning

Trial and error learning	Insightful learning
1. In trial and error learning, the learner responds to the stimuli separately.	1. The learner reacts to a situation as a whole.
2. The behaviour of the learner is either mechanical or purposeless.	2. The behaviour of the learner is well-planned, meaningful and purposive.
3. The total situation is not clearly visible to the learner. He learns in a closed situation.	3. The whole learning situation is visible to the learner. He can see the goal clearly, and learns in an open situation.
4. This process of learning does not involve higher forms of mental abilities. Learning occurs through trials and exercises.	4. Insightful learning involves reasoning, thinking, imagination and other forms of higher mental abilities.
5. Lower animals, infants or idiots learn by this method.	5. Animal's mental ability is to learn by this process.
6. Trial and error learning is gradual.	6. Suddenness is a factor of insightful learning.

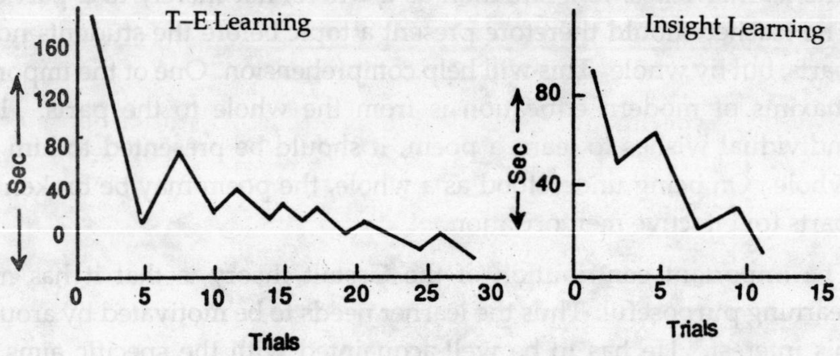

Fig 15.7

The experiments of the Gestalt psychologists show that learning is not the result of trial and error but of insight and the ability to see relationship between the various factors involved in a situation. Koffka suggested that in learning the laws of perception were equally applicable. Following laws govern the process of perception :

1. **The law of whole :** Whatever we perceive, we perceive as a whole. We do not perceive an object element by element into separate parts.
2. **The law of figure and ground :** The situation is perceived with reference to a definite relationship between the figure and the background.
3. **The law of configuration :** We perceive the situation in patterns or configurations.
4. **The law of pragnaz :** It means that tne whole tends to be as good and stable as possible. The mind tends to overlook incompleteness or irregularities.
5. **The laws of organisation :** The organisation of different elements of a situation into a pattern takes place under the following principles :
   (a) The law of similarity.
   (b) The law of proximity.
   (c) The law of segregation.

Criticism : The Gestalt theory is a revolt against the doctrine of associationism. It discards analysis altogether which is not justified. By refusing analytical method, the Gestalt theory opens the way to arbitrary interpretations and unanalysed conceptions.

15.2.8 Pavlov's classical conditioning

Ivan Pavlov (1849–1936), a Russian physiologist, discovered the classical conditioning about the year 1900. He was basically interested in the studies of the glandular secretions involved in the digestive processes. He was awarded Nobel Prize of medicine or physiology on his research on digestive process in 1904.

Pavlov's experiment : Pavlov made experiments with a hungry dog and evoked his salivary reflex by conditioning stimuli. He kept a dog hungry for a few days and before giving it food, he rang the bell. When the food was given and the bell was rung, there was automatic secretion of saliva from the mouth of the dog. This process of presenting the food accompanied with the bell was repeated several times. The amount of saliva secreted was measured.

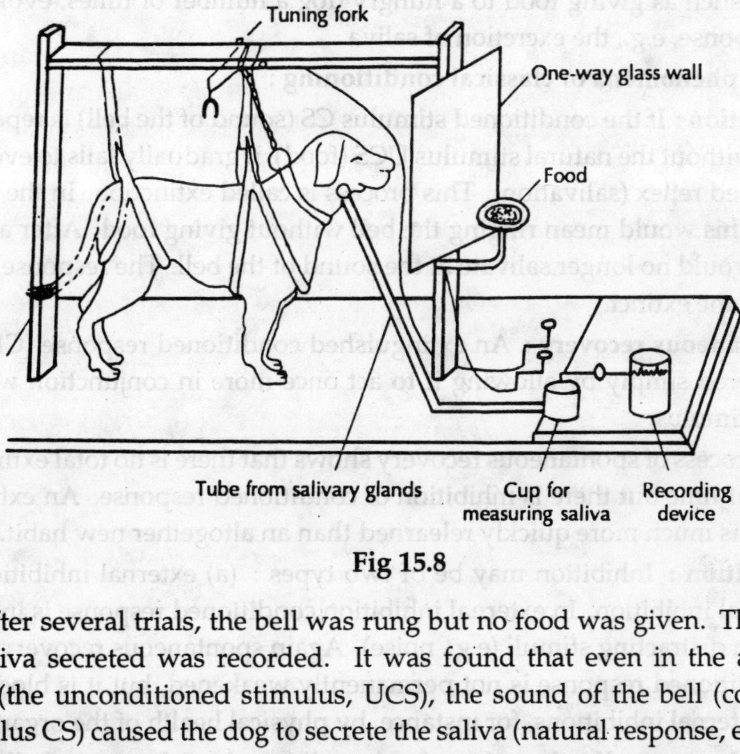

Fig 15.8

After several trials, the bell was rung but no food was given. The amount of saliva secreted was recorded. It was found that even in the absence of food (the unconditioned stimulus, UCS), the sound of the bell (conditioned stimulus CS) caused the dog to secrete the saliva (natural response, established by connecting UCS). A conditioned response was the natural stimulus with an artificial stimulus.

Diagrammatic representation of the classical conditioning is given below :

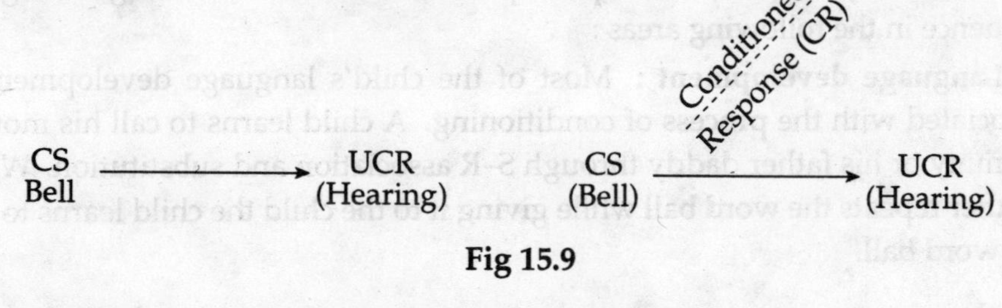

Fig 15.9

We may define classical conditioning as a process in which a neutral stimulus, by pairing with a natural stimulus, acquires all the characteristics of natural stimulus.

In the above diagram, ringing of the bell is neutral stimulus to elicit the response of salivation but by pairing with food a number of times, it acquired the characteristics of food and elicited the response of salivation when presented alone.

Pavlov found that any substitute stimulus, such as, the application of heat or cold to the skin, the shining of an electric bulb, connected with the natural stimulus such as giving food to a hungry dog a number of times, evoked the same response, e.g., the excretion of saliva.

Some phenomena of classical conditioning :

Extinction : If the conditioned stimulus CS (sound of the bell) is repeatedly applied without the natural stimulus UCS (food), it gradually fails to evoke the conditioned reflex (salivation). This process is called extinction. In the case of the dog, this would mean ringing the bell without giving food. After a while, the dog would no longer salivate at the sound of the bell. The response would have become extinct.

Spontaneous recovery : An extinguished conditioned response (CR) may be recovered simply by allowing it to act once more in conjunction with the natural stimulus.

The process of spontaneous recovery shows that there is no total extinct due to lapse of time but there is inhibition of conditioned response. An extinction response is much more quickly relearned than an altogether new habit.

Inhibition : Inhibition may be of two types : (a) external inhibition and (b) internal inhibition. In external inhibition conditioned response is inhibited by certain distracting stimuli (e.g., noise). Again spontaneous recovery shows that conditioned response is not permanently weakened, but it is blocked by certain internal inhibitions, for instance, by physical health of the organism.

Stimulus generalisation : An animal conditioned to salivate to a bell, would also salivate to sound of a buzzer. Thus the animal tended to generalise the conditioned response to stimuli that were different from, but somewhat similar to the one to which it was specifically conditioned. It was found that the greater the similarity between stimuli, the greater the generalisation between them.

Pavlov's contribution : The principles of classical conditioning has a great influence in the following areas :

Language development : Most of the child's language development is associated with the process of conditioning. A child learns to call his mother mummy or his father daddy through S–R association and substitution. When mother repeats the word ball while giving it to the child the child learns to say the word ball.

Thus the principles of conditioning are used to teach alphabets.

Habit development : Children learn some good habits such as cleanliness, punctuality, early rising etc. through the principles of conditioning.

They also learn some good manners, such as how to behave with elders and classmates through the process of conditioning.

Breaking bad habits : Bad habits, such as nail biting, carelessness, errors in writing etc. can be eliminated by using the principles of deconditioning.

Development of fear : Fear, phobias, anxiety and other mental abnormalities develop through the process of conditioning. If a child is punished repeatedly for his failure to work out sums correctly, he develops fear for the subject. Often a teacher with his defective methods of teaching or bad temper may condition a child to develop distaste toward the subject.

In fact, most of our habits, attitude and interests are fashioned through conditions. On the other hand fears and phobias, unhealthy superstitions and attitudes—all may be eliminated through deconditioning.

15.2.9 Lewin's field theory

Kurt Lewin (1890–1947) was a German psychologist, who spent his last years in teaching in the USA. His system was explained in a book and a monograph, Principles of topological psychology (1936) and the conceptual representation and measurement of psychological forces (1938).

Basic concepts of field theory :

Topology : Topology is a geometry of spaces, in which concepts like inside, outside and boundary are used. Lewin thinks that many psychological situations are structured in that way.

Vector : The term vector is used in mechanics to describe the resolution of forces. A vector is indicated by an arrow. The length represents its force and the direction represents the line of application. Since many facts of dynamic psychology can be explained in terms of conflict, the use of vectors may be justified.

Life space : Life space of a person is the psychological field in which he moves. The life space of a person is influenced and conditioned by physical and social environment. My life space may be different from that of yours in identical situation.

Often life space corresponds closely to real world with which the individual is in contact. But when the individual lives in the world of fantasy or day-dreams, he is out of touch with reality.

Valence : Lewin called goal-attractiveness valence. There are two types of valences operating in one's life space. When an individual is attracted by an object, that object has positive valence. But when an individual is repelled by an object in life space, the object is said to have a negative valence. The same object carries different valences for different people because of their different perception in life space.

Now conflict may arise due to the presence of several valences in life space. Lewin describes three kinds of conflict :

1. Two positive valences, e.g., a boy has to choose between a film show and a picnic.
2. Two negative valences, e.g., a boy is threatened by punishment if he fails to do his home task.
3. A simultaneous positive and negative valence, e.g., a child is offered a reward for a homework he does not like to perform.

Learning theory of Kurt Lewin :

Change in cognitive structure : According to Lewin, learning means a change in one's cognitive structure. In the beginning, the life space of a child is less differentiated. But as the child grows up and learns more, his field of perception becomes more and differentiated. His life space becomes gradually more structured.

An unstructured region of life space indicates problem. When the problem is solved through learning, the life space become structured. Let us give an example : Suppose a child C stands in a particular place of the field. He tries to reach food F, but there is an obstacle O in between him and the food. The child feels an urge for reching the goal F. He attempts to reach F through T–E process. Finally, he finds out the right path and secures the food. Thus his problem is solved. His old cognitive field undergoes a change and a new field is created.

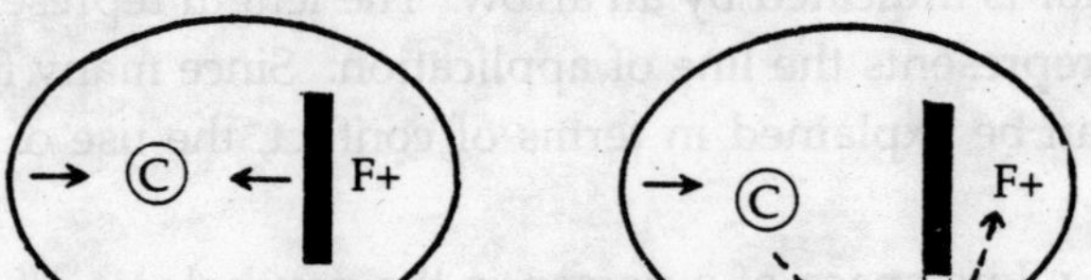

Figure I Figure II

Fig 15.10

Learning and repetition : Learning is a required change in one's cognitive structure. This change may be brought about with repetition. But too much repetition as advocated by Thorndike does not help learning. Moreover, repetition may lead to psychological satiation with accompanying disorganisation of the cognitive structure. Thus, instead of excessive repetition, the structure may get changed with better organisation and arrangements.

Rewards and punishment : Lewin highlighted the role of both punishment and reward in teaching-learning-process. The purpose of punishment is to keep the learner engaged in a task which he dislikes. Activities controlled by the threat of punishment give rise to mental conflicts in the learner. So, excessive punishment should be avoided.

Rewarded activities, no doubt, become interesting and liked by the learner. But tempted by the reward, the learner may take recourse to improper means of cheating without doing the demanded task. So, judicious use of punishment and reward is advocated.

Success and failure : According to Lewin's theory, success or failure depends upon one's ego involvement and level of aspiration.

The success experience on the part of a learner shows the following possibilities :

1. Reaching a goal constitutes a success.
2. Getting within the region of the goal may be a success experience.
3. Making noticeable progress toward a goal may constitute a success experience.
4. Selecting a socially approved goal may in itself provide a success experience although no efforts are made to reach the goal.

Level of aspiration : The level of aspiration, according to Lewin, is an important factor in teaching-learning-process. It is set according to the learner's interpretation of his own achievement. However, there are individual differences in setting level of aspiration or setting of goal. Learners who are realistic set their goals according to their capability. But unrealistic learners may set goals too high to achieve. On the other hand, to avoid the possibility of failure, some learners may set goals too low. In fact, too high or low level of aspirations discourage learning.

Motivation : Motivation is attraction towards a goal. It has very important place in learning-process. Lewin introduced the concepts of ego involvement, the role of valences and the level of aspiration to interpret motivated learning.

However, attractive goals may lose their attraction if the activity related to them is repeated to the point of satiation. Again, an originally unattractive goal-may become attractive through a change in the meaning of the goal related activity. This principle may be utilised in many teaching methods to induce motivation in learners. For example, a child who has no attraction for mathematics may be told a story in which mathematics is the favourite subject for his hero.

Memory : According to field theory, tasks which do not serve any worthwhile purpose in life are forgotten. Because of psychological tensions, unfinished tasks are remembered better than the finished tasks. Again, tasks which satisfy our many needs are remembered better than the tasks which lead to the satisfaction of only one need.

Summary

Learning is the modification of behaviour through experience and training. By way of experimental studies. Thorndike discovered three major laws of learning : The Law of Effect, The Law of Exercise and The Law of Readiness. Thorndike's laws of learning are of great significance in the field of education.

Watson regarded psychology as a science of behaviour and not a science of experience. He explained the process of learning by the law of exercise, the law of use, the law of disuse, the law of frequency and the law of recency. Watson had a strong belief in environmentalism.

Guthrie propounded a theory of learning-based upon contiguous conditioning. In fact, Watson and Pavlop prepared a background for the exposition of contiguous conditioning.

According to Guthrie movement is an essential part of learning. The gap between the stimulus and response is filled in by movements. Guthrie considered drill or practice essential for it leads to improvement. He examined the role of motives and rewards in learning and concluded that motives and rewards merely accelerate the movements in learning. He stressed the importance of cue in learning.

Based on the findings of a series of experiments, Skinner concluded that behaviour is shaped and maintained by its consequences. It is operated by the organism and maintained by its results. The occurrence of such behaviour is known as operant behaviour and the process of learning as operant conditioning. In operant conditioning S–R connection takes place on the basis of Law of Effect. To shape the behaviour of an organism according to the desired goal, Skinner put forth the idea of planning of schedules of reinforcement. The theory of operant conditioning provides valuable methods for training individuals to learn complex behaviour.

Hull tried to study human behaviour and learning-scientifically and avoided all references to consciousness. He was deeply interested in the habit formation as well as the nature of reinforcement. In this connection he points out the role of need-reduction in reinforcement. He believed that the individual had a hierarchy of needs and they required necessary response to be satisfied. Hull considered need-reduction as a kind of reinforcement. When there is a reduction of need S–R connections are reinforced.

Hull threw light on the nature of motivation and explained it in relation to need-reduction. He has propounded the principle of secondary reinforcement which has been applied in teaching to a great extent.

Hull's theory of learning is helpful in understanding the process of forgetting. Forgetting occurs on account of disuse and fatigue. When forgetting occurs due to fatigue, Hull calls it reactive inhibition.

Pavlov established a conditioned response by connecting a natural stimulus with an artificial stimulus. If the C–S is repeatedly applied without UCS, extinction of the conditioned reflex occurs. However, an extinct response may be quickly relearned by allowing it to act once more in conjunction with the natural stimulus. The principle of classical conditioning has a great influence in language development, habit formation and breaking undesirable habits.

The sign Gestalt theory of learning assumes that learning is purposeful and meaningful. It is a meaningful activity performed in terms of a kind of map which has many signs to guide the learning-process.

This theory stresses the role of goal and movement towards the goal. The movement towards that goal depends upon cues and signs which indicate the path leading to that goal.

In the process of learning, there are certain intervening variables. Tolman discussed the nature of variables as well as individual differences. According to him, every intervening variable is related to some environmental variable.

In sign-learning there are three types of situations which indicate that reward expectancy, place-learning and laten-learning are involved.

Gestalt psychology appeared as a revolt against the analytical psychology of Wundt. Analytical psychology emphasises the elements of experience and behaviour. But the fundamental aspects of Gestalt theory is that every kind of experience or behaviour is a Gestalt, which cannot be analysed into elements. The behaviour of an individual does not consist of a sum of reflexes. Our brain also functions as a whole. When an irregular figure with gaps is seen, there are unbalanced tensions in the brain. The brain receives a closed figure with tensions restored to equilibrium.

Learning consists in performing a new movement by which the gap between the present situation and the goal may be bridged. Perceptual reorganisation of the situation is necessary for learning a new movement to master a novel situation. The Gestaltists hold that chimpanzees learn by insight and not by trial and error. They have the power of seeing the point. They can see the pattern of a situation.

Learning according to Lewin's field theory is a process of perceptual organisation or reorganisation of one's life space. The field theory attaches importance to insight in all types of learning. Lewin highlighted the importance of both reward and punishment in teaching-learning-process. According to him, level of aspiration is an important factor in the learning process. But too high or low level of aspirations discourages learning.

References

1. Crow, L.D. and Crow, A. : *Educational Psychology,* New Delhi : Eurasia Publishing House, 1973.
2. Gagne, R.M. : *The Conditions of Learning,* New York : Rinehart & Winston, 1970.
3. Guthrie, E.R. : *The Psychology of Learning,* New York : Harper & Row, 1935.
4. Guthrie, E.R. and Horton, G.P. : *Cats in a Puzzle Box,* New York : Rinehart, 1946.
5. Hillgard, E.O. : *Theories of Learning,* New York : Appleton-Century-Crofts, 1976.
6. Hull, C.L. : *Principles of Behaviour,* New York : Appleton-Century-Crofts, 1943.
7. Kohler, W. : *Gestalt Psychology,* New York : Leveright, 1929.
8. Murphy, Gardner : *An Introduction to Psychology,* New Delhi : Oxford & IBH, 1968.
9. Skinner, B.F. : *The Behaviour of Organisms,* New York : Appleton-Century-Crofts, 1938.
10. Tolman, E.C. : *Purposive Behaviour in Animals & Men,* New York : Century, 1932.
11. Woodworth, R.S. : *Psychology,* London : Methuen, 1945.
12. Watson, J.B. : *Psychology from the Standpoint of a Behaviourist,* Philadelphia : Lippin Cott, 1919.

Questions and Assignments

1. Give a critical estimate of Watson's theory of learning.
2. Define reinforcement. What are the various schedules of reinforcement? Explain with examples.
3. What are the main differences between Skinnerian and Pavlovian conditioning?
4. Discuss the theory of learning by reinforcement and point out its application in education.
5. What are the main tenets of theory of learning proposed by Hull?
6. What are the main features of Tolman's theory of learning? In what way is it an improvement over Skinner's theory?

7. Distinguish between Associationist and Gestalt Psychology and give your own estimate of each.
8. How does Gestalt Psychology account for learning in higher animals?
9. Explain the Gestalt Psychology of perception and learning?
10. Estimate the contribution of J.B. Watson, Guthrie, Tolman and Kurt Lewin to education.
11. What are the main differences between classical conditioning and operant conditioning?
12. Compare human learning with animal-learning. What is learning through insight? Show how it is trial and error method carried on at a higher level.
13. What is learning through insight? Explain fully the Gestalt's theory of learning.
14. Analyse Thorndike's theory of learning. Can this theory fully explain human learning?
15. Discuss Re-inforcement theory of Skinner.
16. Explain Kurt Lewin's Field Theory of learning.
17. Write notes on :
    (a) Operant.
    (b) Shaping.
    (c) Generalisation.
    (d) Place learning.
    (e) Discrimination.
    (f) Latent learning.
    (g) Movement-produced stimuli.
    (h) Programed instruction.

Chapter 16

The progress of learning

Introduction : The progress of learning depends on factors such as interest, attention, amount of practice, fatigue, method of learning, physiological conditions, maturation and so on. There are individual differences in the ability of learning. Again the same individual may also have varying progress under different conditions.

16.1 Plateau of learning

There are various types of learning curve. But in most of the curves following characteristics may be observed :

1. In the beginning, there is rapid progress in the acquisition of the new skill. This is due to attention and interest of the learner in the initial stage.
2. The initial progress is followed by a period in which no improvement is visible. This period of no improvement is called plateau. This period of stagnation is apt to discourage the learner.
3. At the end of the plateau period learning improves and the curve rises at a rapid rate.

16.2 How do plateaus occur

Plateaus in learning curve mainly arise due to two causes :

1. After a few days of practice in any mechanical type of work, interest begins to slacken. The monotony of the task makes it boring.

2. Plateaus may indicate a period of consolidation. There may be a certain difficult element in the task which blocks progress. At this period the learner is required to make new co-ordinations in order thar improvement takes place.

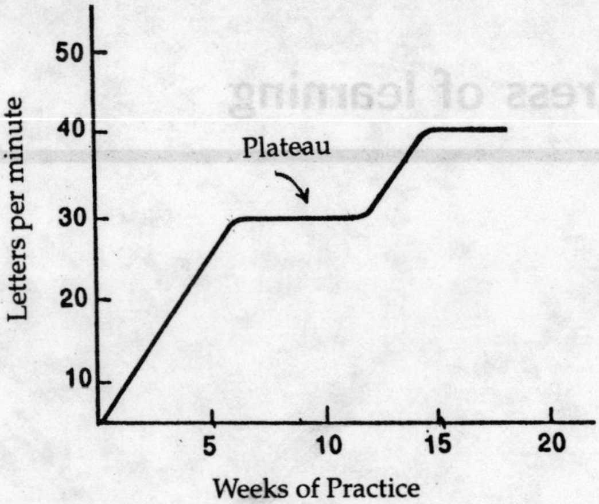

Fig. 16.1

16.3 How to overcome plateaus

Plateaus may develop because of lack of interest and boredom. These may be broken by the following ways :

1. Changing the old method of attack.
2. Distributing the period of work judiciously to avoid boredom and fatigue.
3. Providing proper incentives.
4. Making the goal of learning clear to the learner. They may be reminded of the gain they would have after the completion of the task.

In all types of learning curve plateaus may not appear, although a learner's progress from his initial score to his practice level shows irregular ups and downs.

16.4 Learning and fatigue

When learning is continued for a considerable period of time fatigue sets in. Fatigue may be physical or mental. The muscular fatigue sets in readily by mechanical type of work, such as, weight lifting on the ergograph. There may be an actual accumulation of metabolic wastes in the muscles involved. However, for some tasks like doing long multiplication fatigue may set in. But in such task there is very little evidence that the work has clogged the system with waste products. Tl.is sort of fatigue is called boredom.

16.4.1 Causes of fatigue

Fatigue may be caused due to following reasons :

1. Lack of oxygen.
2. Presence of toxin.
3. Exhaustion of the energy producing compounds.

16.4.2 Remedy for fatigue

The remedy for fatigue are as follows :

1. **Change of work :** When certain centres of brain are fatigued by a particular kind of activity and if that activity is changed, other centres become active, while the former ones get rest.

   Thus, in schools, it is better to alternate mental work with handwork. Mathematics should be followed by drawing or games to avoid boredom.

2. **Taking nourishment :** Food containing sugar is helpful in replenishing energy. Tea and coffee removes fatigue for the time being. So, during recess period, students should be given milk, plantain, gram, sweet fruits, etc., to ward off fatigue and boredom of classroom teaching.

3. **Creating interest :** Monotonous teaching for a long period kills interest. So, teacher should adopt such methods of teaching which interest the child and eliminate boredom.

4. **Forming habits of work :** Habit is a great help to hard work. When a pupil in the beginning is asked to solve certain mathematical exercises, he feels soon tired. But when he is habituated he does not feel boredom to work out harder problems.

5. **Sleep :** Sleep is a great remedy for fatigue. During the rest provided by sleep, the toxins are removed and the store of the energy-producing compound is replenished.

16.5 Learning and maturation

Maturation is the process of natural growth. According to Baldwin, maturation is an increase in competency and adaptability. Biggie and Hunt defined maturation as a developmental process within which a person, from time to time, manifests different traits.

Learning and maturation are closely connected. A child must attain a certain level of maturation before certain kinds of learning occur. For instance, a six-month old baby cannot learn how to swim because he is not mature enough to do so. Training without proper maturation is never effective.

16.5.1 Types of maturation

A.I. Gates classified maturation into two types :

1. Maturation of structures in the Gross.
2. Maturation of Specific Neural Connections.

The first type includes the growth of muscles, bones, glands and other bodily organs in a general way. Walking and many other activities cannot be carried out until a child's organism has reached a certain maturity level.

The second type of maturation makes possible a number of complex, coordinated reactions, e.g., sucking and swallowing food, crawling and making vocal sounds appear only when certain patterns of synaptic connections in the nervous system have reached a minimum stage of maturity.

16.5.2 Experiments on relative influence of maturation and learning

1. **McGraw's experiment :** McGraw took children of the same age and divided them into two groups—(i) Experimental group and (ii) Control group. He conducted experiments on these two groups and found that activities like crawling, walking, etc., which depend on maturation are not influenced by training. They would appear in proper time without waiting for any external training.
2. **Hillgard's experiment :** Hillgard trained the children of his experimental group in paper-cutting, button fitting and other activities for twelve weeks. His control group, however, did not receive any training. After twelve weeks it was observed that the ability of the experimental group excelled the control group in their performances. After that the children of the control group were given training in those activities for a week. At the end of the training it was found that the boys of the control group has earned the same capacity as the boys of the experimental group.
3. **Gessel's experiment :** Gesell and Thompson conducted an experiment on identical twins T and U to determine the relative influence of maturity and learning in stair-climbing. T and U were of the same age and otherwise equal. Twin T was given daily training in stair-climbing for six weeks at the age of forty-six weeks. During this time U did not get any training. At fifty-two weeks, twin T climbed the stairs in twenty-six seconds. Twin U at the age of fifty-three weeks, without any previous training, climbed the same stair case in forty-five seconds. Obviously, the difference between the two records represents the effect of the six weeks of training the twin T.

The experiment continued further and U was given training for two weeks while T received no such training. After two weeks of training U climbed the stairs in ten seconds. This show that the climbing performance of U at fifty-five weeks was far superior to that of T at fifty-two weeks. Thus U's advantage of two weeks in maturity outweighs T's advantage of four weeks of training.

Thus, these experiments show that education, if introduced too early before maturation, may be largely wasted, (Gates).

Learning is a process of development, which has certain specific characteristics. For instance, an individual cannot learn without motivation, need, attention and practice.

In maturation the learner has hardly any scope for self-activity. Maturation is not brought about by organism's need or drive. Learning is a mental process, where as maturation depends upon natural physical growth. However, maturation and learning are not two opposite concepts. Both maturation and learning are necessary for proper development of the child.

Comparison between maturation and learning

Maturation	Learning
1. Maturation depends on natural process of innate structural and neural growth.	1. Learning depends on efforts. It is effected through interaction with environment.
2. Maturation does not depend on past experiences.	2. Learning often depends on past experiences.
3. Maturation involves physical changes.	3. Learning brings about mental changes.
4. Maturation does not depend on motivation and need.	4. Learning takes place because of individual's need and drive.
5. Maturation is a physiological process. The individual remains unconscious of changes due to maturation.	5. Mental changes take place through conscious learning process.

16.5.3 Efficiency in learning

Efficiency in learning depends on a number of factors. Some of them may be discussed below :

1. **Will to learn :** Often students are found to be interested more in games than monotonous classroom teaching. In that case, no method of teaching will be effective. You may take a horse to water, but you will not make him drink. There must be will to learn. The learner must put forth his best in the actual work of learning.

2. **Good working environment :** The environment must be conducive to learning. Learning becomes difficult where distractions are excessive. Dingy, damp or suffocating classrooms reduce the efficiency of the students in learning. Thus good working condition is indispensable for successful learning.

3. **Length of the working period :** There is loss of efficiency due to boredom and fatigue when work is prolonged beyond certain period. It is desirable to stop or change the mode of work under such conditions.

4. **Learning by doing :** The learner should not be passive listeners. He should be made always very active. He should prepare charts and diagrams, draw sketches, work on the blackboard, prepare notes and so on.

5. **Vigorous application :** Last but not least, vigorous application is needed to promote learning. Procrastination and dilatoriness are inimical to learning efficiency. Learners should develop the habit of learning within time limit. They should be habituated to sustained work.

Summary

The progress of learning depends on various factors such as method of learning, fatigue, maturation, interest, physiological condition etc. Often the initial progress of learning is followed by a period of stagnation called plateau. Plateaus may be overcome by chaing the method of attach or providing proper incentives to the learner. The progress of learning may also be hampered by fatigue and boredom. They may be overcome by change of work, creating interest, taking nourishment and forming habits of work. Again learning and training without proper maturation is ineffective.

Efficiency in learning mainly depends on will to learn and proper working environment. Learning becomes difficult in a damp, dingy and suffocating classroom. When the environment is conductive to learning, the learner must put forth his best in the actual work of learning.

References

1. Crow, L.D. and Crow, Alice : *Educational Psychology*, New Delhi : Eurasia Publishing House, 1973.

2. Gates, A.I. : *Educational Psychology,* 3rd ed. New York : Macmillan, 1948.
3. Sorenson, H : *Psychology in Education,* New York : McGraw-Hill, 1964.
4. Stones, E : *Psychology of Education,* Methuen, London, 1984.

Questions and Assignments

1. On what does efficiency in learning depend? How can the devices of effective learning for the education of the child be used?
2. What is Platen of Learning? Why do the plateaus arise? How can they be overcome?
3. Distinguish between physical and mental fatigue. Discuss how mental fatigue can be got rid of.
4. *Change of work is rest*—How far is this principle true? Discuss.

Chapter 17

Programmed learning

Introduction : Nowadays, the demand for mass education has created a number of problems in educational system of our country. Previously, a few traditional methods of teaching were enough for the limited number of students in our schools. But at present, on account of industrial development and influx of students as a result of population explosion, use of latest teaching equipments and improved teaching techniques have become indispensable in our educational system. Particularly, to cope with the influx of students and shortage of teachers, the new technology of programmed learning has been evolved.

In 1953, B.F. Skinner of Harvard University first explained the concept of programmed learning in his book, "The Science of Learning and The Art of Teaching." Based upon his theory of operant conditioning he developed a teaching-machine and evolved a teaching-learning process which is popularly known as programmed instruction or programmed learning.

Presently, programmed book is helping the students to learn in auto-learning method and various types of teaching-machines are being used in America and other advanced countries as teaching-aid.

The sole object of programmed learning is to improve the teaching-learning process. It may be defined as a process of arranging material to be learned in a series of small steps designed to lead a learner through self-instruction from what he knows to the new and more complex knowledge and principles. The subject matter is divided into meaningful segments of information and, in each segment, the learner is motivated through reward.

17.1 Characteristics of programmed learning

1. In programmed learning, learning material is divided into small steps according to logical sequence. Logically one step is related to the next one. Each step or segment is known as *frame.*

2. Each frame contains certain information. The learner can correctly answer the question on the information.

3. The learner can compare his response with the correct response given at the end of the frame. Thus providing immediate confirmation is an important factor in the process of auto-learning.

4. Each frame of the program is prepared with great care and presented one at a time.

5. As the frames are constructed according to the interest and ability of the learner, he remains active and motivated throughout to complete the program.

6. In programmed learning each learner proceeds at his own space according to individual difference. He is not forced to complete the program with other members of his class.

7. In this method the learner can evaluate his performance and the teacher can also assess the progress of the learner. Moreover, the teacher can modify the program in the light of performances by the learner.

17.2 Program construction

While preparing a program following points are to be noted :

1. Those important units which appear to be harder and complex should be selected only for programming, instead of the entire learning material.

2. The learner's age, sex, name and address are to be noted.

3. The objective of the program should be clearly expressed in behavioural term. The terminal behaviour which the learner would be able to show at the completion of the program should be mentioned. e.g., the learner should be able to write the correct answer, he should give the verbal answer or he should be able to give practical demonstration etc.

4. Previous knowledge of the learning material is to be ascertained through short questions.

17.2.1 Organisation of the material

The learning material is divided into small frames according to logical sequence. In the beginning, the learning material along with a number of small objective-questions are given. The answers to these questions are given either at the end of the page or in the next page of the book.

In the beginning, the size of the frames will be shorter but gradually they may be longer.

In case of a difficult frame additional stimulus may be provided which will raise the probability of correct response. This is known as *prompting*.

17.2.2 Try out

Following the above principles the first draft of the program is prepared. Then the program is tried out in three following phases :

1. The first draft of the program is tested on an individual. The reactions of the individual are carefully noted and the program is modified accordingly. Some frames may be eliminated and replaced by new frames or some complex frames may be broken into smaller frames.
2. Thus, after individual try out the program is tested on a small group of students of the class for which the program is meant.
3. After modification of the draft program on the observations of the small group, the program is finally administered in actual classroom conditions.

17.2.3 Evaluation

Finally, how far the students learnt from the program may be tested by small objective questions. These evaluative questions are set at the end of the program.

17.3 Presentation of program

Generally programmed material is presented either through programmed text or thorough teaching-machine. The teaching-machine may be simple or highly complicated. They are very costly. In this poor country where classrooms are overcrowded, it is not possible to make use of these costly machines. Instead, we can of course use programmed texts in the class as an aid to auto-instruction.

17.4 Types of programming

Programmed material can be presented in the following conventional style : (1) Linear program; (2) Branching program; (3) Mathetics program and (4) Adjunct auto-instructional program.

17.4.1 Linear program

Linear program was developed by B.F. Skinner. After experiments on rats and pigeons, Skinner established that, both animals and human beings can be led to desired goal by presenting carefully structured material in small steps provided each step is rewarded by favourable experience.

In linear program the learner proceeds in a series of short steps which ensure a high rate of correct response to the frames. The process of learning through linear program may be explained as follows :

Linear Model

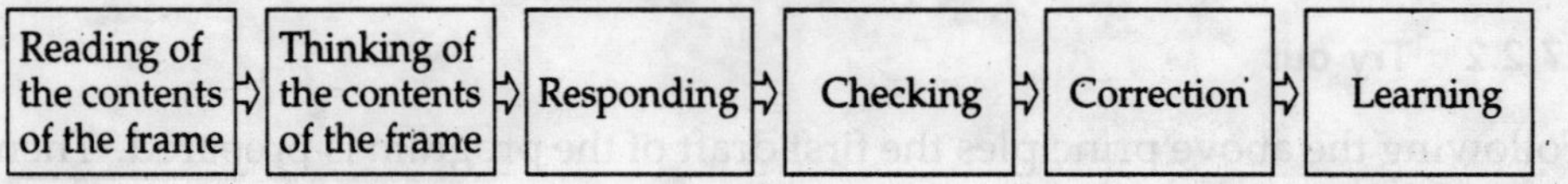

Fig. 17.1

In a linear program, responses are controlled by the programmer. The learner has no freedom to respond in his own way. However, he can immediately compare his answer with the answer of the program. There are provision for prompts or cues in the program to facilitate learning.

17.5 Limitations of linear program

1. It can be used in limited areas where the performance is measurable and observable. It cannot cover the whole syllabus. Difficult portions of science and mathematics can best be taught through linear program.
2. It is alleged that as freedom of choice is limited in this type of program, the creative thinking of the learner is inhibited.
3. Linear programming is mechanical. It does not properly motivate the learner and learning becomes dull and monotonous.
4. It can be used in limited areas of learning only. The language skill, for example, cannot be developed through this method.
5. Only trained and experienced person can develop a good program book. Such persons are not easily available.
6. In case of program book the learner may copy the correct response given in the book without going through the frames.
7. Preparation of program material is too much time-consuming and the electronic teaching-machines are costly also. In fact, it is not possible to provide every student of a big crowded class with teaching-machine. However, a good programmed book will enable a learner to master hard and complicated materials.

17.5.1 Branching program

The branching program was developed by Norman A. Crowder. In this type of program, frames are of large size and may consist of two to three paragraphs.

The questions are of multiple choice type and students have to make choice. If the learner can select correct response, his response is confirmed and in case of wrong response, he is routed to material which explains the cause of his mistakes.

The process of learning through branching program may be shown as follows.

Branching Model

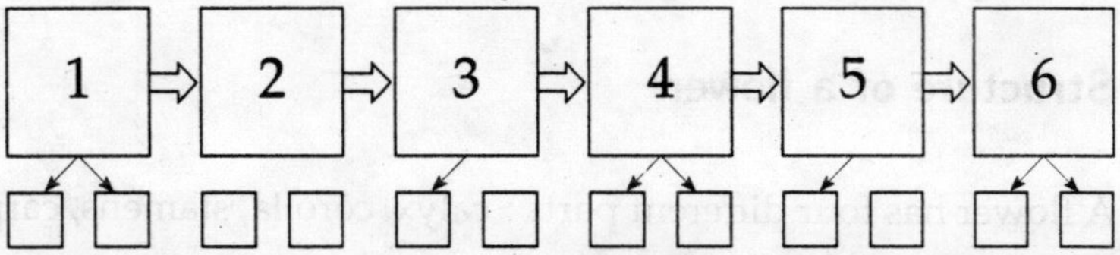

Fig. 17.2

Characteristics of branching program : In this type of program, learners have freedom to select their own path of action. They control the exact sequence to be followed.

The important feature of branching program is that the material presented is directly controlled by the learner's performance in responding questions. When the errors are detected the learner is routed to the frame which explains as to why he is wrong. Thus the learner comes to know the cause of his mistake.

Limitations of branching program : The cost of construction of such program is very high. Moreover, it cannot cater to the needs of all individuals. This type of program cannot be used in lower classes because small children cannot understand its mechanism.

17.5.2 Mathetics program

This type of program has been developed by Thomas F. Gilbert. It is just the reverse of Skinner's linear program. In Skinner's linear program the procedure followed is from parts to the whole, whereas in mathetics program the procedure is from the whole to the parts.

17.5.3 Adjunct auto-instructional program

Prof. S.L. Pressey has developed this program. This type of program is used along with the lesson as and when necessary. Particularly, in case of a complicated lesson, this type of program is very useful.

17.6 A model of a program

A brief draft of a program on the structure of a flower is shown below. Each frame is clearly written on a card and properly arranged to form a program book.

This program book on structure of a flower is presented before the learner. Going through this book the learner will have an idea of the structure of a flower. He will be able to show the different parts of a flower, label the picture and answer questions relating to the structure of the flower.

17.7 Structure of a flower

Step 1. A flower has four different parts : calyx, corolla, stamens, carpel.

(a) How many parts a flower has?

(b) The different parts of a flower are : calyx, stamens, carpel, — —

Correct response : (a) four, (b) corolla.

Step 2. See the picture (A) on the left-side and observe carefully its different parts. Label the picture on the right-side (B).

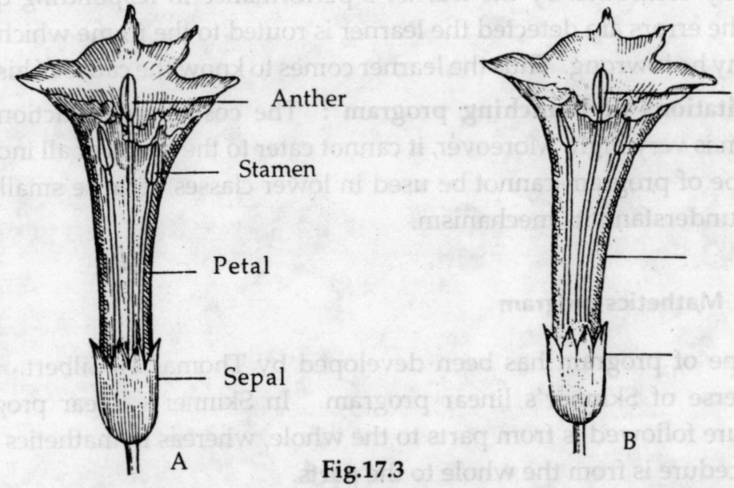

Fig.17.3

Step 3. Sepals are green in colour. They have close resemblance with the leaves.

The colour of the sepals is : red/yellow/ green (underline the correct one).

The sepals have close resemblance with — —

Correct response : (i) green, (ii) leaves.

Step 4. Stamens are the male organs of the flowers. Each stamen consists of filament and anther (see Fig. 17.4).

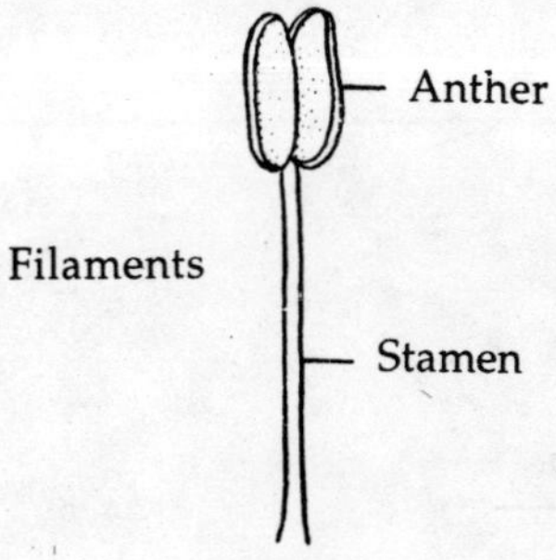

Fig.17.4

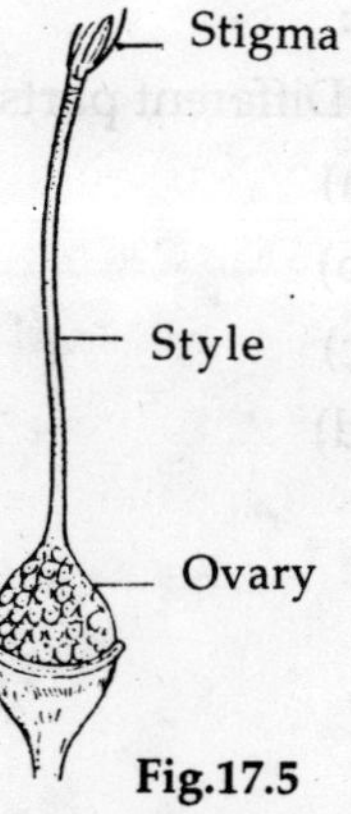

Fig.17.5

The anther possesses pollen sac which contains pollen mother cells.

(i) Stamens are : male organs, female organs. (Tick the correct one).

(ii) Each stamen consists of — and —.

(iii) Pollen sac contains —.

Correct response : (i) male organs, (ii) filament, anther, (iii) pollen mother cells.

Fig.17.6

Step 5. Carpels are the female organ of the flower :

Each carpel consists of three parts :

(i) Stigma, (ii) style, (iii) ovary.

(see fig. 17.5).

(i) Female organ of the flower —

(ii) Each carpel consists of (i) —, (ii) — (iii) —.

Response : (a) carpel, (b) (i) stigma, (ii) style, (iii) ovary.

(iii) Label correctly :

Fig.17.7

Step 6. Label the different parts of the flower correctly.

Post test :

Q. (1) Different parts of the flower are :

(a)

(b)

(c)

(d)

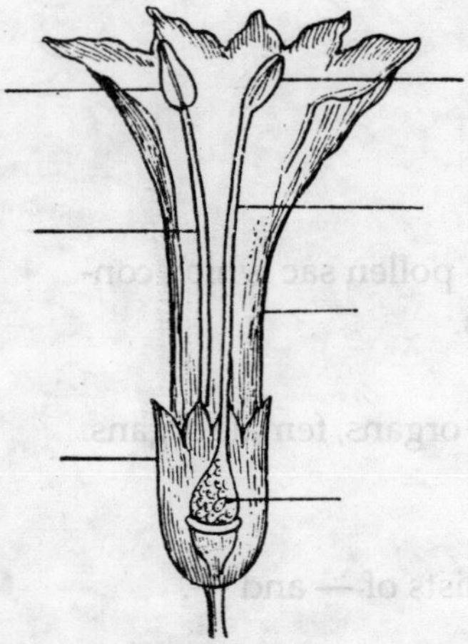

Fig. 17.8

Q. (2) Tick the correct one : The colour of the calyx is : red/green/black.

Q. (3) Carpel has three parts :

(i)

(ii)

(iii)

(4) Stamen has two parts : (i) Filament, (ii) —.

(5) Label different parts of the given flower (Fig. 17.8) :

17.8 Use of programmed instruction

Programmed material in different subjects is now widely used in U.S.A. and other developing countries for the benefit of students.

Programmed instructional material may be used in the following areas :

1. Both in secondary and primary level programs may be used in selected areas. Particularly, difficult portions of mathematics and science can be taught through programs.
2. Programmed materials can be used in teacher's training colleges also.

3. Programmed material may be successfully used for improving the knowledge of non-formal students.
4. Those who continue their higher education through correspondence course, may be supplied with programmed materials for self-study.
5. Programmed material may be used to enrich the knowledge of gifted children. Also special programs can be developed for exceptional and deviant children.
6. Programmed materials are now used in vocational training centres also.
7. Programmed materials are now widely used in banks and air force to keep the personnel abreast of new developments in those fields.

17.9 Role of teachers

Considering the great importance of programming it may appear that if the system of auto-education is introduced through programmed learning in our schools, there will be no need of teachers at all. Pushing the button of teaching-machine will simply solve all problems of the learners. They will proceed at their own space according to their ability and learn everything from the program without the help of the teacher.

But it is an absurd idea. We cannot dispense with our teachers. The importance of the role of teachers has not been at all diminished with the advent of programmed instruction. In the traditional method the teacher has to plan his lesson, explain the subject matter and put questions to the learners to ascertain their knowledge. When needed he has to explain certain problems on the blackboard by drawing figures and graphs. In the program learning technique the teacher has no such role to play.

In teaching through program the teacher has to act as Director, Analyst and Tutor. The help of a teacher in planning and developing a program is extremely needed. The teacher modifies his program on the basis of the mode of responses of the learner. Besides these, the teacher has to explain and discuss certain points of the program. The teacher has to do these jobs with skill. That is, on the whole, the monitoring of the program is a responsibility of the teacher.

Summary

B.F. Skinner developed a teaching-learning model, which is known as programmed learning. Programmed learning is a learner-oriented system in which learning material can be presented to help auto-instruction. It is widely used in America and other advanced countries. Programmed materials can be presented to the learner either in book form or through a machine. As teaching-machine is costly, we can profitably use well-planned programmed books in different subjects. A well-developed program serves better than an incompetent teacher.

Specially when teachers fail to explain certain difficult portions of science and mathematics within limited school hours, Programmed book may serve as supplementary book.

References

1. Chauhan, S.S. : *A Text Book of Programmed Instruction*, 2nd edition. Sterling Publishers (P) Ltd. New Delhi, 1985.
2. Edward, F.O'Day : *Programmed Instruction : Techniques and Trends*, Appleton-Century. New York, 1971.
3. Fry, Edward B. : *Teaching Machines and Programmed Learning*, McGraw Hill. New York, 1963.

Questions and Assignments

1. What is programmed instruction? Discuss its various implications as educational techniques. How does it differ basically from conventional aids?
2. What are the fundamental principles of programming?
3. What is programmed learning? Discuss the various aspects of this system of instruction.
4. What are the different areas of our education where we can use programmed instructional material?
5. Discuss the advantages and limitations of programming.
6. Write notes on:

   (a) Auto-instruction

   (b) Branching program

   (c) Teaching machines.

Chapter 18

Creativity

Importance of creative thinking : Man does not live by bread alone. He is endowed with the most unique power of creative thinking. He always wants to create, something new. He is not a mechanical computer. He is blessed with the capacity to imagine and to think.

Various scientific inventions of today, means of transportation such as, ships, trains, tram, cars, motor cars, aeroplane, and means of communication such as telegraph, telephone, radio, etc. all are the inventions of creative mind.

There are creators of art, painting and architecture, designers of buildings and of clothing, etc.

Skyscarppers, bridges, irrigation system, radar, television, cinema and other scientific inventions testify to the creative genius of mankind.

It is rightly said that survival of a democratic society is intimately linked to a people capable of making wise selections through critical analysis.

18.1 Defining creativity

The term creativity has been defined in various ways. Some of these definitions are :

1. Stein (1974) states that creativity is the process which results in novel work that is accepted as tenable to useful or satisfying to a group of people at some point in time.

   It is a process of hypothesis formation, hypothesis testing and the communication of results. Creative acts terminate in the production of objects which are distinctive.

2. According to Bartlett (1958), creativity is an adventurous thinking or a getting away from the main track, breaking out of the mould, being open to experience and permitting one thing to lead to another.
3. According to Wallach and Kogan (1965), creativity lies in producing more associations and in producing more that are unique.
4. According to David Ausubel (1963), creativity is a generalised constellation of intellectual abilities, personality variables and problem-solving traits.
5. According to Spearman, creativity is the power of the human mind to create new contents by transforming relations and thereby generating new correlates.

Creativity is the ability to invent and develop new and original ideas, especially in an artistic way (Collins English Language Dictionary).

Most of the definitions of creativity emphasize novelty or newness as the important factor of creativity. The creative thinker is capable of exploring new areas and making new observations, new predictions and new inferences.

18.2 Nature of creativity

1. Creativity is not a single dimension of personality. It is made up of a number of traits which can be determined by the technique of factor analysis.
2. Creativity indicates the power of an individual to produce something new or unusual. But all individuals may not invent entirely a new idea or object. The ability to reshape or rearrange the already known facts may also be regarded as creativity of an individual. All kinds of planning and construction of new things involve creative thinking.
3. According to MacKinnon (1963), the most important characteristic of creative persons is that they are intelligent and original in thought and action. But in fact, there is hardly any positive correlation between intelligence and creativity. It has been found that persons having low I.Q. in intelligence test often produce something very original. According to Kitano and Kirby (1986), an individual can be extremely bright but uncreative, or highly creative but not necessarily intellectually gifted. However, a creative person must have a minimum level of intelligence above the average.
4. Divergent thinking is considered to be an important characteristic of creative persons. Taylor (1963) noted the importance of divergent thinking, especially in production of ideas, fluencies, flexibility and originality.

5. Creativity is considered as a God-given gift and an innate endowment. Only a very few can think creatively. But we cannot ignore the influence of training and education on nurturing creativity. The old myth that creativity is the function of superior genes has been exploded. Now it has been established that every individual is creative—in a greater or lesser degree. So, the development of creativity cannot be left to chance alone.

Creativity depends upon two factors : (a) Good inborn talent, as well as (b) Good cultural environment. Thus creativity may be considered as the product of both heredity and environment.

18.3 Theories of creativity

There are several theories of creativity. Some of them may be discussed here.

18.3.1 Creativity is inborn

According to this theory creativity is innate and hereditary. It cannot be produced by training or education. Great scientists like Einstein or Newton were born with extraordinary innate talent. No training can produce a second Einstein. Dr. Sandra Witelson, the Mc Master University neuro Scientist, studied brain structure of Einstein. He found that although Einstein's brain was no bigger than average men, there was no parietal operculum in it and this led to the inferior parietal lobe becoming 15% bulkier. The inferior pareital lobe is the seat of mathematical and visual reasoning. The genius, therefore, was destined to hit upon big ideas. Does not this recent finding imply that geniuses are only born, not made?

18.3.2 Creativity is acquired

The power of creativity is acquired and nurtured like other qualities of human being. Creativity is the product of culture and environment. Proper environment inspires the creative mind, while lack of opportunities cripples it.

18.3.3 Creativity is equivalent to insanity

A highly creative person's behaviour is often eccentric. He often behaves like an insane.

Creative persons are mostly introvert in their behaviour. But to say that creative persons are abnormal is quite incorrect. No positive correlation has been established between creativity and insanity.

18.3.4 Creativity is the expression of repressed sexual desires

According to Freud, all creative works of art are the expressions of repressed sexual desires. Creativity, according to the psychoanalysts, provides an opportunity for catharsis of libidinal energy. The subconscious mind plays an important role in the creative expression of an individual.

18.4 Characteristics of creative person

It is difficult to present uniform personality traits of a creative person. The psychologists like Cattel, Foster and Torrance have produced different lists of traits attributed to the creative persons, some of which may be enumerated below :

1. Capability of divergent thinking.
2. Flexibility and originality of ideas.
3. Foresight.
4. Good memory and intelligence.
5. A creative imagination.
6. Ethical sensitiveness.
7. Enthusiasm for solution of problems.
8. Ability to work out details of a plan.

18.5 Stages in creative process

There are four stages of creative process : 1. Preparation. 2. Incubation. 3. Inspiration. 4. Verification.

Preparation : In this period facts are collected from past experiences.

Incubation : This is a period of no progress. But in the unconscious mind search goes on to find a solution of the problem.

Inspiration : In this stage new pattern towards the solution of the problem seems to emerge all on a sudden, when the individual is occupied with something else.

Verification : In this stage the inspiration is checked to find out whether the solution appeared is consistent with reality.

18.6 Tests of creativity

Creativity is not a single trait of personality. It is composed of a number of traits which can be determined by a multi-dimensional approach, such as, intelligence tests, personality tests, interest inventories, aptitude tests etc.

There are many standardised tests for determining creativity and some of them are :

1. Guilford's divergent thinking instruments.
2. Minnesota tests of creative thinking.
3. Wallach & Kogan creativity instruments.
4. Torrance tests of creative thinking.

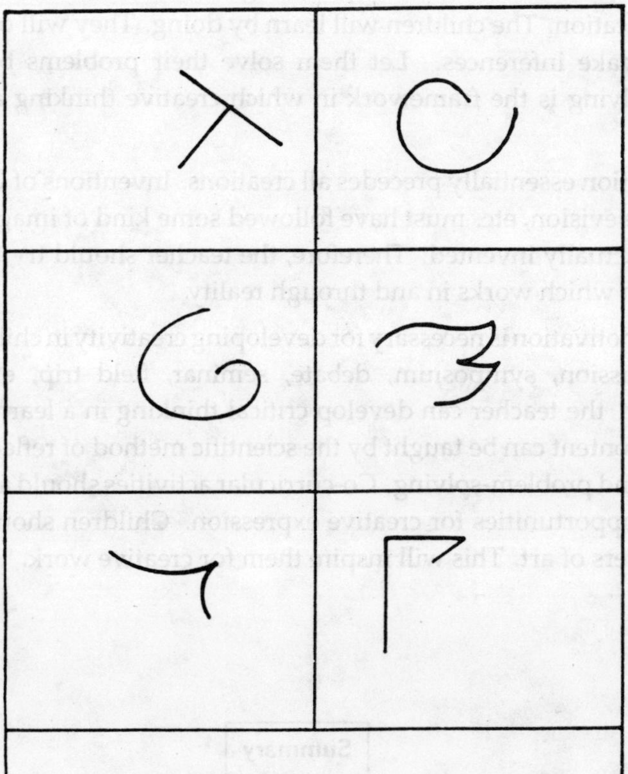

Sample Items from the Torrance tests of creative thinking

(Figural form)

Fig. 18.1: Creativity picture completion test.

Like intelligence tests, creativity tests include both verbal and non-verbal activities. For example, in picture completion test of Torrance, the subject is asked to complete some figures, at the same time, to make them meaningful and provide a suitable title for each figure.

18.7 Creativity and education

Like other qualities creative ideas need to be nurtured. Education can play significant role in the development of creative efficiency.

Many children have latent creative talent but often social pressure discourages them. In the traditional system of education children have very little scope for creative thinking. The function of the teacher is only to stuff their brain with facts and information. But, according to Whitehead, a merely well-informed man is, surely, the most useless bore on God's earth. He has said, "From the beginning of his education the child should experience the joy of discovery."

The teacher should remain in the background and create an environment of auto-education. The children will learn by doing. They will observe, collect data and make inferences. Let them solve their problems by themselves. Problem-solving is the framework in which creative thinking and reasoning take place.

Imagination essentially precedes all creations. Inventions of Gramaphones, Wireless, Television, etc. must have followed some kind of imagination before they were actually invented. Therefore, the teacher should try to cultivate an imagination which works in and through reality.

Strong motivation is necessary for developing creativity in children. Through panel discussion, symposium, debate, seminar, field trip, excursion, role playing, etc. the teacher can develop critical thinking in a learner. In fact, all curricular content can be taught by the scientific method of reflective thinking, reasoning and problem-solving. Co-curricular activities should also be used for providing opportunities for creative expression. Children should be allowed to visit centers of art. This will inspire them for creative work.

Summary

Man is endowed with the unique power of creative thinking. Creativity is defined as the ability to invent and develop new and original ideas. Divergent thinking is considered to be an important characteristic of creative process by Taylor.

There are several theories of creativity. The theory considering creativity as something inborn and innate cannot be accepted. In fact, creativity is the product of both heredity and environment. Similarly, the theory which considers creativity as equivalent to insanity may be rejected.

For determination of creativity various types of standardised tests are used. The Minnesota tests of creative thinking and Torrance Tests of creative thinking are examples of creative tests.

Education plays an important role in the development of creative ability. Both through curricular content and cocurricular activities creative thinking can be nurtured in children. They should be given adequate freedom to solve problems in their own way. Originality in any form should be encouraged by the teachers and parents.

References

1. Bartlett, F.C. : *Thinking—An Experimental and Social Study,* London : Allen & Unwin, 1958.

2. Kitano, M.K. and Kirby, D.E. : *Gifted Education : A Comprehensive View,* Boston : Little Brown, 1986.

3. Gowan, J.C., Demos, G.D. and Torrance, E. : *Creativity,* John Wiley & Sons. Inc. New York. London, Sydney.

4. Mongal, S.K. : *Advanced Educational Psychology,* Prentice-Hall of India Private Limited. New Delhi 100 001, 1997.

5. Stein, M.I. : *Stimulating Creativity,* Vol I : Individual Procedures. New York : Academic Press, 1974.

Questions and Assignments

1. Define creativity. Can creativity be equated with insanity?
2. Discuss different theories of creativity.
3. Describe the importance of creative thinking.
4. What is the psychoanalytical theory of creative thinking?
5. What are the different stages of creative process?
6. What are the characteristics of creativity? How can creativity be tested?
7. Describe the role of teachers in developing creativity in children.
8. How creative potential be identified?
9. To be creative, is it necessary that a person must have a high level of intelligence?

Chapter 19

Attention and interest

Meaning : The word attention is frequently used in our day-to-day conversation. A teacher while teaching in a class calls for his students' attention to what he is saying. Parents ask their children to be attentive to their lesson. Thus, attention is taken to be a mental faculty and we believe that through proper effort and exercise we can increase the power of attention. But this notion is not correct.

Kulpe considers, attention as a state of consciousness. Bentley equates attention with clearness. He says, attention is a name for the attribute of clearness.

According to Titchner, attention is identical with sensory clearness. He preferred the word attensity, an attribute of sensory experience. By attensity he meant what is often called clearness, vividness or prominence. In the opinion of McDougall, attention is merely connation or striving considered from the point of view of its effect on cognitive process.

According to Stout, attention is connation determining cognition. Ross thinks that, attention is a process of getting an object or thought clearly before the mind.

According to Dumville, attention is the concentration of consciousness upon one subject rather than upon another.

Woodworth has emphasised the selective process of attention. Woodworth says : We are usually immersed in a sea of potential stimuli, each of which is capable of eliciting one or more responses. Yet we behave in a consistent and integrated fashion; irrelevant or conflicting stimuli do not generally elicit responses that would interfere with the present course of action. This selective factor has long been designated by the term attention.

The behaviourists have rejected attention as a mere traditional mentalistic concept. The Gestalt psychologists also have regarded any force of attention as extraneous to the field forces which, in their view, are the dynamic factors in human activity. Titchner and Gestalt psychologists have both neglected the functional aspect of attention.

19.1 Characteristics of attention

1. **Clarity of perception :** Attention is a process of focussing of consciousness on an idea or object of thought. Therefore, it consists in getting an object of thought clearly before the mind. Out of a number of stimuli that are present in our normal state of consciousness, some are more vivid, others are dim. Those which are vivid are at the focus of our consciousness, those that are less vivid are said to be at the margin. For instance, if we are looking at a bowler in a cricket match, the bowler is at the focus of our consciousness and the rest of the players remain at the margin. Thus clarity of perception is an important attribute of attention.
2. **Selectivity :** At any moment numerous stimuli act upon our sense organs. All these make a bid for our attention. We continuously select some of them and attend to them. We leave other stimuli unnoticed. Thus attention has two aspects—positive and negative. Selection is the positive aspect of attention. Rejection is the negative aspect of mind.
3. **Shifting :** Attention is highly shifting or mobile in nature. It shifts from one object to another and cannot be fixed on an object for more than eight or ten seconds. If we hold a watch near the ear, we will hear a comparatively loud sound and then a faint sound, though the sound of the ticking of the watch does not vary. This change in our hearing the sound is due to fluctuation of attention.

   You can study the process of shifting of attention by using Kohler cross. Look at the figure with the black as the cross and the white as the background. Record the moment when a shift occurs, the white becoming the cross and the black the background.

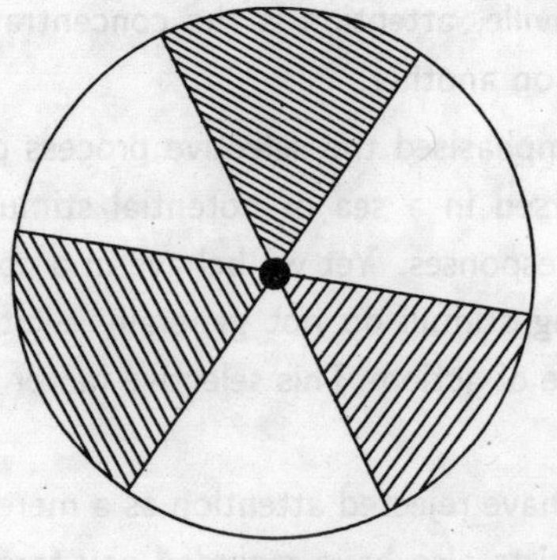

Fig. 19.1

4. **Motor adjustments :** Attention involves certain motor adjustments. James and Ribot regard these physical changes as attention. Indian Yogis also practise various Asanas for concentration of mind.

   In sensory attention, the whole body is adjusted to the object of attention. For instance, when we watch a game, we crane our neck and adjust the whole body to the object of attention. Sensory attention is always accompanied by accomodatory movements of the concerned sense organ. When a person strongly attends to any object, he becomes tense, his brow wrinkles, his fists are clenched. In very close attention to sensible objects our body becomes tense and motionless.

   There are certain other movements due to individual peculiarities. Some persons compress their lips, some scratch their heads, some pull their beard.

   In ideational attention also there is slight adaptation of the sense organs concerned with the objects. If we attempt to recall the image of a temple seen long ago, our eyes tend to turn in the direction of the imagined temple. In recalling a taste we make slight movements of the tongue.

Thus, from the above discussion we find certain important characteristics of attention :

1. Attention is essentially a process, and not a product.
2. It helps in our awareness of our environment.
3. This awareness is selective.
4. At any time, we can concentrate on one particular object only.
5. Attention is highly shifting or mobile in nature.
6. Attention is not merely a cognitive function but is essentially determined by emotional and connative factors of interest and attitude.
7. Attention involves certain sensory and motor adjustments.

19.2 Kinds of attention

William James divides attention into : (a) Immediate and (b) Derived attention. Attention is immediate, when its object is itself interesting. When we attend to the delicious dishes in a feast, our attention is immediate. But when we attend to a lecture in mathematics without feeling any interest in it but only to pass an examination, our attention is derived.

Angel distinguishes between analytical and synthetical attention according to its function. When one attends to a tree and analyses it into its component parts, e.g., roots, branches, leaves etc., his attention is analytical. But, when he attends to the roots, branches, leaves etc., and combine them into a complex whole (tree) his attention is synthetical.

Again, attention may be divided into sensory and ideational attention according to the nature of its objects. Sensory attention is attention to sensible object. When we attend to a house or a tree, our attention is sensory. Ideational attention is attention to ideas, thoughts, emotions and volitions.

Thus, psychologists have classified attention in a variety of ways. However, Ross (1951) has given a more acceptable classification.

Table 19.2 : Classification of attention.

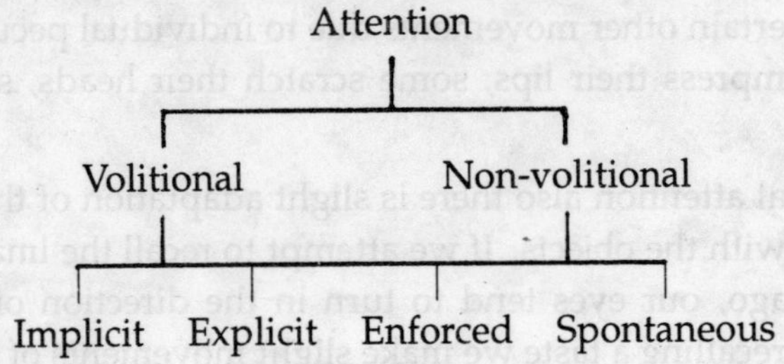

19.2.1 Volitional attention

Volitional attention involves a conscious effort of will or volition. When a single effort of will is required, attention is called implicitly volitional. But when more than one effort of will is required attention is said to be explicitly volitional. For instance, when a student attends to a lecture in the class in spite of some noise outside, he has voluntary attention. If the student having made up his mind once keeps on listening to the lecture, his attention is implicitly volitional. But if he has to struggle hard to continue to be attentive and has to make several efforts to bring his mind to the task, the process will be called explicitly volitional. In explicit volitional attention, attention is obtained through repeated acts of volition.

19.2.2 Non-volitional attention

It is spontaneous and does not involve an effort of volition. Non-volitional attention is sub-divided into : (a) Enforced non-volitional and (b) Spontaneous non-volitional. The attention which is aroused by our instincts is called non-volitional attention. For example, a young man while occupied in reading a book, his attention to a young girl may be termed as enforced non-volitional attention.

The spontaneous non-volitional attention is aroused by our sentiment. We pay spontaneous attention to the objects around which our sentiments have already been formed. For example, when we attend to a patriotic song, it becomes spontaneous non-volitional attention.

Non-volitional attention appears early in life, because it does not involve an effort of the will and it is directed towards interesting objects. It is determined by native interest.

For building character of a grown up student, it is the volitional attention that has to be made use of. The sentiment of self-regard has to be appealed to.

However, for teaching small children, the teacher should make as little use of volitional attention as possible. He should take the aid of innate dispositions.

19.2.3 Conditions of attention

The conditions of attention are classified as objective and subjective.

Objective conditions : The objective conditions are found in the attributes of the stimuli that act on the sense-organs. They are :

1. **Intensity :** Loud sounds, bright colour and dazzling light attract attention. Large objects, coloured pictures command the attention of the students better than small objects and pictures without colours. The teacher who speaks loudly commands the attention of the students than the one who speaks in a low voice.

2. **Size :** Size is an important condition of attention. The advertiser uses large type to attract the attention of the prospective customers. Full page or half page advertisements in the newspapers easily attract our attention. But small advertisements escape our attention. The full moon easily attracts our attention but small stars may not attract our attention.

3. **Novelty :** Teachers who are shouting all the time do not command the attention of the class when their voice becomes familiar to them. But, when a new teacher comes and speaks, the attention of the students is attracted. The advertiser uses coloured lights and pictures to attract the attention of customers.

4. **Change :** Change brings novelty with it. The teacher who changes the devices of his teaching, captures the attention of the class much more than the one who does not. To control the attention of the class, change of voice, repetition, pause, emphasis, gesture sometimes become necessary.

   However, the change must not be too gradual if it is to be effective; it must have a degree of suddenness. If a noise suddenly drops into calmness, it is bound to attract our attention. We do not notice the ticking of a clock on the wall but it arrests our attention as soon as it stops.

5. **Movement :** The objects that move capture our attention more easily than those that remain stationary. A motor car or a train is more likely to attract attention while running than when it is not in motion. Advertisements by means of moving electric lights easily catch our attention.

6. **Repetition :** If a stimulus is repeated, it is likely to draw our attention. The teacher repeats the same lesson over and over again to attract the attention of the students. He repeatedly writes a difficult word on the board to attract the attention of the class.
7. **Isolation :** When one particular stimulus is kept isolated from other stimuli, the isolated stimulus shall attract our attention. If an advertisement is placed with a number of advertisements, then it will escape our attention. But if the advertisement is placed in a separate place it will captivate our attention.
8. **Contrast :** Contrast is a distinct factor of advantage. A tall man by the side of a short man or a white man in the midst of dark coloured men is sure to attract our attention.
9. **Duration :** If the stimulus lingers for sometime, it is very likely to catch our attention. A song, if continued for a minute, may escape our notice. But, if it is continued for half an hour, it is very likely to capture our attention.
10. **Definite form :** What is vague does not catch our attention. A clear picture catches the attention of the students much more than a hazy one.

19.3 Subjective conditions

The subjective or mental conditions of attention are :

1. **Interest :** We attend to those objects which interest us. Those who are interested in games will naturally attend to the news of matches in the newspaper. Those who are interested in film shows will attend to the cinema page of the newspaper. An able teacher draws the attention of the class by making his lesson interesting.
2. **Instincts :** Different instincts compel attention to their specific objects which excite them. Thus, when we are hungry we attend to bread and food. A bird attends to the materials of a nest-building before laying eggs. A mad dog captures our attention because of our innate fear. Thus different instincts compel attention to their specific objects which excite them.
3. **Emotion :** Attention is determined by emotions. A lover, for instance, attends only to the good qualities of his beloved. But we attend only to the bad qualities of our enemy. In intense emotions we often attend to minute details which pass unnoticed at normal moments.
4. **Training and habit :** Previous experience and training facilitate attention. Training builds up habits. A geologist attends to the peculiarities of minerals and a zoologist attends to peculiarities of animals because of previous education and habit.

5. **Desire :** Desire leads attention to its object. Often feeling of want gives rise to desire. Objects of our desire are apt to attract our attention. Generally we hear or see what we want to hear or see.

Some other factors of attention are :

1. **Social influence :** A child often imbibes certain ideas from his family and society. He develops certain sentiments in course of social contact. He owes his moral and religious sentiments mostly to the influence of his family and society. Thus, a Christian attends to a church or a Hindu attends to a temple because of social influence.
2. **Hereditary disposition :** Certain traits of an individual, e.g., taste for music, are said to be inherited from the parents. A person who inherits religious disposition from his parents naturally takes a keen interest in religion and attends to religious discourses. Thus, heredity may determine attention.

Watson thinks that, objective conditions alone capture attention. But McDougall holds that, subjective conditions are more significant than the objective conditions of attention. In actual experience, we find both objective and subjective conditions co-operating in determining attention. But the subjective conditions dominate the objective conditions. We attend to intense, sudden and novel sense-impressions because they excite in us curiosity, fear or both. A sound which is very loud does not sometimes attract our attention, whereas gentle taps at the door, if significant, catch our attention. So, the objective conditions in themselves are not enough to determine attention. They are controlled by the subjective conditions. The objective conditions are ineffective without the subjective conditions.

19.4 Attention and interest

Meaning of interest : Interest means what matters. While attention is selective activity of the mind, it is determined by interest. It is a mental structure which supplies the driving power needed for connative activity. Interest, according to Drever, is a disposition in its dynamic aspect.

Relation with attention : According to McDougall, "Interest is latent attention and attention is interest in action." Ross supported the view of McDougall and said that, attention and interest are the two sides of the same coin.

When we speak of an interest, we refer to an affective disposition. An interest is not an affective experience. It is of the nature of a disposition. It is structure of the mind, not a function of it.

Interest is a subjective condition of attention. The greater the interest, the greater the attention. But attention is not always accompanied by interest. We attend to many things in which we do not find any interest. In fact, attention and interest do not always go together. They are not identical with each other.

Span of attention : How many things can be attended to at once? In a strict psychological sense only one object, idea, or fact can be the centre of consciousness at one particular moment. Hence, we can attend to only one thing at a time. However, we see some people who can attend to more than one task at the same time. But this is wrong. Here, there is a rapid shifting of attention from one task to another. Jelias Calesar and Michael Madhusudan used to dictate to several secretaries at a time. This could be done only by the rapid shifting of attention from one task to another.

Experiments : Experiments have been made to find out as to how many objects an individual can attend to at the same time.

The span of visual attention is measured by an instrument called Tachistoscope. It consists of a wooden screen having a window in the middle. A number of letters, digits or dots are presented through the window. The exposure is quite short, generally one-tenth of a second. The subject can attend to only four or five items, if the items are not grouped into familiar units. But if the items are grouped into meaningful wholes, for example, letters are arranged into words, a large number of items can be perceived at once.

The experiments of Glanville and Dallenbach on span of attention show the following results :

1. Number of dots 8.8 inches.
2. Number of letters 6.9 inches.
3. Number of geometrical figures 3.8 inches.
4. Coloured geometrical figures 3.0 inches.

The span of auditory attention is measured by metronome. Experiments have shown that an adult subject can perceive eight sounds given rapidly in succession, when sounds are given in a rhythm, a much larger number of sounds can be perceived.

The significance of span of attention : The experiment on span of attention does not prove that we can attend to many things at the same time. At any time we can be aware of only one thing. These experiments, in fact, measure our power of remembering the different units once seen.

We can attend to a general subject containing elements for several hours. The duration of attention depends upon the nature of the material, the interest of the observer, and other conditions. But we can attend to one object exclusively for only a second. There is shifting of attention within sustained attention which may continue for a long time. Now, under control of a purpose or interest, attention shifts frequently but is confined within narrow limits.

Distraction : When we attend to one thing, often our attention is distracted by other things. When a student reads a book, his attention may be diverted to music in an adjoining house. Any thing that interferes with attention is called distraction. Distraction causes inattention. Woodworth defines distraction as a stimulus that attracts attention away from the thing to which we mean to attend. Often a distraction destroys the efficiency of attention.

Distraction may be overcome in the following ways :

1. Distraction may be overcome by throwing greater energy into the task at hand. For instance, while reading, you may read aloud to drown the distracting noise.
2. Distraction may be overcome by forming a habit of inattention to the distraction. Distractions will loose their force automatically when one is absorbed in an interesting task.

Distractions cannot be overcome by directly fighting them. A conscious effort to get rid of distractions, in fact, keeps them in the foreground of consciousness.

However, it is wrong to assume that distractions always destroy the efficiency of work. At times they increase the efficiency of work instead of decreasing it. Experiments show that distraction act as a stimulus to greater effort and by this effort the distraction is overcome. When distracted, the individual gets an incentive to act. Of course, when the distraction is violent, it decreases efficiency of work because our mental energy fails to cope with it.

Fluctuation of attention : Attention is highly shifting in nature. It shifts from one object to another and cannot be fixed on an object for a long time. The focus of attention generally keeps changing—making the process of attention flexible.

The phenomenon of fluctuation of auditory attention may be studied by holding a watch near the ear of the subject. He does not continuously hear the sound of the watch with same intensity. At times he is able to hear the ticking of the clock, but at other times the sound disappears. This change in hearing the sound is due to fluctuation of attention.

Experiment : The study of fluctuation of visual attention can be studied with the help of a Masson's disc. The Masson's disc consists of a circular cardboard having five patches of ink put in a line along one radius (see Fig. 19.3). The circular disc can be rotated by an electric motor. When the disc rotates, each dot appears to the subject a circle. The subject is asked to concentrate on any one of the grey circles on the rotating disc and to report when the circle is visible and when it becomes blurred or disappears. From the smoked-drum of Kymograph a picture of positive phase and negative phase of attention of the subject will be obtained.

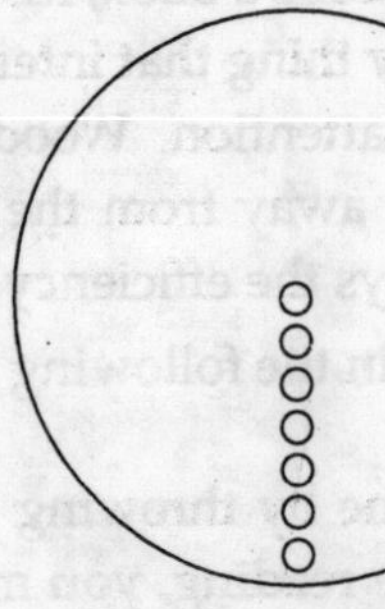

Fig. 19.3: Masson's disc.

It is seen from the above experiments that the rate of fluctuation of attention is 8–10 seconds. That is, we cannot attend to an object for more than ten seconds. Some scientists think that, such fluctuations take place due to frequent contraction of the ciliary muscles of the eye. But it has been seen that fluctuation of attention takes place even when ciliary muscles are rendered inactive by using atropine.

Sustained attention : Sustained attention consists in focusing the mind on an object for a considerable period of time. Woodworth says, "To sustain attention is to concentrate one's activity continuously upon some object or happening or problem."

In case of sustained attention, the activity goes on without interruption and serious distraction. One striking example of sustained attention is to be found in an astronomer sitting with his eyes fixed on a particular star while looking through his telescope.

In order to hold attention to a task for a considerable period of time favourable environmental conditions for work is a primary need. Moreover, genuine interest in the task is to be developed in the individual. His will-power for sustained work should equally be developed.

Lack of interests, fatigue and presence of distraction are some of the obstacles in the path of sustained attention. So, these are to be avoided by all means.

Educational implications : In the problem of securing attention of the educand to the lesson lies the whole problem of education. Children attend to those things which interest them. The main determinant of their attention is interest. Therefore, the teacher, instead of dull and drab lectures, should try to make his lessons interesting.

The child's interest varies at different stages. The teacher should study them. He should know about the primitive springs of action, that is, instincts and the innate tendencies.

The teacher should illustrate topics with concrete examples. Nothing should be presented to the child for which there is no preparedness in his mind to receive. The teacher should proceed from known to unknown. What is totally unfamiliar to the class can seldom interest it. The topic of instruction should be related to the already existing dispositions in the mind of the child. The teacher should appeal to his instinct of curiosity, of constructiveness, of play or of pugnacity.

Teaching—in order that it may be effective, must be interesting. But this does not mean that the teacher should always cater to the whims of the child and appeal to the instincts of curiosity, pugnacity or other instincts to capture attention of the child. The teacher may start with the natural impulses, but he must ultimately take help from the derived interests of the child. The child should be gradually trained to have sustained attention.

While teaching children, distraction should be kept away, so that they can concentrate on their study. In fact, securing of the absence of distractions, while the children are engaged in their study, is of prime importance. A teacher can fight distractions to the attention of the boys only by making his lesson more interesting.

In the primary stage the child has only non-volitional attention. His attention is guided by instincts. As he grows up we must try to develop volitional attention in him. Gradually he must be taught to attend abstract ideas. In the primary stage the teacher may use various teaching aids to make his lesson interesting and capture thereby the attention of the child. But in the secondary stage the teacher should make an effort to develop thinking and reasoning power in children as because no learning can be effective without these abilities. Students should learn to work hard and concentrate their attention on what is abstract or difficult. They have to put forth volitional attention in order that they make progress in learning. The doctrine of soft pedagogy is psychologically unsound. The teacher may start with the natural instincts but he must soon take help from the derived interests of the child. He is gradually to be trained to master attention by an effort of will.

Summary

Attention is intimately related to the process of learning. The process of attention consists in getting an object of thought clearly before the mind. According to Dumville, attention is the concentration of consciousness upon one subject rather than upon another. Woodworth has emphasised the selective process of attention. Attention is highly shifting. It involves certain motor adjustments. The process of attention includes both physical set and mental set.

Attention may be divided into immediate and derived. Attention is immediate when its object is itself interesting. But when we attend to an object or a task which is not interesting to us but which will serve a particular purpose, our attention is derived.

Ross has classified attention into volitional or voluntary and non-volitional or involuntary. Volitional attention involves a conscious effort of will. Non-volitional attention is spontaneous and does not involve an effort.

Attention is guided and controlled by objective and subjective conditions. The objective conditions are : intensity and size of the stimulus, novelty, change, movement, isolation, contrast, duration, definite form etc. Subjective conditions are : interests, motives, instincts, emotion, habit and other internal factors.

Attention and interest are closely related. They are said to be the two sides of the same coin. Interest is a subjective condition of attention. The greater the interest, the greater the attention.

Normally, we can attend to only one thing at a time. But people like Caeser may attend to more than one task at the same time. They possess a larger span of attention. The span of attention may be defined as the size to which the perceptual field of an individual can be effectively organised in order to enable him to attend to a number of things in a short duration. The span of visual attention is measured by an apparatus called Tachistoscope.

One of the characteristics of attention is that it is highly mobile and shifting. The study of fluctuation of attention can be studied with the help of a Masson's Disc. The experimental results show that the rate of fluctuation of attention is only 8 to 10 seconds.

Distraction interferes with attention. It causes inattention. The external sources of distraction are : noise, improper lighting, etc., and internal distractions are fatigue, bad health, emotional disturbances, etc. Thus, to achieve best results in the process of learning, all such forces of distraction should be overcome. A teacher can fight distractions to the attention of the pupils by making his lesson more interesting.

References

1. Dumville : *The Fundamentals of Psychology,* 3rd ed, London : Univ. Tutorial Press, 1938.
2. Sinha, J.N. : *A Manual of Psychology,* New Cental Book Agency, Calcutta 700 009, 1984.

3. Morgan, J.B. and Gilliand, A.R. : *An Introduction to Psychology,* New York : Macmillian, 1942.

4. Ross, J.S. : *Groundwork of Educational Psychology,* London : G.G. Harrup & Co. 1951.

5. Mangal, S.K. : *Advanced Educational Psychology,* Prentice-Hall of India. New Delhi, 1997.

6. Woodworth, R.S. : *Psychology,* London : Methuen, 1945.

7. Woodworth, R.S. : *Experimental Psychology,* New York : Holt, 1954.

8. Murphy, Gardner : *An Introduction to Psychology,* New Delhi : Oxford & IBH, 1968.

9. Sorenson, Herbert : *Psychology of Education,* New York : McGraw Hill, 1948.

10. Gates, A.I. : *Educational Psychology,* 3rd ed. New York : Macmillan, 1948.

11. Travers, R.M. : *Educational Psychology,* New York : Macmillan, 1973.

Questions and Assignments

1. Define Attention and point out its characteristics. Discuss—Interest is latent attention and attention is interest in action.
2. What are the different stages of attention? Is volitional attention possible without interest?
3. Describe the various conditions of attention with illustrations.
4. What are the educational implications of attention? How can a teacher make his pupil attentive?
5. Write notes on the following:

   (a) Span of attention.

   (b) Fluctuation of attention.

   (c) Interest.

   (d) Inattention.

   (e) Distraction.
6. What are the conditions of attention? How can a teacher secure the attention of the class?
7. Discuss the relation between attention and interest. How can an abstract lesson be made interesting?

8. Point out the distinction between voluntary and non-voluntary attention. How can attention be controlled?

9. What is the best way of dealing with a distracting situation arising during the course of a lesson? What advice would you give to a student to fight his own distractions?

10. Distinguish between spontaneous and voluntary attention. How does the child's attention differ from the adult? Explain fluctuation of attention.

Chapter 20

Emotion

Introduction : The word Emotion is derived from the Greek word 'Emovere', which means excitation. Emotion is a stirred up state of body and mind. When a person acts under emotion, he loses his mental balance.

From the point of introspection, it is a kind of sensation originated from certain physical changes. From the point of behaviour, emotion is a stirred up physical state of an individual. Fear, anger, joy, sorrow, hate are instances of emotion.

20.1 Nature of Emotion

1. Emotions are complex affective states from perception, memory or imagination of a situation. For example, when a mad dog chases us we run away out of fear. Emotions may arise from ideas and thoughts also.

2. Emotions are tinged with feelings. Both of them are affective experiences. Some emotions (e.g., joy, elation) are pleasant. Some other emotions (e.g., fear, sorrow) are unpleasant. The core of an emotional experience is feeling. When feelings are violent and the composure of our mind is disturbed we have no longer feelings but emotions.

3. Wide range is another characteristic of emotion. Emotions can be aroused in the young as well as in the old. The child gets angry if you snatch away his dolls; a man gets angry if somebody criticises his conduct. Even the animals are not free from emotions.

4. Emotion is a function of the whole organism. In it the organism as a whole is aroused.

5. Emotions are closely associated with physiological disturbances in our body. Peculiar organic sensations are aroused along with an emotion. An emotion produces diffused organic reverberations in the internal organs. According to William James, *emotion is simply organic sensation* and nothing else. He says, "If we fancy some strong emotion and try to abstract from our consciousness of it all the feelings of its bodily symptoms, we find, we have nothing left behind."

6. Morgan has pointed out the *swing of an emotion* as an important characteristic of emotional experience. The emotional mood may not persist in the original form. Anger may yield place to fear or love as the changes in the environment take place.

7. Emotions are parasitical in nature, and are based on instincts. Stout has stressed this point. McDougall holds that an emotion is a conscious correlate of an instinctive action. He gives the following pairs of instincts and emotions correlated to each other :

Instinct	Emotion
1. Instinct of escape	Fear
2. Instinct of combat	Anger
3. Instinct of repulsion	Disgust
4. Instinct of curiosity	Wonder
5. Instinct of sex	Lust
6. Parental instinct	Tender emotion
7. Instinct of submission	Inferiority
8. Instinct of assertion	Superiority
9. Gregarious instinct	Loneliness
10. Instinct of acquisition	Ownership
11. Instinct of construction	Creativeness
12. Instinct of laughter	Amusement

8. Violent emotions affect our reasoning and thinking capacity. Under the influence of anger an individual may kill others or may commit suicide. Many undesirable types of personalities are formed because of wrong training of emotions.

Woodworth mentions the following factors of an emotion :

1. The individual's intellectual perception of a situation.
2. His motor set for a certain overt activity such as escape from danger.
3. The organic state in some emotions, though perhaps not in all, depends largely on the autonomic nerves and their centre in the inter-brain.
4. A mass of organic muscular sensations produced by the internal organic activity.
5. The individual's inability to cope with the situation for the time being.
6. Pleasure or pain, excitement or numbness, tenseness or relaxation.

20.2 Kinds of emotions

According to Watson, basic emotions are : fear, anger and love. A child gets afraid on hearing a loud sound. He becomes angry when his movement is restricted. On getting a toy he expresses his joy.

Wundt has divided emotion into three dimensions : pleasant–unpleasant, excitement–calmness and expectation–release. Different kinds of emotions are the product of these three emotions.

McDougall classifies emotions into three kinds : 1. Primary emotions. 2. Secondary emotions and 3. Derived emotions.

1. **Primary emotions** are the elementary correlates of instincts. Fear, anger, disgust, distress, lust, curiosity, etc., which arise from the instincts of escape, combat, repulsion, appeal, sex, wonder, etc. are primary emotions.
2. **Secondary emotions** are the combinations of two or more primary emotions. For example, scorn is a blend of anger and disgust. Similarly jealousy, revenge, gratitude, etc. are blended emotions.
3. **Derived emotions** are the complex feelings. They are neither primary emotions nor blended emotions. They are related to desires, confidence, hope, anxiety, regret, despairs are derived emotions.

20.3 Organic changes in emotions

Emotions and automatic nervous system are intimately connected. The autonomic system is a part of the general nervous system.

There are three divisions of autonomic system—upper, middle and lower. The cranial division connects the brain with the iris muscle of the eye, causing it to contract and with the salivary glands, causing them to secrete saliva. Its other nerves connect with the muscles and glands of the stomach. The other nerves connect with the heart.

The sympathetic division is connected with the central part of the spinal cord. The sympathetic nerves, which run from the spinal cord, have the opposite effect on the heart and the stomach. They hasten the heart-beat and arrest stomach activity. Fear, anger and other strong emotions are connected with those internal changes brought about by stimulation of the sympathetic division.

The sacral division connects the spinal cord with the genital system. The action of sympathetic nerves is opposite to the cranial and the sacral nerves.

The sympathetic part is involved in strong emotions such as fear and anger. The cranial and part of the sacral division are involved in mild, pleasant states. Part of the sacral division is concerned with lust and sex excitement.

Strong emotions are accompanied with palpitation of the heart, increased breathing, rapid circulation of blood and rise in blood pressure. These organic changes can be measured by various scientific apparatus.

Blood pressure is measured by **sphygmomanometer.** During anger, blood pressure increases, while during pleasure and joy it decreases.

During emotion breathing changes. The change of breathing can be determined by **pneumograph.**

In mild fear, surprise and the like, there is a momentary change in the electric condition of the skin, which may be determined by Psycho-Galvanometer.

The organic changes in the stomach and the intestine can be known by X-ray examination. The change in brain-wave is detected by Electroencephalograph.

20.4 Emotion and feeling

Feeling arises from sensation. But it is a diffuse mass of unanalysed sensations. Feeling is always accompanied by mental processes, such as perception, memory, imagination and emotion.

Feelings are simple sense-feelings of pleasure and pain. They arise from sensations. They are peripherally excited. But emotions are complex affective states. They are centrally excited. They are higher and more complex affective states. The pain of hearing a noise is a feeling, but the pain of grief is emotion.

A feeling is expressed in relatively restricted nervous excitement. While an emotion is expressed in wide-ranging excitation involving the voluntary muscles and the viscera.

Both feelings and emotions are affective experiences but they differ in some respects.

Table 20.1 : Comparison between Feeling and Emotion.

Feeling	Emotion
1. Feelings are peripherally excited.	1. Emotions are centrally excited.
2. Feelings arise from sensations.	2. Emotions arise from ideas and thoughts.
3. Feelings are simple sense feelings of pleasure and pain.	3. Emotions are complex affective states from perception, memory or imagination of a situation.
4. Feelings involve no physical change.	4. Physical changes are well-marked in emotion.
5. Feelings are not connected with any of the instincts.	5. Each emotion is connected with an instinct. Emotions are parasitical and based on instincts.
6. Feelings are not aroused by critical situations.	6. Emotions are aroused by emergencies.
7. An individual is not overwhelmed by a feeling.	7. An individual is overwhelmed by an emotion and its reactions.

20.5 Theories of emotion

Commonly, it is believed that an emotion arises from the perception, memory or imagination of a situation and is expressed in organic changes. Thus, according to common belief, first there is perception, ideation or thought of a situation. Then an emotion arises out of it and then the emotion is expressed in organic changes. Thus, emotion appears before physical changes. When we perceive a snake it excites fear in our mind, the emotion of fear gives rise to trembling and running away. The sequence of organic changes and emotions are as follows :

Perception of the situation ⇒ Emotional experience ⇒ Organic reactions

20.5.1 James-Lange theory

William James and Lange propounded just an opposite view of emotion. According to them, the sequence of organic changes and emotion are as follows :

Perception of the situation ⇒ Organic changes ⇒ Emotional experiences

The perception of an object produces organic changes in the internal organs. These are reported to the brain by sensory nerves and produce organic sensations. These organic sensations together with the perception of the object are called emotions.

James says, "My theory is that the bodily changes follow directly the perception of the exciting fact, and that our feeling of the same changes as they occur is the emotion. Common sense says, we lose our fortune, are sorry and weep; we meet a bear, are frightened and run; we are insulated by a rival, are angry and strike. The more rational statement is that we feel sorry because we cry, angry because we strike, afraid because we tremble, and not that we cry, strike or tremble because we are sorry, angry or fearful as the case may be."

Thus, according to James, "An emotion is a mass of organic sensations due to organic changes in the internal organs following upon the perception of an exciting object. Emotion is simply organic sensations and nothing else."

James gave the following arguments in favour of his theory of emotion :

1. We cannot think of an emotion without an organic expression. We cannot think of an anger without frowning, grinding of teeth etc. If we fancy some emotion and then try to abstract from our consciousness of it all the feelings of its bodily symptoms, we find we have nothing left behind, out of which the emotion can be constituted and that a cold and neutral state of intellectual perception is all that remains.

2. Suppression of organic expressions leads to the suppression of corresponding emotions. Refuse to express an emotion, and it dies. (James).

3. The use of alcohol and other stimulants produces certain emotions such as courage, hilarity etc. Here organic conditions are the causes of emotions.

4. Artificial production of organic expressions produces the corresponding emotions. Actors sometime, truly feel angry or sorry by producing the expressions of anger or sorrow while acting.

5. Certain organic disturbances produce certain emotions, e.g., disorders of the liver produce gloom and irritability, nervous diseases produce despondency and fear.

6. In lunatic asylums different insane persons display different emotions of anger, fear, melancholy etc. in the same environment. James holds that these objectless emotions are produced by pathological conditions of the organism. These emotions are nothing but feelings of bodily states, and they have purely physical causes.

20.5.2 Criticism of the James-Lange theory

Sherrington, Cannon, Bird and some physiologists have severely criticised the James-Lange theory of emotion. James-Lange theory is criticised on the following grounds :

1. An emotion is not identical with its expression. If an emotion and its expression always go together, they may be inseparable correlates. They may not be identical with each other. The organic expression does not constitute the whole emotion.
2. If organic expressions constitute the emotions, the same emotions should have the same organic expressions. But in fact, different emotions have the same organic expression. For example, shivering is an expression of fear. But when we shiver from cold, we feel no emotion of fear.
3. The so-called pathological objectless emotions are not really objectless or unmotivated. They are not emotions but emotional moods. They are the persisting after-effects of certain emotions felt by the lunatics in the past. They are not entirely due to organic disturbances.
4. James holds that mere objects being perceived immediately produce organic reflexes. But if organic reactions were mere reflex actions, the same response would be evoked by the same stimuli. There is uniformity of responses in reflex actions. But, in fact, the responses are different according as objects are perceived in different contexts. Ward says, "Let James be confronted by a caged bear and next by a bear at large; to the one object he presents a bun and to the other a clean pair of heels."
5. James ignores the parasitical character of emotions. Emotions are based on instincts. The removal of a kitten from its mother only does not excite anger in the mother cat. But her maternal instinct is thwarted.
6. Sherrington cut the sensory nerves of the dog carrying nerve impulse from the trunk to the brain and deprived it of all visceral sensations—still the dog exhibifed the symptoms of anger, joy, disgust and fear.
7. Cannon severed the sympathetic nerves of a cat and showed that still the cat performed the overt behaviour and expressive movements of anger.

In another experiment Cannon injected adrenalin to a person to evoke artificial physical excitement but he found that no emotion in real sense appeared in the person.

Dana spoke of a woman patient who after an accident lost all connections between her autonomic nerves and brain. This woman remained alive for a year and she showed emotions of sorrow and joy, love and hatred as usual.

20.6 Cannon-Bird theory

According to Cannon (1927) and Bard (1934), Thalamus is really the seat of emotion. Emotion and physical changes take place simultaneously and one is not dependent on the other. Thalamus (or Hypothalamus) control emotion and physical changes. Hypothalamus works in three ways :

1. Emotional impulse from receptor goes to the hypothalamus through afferent nerve.
2. From hypothalamus a part of the impulse passes to the brain. Here the nature of the emotional experiences is determined.
3. Again, from hypothalamus, a part of the impulse passes to muscles, viscera and other organs of our body.

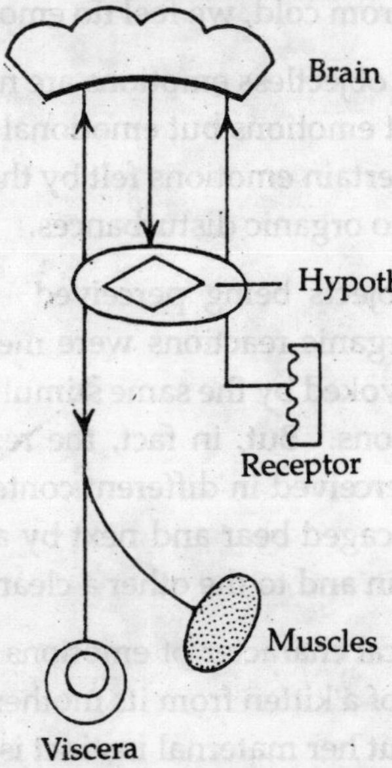

Fig. 20.2: Hypothalamus controls emotion.

Bard removed the cortex and thalamus of some animals and left only the posterior part of the hypothalamus and found that they still showed rage. But when he removed the hypothalamus, they failed to show the integrated rage pattern.

Thus he proved that the hypcthalamus was necessary for the expression of rage.

20.6.1 McDougall's theory of emotion

McDougall holds that emotions are functions of instincts. McDaugall gave a list of 14 pairs of instincts and emotions correlated to each other. He defines instinct as an inherited or innate psycho-physical disposition which determines its possessor to perceive, and to pay attention to, objects of a certain class, to experience an emotional excitement of a particular quality upon perceiving such an object and to act in regard to it in a particular manner or, at least, to experience an impulse to such an action. According to Mc Dougall primary emotions are based on instincts; every specific instinct has specific primary emotion attached to it.

McDougall's theory is very attractive but his list is unscientific. Though emotion and instinct are closely connected with each other, we cannot hold that corresponding to every instinct there is an emotion and corresponding to every emotion there is an instinct. There are many instincts which are not accompanied by any specific emotions. Further, the same emotion may include a variety of instinct in its system. Again, the same expression may be connected with different emotions.

From the above discussion it is clear that no one single theory of emotion is complete in itself. The common view of emotion does not consider physical reactions during emotional experiences as important. Whereas, Sherrington and Cannon's experiment expressed doubt about James-Lange theory. As the behaviourists have entirely neglected the mental processes involved in emotion, their theory also cannot be accepted.

20.7 Analysis of emotions

1. **Anger :** It is an emotion excited by the thwarting of an instinct. According to McDougall the emotion of anger is the affective aspect of the combat instinct. A child becomes angry if his toy is taken away. A man becomes angry if he is insulted.

   In anger our body assumes an aggressive attitude. It is expressed in a violent motor discharge. It is expressed in grinding the teeth, kicking, striking, howling, frowning, etc. If a person is constantly subjected to fits of anger, he may soon suffer from many kinds of formidable diseases.

2. **Fear :** Fear is excited by the apprehension of a dangerous situation. According to McDougall fear is the affective aspect of instinct to escape. It arises from the perception of an object which caused pain or injury in the past.

   Fear is excited by a sudden loud sound or a blinding flash of lighting. A sudden and intense impression excites fear.

   Fear is expressed in quick palpitation of the heart, trembling, drooping of the limbs, running away, etc. Extreme terror causes immobility of the body.

The normal functioning of the thyroid gland is affected both by fear and anger. A constant arousal of these states may tear down our physical health. A general state of fear makes us liable to all kinds of ill-health.

3. **Love :** McDougall calls love the emotion of lust. It is the emotion arising from the sex instinct. Love means a permanent emotional disposition which is manifested in tender emotion.

   Love has two elements, namely, attachment and sympathy. Attachment consists in fondling or caressing. Sympathy is expressed in sharing the emotion of others.

   The emotion of love is conducive to life, while anger and fear are conducive to death.

4. **Hate :** According to McDougall, hate is a compound emotion consisting of anger, fear and disgust. The object of hatred provokes us, frightensus, and repels us. A powerful person who insults you excites anger in you. Though angry, you cannot dare fighting him. He is too powerful for you. So he excites fear in you. This fear is again complicated by disgust for the person.

   Hate is the opposite of love. It makes a person withdraw from the presence of the object of hate. While love is an expanding emotion, hate is a contracting emotion.

5. **Joy :** It arises from the attainment of a cherished object. When the desired object is attained, it gives rise to joy. It is expressed in a general heightened tension of the entire body. Erect posture, throwing out the chest, laughing, jumping, smiling face, brightness of the eyes are the expressions of joy.

6. **Sorrow :** Sorrow arises from the loss of a cherished object. When we are deprived of our cherished objects we feel sorrow. The expressions of sorrow are the opposite of those of joy. Drooping, retracting the chest, general relaxation of the bodily tension are the expressions of sorrow.

20.7.1 Are the emotions native or acquired?

The emotions depend on complex native patterns of response. Facial expressions, changes in breathing and other characteristics of fear and anger appear immediately after birth. Joyful expressions are also found to appear at an early age. Some psychologists consider joyful emotions and the sex emotions as same thing. But this is not correct. The only way of arousing the sex emotions is the stimulation of certain erogenous zones. Among adults, enjoyment results from innumerable situations and they cannot be distinguished the native from the acquired sources.

20.7.2 Development of emotion

According to Watson, three kinds of emotions are seen in newborn infants—anger, fear and love. The expression of these emotions are very strong in infants and they cannot control their emotional outbursts like adults. Most of their activities are guided by emotion.

As the infants mature they exhibit such emotional responses as crying, weeping, smiling and laughing. They appear almost at the same age in all children even when they are not allowed opportunities to imitate others.

Maturation and learning both play an important roles in the development of emotion. With the age of the child early pattern of emotional expression changes. By the end of late childhood the child learns to control his emotional expression in social situations. The emotional responses of the child become less diffuse, random and undifferentiated. Joy, pleasure, love, curiosity, grief and affection appear in childhood.

When the child reaches the adolescent stage he experiences a number of emotional upheavals. His emotional development becomes complex.

20.7.3 Training of emotions

Emotion plays an important role in our individual and social life. Our physical as well as mental health depend to a great extent on emotional expressions.

We know that when an emotion is aroused the endocrine glands begin to work vigorously. A depressing emotion usually retards the flow of the hormones that help digestion. So, if an individual is frequently visited by such an emotion, chronic indigestion may occur. The normal functioning of the thyroid gland is affected both by anger and fear. So, frequent arousal of these states tear down our physical health.

The study of personality shows that many undesirable types of personalities are formed due to a wrong training of the emotions.

Due to defective training a child may suffer from emotional repressions in early childhood. These repressed emotions may cause several mental diseases in later life.

Psychoanalysis has devised a technique of digging out these repressions and, through catharsis, has been successful in curing mental diseases.

Thus, whether we take the aim of education to be the development of the individuality or social efficiency, the training of emotion of the child is essential. They should have proper emotional maturity with the increase of age.

20.8 How to train the emotion of the child

A great deal of our misery is due to misdirected emotions. A happy man is he who has well-trained emotions.

Some of the principles of training the emotions of the child may be discussed below :

1. **Redirection :** With regard to the training of emotions we must keep in mind that no emotion is harmful in itself and none of them is to be unconditionally repressed. It is mostly its use that is bad or good. For example, although anger uncontrolled or misdirected is very much harmful, it supplies an organism the energy to fight for a righteous cause. Thus, show of anger at proper moment is very much desirable. It is not bad to be angry with the antisocial elements, who work to destroy the very fabric of our society.

   What is true of anger is equally true of fear. The child should never have irrational fears. He should not be afraid of darkness, ghosts or closed spaces. But he should fear God and obey the rules and regulations of the social institutions. Without such fear, there will be chaos and there will be no social order or moral discipline.

   A child may be afraid of reading Sanskrit or grammar, but if the teacher can explain clearly the difficult portions of the subject, the child may feel interested in it.

   The child is fond of his mother. So he loves all that is concerned with the name of the mother. Love for the mother may be associated with the love for the motherland. Thus, the sentiment of patriotism and sentiment for great men may be built up. These are all instances of redirection of emotions towards desired goal.

2. **Sublimation :** Sublimation of emotions is the process of redirecting emotions to worthy ends. The emotions—instead of being directed towards unworthy objects are directed to those that are thought to be socially useful.

   Many emotions which would otherwise create a chaotic state of the mind may be sublimated through music and painting. Therefore, to build up a sound personality of the child, the teacher should redirect his emotions to the useful forms of artistic pursuits.

20.8.1 Conditioning of emotions

Watson demonstrated that irrational fears of the child may be removed through conditioning. If a fearful stimulus is paired with a pleasant stimulus then fear is eliminated. A child who is afraid of doing sums may be given easy sums to do and for each correct sum prizes given, then his fear for sums will disappear.

Mental occupation : It is said that idle brain is a devil's workshop. When the child is engaged in some rigorous activity, most of his energy is being consumed in that occupation. He has no energy left to indulge in any undesirable emotional outburst.

Therefore, children should be kept busy with various types of creative and productive work.

Catharsis : It is not possible to keep the child always engaged in serious type of work. There should be opportunities for laughter, play and fun. Through various functions and festivals of the school, their pent-up emotions should find expression.

Inhibition : Lastly, the undesirable forms of emotional expressions of the child have to be curbed. Without this there would be a chaos in the society. Teachers should not allow children to indulge in back-biting, or to use obscene jokes against their classmates. Bad emotions are to be carefully checked for harmonious development of the child.

In brief, a few suggestions may be made for training of emotions of the child :

1. Provide proper environment in home and school, so that children are encouraged to express their feelings.
2. Provide opportunities to participate in music, crafts, games and cultural activities.
3. When pupils show emotional outbursts, treat them calmly.
4. Respect the individuality of the child.
5. Games and other physical activities appropriate to the age-levels of children should be organised.
6. Emotional energy of the child should be properly sublimated in useful channels.

20.9 Abnormalities of emotion

Abnormalities of emotions are due to maladaptation of personality to the environment. Some of the abnormalities of emotion and their causes may be discussed below :

Depression : In depression the patient feels sad and miserable. The feeling of inferiority is the cause of his unhappiness. Depression results when the patient fails to adjust himself to the environment. According to the psychoanalysts repeated failures to express the repressed emotions result in the regression to infantile experiences.

Apathy : In apathy the patient is averse to take any interest in the outside world. Apathy is utter lack of emotion. In *emotional dementia* the patient sits in a corner with face devoid of expression and head hanging down. He cannot cope with the complex environment and relapses into the past infantile experience.

Mania : In manic depression the patient is abnormally cheerful and over active. He cannot stick to an occupation for long. He takes up one job, gives it up immediately and starts another job. Often his cheerfulness changes into violent outburst of anger at the slightest provocation. The patient suffers from delusion and hallucinations.

Involution melancholia : In involution melancholia the patient suffers from extreme sadness and guilt feeling. Sometimes he is haunted by the delusion of persecution and death.

Involution melancholia may occur in old age when physical degeneration takes place. The patient becomes weary of life and may relapse into infantile regression.

20.10 Educational implications of emotional development

Emotion is an important phase of a child's mental life. His behaviour is mostly guided by emotion. So, with the increase of age, his intense emotions are to be controlled and guided by social needs. In this respect the teacher's responsibilities are : (i) To control outbursts of undesirable emotions of the child and (ii) To provide opportunities for expression of normal, desirable emotions of the child.

The aim of education is the harmonious development of the child's personality. Emotions are the important aspect of personality. They determine to a great extent the physical and mental health of the child. They also determine whether an individual will be liked in society, will gain the admiration of his neighbours or will be treated as a nuisance. A person of irritable nature or one suffering from mental depression is seldom liked by anyone. Therefore, a child's emotion should be sublimated and redirected to those that are thought worthy by society. Instead of repression, the emotions of the child should be properly directed to desirable goals.

20.10.1 Redirection of anger

Anger is a natural emotion excited by the thwarting of an instinct. If the child is not fed when he is hungry, he will be angry. He becomes angry when his toys are snatched away from him or he is detained in a room for sometime.

However, misdirected outbursts of emotion of the child is to be controlled by education. When a child shows emotional outbursts, the teacher should treat him calmly and intelligently. He must try to understand the cause of the child's anger and correct him accordingly. The child may be angry because of his failure. In that case, the teacher should encourage him to acquire the skill so that he can conquer his failure. The teacher should avoid criticism and harsh command at this time. Monotony of work often may be a cause of anger. So, novelty and change should be introduced in his work. The result of outburst of anger is bad. This should be explained to him when he is in normal mood.

One thing, however, the teacher should bear in mind that all emotions are not bad in itself. The emotion of anger supplies energy to work. It motivates the organism to act. Instead of continuous praise, a mild criticism or rebuke may be helpful to motivate a child to work.

20.10.2 Elimination of fears

Fear is an emotion excited by the apprehension of a dangerous situation. It arises from the perception of an object which caused pain or injury in the past. In fear, the bodily attitude is one of withdrawal. Fear is expressed in trembling, running away etc. A general state of fear makes one liable to all kinds of ill-health.

Thus, fear is an undesirable and harmful emotion. The child should be free from irrational fears. But these cannot be eliminated by criticism, taunt or rebuke. The causes of fear are to be analysed and then tackled with care.

20.10.3 Some suggestions for elimination of fears

1. Often fear appears due to ignorance. Children who are afraid of learning Geography show disgust when asked to read the subject. Their fear may be eliminated if the teacher applies suitable methods to make the lessons on Geography interesting.

2. To eliminate fear from child's mind, his self-confidence has to be built up.

3. Conditioning may often give rise to irrational fears. If for every error in mathematical sums the child is punished, he will naturally develop fear for the subject. To eliminate the fear, the teacher should give him easy sums in the beginning and introduce difficult sums step by step. Correct responses should be reinforced by suitable prizes.

4. The teacher should avoid telling children stories of terror. He should hold before them the ideal characters of heroes and great men who were brave.

However, we should bear in mind that though irrational fears are to be eliminated some amount of fear is a necessity. The fear of punishment forbids a child to engage himself in delinquency and other antisocial acts. The fear of punishment forbids the children to indulge in obscene jokes or grow quarrelsome. Of course, punishment is a negative method for controlling fear.

Summary

Emotions are complex affective states from perception, memory or imagination of a situation. Emotions are tinged with feelings. Both of them are affective experiences.

Wide range is another characteristic of emotion. Emotions can be aroused both in young and old. Even the animals are not free from emotional expressions.

Emotions are parasitical and are based on instincts. Mc Dougall gave a list of instincts and emotions correlated to each other.

Strong emotions are accompanied with palpitation of the heart, increased breathing, rapid circulation of blood and rise in blood pressure. These organic changes are measured by various scientific apparatus.

The important theories of emotions are : James-Lange theory, Cannon-Bird theory and McDougall's theory.

Abnormalities of emotions are due to maladaptation of personality to the environment. Depression, apathy, mania, melancholia are some of the abnormalities of emotions.

Emotions play an important role in our individual and social life. Our physical and mental health depend, to a large extent, on our emotional expressions. So, training of emotions of the child is essential through redirection, sublimation and mental occupation.

References

1. Bhatia, H.R. : *Elements of Educational Psychology,* Calcutta : Orient Longman, 1968.

2. Thorpe, L.P. and Katz, B. : *The Psychology of Abnormal Behaviour,* New York : Ronald Press, 1961.

3. Munn, N.L. : *An Introduction to Psychology,* Delhi : Oxford & IBH, 1967.

4. Stout, G.F. : *A Manual of Psychology,* London : U.T. Press, 1938.

5. Woodworth, R.S. : *Contemporary Schools of Psychology,* London : Methuen, 1965.

Questions and Assignments

1. What is Emotion? Discuss the nature of emotion.
2. Describe the general characteristics of emotional behaviour.
3. What do you understand by basic emotions? How many basic emotions are there?
4. Discuss the James-Lange theory of emotion. Analyse the emotions of fear, anger, love and hate, pointing out their characteristic differences in expressions.
5. How are emotions related to instincts?—Discuss.
6. What is meant by training of emotions? How would you train the emotions of a child under your care?
7. Describe the physical and mental changes in emotion.
8. What is meant by sublimation of an emotion? Explain with suitable examples.
9. "Each emotion is a sensation mass and each is at the same time a motor set" (Woodworth). Explain.
10. How does mental occupation help in enabling a man to control his emotions? What mental occupation will you recommend to an infant and adolescent?
11. We do not tremble because we are afraid but we are afraid, because we tremble. Is that the correct order of events? Discuss.
12. "Let James be confronted first by a caged bear and next by a bear at large; to the one object he presents a bun and to the other a clean pair of heels." (Ward). Discuss the statement.
13. "The great instincts of human nature have all their accompanying and typical emotions." Explain the statement with special reference to fear and anger.
14. Write notes on:
    (a) Transfer of emotion
    (b) Sublimation
    (c) Emotion and feeling
    (d) Cannon-Bird theory.
15. Discuss the role of emotion in the education of the child. In this connection discuss the role of fear and anger in children.

Chapter 21

Memory: Remembering and Forgetting

Introduction : Whatever we learn or experience should be somehow retained in the mind so that it can be used in future. This faculty of mind to store the past experiences and to revive them when we need is known as memory. Ryburn (1956) considers memory as a faculty to store experiences in our mind. He says, "The power that we have to store our experiences and to bring them to the field of consciousness sometime after the experiences have occurred is termed memory."

Watson consider, memory as repetitive functioning of already acquired habits. But this view is too mechanical and cannot be accepted.

A good memory should reflect an ideal revival. As Stout says, "Ideal revival in which the objects of past experience are reinstated in the order and manner of their original occurrence as far as possible." The word memory is taken sometimes in the sense of retention. But Stout emphasises that it is better to confine memory to ideal revival.

Ross synthesised the different views of the psychologists thus : Memory is a complex process involving the establishment of disposition, their retention and the recalling of experiences that have left behind them. According to Ross, "Memory cannot be viewed merely in terms of revival of past experiences. It is a complex process involving four factors : 1. Learning. 2. Retention. 3. Recall. 4. Recognition."

21.1 Factors of Memory

1. **Learning :** Learning is a process of forming associations among ideas in the mind. We learn facts in their proper context more easily than isolated facts. Physiologically, learning consists in forming connections between neurons.

Those materials which are learnt well are retained in our mind for long. Meaningful materials are not easily forgotten.

2. **Retention :** Anything learnt is retained by the mind in the form of psychological or physiological dispositions. Retention is determined by three important conditions. These are frequency of impressions, their recency and the interest with which they are received. The more often is an impression repeated the deeper does it becomes and it is likely to be retained for a long time. Recency is also an important factor of advantage to retention. Usually we have vivid memories of things that occurred a few days ago.

   Interest is an important factor determining interest. We do not retain all things equally well. We remember things in which we are interested. A student who has interest in games remembers the names of all the important players of different teams. But the same student may have very bad memory of his school lessons.

3. **Recall :** Recall is reproduction. It consists in the revival of past experiences. It is reinstatement of past experiences in the same order.

   What is well-retained is easily recalled. For better recall, associative links among several ideas should be formed.

   There are three laws of Association of ideas : (a) The Law of Contiguity, (b) The Law of Similarity and (c) The Law of Contrast.

   (a) The **Law of Contiguity** states that the two experiences which occur one after another get associated with each other in such a way that when one is recalled the other is also recalled.

   (b) The **Law of Similarity** states that similar events and facts become linked with each other so that one easily reminds the other. The activities of Swami Vivekananda remind us those of Ramkrishna.

   (c) The **Law of Contrast** states that the contrasted characters get associated with each other so that one reminds the other that stands in contrast with it. A specially vicious man may remind us of a specially virtuous man.

4. **Recognition :** Without recognition memory is not complete. Recognition means knowing the object again. It is the feeling of familiarity which accompanies the revival of past experiences. Definite memory must involve definite recognition. Recognition depends upon association and the sense of familiarity. It gives us a feeling of relief which is pleasant. We forget the name of a person and are unable to recall it. But if the names of a number of persons are mentioned and the name of the person happens to be there, then, aided by the perception of it, we recognise it.

21.2 Conditions of memory

Memorisation involves two important factors : 1. Retention and 2. Recall.

Hence the conditions of memorisation are the conditions of retention and recall.

1. Conditions of retention depend upon the following :

(a) **Physiological conditions :** A healthy condition of the body and the brain during the learning process is conducive to retention. Fatigue is unfavourable to retention and recall. Lessons learnt in fatigue or illness cannot be recalled easily.

(b) **Physical conditions :** The physical conditions of retention are :

(i) **Intensity of the stimulus :** A loud sound, a bright light, etc. produce deep impressions on the mind and these are retained for a long time.

(ii) **Clearness and distinctness** of the stimulus help retention.

(iii) **Recency of the stimulus** is also a condition of attention. The impression of a recent experience can easily be retained.

(iv) **Frequency of stimulus** is another condition of retention, e.g., if a story is repeated many times, it is retained in our mind.

(v) **Duration of the stimulus** is a condition of retention, e.g., a musical sound which continues for sometime produces deep impression and can be retained.

(vi) **Significant events** in our life, such as death of our close relatives, are retained long in our mind.

(vii) **Interesting** episodes are easily remembered. The lesson, which are attractive are remembered well. Poems are remembered longer than nonsense syllables.

(viii) **Amount of material :** The longer lists of learned materials are better retained than the shorter lists. The results of Ebbinghaus experiment with nonsense syllables (Table 21.1) show that the greater the number of words in the list, the greater is the percentage of retained materials.

Table 21.1

No. of words in the list	No. of readings	Time (sec.)	P.C. retained
12	17	82″	35%
24	44	422″	49%
36	55	792″	58%

(ix) **Amount of learning :** Ebbinghaus conducted experiments with a list of sixteen nonsense syllables and found that overlearned materials are better retained (Table 21.2).

Table 21.2

No. of readings	16	24	32	64
P.C. of retention	16%	24%	32%	64%

To investigate the influence of overlearning on retention, Kruegar conducted an experiment with a list of twelve noun words. The results of his experiment are shown graphically :

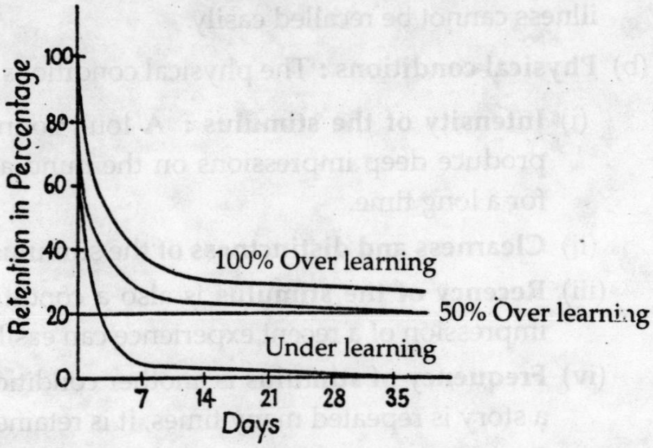

Fig. 21.3

(c) **Mental conditions :**

(i) Attention is a mental condition of retention. The greater attention is paid to the original experience, the greater is the power of retention.

(ii) Interest is another condition of attention. If a person has deep interest in games, he can retain the names of players of various groups.

(iii) Intention to remember is also a condition of retention. When an examinee learns his lesson with the intention to remember it, he can retain it. Minor details of our past experiences cannot be remembered, because we did not intend to remember them.

(iv) Massive experience is a condition of retention. For instance, we cannot forget the experience of our parents' demise.

Apperception : If a person thoroughly understands a subject and the logical connection among its different parts, he can retain it easily. Thus cramming is not useful, as because it does not require intelligent understanding.

2. **Conditions of recall :** Recall or reproduction depends upon retention. What is well-retained is easily recalled.

Hence, condition of retention are also conditions of reproduction :

(a) A healthy and fresh conditions of the body and mind is favourable for correct recall of past experiences.

(b) Recall depends upon bonds of association. Bonds of association have been established among the subconscious traces of past experiences. The sight of the school in which we read brings back many delightful memories of our teachers and classmates.

(c) Recall depends upon the influence of the context. The entire context determines which of several possible ideas will be revived at a particular time.

(d) Recall depends upon the dominant interest at the time of revival. The sight of a book may remind you of its price, or the shop from which it was purchased, or the person who presented it to you as a gift.

(e) Recall depends on mental effort. A student recalls the right answer in the examination hall by applying mental effort.

21.3 Improvement of memory

In the past, it was believed that memory is one of the faculties of the mind and it can be improved by exercise. Raymont points out that improvement of memory is to be sought, not in rote learning but in clear thinking, orderly arrangement, lively interest and close attention. The attention and interest with which a thing is learnt, determine recall. Again, interest depends upon the understanding of the materials to be learned. Meaningful materials are learnt more rapidly and retained for longer time than nonsense material. Hence comprehension of meaning is a great aid to memory. Thus a fact may be well-remembered by the students if the teacher can create interest in it, explain its meaning fully to them and associate it with a number of other facts.

To be brief, the power of retention is an innate ability and it cannot be increased through exercise. But there are certain economical methods which help memorisation.

21.4 Economical methods of memorising

1. **Intention to learn :** Strong determination is required for effective learning. We can remember those things only which we note carefully and intend to remember. For successful learning, the will to learn is necessary.

2. **Comprehension of the meaning:** Cramming is not effective in recall. The meaning of the materials to be learned has thoroughly to be understood. To improve retention of his pupils, the teacher should use the method of making the subject matter meaningful.

3. **Recitation :** Repeated recitation is of great advantage for permanent memory. The learner should read his lesson twice or thrice and then recite it to himself, prompting himself when he fails. This active recitation method takes less time to memorise. An experiment conducted by Gates shows the effect of recitation. The results of the experiment are given below.

Table 21.4

Percentage of time devoted to recitation		Percentage of 16 syllable recalled	
		Immediately	After 4 hours
1.	0	35	15
2.	20	50	26
3.	40	54	28
4.	60	57	37
5.	80	74	48

4. **Intelligent learning:** Unintelligent rote learning is not helpful in retaining materials. Intelligent memorising of a visible material and grasping the meaning of the whole matter is far more effective. Learning through logical thinking is helpful in memorisation.

5. **Overlearning :** Learning after one correct reproduction is called over-learning. Overlearning helps retention.

6. **Forming associations :** For the retention of the learning of material, associative links among several ideas should be formed.

7. **Grouping :** Grouping of materials help memorisation. For instance, it is difficult to remember the number 8 4 9 7 3 8 9 3. But if we group the numbers as 84, 97, 38, 93, the full number will be easily remembered.

8. **Memo technique :** Sometimes mnemonics are devised to help memory. For instance, the word VIBGYOR is made to stand for the seven colours that constitute the ray of sunlight.

9. **Learning by doing:** Children learn more by doing than passively listening to the teachers. Particularly in lower class, the teacher should follow the principle of learning by doing. Learning experiences thus acquired will be remembered for a longer period.

10. **Learning by whole :** The whole method is used when one tries to learn a poem by reading the whole of it at a time. The merit of the whole method consists in the fact that the last word of the first stanza becomes connected with the first word of the next. The mind, therefore, easily passes from one stanza to another in the process of recalling it. Again, the connected sense of the whole piece also help recall.

    However, that does not happen in the case of *Part Method,* which consists in learning a poem stanzawise. In case of this method the last word of a stanza, by the law of contiguity, associated with first word of the very same stanza. It becomes then difficult to cut off this link and pass over to the next stanza.

    In some cases, *mixed method* has been found to be the most useful. In the mixed method, a stanza of a poem may be committed to memory and then we may pass over to the next, after this the two stanzas may be read together and thus the entire poem may be learnt in this process. Or, we may read a poem up to the place where the difficulty occurs. Then to master the difficult one, we repeat it and then proceed on further with the previously learnt part.

    According to Winch, "the children above twelve learn quickly by whole method. Whereas, those who are below that age, profit by part method."

Table 21.5 : Comparison of Whole method and Part method

Whole method	Part method
1. This method is useful when the learning material is short and requires less time. It lacks the incentive which one gets from appreciating one's own success in mastering a part of the material.	1. The method is useful when the learning material is a long one. When committed to memory in parts, the appreciation of partial success will itself lead one to continued effort.
2. Comprehension of the meaning of the material becomes easier because of proper associations.	2. Lack of proper associations between different parts makes comprehension difficult.
3. Produces fatigue and boredom.	3. Does not bring fatigue or boredom.

11. **Spaced learning :** Learning should be spaced rather than unspaced or massed. Continued repetition in unspaced learning makes the work boring and the interest is killed. While, spaced learning gives time for the assimilation of the subject matter learnt.

The adjoining table gives the results of **Jost** with regard to his experiments on spaced and unspaced learning.

Table 21.6 : Spaced and Unspaced learning

Distribution of 24 readings	Total score of B	Total score of M
8 readings a day for 3 days	18	17
6 readings a day for 4 days	39	31
2 readings a day for 12 days	53	55

Table 21.7 : Comparison of Spaced and Unspaced learning

Spaced method	Unspaced method
1. This method gives time for the assimilation of the subject matter learnt. Freshness is another advantage of the method.	1. In this method attention flags and interest diminishes.
2. Learning becomes strengthened and learning experience last longer by this method.	2. This method helps immediate memory but experiences does not last for long.
3. Spaced learning is not advantageous. When the subject matter is short and simple.	3. This method is useful when the subject matter is short and simple. Instead of reading twelve digits once a day, Lyon learnt the digits by continued repetition and memorise it in shorter time.
4. In case of solving difficult problem, effort should be continuous. In this case, this method is not useful.	4. In case of difficult problem, continued effort is necessary. Cook and Stagner adopted this method in solving problems and got better result.

12. **Technique of Thomas and Robinson (1972) :** They devised a strategy for effective learning and memorisation. This technique involves sequenced steps, which are survey, question, read, reflect, recite and review.

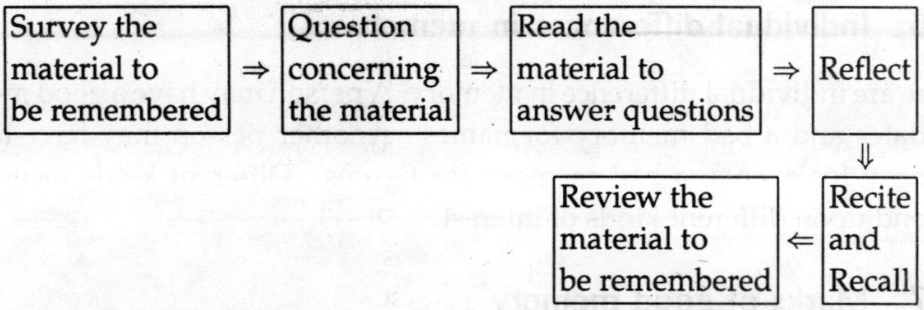

21.5 Training in memory

Memory cannot be improved by training though we are keen to improve it. It cannot be trained by any kind of exercise. Memory has four factors : Learning, Retention, Recall and Recognition.

Retention is innate and cannot be improved. Recognition also cannot be improved by training. The remaining two factors—learning and recall—can be improved by training. For effective learning and memorisation, there must be will to learn, close attention and a judicious selection of methods of memorisation, which have been discussed in detail.

Recall becomes difficult when associative links between previously learnt ideas are broken. Fear and doubt may paralyse recall. So, to recall something, one should be free from excessive anxiety, fear and doubt.

The easy and confident mood wards off doubts and distractions. Auto-suggestion is very important to gain self-confidence.

Moreover, we should not strain for too long to recall anything. It is better to drop the matter for a while. After allowing a little time to relax, we should come back to it afresh. The interference by this time would have automatically died out. When a student fails to get the right answer of a problem sum in mathematics by repeated attempts, let him leave the task and do something else. After a while, let him take up the task. He will do better then. Munn gives some suggestions for memory training :

1. Learn with the intention to remember.
2. Pay close attention to what you learn.
3. Make use of images while you learn.
4. Form associations between what you learn and other things.
5. Make use of rhythm.
6. Do not cram. Learn the same material at intervals.
7. Recite the learned material to your self.
8. Rest or sleep after you have studied.
9. Read the whole chapter and then study its parts.

21.6 Individual differences in memory

There are individual difference in memory. A person may have a good memory for dates and a bad memory for names. Another person may have a good memory for events, a bad memory for figures. Different kinds of memory depend upon different kinds of interest.

21.7 Marks of good memory

Rapidity of learning is a mark of good memory. A student who can learn his lesson quickly is considered to possess good capacity for memorisation. But rapidity of learning only cannot be considered as a mark of good memory. He who learns quickly and forgets quickly cannot be taken as to possess good memory.

The power of retaining for a long time is a more important mark of memory than the power of learning quickly and easily.

Again, if the retained material cannot be recalled quickly and accurately, it is useless. Often the minds of some people are packed with all sorts of information, but they fail to recall any of them when it is urgently needed. Such power of memorisation is worse than useless. So, serviceableness is an important mark of good memory.

According to Stout, "the marks of good memory are : ease and rapidity of learning or memorising, permanence of retention, rapidity of revival, accuracy of the actual recall and serviceableness of the revival or its relevance to purpose."

Rapidity of learning depends to a great extent on congenital interest. The length of time during which the learned material is retained also depends largely on interest. An examiner retains the learned details till the examination is over. Promptness and accuracy of recall depends on strong suggestive forces and well-formed associations.

The serviceableness of memory depends on forming the right kind of associations and organised knowledge. An individual with systematised knowledge can readily recall the proper thing at the proper moment.

21.8 Types of memory

Memory has been classified by Psychologists into various types according to its nature and the purpose it serves. We will discuss here some of the important types :

1. **Short-term and Long-term memory :** The material learned may be recalled immediately or after a very short time. The short-term memory of an individual can be determined from the experiment on the span of memory. It has been found that average memory span can be expressed

as 7 ± 2, i.e., an adult can normally recall 7 items, but he may be able to remember as many as 8 or 9 or only 5 or 6. However, the short-terms memory span can be increased by grouping. For instance, the number 869368273 may be remembered when arranged as 869, 368, 273.

Unlike short-term memory, the material learned may be recalled after a lapse of time. This type of memory is called long-term memory, which depends upon the laws of association. The more the learned material is associated with other ideas in the mind and wrought into the system of knowledge, the greater is the permanency of memory. With the help of long-term memory we store, retain and recall the most important incidents of our life at a second's notice, such as the date of marriage or the death of a close friend.

2. **Rote Memory and Logical Memory :** Mechanical repetition of experience without intellectual comprehension is known as rote memory. It is cramming. While Logical memory depends upon understanding and assimilation. It does not depend upon mere repetition. When a student thoroughly understand a mathematical problem, he can easily retain and reproduce it on proper occasion.

3. **Habit memory and pure memory :** According to Bergson "there are two types of memory, habit memory and pure memory." Habit memory is related to the body, and pure memory to the mind. Habit memory is the result of verbal repetitions. It consists in mechanical habit formation. True memory depends on association and interest. Habit memory is rote memory, whereas true memory is logical memory.

4. **Photographic memory :** Photographic memory or eiditic imagery stands for a kind of memory possessed by a person who can recall a scene in photographic detail. He can give a vivid description of a past incident as if he is seeing it before his eyes.

5. **Passive memory and active memory :** When past experiences are recalled without an effort of the will, we call it passive memory. For example, the sight of a delicious mango, spontaneously reminds us of its sweet taste. But when we remember a past incident by an effort of the will, our memory becomes active. We try to recollect a forgotten incident by an effort of the will and succeed at last in recollecting it.

21.9 The experimental study of memory

1. **Materials used :** Verbal materials like serial list, paired-associate lists and connected discourse.

(a) A serial list is composed of words such as

BAT, SET, LOT, RENT, etc.

Numbers : 42, 73, 98, 67, etc.

Nonsense syllables : TAB, DUS, LEB, MEEV, HOOL, CRAD, LATUK, POLEF, DEFIS, etc.

(b) A paired-associate list consists of a series of paired words of meaningful or nonsense syllables :

Meaningful words : LEG–CAT, BOOK–FOOD, DOLL–CORN.

Nonsense words : THOG–CHUZ, GLES–FEPO, GABAB–MATUK, SOLEF–DARUP, etc.

(c) **Connected discourse :** This includes paragraphs or passages from a piece of literature which can be broken up into phrases or ideas and can at least be counted.

2. **Apparatus :** Ebbinghaus (1885) presented a list of nonsense syllables before the subject and kept time with a metronome. But this procedure had certain defects. Muller and Schumann (1894) standardised the procedure by pasting the list of syllables around a rotating drum behind a screen and exposed one syllable at a time through a little window in the screen.

The subject is asked to recall as many words as possible. The procedure is repeated and the number of trials and the time taken to learn is recorded (see Fig. 21.8).

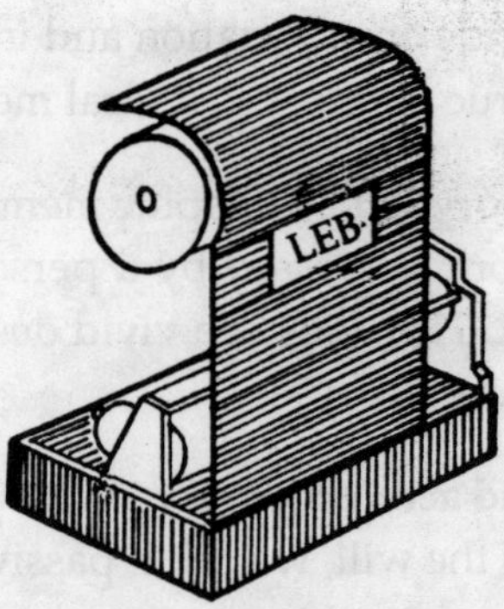

Fig. 21.8: Memory drum.

3. **Method of measurement :** Ebbinghaus devised three important methods for measuring memory : (i) Learning method, (ii) Saving method and (iii) Prompting method.

(a) **Learning method :** In this method, the subject is shown a list of verbal material. He tries to remember the material over a number of trials. After each trial, the subject has to write down all the words of syllables he remembers. The better a person's retentive power, the lower would be the number of trials required by him for remembering the complete list.

The learning method has the advantage of being applicable to a great variety of material which need not be divisible into separate items. It is scored as a whole.

(b) **Saving method :** When the subject has learned all the words correctly by learning method, the saving method is employed. The subject is given a period of rest, say a week. During this period, naturally, he forgets some of the material he has already learnt. He is then allowed further trials to relearn the material. The number of trials saved in the relearning process is the measure of the power of retention.

(c) **Prompting method :** After one or a few presentations of the list, the subject attempts to recite. He is quickly prompted whenever he hesitates and corrected whenever he makes an error. The list is gone through in this way time after time until the subject successfully recites it without prompting.

(d) **Other methods :** Besides these methods devised by Ebbinghaus, there are some other methods of measuring memory. Some of them are : (i) The Method of retained members, (ii) The Reconstruction method and (iii) Recognition method.

(i) **The method of retained members :** It was first used by Bolton (1892). In this method, the quantity of material presented before the subject must exceed the memory span. The amount of material reproduced by the subject is the score. For a given experiment, the length of the presented list of numbers or words should be standardised. This method is convenient and can be used with a variety of material.

(ii) **The reconstruction method :** Munsterberg and Bigham (1894) first devised this method. In this method, the materials are presented in a certain arrangement. This arrangement is then broken up and the subject is instructed to reconstruct the original order. The trials are continued until the subject is able to make a perfect reconstruction. The score is determined by the time or number of trials needed to reach a standard of mastery.

(iii) **The Recognition method :** In this method, after learning, the known materials are mixed with unknown materials and presented to the subject. The subject is asked to select the known materials from the mixed stimuli. For instance, 10 pictures are shown one at a time and then shuffled with 10 other pictures and the whole 20 shown one at a time. The subject responds YES or NO to each picture.

The memory score is then determined by the following formula

$$\text{Score} = \frac{\text{Right} - \text{Wrong}}{\text{Total number of pictures}}$$

21.10 What is Forgetting?

All that we learn are not totally retained in our memory. It is found that students forget most of the knowledge imparted in school after a short lapse of time. In our daily life also we often fail to recall important information wanted urgently.

Munn (1967) says, "Forgetting is the loss, permanent or temporary, of the ability to recall or recognise something learned earlier."

According to Mangal (1997), "forgetting is just the opposite of remembering and is essentially a failure in the ability to reproduce experienced or studied material."

Though forgetting is termed a failure, it has its utility in our life. In fact, both the processes of memorisation and forgetting are essential. Unless we forget unimportant and trifle matters, we cannot retain and recall new experiences. A student who has learnt inadvertently some erroneous things and does not forget them, will never learn the correct thing. Our life is full of many painful incidents, but if we do not forget them, our life will be miserable. So for keeping up our mental health, we need to forget them. Thus forgetting is an essential condition of memory (Ribot).

21.10.1 Ebbinghaus's experiment

Ebbinghaus (1885) first studied the process of forgetting with a list of nonsense syllables. The result of the experiments show that after 20 minutes 58% of the material learnt is remembered. After one hour 44%, after one day 34% and after 31 days only 21%. The results in terms of the percentage of material retained and forgotten with the lapse of time were as follows :

Time elapsed	P.C. retained	P.C. forgotten
20 minutes	58%	42%
1 hour	44%	56%
1 day	34%	66%
2 days	28%	72%
6 days	25%	75%
31 days	21%	79%

The data may be plotted as a graph as shown in fig. 21.9.

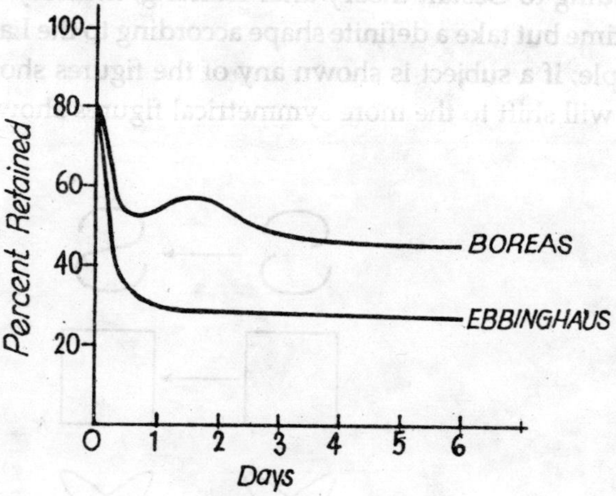

Fig. 21.9

From the graph we find that forgetting is most rapid immediately after learning. Gradually, the curve of forgetting gets flat and never reaches the base line. Thus we may conclude that (i) there is something retained in our mind for all the time, (ii) Revision of a material is most economic in memorising it immediately after it is learnt.

Following Ebbinghaus, Boreas and other psychologists conducted experiments on the rate of forgetting and got identical results.

21.10.2 Theories of forgetting

On the basis of extensive research and investigation, a number of theories of forgetting have been formulated. Some of the important theories are :

1. **The theory of decay :** Forgetting is due to lapse of time. Some psychologists believe that learning involves certain neurological changes, leaving certain memory traces (engrams) in the brain. Through disuse, these traces get weaker and finally fade away.

   However, this trace decay theory is an old view and has been disproved because of the fact that numerous activities of our life such as cycling and swimming are not forgotten even after long years of disuse.

2. **Theory of Retroactive inhibition :** This theory holds that we forget because of interference. If a bond of association between A and B is formed through learning, and just after this a bond between C and D is formed, then the formation of the latter bond tends to inhibit the former.

   Proactive inhibition is just the opposite of retroactive inhibition. In proactive inhibition, the old learning (A–B) works forward to disrupt the memory of what we learn afterwords (C–D).

3. **Trace-change theory :** Memory tends to change in specific ways. According to Gestalt theory after learning, memory traces do not decay with time but take a definite shape according to the Law of Pragnang. For example, if a subject is shown any of the figures shown, his memory of them will shift to the more symmetrical figures shown in the right hand side.

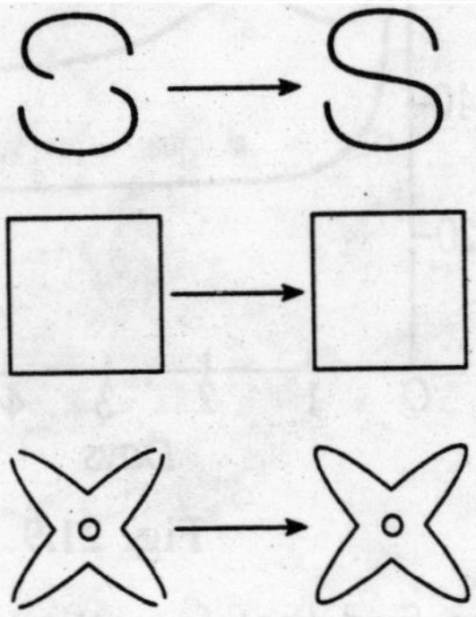

Fig. 21.10

4. **Theory of repression :** Abnormal or morbid forgetting cannot be explained by the above two theories. These may be explained by Freud's psychoanalytic school according to which forgetfulness is the product of repression or the desire to forget. Unpleasant and painful memories, which hurt our self-respect, are repressed and forgotten. Sometimes forgetfulness is motivated and intentional. For instance, we forget to attend a marriage party which we do not want to attend.

   People under a serious emotional shock, often forget their own names. Amnesia due to repression occurred amongst many soldiers who suffered intensely during World War I.

   Forgetfulness of a certain painful incident may be brought about by hypnotic suggestion to forget it. The subject under hypnosis forgets the incident and fails to recall it.

21.10.3 Causes of forgetting

Forgetting is usually due either to lack of attention and interest or lapse of time. Besides these, there are some other causes of obliviscence.

1. **Lack of practice :** What is learnt or experienced is forgotten due to lack of practice (Law of Disuse). Drill, practice or repetition of a learning succeeds in preventing decay.
2. **Retroactive inhibition :** The main reason of obliviscence is retroactive inhibition. According to McGeoch, learned materials are forgotten due

to retroactive inhibition. That is, the acquisition of new learning works backward to impair the retention of the previously learned material. However, the interference depends on numerous factors. They are :

(a) **Effect of sleep :** From the experiments of Jenkins and Dallenback, we come to know that sleep, immediately after learning, helps retention.

Table 21.11: Results of Dallenback's experiment.

	(Percentage of Recall)			
	After 1 hour	After 2 hours	After 4 hours	After 8 hours
In awakening state	46%	31%	22%	7%
In sleeping	70%	54%	55%	56%

(b) **Similarity of materials :** Inhibition is greater when there is close similarity between two learned materials. For instance, inhibition will be greater when two English poems are learned one after another. But it will be less when an Algebreical problem is learned after an English poem.

(c) **Amount of interval :** If the interval between learning of two materials is too short, then the process of consolidation is impaired and percentage of recall becomes less.

(d) **Overlearning :** Overlearning of a material resists inhibition.

(e) **Consolidation :** When the newly formed traces are disturbed and no time is allowed for consolidation, they will be wiped out. Muller and Pilzecker lend support to the consolidation theory.

(f) **Emotional blocking :** Fear and anger may paralyse recall. Stage fright often prevents the recall of many a well-learnt speech of an orator. During examination, some students may suffer from emotional blocking, causing thereby total obliviscence.

(g) **Effect of transfer :** When two materials are learned, they mingle with one another so much so that when we try to recall one material, some parts of the other material also come to our mind and create confusion. This impairs retention and hampers recall. The greater the similarities between the two kinds of materials, the greater the amount of transfer and consequent loss of recall. Many psychologists support this theory of Decamp and Webb.

(h) **Effect of repression :** Freud first used the term repression to describe the tendency to forget anything associated with painful experiences. Amnesia due to repression occurs in soldiers, who forget the experiences which hurt their self-respect.

(i) **Effect of drug :** Excess use of drug or liquors often impair recall.

(j) **Shock Amnesia :** Amnesia is often caused by an accident. A person was thrown off a carriage which collided with a military truck. On account of brain injury, he could not remember what happened immediately before the accident.

(k) **Want of association :** When associative links between previously learnt materials are broken, recall becomes difficult. Thus, at times, we fail to recall the name of certain person whom we know well.

According to Watson, want of language or want of Verbal association brings about obliviscence. We cannot remember the incidents of our early childhood due to lack of verbal association.

(l) **Fatigue :** If we learn something during fatigue or illness, we easily forget them. This lapse of memory is due to lack of interest.

21.10.4 Abnormalities of memory

There are certain disorders of memory, viz., amnesia, hypermnesia and paramnesia.

1. **Amnesia :** Amnesia is sudden loss of memory. It is an abnormal form of forgetfulness. Amnesia may be divided into : (a) Partial amnesia and (b) General amnesia.

(a) Partial amnesia is loss of memory for particular things. One may lose visual memory, auditory memory if visual area or auditory area is injured.

(b) General amnesia may be : (i) temporary, (ii) periodical, (iii) Progressive and (iv) congenital.

(i) Temporary amnesia is often caused by an accident or overstrain. There is a loss of memory of the knowledge of events immediately preceding the accident. Wounds from accident and war cause *Traumatic amnesia.* The epileptic patient cannot recall events that occur prior to a seizure. These are called Retroactive amnesia.

(ii) Periodic amnesia is found in double personality. A man meets an accident, suddenly forgets his home and his friends, goes to a distant place, sets up a shop there, and behaves like an entirely different person. Then after few years, he gets up in the morning and suddenly recalls his past life. This is a Periodic amnesia.

(iii) Progressive amnesia is found in old age. Old persons first forget their recent experiences and then gradually other experiences of earlier life. They may forget the names of their children, and even their own names.

(iv) Congenital amnesia is found in idiots and imbeciles. Their forgetfulness is due to the inherent defects of their brains.

2. Hypermnesia is a sudden abnormal increase of memory. A person suddenly remembers the language learnt during infancy. Some rare persons with prodigious memory can remember pages of a book after reading them only once. Some persons can remember many digits after hearing them once.

3. Paramnesia is false recognition. Sometimes we feel that we have previously been in the place where we are at the moment, though we could not possibly have been in this place before. Again, sometimes we feel that we have previously said the words we are now saying, though we are sure that we could not have spoken such words.

21.10.5 Memory and imagination

Memory and imagination are similar mental process, in many respects but they are really different. Memory is the exact reproduction of the contents of past experience in the same order in which they were experienced in the past.

Imagination consists in reproducing the contents of past experience and arranging them in a new order different from that in which they were originally experienced.

Memory looks backward, whereas imagination looks forward. In memory only the past experience is reproduced, while in imagination a new creation is being made. Memory involves the capacity of reproduction, whereas imagination requires the capacity of creation. This is why often memory is called reproductive imagination.

Woodworth calls imagination mental manipulation because an individual rearranges facts previously observed and recalled at present into a new pattern in imagination. For imagination, proper memory is needed. You perceived roses and blue colour in the past, but never blue roses. But you can recall the image of a rose and the image of blue colour and conjoin them into the image of a blue rose. Thus a centaur is composed of horse and man and mermaid of fish and woman.

21.11 Laws of association

Recall depends on retention. What is well-retained is easily recalled. For this, associative links among several ideas should be formed. There are three Laws of Association : 1. The Law of Contiguity. 2. The Law of Similarity and 3. The Law of Contrast.

1. **The Law of Contiguity** states that two experiences which occur together, or which closely follow one another, tend to cohere and form an association in such a way that when one is recalled, the other is also recalled. If A has always been perceived together with B, or immediately after B, then the perception of the idea of B will revive the idea of B.
2. **The Law of Similarity** states that similar experiences become linked with each other so that the one easily reminds the other. A photo reminds us of the person whom it represents.
3. **The Law of Contrast** states that the contrasted characters get associated with each other, so that one reminds the other that stands in contrast with it. Prosperity reminds a person of his days of adversity. The heat of summer suggests cold of winter.

While teaching, the teacher should avail of these laws of association so that learning materials are well-retained in the mind of the students. The associative links have to be formed by consciously directing the attention of the students to points of contiguity, similarity and contrast.

Summary

Memory is the exact reproduction of the past experiences in the same order in which they were experienced in the past. In involves four factors—learning, retention-recall and recognition.

Memory may be classified into : short-term and long-term, rote memory and logical memory, habit memory and pure memory, passive memory and active memory.

Ebbinghaus devised three methods of measuring memory : learning method, saving method and prompting method.

Rapidity of learning is a mark of good memory. Retained material should be recalled rapidly and accurately. Memory, to be good, must be serviceable.

Economy in memorisation may be achieved by adopting proper methods such as recitation, grouping, forming associations, intelligent learning, learning by doing, using memo techniques, learning by whole, etc.

Improvement of memory is to be sought not in rote learning but in clear thinking, orderly arrangement, lively interest and close attention. Factors like the learner's interest and attention, use of association, the methods of learning, a good learning environment, emotional state of the learner, etc. are important for achieving best results in memorisation.

Forgetting is just the opposite of remembering. It is essentially a failure in the ability to reproduce experience or studied material.

Natural forgetting can be explained by the theory of decay of traces in the brain through disuse. According to the theory of Retroactive Inhibition, we forget things because of the interference of other materials.

In Proactive Inhibition, earlier learning interferes with the later learning. In Retroactive Inhibition, later learning comes in the way of earlier learning.

The theory of repression explains morbid or abnormal forgetting. The term repression describes the tendency to forget anything associated with painful experiences. Amnesia is often caused by an accident.

References

1. Munn, N.L. : *An Introduction to Psychology*, Delhi : Oxford & IBH, 1967.
2. Morgan, J.B. and Gillilend, A.R. : *An Introduction to Psychology*, New York : Macmillan.
3. Mangal, S.K. : Prentice Hall of India Pvt. Ltd. New Delhi, 1997.
4. Ryburn, W.M. : *Introduction to Educational Psychology*, London : Oxford Univ. Press, 1956.
5. Sinha, J.N. : *A Manual of Psychology*, New Central Book Agency, 8/1 Chintamoni Das Lane, Calcutta, 1978.
6. Woodworth, R.S. and Schlosberg, H. : Methuen & Co. Ltd. London, 1955.
7. Bhatia, H.R. : *Elements of Educational Psychology*, Calcutta, Orient Longman, 1968.
8. Stout, G.F. : *A Manual of Psychology*, London : University Tutorial Press, 1938.

Questions and Assignments

1. What are the factors of memory? Distinguish between perception and memory.
2. Describe the stages in the process of memorisation.
3. What are the conditions of remembering? Discuss fully.

4. How does interest determine memory? Do we always remember things which we are interested in?
5. What are the marks of good memory? Can memory be trained? Discuss.
6. Why do we forget? What are the different causes of forgetting? Is forgetting an evil?
7. What are the conditions of forgetfulness? How would you recollect a forgotten name? Bring out the factors which influence forgetting.
8. Explain some economical method of memorising. Describe some of the experimental studies on memorising.
9. Elucidate the various factors of memory and show their intimate relation to each other.
10. What kind of memory will you encourage among your students? Point out the value of rote memory and associative memory in class teaching.
11. What are the best way of memorising a poem? Why does recitation method prove more effective than continuous learning?
12. Write notes on :

    (a) Memory span

    (b) Eidetic image

    (c) Positive and Negative after-images.

    (d) Amnesia

    (e) Aphasia

    (f) Paramnesia.
13. Why is it that we forget something just when we want it most? How can such forgetting be prevented?
14. What is the secret of memorising? What practical hints will you give to a student to memorise facts of history or geography?
15. What is the best way of improving memory? Discuss the value of memory exercises in this connection.
16. "Improvement of memory is to be sought not in rote learning but in clear thinking, orderly arrangement, lively interest and close attention." Explain.
17. Write notes on :

    (a) Retroactive Inhibition.

    (b) Overlearning

    (c) Memory training

    (d) Rote memory and Immediate memory.

    (e) Active memory and Passive memory.

18. What are the general conditions of Retention and Reproduction? Account for retention of past experiences.

19. Discuss the advantages and disadvantages of cramming.

20. Distinguish between :

    (a) Recognition and Recall

    (b) Space and Unspaced repetition

    (c) Whole and Part learning.

21. State the doctrine of association of ideas. Explain the different types of Association in psychology and describe the part played by them in mental life.

Chapter 22

Attitude and Interest

What is attitude? Although the word attitude is used too frequently in everyday conversation, it cannot be wholly described by a single numerical index because of its complexity and variability. G.W. Allport after a careful consideration of various senses in which it has been used, proposes the following definition :

An attitude is a mental and neural state of readiness, organised through experience, exerting a directive or dynamic influence upon the individual's response to all objects and situations with which it is related.

Thurstone defines an attitude as the degree of positive or negative affect associated with some psychological object. By a psychological object, Thurstone means any symbol, phrase, slogan, person, institution, ideal, or idea toward which people can differ with respect to positive or negative affect. Krech and Crutchfield view attitude as an enduring organisation of motivational, emotional, perceptual, and cognitive process with respect to some aspect of the individual's world. An enduring organisation of psychological processes implies a consistency of response patterns. To Likert, attitudes are simply dispositions toward overt action.

However, broadly conceived, attitude denotes an adjustment of an individual toward a selected aspect of his environment. A social attitude means consistency in response to social objects. It is primarily a way being set toward or against certain aspect of the society. It indicates our feelings for or against some social institutions, or social issues, such as, attitude towards divorce or dictatorship.

In the formation of attitude of an individual, the influence of family, community and association is very significant.

22.1 Influence of family

Of all the basic social institutions, the most responsible for the harmonious development of the child's body and mind is our family. Though at present the family life is passing through a period of stress and strain on account of divorce, desertion and other causes, it is still regarded as the primary group responsible for training children in the art of living and moulding their attitudes in various ways.

The phenomenal advances of science and technology in modern age have tremendously shaken up the family life of Western countries. In India, where society is still dominantly agrarian, social problem of this nature has not yet reached the same dimensions. The age-old joint family system in India has survived the shock of many social changes and it is not unusual to find here the peaceful co-existence of five or six brothers (with a multitude of noisy children!) in a single family.

An Indian family generally comprises, besides parents and their children, number of near and distant relatives of parents, and even an old servant or maid-servant may become an integral part and a life-member of the family. The head of the family may or may not necessarily be any of the child's parents. The grandfather or grandmother or even the widow aunt may be the mistress of the family and she may act as cashier-cum-administrator of the home. In such a well-knit family, children receive a large number of playmates of the same age and they receive wide scope for social training.

22.2 Influence of association

As the child develops, his circle of contact widens and with each succeeding year, his interest in playmates outside home and family increases. His interest in individual games give way to group games. His chums, particularly the leader of the group, exert considerable influences on his conduct. The child being extremely suggestible the leader of a gang may, through action and speech, tend to destroy some of his favourable social attitudes and create certain adverse ones in its place.

22.3 Influence of community

Many of the attitudes are acquired as second hand from social interactions. Adults pick up most of their social and political attitudes from newpapers.

As the child grows older, he is taught by adult members of the family to conform to the moral standards set by the community. He is induced to follow a large number of taboos, regulations and standard practices. This sort of moral control is essential for the survival of a society. To fulfil this purpose, society calls upon its institutions, particularly the home and the educational agencies.

Education uninspired by moral and spiritual values is directionless, says the Education Policies Commission, National Education Association of the United States. Dr. Radhakrishnan defines education as initiation into the life of spirit, a training of human souls in the pursuit of truth and the practice of virtue.

Social changes in the modern age have shattered to a large extent the moral code of every society. Corruption in high places on the national and local scenes, horror comics, pornographic literature and other crime provoking books create an attitude within the child that makes him more susceptible to delinquency than he might otherwise be.

22.4 Formation of Attitude

Like other features of mental life, attitudes also grow and develop. Allport has distinguished four common processes involved in the making of attitudes :

1. Integration of various specific responses of a similar type into a definite pattern of mental state.
2. Individuation of a definite mental set.
3. The effects of some trauma of fixation resulting from a starting and dramatic experience. This represents a sudden change in the mental state caused by some vivid experience, e.g., the student abandons medical career because of repugnance to dissection.
4. Readiness for adoption through imitation. By way of imitation some sort of readiness to adopt an ideal develops. Thus attitudes are caught as often as they are taught.

Attitudes are flexible. The largest single factor in changing attitudes is the propaganda. Besides this the Television, Radio, Cinema and Newspapers have been found to possess an amazing power to shake attitudes. But attitudes are considered to be emotionally toned predispositions towards objects and ideas. They are said to be somewhat lasting generalisations of experiences such as, attitudes towards widow marriage. Early marriage and democracy. Therefore, attitude of a person towards certain social factors are measurable.

22.5 Methods and techniques of measurement of attitude

The attitude of a person or a group is a complex affair. Following LaPiere, Lundberg has classified the attitudinal behaviour into four categories :

(a) Overt, symbolic, which includes the acts of speaking, writing and gesturing;

(b) Overt non-symbolic, which includes such directly significant acts as driving a car and closing a door;

(c) Covert-symbolic, or what is commonly designated as thought;

(d) Covert-nonsymbolic, or what is usually described as feeling states and emotions.

In the above classification only class (a) is measurable. Class (b) is not attitudinal. Class (c) and (d) are attitudinal but cannot be measured. We are interested in the particular form of attitudinal behaviour which takes the form of opinions expressed in language and is, therefore, measurable. When language or verbal opinion is taken as indicator of attitudes of a person, we try to know his attitude by means of the opinion expressed by him.

Bert F. Green describes six principal measuring techniques :

1. The judgement methods;
2. The method of summated ratings;
3. Scalogram analysis;
4. The unfolding techniques;
5. Latent structure analysis;
6. Rating methods.

It seems unnecessary to discuss the lengthy procedures of all these scales.

We discuss below in detail the technique of summated ratings or Likert Technique only.

22.6 The technique of summed ratings

The fundamental steps in constructing a Likert-type attitude scale are :

1. A series of statements relating to the attitude object in question are collected. The test items are carefully edited to eliminate ambiguous, irrelevant and otherwise faulty items. Moreover, the statements are so constructed as to indicate clearly a position for or against the point at issue.

2. The items are then drawn up in the form of an attitude test, each item being given multiple response categories of : (a) strongly agree, (b) agree, (c) undecided, (d) disagree, (e) strongly disagree.

   In the five point continuum weights of 1, 2, 3, 4, 5 are assigned in proper order, the direction of weighting being determined by the favourableness or unfavourableness of the statements.

3. A large number of subjects are requested to check their attitude on the original list of statements.

4. A total score for each subject taking the test is obtained by summing the value of each item that is checked.
5. As a basis for determining the selection of items for the final scale, the discriminative value of each item is computed. This is done by obtaining the difference between the average scores for each item when the total scores are arranged in quartiles.
6. The final attitude scale is then constructed by selecting 20 to 25 items from the total list which show the greatest discrimination.

The Likert technique is less time-consuming, can be scored easily and is more diagnostic. Again, it yields reliabilities as high as those obtained by other techniques with fewer items. These advantages of the Likert method make it theoretically more attractive than the other scales.

Examples of a few statements in attitude scales :[1]

1. Too many brothers or sisters mean unhappiness at home.
2. Parents do not treat all children alike.
3. Boys suffer much in absence of their mother.
4. It is the friend who shows the gateway to hell.
5. We should love our friends more than anyone else.
6. Freedom of expression is lost when we are in a group.
7. If we want to earn money we should give up the path of righteousness.
8. On no account we should try to deceive others.
9. Those who always speak the truth can never shine.
10. Those who believe in God are really happy.
11. Heaven and Hell are the two words of the fool.
12. Religion should have no place in our practical life.
13. God keeps strict vigilance over our actions.
14. People who do not believe in God prosper nowadays.

22.7 Attitude and interest

An attitude is primarily a way being set toward or against certain aspect of the society. It indicates our feelings for or against some social institutions, or social ideas. But interest is a particular kind of sentiment centering round certain objects.

Interest is always positive. You may be interested in games or in reading novels. This sentiment is always positive. But your attitude towards religious

---

[1] These statements are quoted from 'Social Attitude of Delinquents and Non-delinquents' by *Dr. S.K. Chatterjee.*

practices may be either positive or negative. Again you may have interest in something, but your attitude may not be favourable to it. For instance, you have interest in smoking, but your attitude towards smoking may be unfavourable.

Interest is often guided by our instinct. Prof. Stout describes interest as affective-connative aspect of instinct. A child feels interest in picture and doll because of acquisitive instinct. But attitude is not guided by such instincts. Attitude has certain special characteristics.

According to Ross Stagner, attitude has always three special characteristics : (i) It has direction, (ii) It has intensity and (iii) It centers round an object.

Attitude always develops towards certain objects of the environment. For example, we may have certain permanent attitude towards the Jews or the Pakistanis, birth control or early marriage, idealism or pragmatism and so on.

Attitude has a direction. Our attitude may be negative or positive towards an object or idea. For instance, the teacher who gives severe punishments for small offence is not liked by students. They develop negative attitude towards him. But the teacher who is affectionate towards the students are liked by them. They develop positive attitude towards him.

Again, our attitude towards certain object or idea may be intensive or mild. The intensity of attitude controls our behaviour.

22.8 Importance of attitude in education

Attitude is formed through our education and experience. So, the teacher's responsibility is to create proper attitude in the students towards different objects and ideas. He must be careful so that no undesirable information and experiences are given to the pupils. Often friends and classmates influence to form wrong attitudes in them which cannot be changed so easily. So, before such permanent attitudes are formed, association of the pupils concerned should be immediately changed. Moreover, books, periodicals, journals and political address by leaders help to form perverted attitudes. In such cases, the teacher should hold out the total picture of the situation before the students and encourage proper reasoning and thinking. Nothing should be imposed on them against their free will.

The teacher should try to create favourable attitude of the students towards curricular and co-curricular activities of the school. The teacher should also be conscious of his own behaviour so that no negative attitude develops against him.

Proper development of social attitude in children is another responsibility of the teacher. Proper attitude towards social customs and rituals of different communities should be formed. Through different social and cultural functions, the teacher should encourage the students to form ideal attitude towards different communities.

Summary

An attitude is a mental and neural state of readiness. It is not hereditary. It develops through interaction with the environment. Attitude has three characteristics : (i) an object, (ii) direction and (iii) intensity. Our attitude may be favourable or unfavourable towards and object or idea.

Attitude and interest are not equivalent though there is some similarity between them. Interest is guided by instincts but attitude of an individual is created by friends and association, newspapers, books and journals, etc.

Attitude can be measured by different techniques of which the judgement method, method of summated ratings, Scalogram analysis, rating methods are important.

References

1. Allport, G.W. : Attitudes. In C. Murchison (Ed.) *A Handbook of Social Psychology,* Worscestor, Mass; Clark University Press, 1935.

2. Corey, S.M. : *Professed Attitudes and Actual Behaviour,* J. Educ. Psychol, 1937.

3. Edwards, A.L. : *Techniques of Attitude Scale Construction,* New York, Appleton Century Crofts Inc. 1957.

4. Ferguson, L.W. : *The Measurement of Primary Social,* Attitudes, J. Psychol, 1940.

5. Goodie, W.J. and Hatt, P.K. : *Methods in Social Research,* New York : Mc Graw Hill, 1952.

6. Likert, R. : *A Technique for the Measurement of Attitude,* Archives of Psychology, 1932.

7. Remmers. H.H. : *An Introduction to Opinion and Attitude Measurement,* New York : Harper, 1954.

8. Sherif, M. and Sherif, C.W. : *Social Attitude : An Outline of Social Psychology,* London : Hogarth Press, 1950.

Questions and Assignments

1. Define attitude. How is attitude distinguished from interest?
2. What is attitude? How can it be measured? Describe any attitude scale in brief.
3. Discuss the importance of attitude in the education of the children.
4. Write notes on :

   (a) Likert scale

   (b) Rating method

   (c) Attitude and Interest.
5. How can you measure attitude? Describe Summated Ratings method.
6. Prepare a list of statements on attitude of a child towards his family.

Chapter 23

Aptitude and Interest

Meaning of aptitude : According to Freeman (1971), an attitude indicates capacity of an individual to acquire some specific knowledge, skill or set of organised responses, such as the ability to speak a language, to become a musician or to do mechanical work.

Bingham in his book 'Aptitude and Aptitude Testing' (1937) remarked, "An individual's potentialities are not all equally strong. One learn to do certain things more easily and better than other things, and can develop greater interest and satisfaction in some kinds of activities than in others."

Intelligence tests measure the general ability (g) of a person, while aptitude tests measure certain specific abilities (s). Aptitude tests predict the future potentialities of a person. These tests help us in selecting individuals who show talent in early stage and readily respond to training. For example, when we say that Somnath has musical ability, we mean two things : (i) Somnath has specific ability for music and (ii) If this specific ability is trained, his skill for music will increase further.

However, individuals differ from one another in their performance in any field of human activity such as mechanical work or art work. It is found that structure of hand and finger makes one skilful in typing and in playing on piano and persons with short hand and thick fingers cannot show such dexterity. But physical inferiority can be overcome through greater devotion, intensive interest and proper training. Thus, aptitude is the product of interaction between heredity and environment.

For many types of work, aptitude has little correlation with intelligence. In vocational guidance or in selecting personnel, it is more important to know about those non-intellectual abilities of a person than to know his I.Q.

Thurston (1935) and his associates have identified nine primary mental abilities through factor analysis. They are :

1. Verbal Fluency (V).
2. Spatial (S).
3. Numerical (N).
4. Memory (M).
5. Word fluencey (W).
6. Inductive reasoning (RI).
7. Deductive reasoning (RD).
8. Perceptual ability (P).
9. Problem-solving (PS).

23.1 Specialised aptitude tests

Various types of aptitude tests have been developed by psychologists for assessing potential ability of a person in an activity of a specialised kind. Some tests of specific aptitude are as follow :

1. **Clerical Aptitude Tests :** It involves several specific abilities such as, perceptual ability, intellectual ability and motor ability.

   Some of the popular aptitude tests are :

   (a) Minnesota Clerical Test.

   (b) Detroit Clerical Aptitude Test.

   (c) The Clerical Ability Test prepared by the Department of Psychology, University of Mysore, Mysore.

   (d) Clerical Aptitude Test Battery, Bureau of Educational and Vocational Guidance, Patna (Bihar).

   In Minnesota Clerical Test, the aptitude for speedy detail perception is measured. This test has two parts : (a) Number comparison and (b) Name comparison.

   Table 23.1

		Correct	**Wrong**
Examples :	(i)	992786192	992768192
	(ii)	Gargil Grain Co.	Gargal Grain Co.

   The Detroit Clerical Aptitude Test include handwriting, arithmetic, checking, classification, alphabetical filing, knowledge of commercial terms, disarranged pictures, etc.

2. **Mechanical Aptitude Test :** This test was first devised by J.L. Stenquist. In this test, the subject is asked to assemble different parts of bicycle bell, door lock, mouse-trap, etc. This Assembly Test of General Mechanical Ability has been revised at the University of Minnesota and it is now known as Minnesota Mechanical Assembly Test.

3. **Musical Talent Test :** The Earliest Musical Aptitude Test was designed by Seashore. This test assesses the ability of pitch-discrimination, intensity of loudness-discrimination, time discrimination, discrimination of timbre, judgement of rhythm and memory. Total score for these parts are used to develop an individual profile.

4. **The Meier Art Judgement Test :** This test is devised to discover the talent for graphic art. The material of the test consists of 100 pairs of representational pictures in black and white. One member of each pair is a reproduction of a known master-piece, while the other is a slight variation of the original. The subjects are informed about which aspect has been changed. They are asked to select from each pair the one which is more artistic. The number of correct responses is the measure of the subject's aptitude for graphic art.

5. **Tests for Scholastic and Professional Aptitudes :** Aptitude tests have been constructed for selection of students for admission to specific courses as medicine, teaching, engineering, military services, etc. Some of these aptitude tests are : Scholastic Aptitude Test (SAT) developed in USA, Stanford Scientific Aptitude Test by D.L. Zyve, Science Aptitude Test (after Higher Secondary stage) NIE, Delhi, Teaching Aptitude Test by Jai Prakash and R.P. Shrivastav, University of Saugar (M.P.).

23.2 General aptitude tests

At present, instead of employing specialised aptitude tests, multiple aptitude test batteries are used for selection of persons for different professions in America. Two examples of such tests are : (i) The General Aptitude Test Battery (GATB) and (ii) The Differential Aptitude Test (DAT).

GATB comprises written tests for vocabulary, arithmetic, reasoning, computation, assembling rivets and washers, etc.

DAT comprises tests for verbal reasoning, abstract reasoning, spatial relation, numerical ability, mechanical reasoning, clerical speed and accuracy, etc.

The DAT developed by U.S. Psychological Corporation has been adapted in Hindi by S.M. Ojha, National Psychological Corporation, Agra.

Besides these tests described, there are some other tests, such as Dynamometer which measures strength of grip, Ishihara Test to measure colour-blindness, Audiometer to measure hearing ability and tests which measure Motor Dexterity.

Uses of Aptitude tests : All these tests described are not standardised and their reliability and validity cannot be said to be of the highest order. However, they are widely used for the purpose of guidance in selecting subjects in schools, for selection of jobs and for admission of candidates for various types of vocational training.

Aptitude and Interest : Interests are affective-connative dispositions. They are regarded as particular kinds of sentiment centering round certain objects. "Interests are inclinations to attend to or to seek certain stimuli or to indulge in certain activities." (Guilford).

Measurement of Interests : Interests of human being are numerous and at the same time, very complex. However, by psychological inventories, we can measure today even complex interests of a person. For example, let us discuss *Vocational Interest Blank* developed by Strong. The test contains about 400 items. The subject is to respond by saying that he likes, dislikes, or is indifferent to the thing suggested.

Table 23.2: Rating of school subjects.

	Like	Indifferent	Dislike
Algebra	L	I	D
Dramatics	L	I	D
Language	L	I	D
Music	L	I	D
Philosophy	L	I	D

The subject encircles L, I or D according as he likes, is indifferent to, or dislikes each particular item. The score is calculated by statistical method.

Another important test of interest is Kuder Interest Tests. This test is highly reliable and valid and widely used for counselling purpose.

Kuder Interest Tests have three forms :

1. **Vocational form,** which measures ten interest category of individuals.
2. **Occupational form,** which measures a large number of specific occupations.
3. **Personal form** measures ten important interests in different fields.

As many other factors cause success or failure in an occupation other than interests, the results from these tests should not be taken as final in the choice of a vocation.

It has been found that interests vary most with age between the years 20 and 35 but remains fairly constant after this age range.

Summary

Intelligence tests measure the general ability (g), whereas Aptitude tests predict future possibilities of a person. For various types of work, aptitude has no relationship with intelligence. There are many specialised Aptitude Tests such as Minnesota Clerical Test, Stenquist's Mechanical Aptitude Test, Seashore's Musical Ability Tests, Meier Art Judgement Test, etc.

Interest and Aptitude are not identical. One may have interest in cricket game but he may not have the aptitude for cricket playing. Interest is measured by Strong's Vocational Interest Blank and notedly, by Kuder Interest Tests.

References

1. Anastasi, Anne : *Psychology Testing,* Macmilian Publishing Co. New York : 1982.
2. Freeman, F.S. : *Theory and Practice of Psychological Testing,* Bombay : Oxford & IBH, 1971.
3. Guilford, J.P. : *General Psychology,* D. Van Nostrand Co. Inc. New York : 1952.
4. Bingham, W.V. : *Aptitudes and Aptitude Testing,* New York : Harper & Brothers, 1937.

Questions and Assignments

1. Define aptitude. What are the uses of aptitude test?
2. What is aptltude? How will you measure aptitude?
3. Define interest. How is interest distinguished from aptitude?
4. Describe any aptitude test in brief.
5. Write notes on:
   (a) Clerical aptitude tests
   (b) Mechanical aptitude tests
   (c) Kuder interest tests
   (d) Vocational interest blank.

Chapter 24

Problems of Child Delinquency

Introduction : The last few decades have seen many changes in India. Her attainment of freedom from foreign yoke is one of them. But the independence she achieved did not come to her without a long trail of problems—political, social and economic. Before the country could recover from the criminogenic effects of the World War II (1939–1945), the partition line between India and Pakistan was drawn in August 1947. This resulted in historic exodus of lakhs of Non-Muslims from Pakistan and Muslims from India. The after effects of partition, coupled with unemployment, under-employment, poverty, rapid urbanisation and industrialisation and many other factors have abnormally accentuated delinquency trends amongst the juvenile population.

The interesting thing is that not only the number of crime is on the increase but as the old order is changing for the new so the old type of delinquency is changing for the new type. Better brains are now at work and better technical skills in the criminal operations become more and more discernible. This all-round improvement in the technique of juvenile crime is obviously eating into the vitals of our society.

Therefore, there is an urgent need in this country for scientific study of the problem of juvenile crime and until and unless we reach down to the unconscious sphere of the child's mind we can never find a real solution of the problem. Here lies a great challenge to our educators along with other social scientists of today.

24.1 Studies on delinquency in India

Kautilya (321–296 B.C.), the Machiavelli of ancient India, dwelt elaborately on crimes and delinquency in his massive book, Arthasastra. Like Cesare Beccaria, Kautilya thought that the degree of punishment must be servere enough to outweigh the pleasurable effects of the crime. So, he prescribed four kinds of torture (Karma)—six punishments (shat Dandals), seven kinds of whipping (Kasa), two kinds of suspension from above (Upasi Nibandhan) and water-tube (Udaka-Nalikacha). As to persons who had committed grave offences, the form of torture was as follows : burning one of the joints of a finger after the accused had been made to drink rice gruel; heating his body after he had been made to drink oil; causing him to lie on coarse green grass for a night in winter.

Kautilya however, asked not to torture youngsters, the aged and the afflicted persons under intoxication, lunatics, persons suffering from hunger, thirsty persons who had confessed of their own accord, or persons who were very weak.

Manu (200 B.C.), the first legislator of ancient India, classified crime into two categories : 1. Patakas (Minor Offence). 2. Mahapatakas (Major Offence).

Stealing grain, base metals and cattle, intercourse with women addicted to wine, etc., were considered as minor offences, while causing pain to a priest, smelling at wine, cheating and sexual intercourse with an unwilling woman were regarded as major offences. Gambling was strictly prohibited by Manu, because it destroys truth, honesty and wealth. With regard to pickpockets, Narada stated that for the first offence the offender shall have the thumb and the index fingers cut off; for the second, the remaining fingers shall be cut off; and for the third, he shall be put to death. For killing a priest, Apastamba prescribed that the murderer must go to the battlefield unarmed and place himself between two hostile armies to be killed mercilessly by them. With regard to drinking, Daksa asked to pour exceedingly hot liquor into the mouth of a drunkard. In connection with sex offence, Bodhayana observed : He who has bad connection with his teacher's wife shall die embracing a red hot metal-image of a woman. In case a man had an intercourse with an unmarried woman, all his property was to be confiscated by the King.

Thus the works of ancient legislators were primarily limited to the question of reformation of the criminal through penances and physical torture. None of these laws contained any detailed reference to psychological treatment of juvenile delinquents, except an ethical code relating to the treatment of children which states : A parent should not administer any punishment for any offence to a child who is under 5 years of age. Children of such age should be nursed and educated with love and affection only. After the age of 5, punishment may be given in some suitable form such as physical chastisement or rebuke by the parents. Towards the latter half of childhood, however, punishment should be gradually withdrawn and replaced by advice. From the age of 16 upwards, sons and daughters should be treated as friends by the parents.

Under the British rule in India (1757–1947), very little effort had been made to examine the fact about juvenile delinquency. The 1st special law directly related to the treatment of juvenile delinquents in British India was the Reformatory

Schools Act of 1870, which provided for the establishment of reformatory schools where any male juvenile delinquent could be detained by order of the Court from 2 to 7 years. Under the Reformatory Schools Act of 1897, the courts were empowered to send delinquent boys below 15 years of age to such schools.

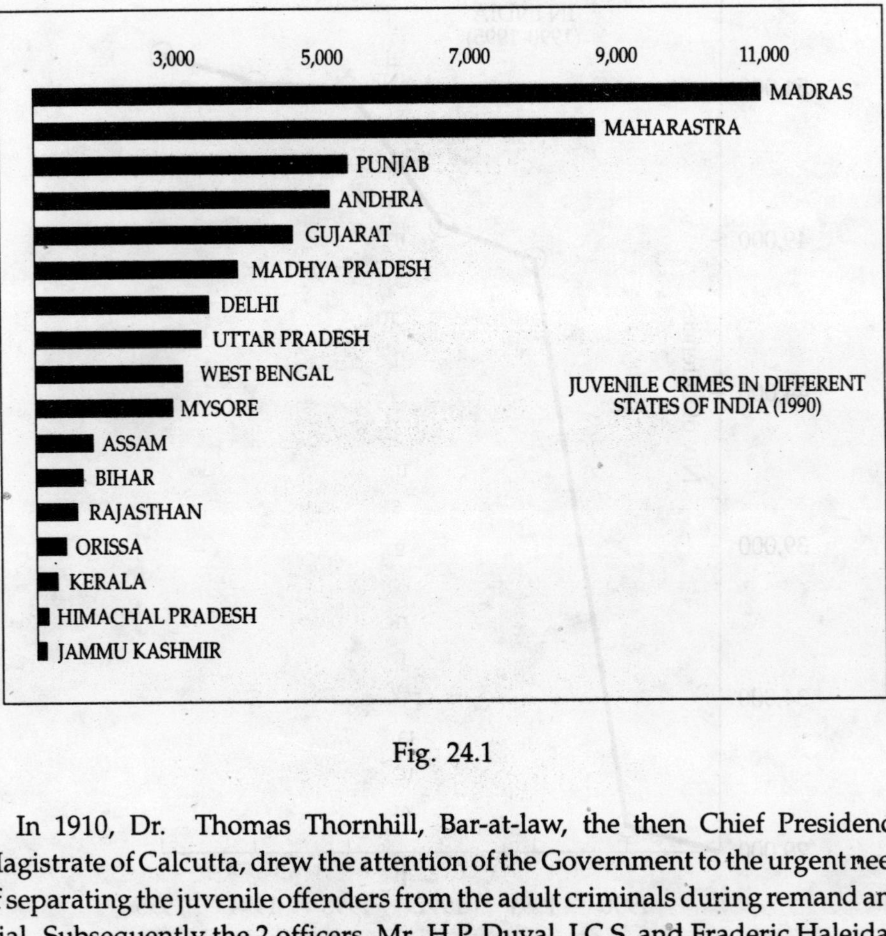

Fig. 24.1

In 1910, Dr. Thomas Thornhill, Bar-at-law, the then Chief Presidency Magistrate of Calcutta, drew the attention of the Government to the urgent need of separating the juvenile offenders from the adult criminals during remand and trial. Subsequently the 2 officers, Mr. H.P. Duval, I.C.S. and Fraderic Haleiday, the then Commissioner of Police, Calcutta, were directed by the Government to conduct a thorough survey of the problem. They submitted a joint report in August, 1912. On the basis of their recommendation, the juvenile court at 85 Lower Circular Road, the first institution of its kind in India, was born on 1 June 1914. However, eight years later, the Bengal Children Act was passed. Under this Act, no child or young person under 16 can be sentenced to death, transportation or imprisonment. From 1922 onwards, there has been no visible effort in this regard, except for minor legal amendments to the existing measures of legislation. In 1953, a special Children Bill was placed before the Indian Parliament and the Children Act was passed in 1960. The Act provides for separate institutions for neglected children and juvenile delinquents. But this Act is yet to be implemented with any seriousness.

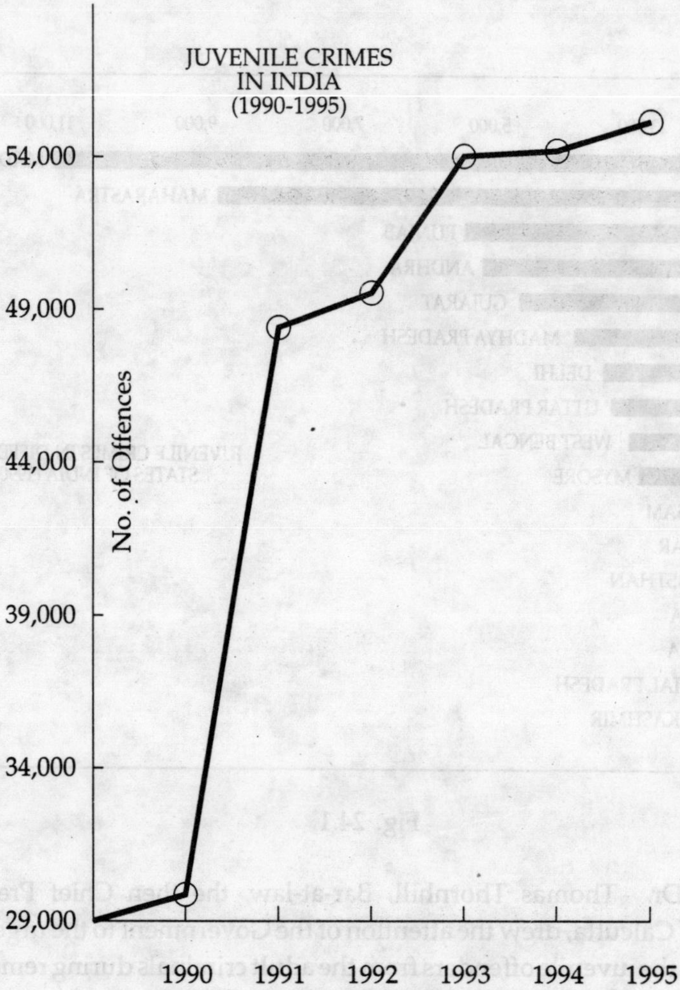

(Computed from the Crime in India)

Fig. 24.2

After the attainment of Independence, public interest in this country has been aroused to some extent in the study and treatment of juvenile delinquents. Foremost amongst the contributions in the post-independence period are the works of Bhattacharya, Bose, Hayat, Kerawalla, Kulkarni, Muhanimad, Mukherjee, Rao, Rohatgi, Sen, Seth, Sethna and Singh. These works are largely limited to questions of aetiology, diagnosis and prognosis in delinquency and crime.

24.2 Understanding the delinquent

The term delinquency is well-known and familiar even to the common people. But it may not be known to all that it is a legal term or a social problem. It is a reflection of conflicts and pressures in an individual in his social settings.

Robinson defines delinquency as any behaviour which a given community at a given time considers in conflict with its best interests, whether or not the offender has been brought to court. But this definition of delinquency is so broad that every child at one time or another is likely to engage in an antisocial behaviour that could be labelled as delinquency.

Tappan defines delinquency as any act, course of conduct, or situation which might be brought before a court and adjudicated. Prof. Burt regards a child to be a delinquent when his antisocial tendencies appear so grave that he becomes or ought to become the subject of official action.

According to Neumeyer, delinquency implies some form of anti-social behaviour involving personal and social disorganisation of the forms and laws of society and the act tends to affect people adversely.

Thus the definitions of delinquency cluster about 2 chief conceptions : (a) the non-adult status of the individuals concerned, (b) that the act is regarded as delinquency according to the laws of the community.

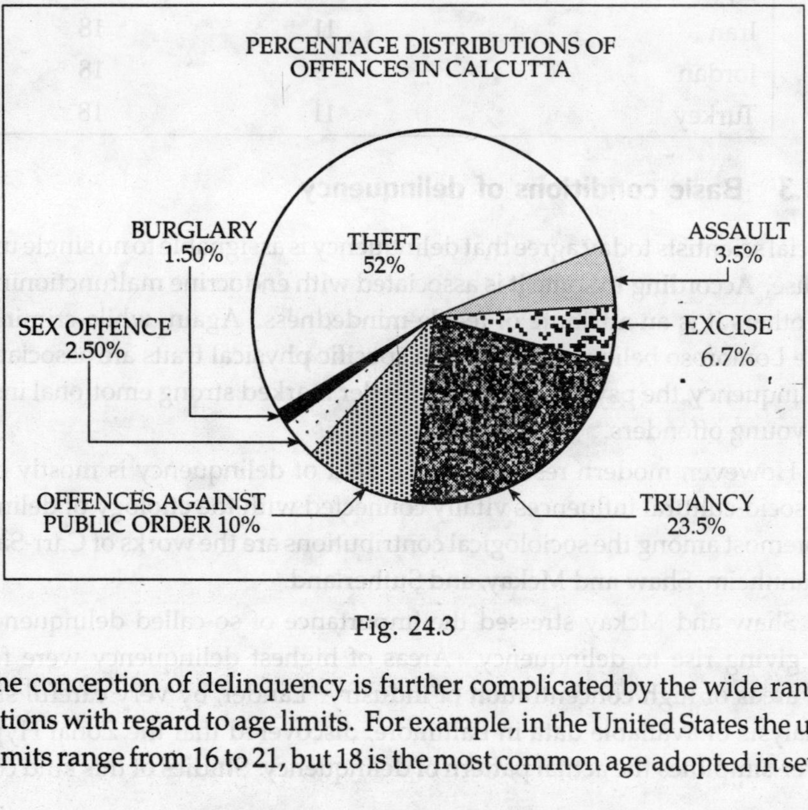

Fig. 24.3

The conception of delinquency is further complicated by the wide range of variations with regard to age limits. For example, in the United States the upper age limits range from 16 to 21, but 18 is the most common age adopted in several states. In Japan Acts, persons under fourteen years of age are not punishable. In certain areas of India and Pakistan—where the Reformatory Schools Act operates—youthful offender means any boy who has been convicted of any offence punishable with transportation or imprisonment and who at the time of such conviction was under fifteen years.

Age limits of juvenile offenders in some of the Asian countries are shown in the Table 24.1.

Table 24.1 : Age Limits of Juvenile Deliquents.

Country	Lower Age limit in years	Upper Age limit in years
Myanmar (Burma)	7	16
Sri Lanka (Ceylon)	7	16
India :		
(a) Where Children's Act operates	7	16
(b) Where Reformatory Schools Act operates	7	15
Japan	14	20
Iran	11	18
Jordan	9	18
Turkey	11	18

24.3 Basic conditions of delinquency

Social scientists today agree that delinquency is assignable to no single universal cause. According to some it is associated with endocrine malfunctioning while to others it is an attribute of feeble-mindedness. Again, while criminologists like Lombroso believed that certain specific physical traits are associated with delinquency, the psychologists like Eissler marked strong emotional instability in young offenders.

However, modern research in the field of delinquency is mostly diverted to socio-cultural influences vitally connected with the etiology of delinquency. Foremost among the sociological contributions are the works of Carr-Saunders, Mannheim, Shaw and Mckay, and Sutherland.

Shaw and Mckay stressed the importance of so-called delinquency areas in giving rise to delinquency. Areas of highest delinquency were found to be areas of high concentration of industry. Lander, by very careful statistical analysis of available data in Baltimore, discovered that the Zonal Hypothesis over-simplifies the actual pattern of delinquency. Studies of this kind could not explain why some boys coming from high delinquency areas appear to develop a resistance to delinquent behaviour, even in the most adverse social setting.

Dirksen and others have described delinquency as a phenomenon of the lower economic strata. Bonger in his Criminality and Economic Condition points out that in order for crimes to be committed, there must exist facilitating environmental conditions. A thief without victims, a bank robber without banks, cannot commit crime, notwithstanding their criminal motives and techniques. Bonger's study indicates that the pressure of a capitalistic system is responsible for delinquency and crime. The studies of Burt and others have been concerned with the effects of poverty. Burt showed that over half of the total amount of juvenile delinquency in London was found in homes that were poor or very poor. Parmalee believed that it was not only poverty but the desire for a higher standard of living which led to crime. One of the most intensive studies of the relation of juvenile court cases to economic trends was made by Bogen. This study indicates that delinquency increases in periods of prosperity and decreases in periods of widespread unemployment and economic distress.

The learning process by means of which an individual associates with a criminal group and studies the various techniques of crime was explained by Sutherland in the theory of Differential Association.

Sutherland stated his theory in certain propositions, and some are :

1. Criminal behaviour is learned.
2. Criminal behaviour is learned in interaction with other persons in a process of communication.
3. The principal part of the learning of criminal behaviour occurs within intimate personal groups.
4. When criminal behaviour is learned, the learning includes :
   (a) techniques of committing the crime, which are sometimes very complicated, sometimes very simple;
   (b) the specific direction of motives, drives, rationalisations and attitudes.

This theory, however, does not offer the basic explanation for the criminal activity of the person under emotional stress, who commits a theft or murders his brother without any special social education for his antisocial behaviour.

In 'Delinquency and Opportunity' Cloward and Ohlin assert that the differential opportunity systems theory provides a new useful way of thinking about delinquency. Delinquency arises from the disparity between what lower-class youths are led to want and what is actually available to them. Cloward and

Ohlin point out that if, in a given social location, illegal or criminal means are not readily available, then we should not expect a criminal subculture to develop among adolescents. To give an example, drug addiction and participation in subculture organised around the consumption of drugs presuppose that persons can secure access to drugs and knowledge about how to use them. In some parts of the social structure, this would be very difficult; in others, very easy.

In 'Delinquent Boys : The Culture of Gang' Cohen emphasises that blocked opportunities to play the male role is an important causal element in delinquent behaviour of the middle class boy. Since mother has been the principal agent of indoctrination of good behaviour, goodness comes to symbolise femininity. As a result, the boy who attempts to assert his masculinity must do so by protests, against his mother's standards of goodness. This, according to Cohen, is the motivation to juvenile delinquency.

Another monumental study which has had tremendous impact on researchers in the field of delinquency is that of the Glueeks called 'Unravelling Juvenile Delinquency.' In this work the Glueeks used a team of psychologists, psychiatrists, social investigators, anthropologists and statisticians. They matched 500 non-delinquents with same number of delinquents on a number of variables such as age, I.Q. social economic background etc. As a result of the investigations, the principal characteristics that differentiate the delinquent from his control are described by the Glueeks as follows :

1. Physically, in being essentially mesomorphic in constitution (i.e., solid, closely knit, muscular);

2. In attitude, in being hostile, defiant, resentful, suspicious, stubborn, socially assertive, adventurous, unconventional, non-submissive (or ambivalent) to authority;

3. Intellectually, in tending to direct and concrete, rather than symbolic, abstract intellectual expression and in being less methodical in their approach to problems;

4. Socio-culturally, in having been reared to a far greater extent than the control group in homes of little understanding, affection, stability, or moral fibre by parents usually unfit to be effective guides and protectors or desirable symbols for emulation; and under conditions unfavourable to the building of a well-balanced and socially adequate character and conscience.

The Glueeks have summarised much of the present knowledge about juvenile delinquency and have made great advances in this field through the publication of their prediction table.

24.4 Certain social determinants in Juvenile Delinquency

It is known to all that the delinquent child does not bring his antisocial tendencies with him from his mother's womb. These he acquires through contact with different social institutions of which the family is the most effective and powerful agency.

24.4.1 The family

A happy normal home is generally regarded as the best insurance against delinquency and crime. On the contrary, it is now a well-known fact that homes broken by domestic discord, play a major part in the causation of crime. Broken home deprives a child parental love, and loss of parental affection means deprivation of the most precious and valued thing in the world. Children need their affection of both the parents. At the same time, they need to realise that there is no discord amongst their parents. There is a specific connection between prolonged deprivation in the early years of the development of an affectionless psychopathic character to persistent delinquent conduct.

In a study of 341 delinquent girls at the Whittier State School in California, Mathews found that more than half were reared in broken homes. In 1930, Sullenger found that about 51 per cent of the 1135 delinquents reported in Omaha came from broken homes. The intensive studies of Burt, Carr Saunder, Wittman, Monahan and others all stress the destructive influence on the child's development of the absence of either parent from the home.

In course of an investigation, the author found that half of the 300 delinquent children studied, came from broken home. The sample of delinquents belonged to different Juvenile jails of West Bengal, who had police record behind them came from home broken by the death of one or both parents or by parental separation (Table 24.1). On the other hand, in the control group (300 normal boys) only 15 per cent of the homes were abnormally structured.

The figures in Table 24.2, however does not correspond very closely tc those reported by other European or American investigators.

Table 24.2 : Family structure

Parents		Delinquents				Controls		
Living together	N	150	%	50	N	255	%	85
Separated		6		2		—		—
Mother dead		54		18		6		2
Father dead		48		16		24		8
Both dead		36		12		15		5
Father re-married		6		2		—		—
		300		100		300		100

χ^2 (Chi-square) = 94.20

$P \angle .01$

This is probably because of the fact that marriage is still considered by the Indians as a sacrament or sanskara, a lifelong union, which cannot be dissolved in this life. This notion, which is strong even in the lower strata of the people, leads to the stability of the Indian family. However, not that divorce or separation never takes place, but such cases are very few.

24.4.2 Discipline by parents

The home, though not broken, may be unsuitable for many reasons such as excessive conflict due to economic strain, alcoholism and erratic discipline.

On the basis of interview data and also from the report of probation officers and social workers, the writer has rated the disciplinary practices of parents of Delinquents and non-Delinquents in Table 24.2.

Table 24.2 : Discipline by parents

Father

Description		Delinquents				Non-Delinquents		
Lax	N	57	%	19	N	12	%	4
Over-strict		75		25		36		12
Over-indulgent		108		36		24		8
Normal (firm but kind)		60		20		228		76
		300		100		300		100

Mother

Description		Delinquents			Non-Delinquents			
Lax	N	81	%	27	N	15	%	5
Over strict		39		13		30		10
Over indulgent		60		20		21		7
Normal (firm but kind)		120		40		234		78
		300		100		300		100

$\chi^2 = 194.48 : P\angle.01, \quad \chi^2 = 101.86 : P\angle.01.$

24.4.3 Drunkenness

One of the features of vicious home is drunkenness. The author has found 25 per cent parents of the delinquents addicted to either wine, toddy, vang, charas, or ganja whereas in normal cases it is only 4 per cent. (Table 24.3).

Table 24.3

Delinquents		Non-Delinquents	
N	%	N	%
75	25	12	4

The introduction of prohibition in India actually caused a considerable fall in the number of crimes committed under the influence of intoxication. There is a strong sentiment in India in favour of prohibition; the vast majority of Hindus do not drink, and Mahatma Gandhi's strong opposition to drinking has still a dominant influence.

24.4.4 Overcrowding

It is generally supposed that delinquents come of larger families than non-delinquents. Overcrowding of the home gives rise to increased competition on the part of the children for parental attention, emotional stress and strain, and other emotional trauma.

Table 24.4 : Number of Siblings

No. of Siblings	Delinquents		Control	
	N	%	N	%
1.	18	6	42	14
2.	30	10	48	16
3.	42	14	51	17
4.	36	12	42	14
5.	45	15	39	13
6.	48	16	18	6
7. or more	81	27	60	20

From the Table 24.4, we find that as a whole, the delinquent boys did come from somewhat larger families than that of the non-delinquents, 58 per cent of the former being one of 5 or more living children as compared with 39 per cent of the latter.

24.4.5 The Companions

The study of crime reveals that in a majority of cases, bad association lies at the root of a criminal career. Cyril Burt and Healy found bad companionship a causative factor in 17.7 per cent and 34 per cent of their juveniles, respectively. Shaw and Mckay found by a study of juvenile court records in Chicago that 88.2 per cent of the boys had been engaged in delinquency in company with others. Similar findings have been reported by the Gluecks. In a study comparing 500 delinquents with 500 non-delinquents in the same area, the Glueeks found that 98.4 per cent of the delinquents associated with other delinquents. While, only 7.4 per cent of the non-delinquents had delinquent associates.

In fact, boys seldom commit delinquencies alone. In course of an investigation, the author has noticed that in a majority of cases child criminals act in a gang.

From the Table 24.5 it is clear that 58 per cent of the delinquents as compared with only 1 per cent of the non-delinquents were members of gangs.

Table 24.5 : Membership in an organisation

No. of siblings	Delinquents		Non-Delinquents	
	N	%	N	%
Members of a gang	174	58	3	1
Members of a club	90	30	237	79
Never belonged to any organisation	36	12	60	20
Total	300	100	300	100

χ^2 (Chi-square) = 237.4; P ∠ .01.

24.4.6 Characteristics of Gangs

The studies of Thrasher, Cohen and Furfey have shed much light into the nature of gang behaviour. It is not for the material gain that the delinquent boys form the gang. If that has been the case, individual stealing instead of collective stealing would have thrived in majority of cases.

Hans Von Henting found elements of self-assertion and love of excitement as deep-rooted incentives in all sorts of property crimes. The boys who are longing for recognition and do not receive it in school or at home take a special pride in their skill when stealing with gang members. Moreover, petty crimes have in them a pleasant colouring of adventure. This makes a strong appeal which draws young criminals to organise the gang. Forced out by the misfortunes of a morbid home, these outcasts of society prefer to take to the life of the road with all its laughter and tears. The eternal gregarious instinct of a social animal unconsciously leads the delinquents to seek associations and friends. Victims of the same evil circumstances flock together. The gang gives them life. It creates a sense of being wanted, so long badly lacking in their lives.

The dull, drab and stuffy home life bears no meaning for them. They agree with none outside their own sphere and thus create an atmosphere of an espirit de corps. Believing none else, they believe themselves. The exchange of mutual sympathy and emotions helps them to build a different world for the comrades in distress, and they soon become strange misfits in society.

Investigation by the author shows that a gang comprised as many as hundred young members with one or more adult criminals at the top. The leaders gave their disciples proper vocational training and guidance, supplied money needed for feasts and purchasing cinema tickets and at times snatched comrades out of the clutches of the furious public with the pretext of handing them over the police.

The author found greater tendency of the young delinquents to seek companions among older youths. This tendency, according to the Gluecks may be associated with the search for a substitute ego-ideal for emulation, since we know that the parents of the delinquents are less affectionate to them and less acceptable as models for emulation than are the father of the non-delinquents. But conscious rejection of their leader is revealed by the fact that as many as 50 per cent of the delinquents, the author studied expressed a marked dislike for their leaders, while 83 per cent of the delinquents were obedient to their leaders of their club. Some of the delinquents openly declared : I hate the leader most. Please, punish me sir, and keep me in this jail as long as you can. If you release me, I will again fall into the clutches of the wicked leader. Probably he will beat me to death once he can get hold of me.

The reasoning for disliking a leader are many :

1. As long as the young offender had worked with the gang without being caught, his faith, his devotion to his group remained unshakeable. But the moment he was caught the esprit-de-corps disappeared and the emotional bond with the leader and other associates of the gang disintegrated resulting in a metamorphosis of the attitude. He started accusing his leader and other associates and poured all his venom against them. This might be due to two reasons :

   (a) It is not solely motivated by gregarious instinct and inherent love for companions that the boy chummed with the delinquents of the gang. In many cases circumstance, like socio-economic conditions at his forced him to accept gang membership. His association with the gang did not really develop any intense emotional link with the members. If he developed any at all it was a weak and superficial link which disintegrated at the slightest shock.

(b) In the juvenile institutions, the little offenders got enough protection, better food, clothing, shelter and a bit of education and social training under better type of persons. The sober effect of all these might have some role to play on their attitudes towards the leader.

24.5 Prevention

While visiting the juvenile jail, the author had occasions to have long talks with the delinquents. Once he found a young delinquent saying with his hands folded and tears rolling from his cheek, "Babu Sahib, please release me from this dungeon. I will never do such thing again, I assure you. I will never mix in evil company. Please give me a chance for reformation. I will go back to my sweet home, where my little sister is weeping for me." Answered the boy while wiping out his tears. After a brief pause, the boy asked, 'Sir, can you give me a job?'

What type of a job, do you mean?—I asked.

'Why, such jobs, as washing of plates or sweeping houses of any kind person, or any sort of manual work you provide.' The boy heaved a sigh.

'There are so many things that stand in our way of becoming good. We are like stray dogs. Who cares for us?' The boy left the author thinking of much what he had said. Is there no way to reform such criminals?

In fact, the problem of juvenile delinquency is one that demands the attention of our society most, because the delinquent child of today may be the dreadful criminal of tomorrow. Dr. Goring found that of 2,204 habitual offenders in the prison, more than 50% had been first convicted before the age of 20. Therefore, early detection and control of the malady is imperative.

24.5.1 Physical punishment

Lombroso suggested that born criminals should be regarded as incurable and all of them should be confined for life in a criminal asylum, or else condemned to death. But a civilised society never accepted this theory, otherwise it could not have spent a lot of money over so many corrective measures. Our society, therefore, thinks in terms of their rehabilitation and not physical liquidation.

24.5.2 Detention

Dr. Cyril Burt, who laid stress on scientific investigation, says to whip a boy, to fine him, to shut him up in a penal institution, because he has infringed the law, is like sending a patient, on the first appearance of fever, out under the open sky, to cool his skin and save others from the infection. With moral disorders as with physical we must find and fight not symptoms but causes. Not before causes have been discovered can cures be advised. The aim of our juvenile courts, therefore, should be to understand the child and to correct those conditions which led to the delinquency. But a peep into any juvenile detention home of West Bengal will show that a large number of children detected for different offences are thrust into the same torture chamber, irrespective of their age and offence. Detaining children in lock-ups without proper classification is obviously harmful, because this system exposes those who have chances of recovery to the vile influence of the hardened criminals.

A petty pickpocket, for instance, may come out of the correction home after confinement with full knowledge of the higher skills of burglary.

24.5.3 Vocational training

Like other states, a Borstal school had been set up in West Bengal at Berhampore, Murshidabad, where about a hundred delinquent boys are provided with various types of vocational training. After completion of the training, some of them have suitable jobs, but many of them have been rejected by the employers simply because they had police record behind them. Obviously, adequate propaganda is necessary to change such attitude on the part of the employer so that the delinquents — after proper vocational training — may find suitable jobs and live as good citizens.

24.5.4 Psychological clinics

For the successful treatment and prevention of juvenile delinquency we need to establish a large number of psychological clinics thoroughout the state. In a psychological clinic, a team of psychologists, psychiatrists and social worker operate. The psychologists and psychiatrists attempt to diagnose the causes of delinquent behaviour and the social workers keep contact with the home. They would often sit together in a conference and discuss jointly about the causes of delinquency and suggest necessary remedies.

24.5.5 Family council

It is now admitted that the reformatories are not proper substitute for home. Recently, in England, the idea of forming Family Council is gaining ground. In India we may also start such councils — at least in some important industri localities. While such council will be represented by the people of all spheres, its important function would be to prepare a list of delinquent children in the locality and adequately help those parents who will agree to take charge of such children.

24.6 Cases from Remand Home

Case No. 1 : Madan belongs to a refugee family. He has one younger sister. The family relationship became defective after the death of his mother. His step-mother was a cruel lady and oppressed him to an extreme measure. One day she gave the boy a plate of ash instead of rice to eat during the time of his hunger. After this incident the boy left his native village, Faridpur, now in East Pakistan. He came to Calcutta and started working as a hotel boy. He worked in the hotel for 15 days but the employer refused to pay him and drove him out under some pretext. He joined a potato shop at Bowbazar. 'K', the proprietor of the shop, sells potato during the day time and deals in illicit liquor at night. The boy used to get Rs. 28.00 only per menses for 'K' as his wages. 'K' asked the boy to remain at his potato shop (or wine shop) at night and taught him how to prepare indigenous liquor from "Mahua flower". Now one night all on a sudden his liquor shop was raided by the police. The boy along with some other workers of the shop was arrested.

Case No. 2 : Tabu stays with his poor illiterate mother in a hut an Manicktola. He does not know who his father is and whether he is dead or alive. When he was very young, a man named Lalu was staying with them and his mother did everything for him. But after some time he left them and another man named Charitra came to stay with them. His mother behaved with Charitra in the same way as she used to do with Lalu. But Charitra too left them. Tabu is told by his mother that Charitra was his real father and he died some years ago. Tabu is told by his mother that Charitra was his real father and he died some years ago. Tabu is not prepared to believe this. Apart from this unhappy situation, however, Tabu's mother is almost mad after him as he is her only son. Though economically poor, she tries to meet all his needs and desires. Tabu is extremely fond of pictures. The mother manages to save some money from her meagre earnings and give some to Tabu to visit pictures. She works as a maid-servant at a number of places in the neighbourhood, wears the old sari for years together and goes without chappals even in hot summer days. Her works keeps her out and away from hime, and Tabu is left all to himself. As the mother says, Tabu was sent to school with he was young, but he played truant and was dismissed because of his misconduct. Since then he refuses to attend school and wanders about in bad company. He and his friends in the neighbourhood have formed a gang. The whole gang has specialised in removing plates of car-tyres and lids of petrol tanks from the cars. The stolen material is then regularly sold at chorabazar and usually the returns of the sale are equally divided among the participants. As Tabu reports, they generally carry out their operations during hot afternoon hours when the Police vigilance is slackened or during late hours of evening when the surroundings are congenial and chances of being detected are comparatively less. The money recovered is spent jointly or individually in enjoying hotel-food, or a cinema show. Tabu's mother is eager to have him back. She wants him to improve and get educated. She deeply feels she should do something good for Tabu but neither does she know the way nor she posses the means to do it.

Case No. 3 : Amal, a thin young lad, belongs to a lower middle class family. His presents are alive. His father is Primary School Teacher. The boy read up to Class V in the Titagarh High School. He says that his mother very badly oppresses him. She beats and kicks him often without rhyme or reason. The boy stresses that she is not his own mother. Under severe oppression he ran away from his house and started working as a coolie at Howrah station. Here he came in contact with a group of anti-socials. The boy reports that one day a man with a heavy luggage alighted fro the Madras Mail and looked about for a collie. The boy agreed to offer him his services. When the boy was about to come out of the gate with the luggage, he was challenged by the Police and was arrested. The owner of the luggage managed to disappear in the crowd. The Police got out of the luggage several bladders containing illicit liquor. The boy pleads not guilty. He strongly desires to go back to his home and meet his younger brother and sisters. He assures to behave nicely in future.

Case No. 4 : Gopal belongs to a poor refugee family. His father died as a result of communal riot in East Pakistan. He sells cigarettes in Howrah-Bandel local train. By means of this, boy earns Rs. 2.00 or Rs. 3.00 daily and thus helps the poor family. The mother of the boy works in a local factory and earns Rs. 80.00 only per month. One day, while he was going back to his home at night, he was kidnapped by two villains and was brought into a dark underground cell, where he met several boys of his age. 'Lalu', the leader of the gang, forced him to adopt the profession of the group. He was taught carefully the technique of picking pockets and other sorts of pilfering. The boy was given shelter, food and sometimes money for purchasing cinema tickets and smoking cigarettes. Gopal does not hesitate to confess his guilt. He accuses his leader and other members of the gang for his misfortune.

Case No. 5 ; Dalu appears meek and mild at the first sight, but behind that gentle look, there is a turbulent and uncontrollable personality. For all his mischievous adventures, running away from home, roaming about with mendicants and stealing, he is often severely punished by his father and is tied up with iron chains by his step-mother. But nothing improve him. He continues stealing money and wandering about freely in the company of his friends. He does not attend school and never cares for any scolding or beating by his parents. He is rebellious and beyond all control.

What has made Dalu such a care-free, revolting, uncontrollable child, is difficult to make out. His mother died when he was every young. His father is illiterate and unemployed. He is not keeping well and gets easily irritated on the slightest excuse. The step-mother and the elder sister work as domestic servants, and remain out of home during the day to earn the bread for the family. As a result, Dalu is left alone without any familial warmth and care and falls easy prey to all the bad influences of slum neighbourhood. His father has lost his patience and he strongly feels that the only was to improve the child is to send him to some institution, where he would be under strict supervision and control.

Case No. 6 : Naru belongs to a lower class family. He woks in a flower shop at Gariahata Market, Ballygunje. His father is a peon in Dharamtala Post Office and his income is Rs. 70,00 only per month. His mother is a maid-servant. The boy is illiterate and dull. He is addicted to all kinds of intoxications—Wine, Toddy, Ganja, Vang and what not. His father is indifferent to home-discipline and he is alcoholic. They boy has been suffering from epilepsy since his early age. He has been implicated in a dacoity case involving twelve thousand rupees plus some valuable jewellery from the house of a rich merchant.

Summary

In recent years much public concern has been caused in our country by the shocking increase in juvenile crime. So far, little progress has been made by the educationists in the intensive study of this social problem.

Social psychologists today agree that delinquency is assignable to no single universal cause. Lombroso (1836-1909) believed that criminals have certain physical features which are inborn. Dirkson (1949) has described delinquency as a phenomenon of the lower economic strata. Bonger's (1916) study indicates that the pressure of a capitalistic system is responsible for delinquency. The studies of Burt and others have been concerned with the effect of poverty. Again, homes broken by domestic discord play a major part in the causation of crime. The study of crime reveals that in a majority of cases bad association lies at the root of a criminal career.

The task of prevention of delinquency is a very complex one. It requires the cooperation of society, home and school. Physical punishment and detention are of no use. School can do a great lot to prevent delinquency by providing proper facilities for curricular and co-curricular activities. Vocational Training Institutes may be set up for the delinquents, so that, after proper vocational training, they may find suitable jobs and live as good citizens. For the treatment of delinquency we need to establish a number of Psychological Clinics, where a team of psychologists and social workers would operate. For prevention of juvenile delinquency, we may establish Family Councils in every district. The important function of the council would be to prepare a list of delinquents in the locality and help the parents who will agree to take charge of such children.

References

1. Bagot, J.H. : *Juvenile Delinquency. Jonathan Cape,* 30 Bedford Square, London, 1941.
2. Bhattacharya, B.K. : *Juvenile Delinquency and Borstals.* S.C. Sarkar & Sons, Calcutta, 1960.
3. Bonger, W.A. : *Criminality and Economic Conditions,* Boston, Little Brown Co., 1916.
4. Burt, Cyril : *The Young Delinquent,* University of London Press, 1945.
5. Chatterjee, S.K. : *Anti-social Activities of Children in Calcutta and Suburbs,* Psychology Department, Calcutta University, 1960.
6. Dirksen, C. : *Economic Factors in Delinquency,* Milwankee Bruce Publishing Co., 1948.
7. Glueck, S. and Glueck, E. : *One Thousand Delinquents,* Cambridge, Harvard University, 1934.
8. Glueck, S. and Glueck, E. : *Unravelling Juvenile Delinquency,* New York, The Commonwealth Fund, 1950.
9. *Government of India,* Ministry of Home Affairs : Crime in India, 1958–1961.
10. Likert, R. : *A Technique for the Measurement of Attitude, Archives of Psychology,* 1932.
11. Merrill, Maud, A. : *Problem of Child Delinquency,* George G. Harrap, London, 1947.
12. Bose, G. : *Delinquency in India,* In Eissler, R.K. (Ed.) Searchlights on Delinquency.
13. Sen. P.K. : *A Peep into the Calcutta Under-world,* Calcutta Police Journal. Vol. 2, Jan-March, 1954.
14. Hayat, A.S. : *A Study of the Juvenile Delinquency,* Dept. of Psychology, Calcutta University, 1950.

15. Kerawalla, *A Study in Indian Crime,* Popular Book Depot., Bombay, 1959.

16. Kulkarni, D.V. : *Juvenile Delinquency Social Welfare in India,* The Planning Commission, Govt. of India, New Delhi, 1955.

17. Mukherjee, B.M. : *Crime in Indian Children,* National Literature Co., Calcutta, 1947.

18. Seth, H. : *Juvenile Delinquency in an Indian Setting,* Popular Book Depot, Bombay, 1961.

Questions and Assignments

1. What is delinquency? How can the delinquents be psychologically helped?
2. Whom would you call delinquent children? How can they be educationally helped?
3. What do you mean by Juvenile delinquency? Suggest some measures that can be adopted to prevent delinquency among students.
4. What is family council? How can such council help a delinquent child?
5. What are the causes of delinquency? Suggest some remedial measures.
6. Write short notes on:

   (a) Family council.

   (b) Psychological clinics.

   (c) Gang and delinquents.

Chapter 25

Habit

Introduction : A habit is the product of repeated voluntary actions. When voluntary actions become habitual, they dispense with the guidance of attention and volition and become automatic. William James defines habit as the tendency of an organism to behave in the same way as it has behaved before. It is performed mechanically like a reflex act.

Habitual actions are not innate but acquired or learnt. They are modes of reactions which are fixed. Instinctive acts also may be repeated and fixed as habits. According to Allport, habit is integrated system of conditioned response.

25.1 Characteristics of Habit

Habitual actions have certain characteristics. They are :

1. **Uniformity :** Habitual actions are uniform actions. Habitual actions are performed in the same way. A person talks or walks in the same way.
2. **Promptness :** Habitual actions are performed promptly. The stronger the habit, the quicker the motor response to the situation.
3. **Accuracy :** Habitual actions are performed not only promptly, but also accurately. The stronger the habit, more precise is the motor response.
4. **Independence of Attention :** Habitual actions are performed automatically without the guidance of attention and consciousness. After having performed an action consciously once or twice or more, amount of attention and efforts are lessened, till it becomes mechanical and forms habit.

5. **Ease and facility :** Habitual actions are performed with ease and facility. As habits are firmly established, they diminish fatigue. The miners, for example, do not feel fatigue when they are accustomed to their work. A small boy makes a great effort in writing the first few alphabets. But afterwards it becomes an easy task for him.

6. **Resistance to change :** The stronger the habit, the greater the difficulty of breaking it. A drunkard finds it difficult to break the habit of drinking. A habitual opium-eater feels an irresistible impulse to take doses of opium regularly. Habits resist modification.

25.2 Relation of Habit with Instincts

Habits and Instincts are alike marked by uniformity and facility. They are both mechanical and accurate. They both dispense with the guidance of volition. But instincts are innate, while habits are learned by repeated voluntary actions. Instincts are said to be racial habits, habits are said to be individual habits.

25.3 Relation of Habit with Emotion

The psychoanalysts hold that behind every habit there is an emotion. The habit does not function unless the emotion is present. Habits can be retained only so long as the emotion behind it is retained. When the emotion disappears, the habit also disappears. An activity becomes fixed, because it yields satisfaction. It satisfies a deep-rooted urge. When it fails to satisfy, it is soon discontinued.

25.4 Importance of habit

Habit is second nature. Habit is the great conservative force with which everybody is endowed. William James says, habit is the enormous *flywheel of society.* They lessen the burden of life. Following are some of the advantages that we derive out of them :

1. **Habit saves our time :** Once a habit is formed we do not require much time to do it next time. A large number of routine-works are performed only by way of habits. Eating, drinking, walking, bathing and toilet, etc. are just done as habits. Had we been required to learn them afresh everyday, it would have become impossible to push life ahead so easily.

2. **Habits prevent fatigue :** Were there no habits, we had to relearn every task on every occasion. This would have caused much fatigue, destroying all our enthusiasm for work.

3. **Habit makes us accurate :** When we become habituated in doing a task, only then the accuracy emerges. Thus accuracy is just the habit formation and its resulting behaviour.

4. **Habit makes us efficient :** Efficiency demands that anything which is to be done should be performed with ease and facility. This can be possible only when performance becomes a habit.

25.5 Limitations of Habits

Acquiring some good habits is nice. But we should not be a slave to habits for the following reasons :

1. Habits are mechanical and stereotyped. They retard the flow of mental energy into new channels. Therefore, adjustment in new situations is not helped by habits.
2. Habits, once formed are difficult to be broken. If some wrong habits is formed in the childhood, it will be difficult to eradicate it in future life.
3. Habits being stereotyped, deprive us of interest. When we perform a task habitually, we experience no feeling of interest in it. Habit discourages initiatives.
4. Habits make a person highly conservative and standardised. We do not much like a person who behaves in the same way at all occasions.

25.6 Teachers' role in Habit formation

Habit has a prominent place in education. The progress of a pupil depends to a great extent upon the formation of good habits. A student should have fixed hours of rising and going to bed, of work, of meals and recreation. It is only in this way that he can discharge his responsibilities of life. Rousseau was incorrect when he declared that the only habit that Emile would form is to form no habit.

The child with good habits has an enormous fund of energy at his command which he can utilise for the purpose of improving himself. The child who has not acquired the habits of cleanliness, punctuality and industry will seldom develop these habits in later life. The child cannot help forming habits.

It is up to the parents and teachers to see whether the habits he forms would be good or bad.

The teacher has to cultivate certain good physical habits in pupils, such as habit of neatness, habit of sitting and standing with right posture, taking regular physical exercises etc. The teacher should also see that students acquire proper habits of attention, of correct pronunciation and correct thinking and reasoning. The teacher should always encourage them to cultivate good habits and praise them for their good habits. Practice makes a man perfect. So the teacher should see that students make their habit firm by constant practice.

The teacher will not only try to cultivate good habits but also see that pupils do not fall victim to wrong habits. However, habits should not be rooted out by force. In that case, it may produce fear, anxiety and nervous tension. Counselling should be done with sympathy and affection.

The teacher should also keep watch on his own habit. Often pupils imitate bad habits of their teacher. The teacher has to hold out good ideals before them so as to create good habits in them and eradicate wrong habits. Let him tell stories to his students about the misery of the persons who contracted bad habits.

25.7 Laws of habit formation

William James has given four laws of the formation of habits. They are :

1. Begin a new habit with a firm resolution. If you make a start with a firm determination, it often carries you along and fixes the habit. It is said, well begun is half done. If you want to rise early in the morning, first make a firm resolve to do it. Often taking a public pledge will enable you to stick to your resolution with greater tenacity. Simple preaching is of no use, prove it by doing.
2. Seize the first opportunity to put the new resolve into practice. No delay or postponment of the action should be allowed. Do not wait for the first day of the next month or the New Year's Day to start to work. If you do so, your resolution will become weak and inspiration will vanish. So strike while the iron is hot.
3. Never allow an exception to occur till the new habit is securely rooted. Efforts should be made until it is deeply rooted in life. Once you have started rising early, continue the action from day to day and never allow a slip or lapse on any pretext. Aristotle rightly said that there is no holiday for virtue.
4. Keep the faculty of effort alive in you by a little free practice every day. In order to cultivate the strength of mind, you should perform a difficult action everyday which requires a great effort of will. Habits make us conservative. But we must be open to new ideas, to new methods. We can best do this by a little practice of doing something new and difficult everyday. Baden Powell laid down the law for the scouts : A scout must do a good turn everyday.

25.8 How to break bad habits

Habits may be good or bad. Good habits should be cultivated. Bad habits should be broken. Though it is difficult, yet certain ways have been found effective in breaking them. They are :

1. Stop the bad habit at once; do not wait for a suitable opportunity. Stop the habit of smoking or drinking at once. According to Angel, "Begin the new regime at once, do not wait for convenient season. If the result be not likely to be physically disastrous stop wholly, do not taper off."

   When a bad habit is not given a chance of expression for a long time and remains in disuse, it is ultimately broken.

2. Cultivate a positive counter-habit. If you are in the habit of going to cinema every evening, try to form the habit of listening to radio music at that time. A drunkard may cultivate the habit of taking hot milk instead of wine at stated times. He should continue the habit until he feels sure that the grip of the old habit is loosened.

3. Try to live in an environment which is favourable to the formation of good habit. Give up the company of the habitual cinema-goers if you want to break the habit of cinema-going. A drunkard must give up the company of drunkards and keep the company of sober people.

4. Bad habits give a feeling of pleasantness. Hence it is difficult to get rid of bad habits. If the repetition of bad habit results in dissatisfaction, the bad habit become gradually extinct.

Punishment, disapproval, criticism and censure for the wrong habit create a feeling of displeasure in child's mind. As a result, he may give up bad habit. But these methods should be used continuously. Otherwise, the case may become more difficult and mental complex or some other abnormality may occur.

25.9 Habit and character

Habits are the foundation of character. Good habits build good character, while bad habits build bad character. Character is the acquired habit of controlling and regulating the natural impulsive tendencies by will or volition. Character is an organisation of habits that are built up through repeated actions. For the acquisition of a proper type of character, the will has to be trained or made strong by exercise.

Development of character : Character formation is decidedly the best aim of education. For acquiring character the strength of will is necessary. One of the important conditions for developing character is to create an atmosphere of freedom. But a cultured person can exercise his freedom properly. Hence his knowledge has to be increased and interests to be widened. Knowledge improves character. For only a man with knowledge can understand the far-reaching consequences of his acts.

But mere knowledge will not suffice to establish the power of self-control or to develop one's character. In spite of knowledge there are men who cannot check themselves from strong temptations. For the development of the character, the will must be exercised according to the light supplied by knowledge.

How to make the will strong? There is no royal road to it. Let the child begin with small things, let him conquer small temptations, and he will be able to conquer the great ones. Let there be built a large number of desirable habits of action by a constant exercise of the will power and then self-control will not seem a Herculean task.

Every small effort of the student requires appreciation and encouragement. He should be encouraged to take part in actions which have a moral value. The teachers should build up moral sentiments in the student by presenting before him situations that require services and sacrifice on his part.

In the development of character and good habit moral instruction should have a prominent place in school curriculum. Instead of direct moral teaching, moral ideas should be communicated indirectly through History and Literature and through fables and stories.

Example teaches better than precept. More is learnt by an individual through conscious and unconscious imitation than through instruction. If the habits of parents and teachers are good, the child will unconsciously pick them up.

Judicious use of punishment is often helpful in the development of habit and character. However, punishment should always aim at reform and not at retribution. These days all progressive educational thinkers condemn corporal punishment. The old Pedagogic doctrine, Spare the rod and spoil the child has yielded place to a new one, Respect the individuality of the child and you will make him good.

In lifting an individually it is neither punishment nor precept but sympathetic understanding and personal touch that count most.

Summary

When a voluntary action is repeated very often, it becomes a habit. Habitual actions are acquired. They are uniform and mechanical and are performed with ease.

Habit is called second nature. It is the enormous *flywheel of society!* Habit saves our time and prevent fatigue. It makes us accurate and efficient. But habit has many limitations. Habits are mechanical and stereotyped. Wrong habits cannot be broken easily. Habits make a person conservative and standardised.

The teacher has to cultivate certain good physical habits in pupils, such as habit of neatness, habit of sitting and standing with right posture, taking regular physical exercises etc.

William James has given four laws of formation of good habits :

(a) Begin a new habit with firm determination.

(b) Seize the first opportunity to put the new resolve into practice.

(c) Never allow an exception to occur till the new habit is well-learnt.

(d) Keep the faculty of effort alive by a little free practice everyday.

Bad habits should be broken by following means :

(a) Stop the bad habit at once.

(b) Cultivate a positive counter-habit.

(c) Line in an environment congenial to formation of good habit.

Habits are the foundation of character. For the development of character, the will must be exercised. The teacher has a very important role in building up the character of his students.

References

1. Sinha, J.N. : *A Manual of Psychology,* New Central Book Agency (P) Ltd., Calcutta 700 009.

Questions and Assignments

1. What are habits? Discuss the characteristics of habits.
2. Define habit. How are habits distinguished from instincts? Explain how bad habits can be eradicated.
3. *The only habit the Emile will form is to form no habit*—how is the statement pedagogically sound?
4. How would you form a good habit in a child? Illustrate your answer with suitable examples.
5. What is bad habit due to? How far does repression succeed in rooting out a bad habit?
6. What is meant by strength of will? How is it related to character?

Chapter 26

Suicide and Current Educational System

Introductino : Suicides have become a regular phenomenon in this country, particularly after the publication of different examination results. Current educational system is being mainly held responsible for such plight. The phenomenon may be discussed from the psychological point of view.

In fact, subject of suicide is a complicated psycho-social phenomenon. No single cause can be attributed to it. It may be due to frustration in educational achievement, conjugal unhappiness, dowry demand, disappointment in love affairs or unemployment. One or more causes may mingle together to lead to such unhappy incident. The causes may be conscious or unconscious, or may be both conscious as well as unconscious.

But in spite of these causative factors, the whole population of different categories of suicide does not resort to such a self-destructive action. All plucked candidates do not commit suicide, neither all frustrated lovers, nor all unemployed persons commit this vile act. A limited few take this course to destroy themselves as a last resort. So there must be certain inherent defects in their personality which leads them to commit suicide. A man of stronger personality can adjust to an adverse situation, while a person of weaker personality succumbs to it. So, let us examine some of the psychological views on causation of suicide and find out some remedies.

26.1 Psychoanalytic view

Suicide may be profitably investigated along psychoanalytic lines. We must find out the hidden motives which prompt a person to kill himself intentionally.

26.1.1 Freud's view

According to Freud, the driving force of the life instinct is libido, which is synonymous with the sex urge or sexuality. It also means love : sexual love, love for friends, love for wives, filial love, love for parents and so on. It also means all kinds of physical pleasures arising out of any of the erotogenous zones. Freud regards sex urge as the dynamic force behind all human behaviour at all stages.

We have urge for life because our libido is attached to our beloved objects such as our wife, children, friends etc. When this libidinal attachment is destroyed we lose all interests in life and commit suicide.

Freud includes life instinct (Eros) and death instinct (Thanatos) in the concept of libido or sex urge. The life instinct is opposed to death instinct. Most people wish to live, while a few individuals have strong death instinct or suicidal tendency. Freud recognised the polarity of the life instinct and death instinct. Often one commits suicide to punish his beloved object.

Repression of sex instincts becomes unavoidable because of social control. But severe control of this instinct brings about the formation of complexes in the unconscious. The psychoanalytic system highlights the importance of sublimation of child's sex instinct through games and social activity. The presence of complex in child's personality may lead to many undesirable consequences. Therefore, the school should organise various co-curricular activities along with curricular activities for releasing pent-up emotions and repressed wishes of the child. We should avoid unnecessary restrictions imposed on the child. They should have freedom for expression of their natural urges. Here comes the importance of *sex-education.*

26.1.2 Adler's view

Alfred Adler, a disciple of Freud, replaced sex instinct advocated by Freud with two important concepts : Power motive and style of life. Every individual has a strong innate urge to dominate to gain superiority over others and to achieve perfection in some field of life. For gaining superiority, an individual strives hard, but he may not always succeed. If he succeeds, he remains satisfied and remains normal. But if he fails, he may develop suicidal tendency. An individual makes efforts to attain mastery over or to compensate for his sense of inferiority and in this masculine protest he resorts to suicide instead of confronting reality. A child may often clamour for becoming the *monitor* of the class, but if his wish is not fulfilled, either he becomes morose or tries to create trouble in the class.

Ones style of life is influenced by ones order of birth in the family. If the child is unwanted in the family, he may develop either neurotic behaviour or he may become a delinquent. Deprivation of parental love often leads a child to become an energetic member of a gang.

In some cases, an individual's style of life may be fashioned according to his physical appearance. If he looks ugly or has some deformity, he may develop feeling of inferiority, because of the physical deformity. If we can develop certain creative power in him, his style of life will change and he will learn to love his life again. So, the function of the school shall be to help the child to have a balanced personality, to develop creativity and social interest. In this process, the pressure of bookish study and examinations on the children should be minimum. The parents also should not burden their children with their own unfulfilled desires.

26.1.3 Jung's view

According to Jung, in whom libido or life urge flows inward are known as introverts. While persons in whom the libido flows outward are known as extroverts. Failures often make one introvert. The cause of suicide lies in the present *failure of adaptation*. Its remedies lie in helping the individual to realise his present position, his aims and aspiration in future. The educational activities of the children should be so designed as to maximise actualisation of their potentialities. Ample opportunities should be provided to them in school for actualising their innate aptitudes.

The teacher should see that the individual does not drift towards the extreme type of introversion and thus develop unbalanced personality. The extroverts should devote sometime to introspection and meditation, while the introverts should be encouraged to take part in extra-curricular activities of the school.

According to Jung, religion has a great influence on one's personality. It gives inner peace by resolving mental conflicts. Religious and moral education, therefore, should form a part of school curriculum.

26.2 Prevention

Failure in examination, fear for loss of prestige, parents' high expectations etc. are some of the common causes of suicide. However, life is not a bed of roses. There shall be failures and associated frustration and agony. Those who commit suicide because of failure in examination are unworthy of living in this competitive society.

We cannot do away with examination system completely, although we can reform it. Some sort of tests are indispensable for mesuring the amount of learning and quality of teaching, selecting for admission to higher courses and for job selection. Tests and examinations have established its firm root in our educational system for its motivating aspect. So pupils have to face it today or tomorrow in some form or other.

Therefore, teachers and parents, instead of criticising the studnets for their failure in the examinatin, should encourages them and help them to gain self-confidence. Thus, their ego is to be made strong by citing examples of Demosthenes, Robert Bruce, Sandow, Kalidas and others who despite failures have achieved success in life by ceaseless effort and perservance. Demosthenes, who was a stutterer, not only overcame stuttering but over-compensated for his inferiority becoming the greatest orator of his age.

Sandow, who was a weakling as a boy, became one of the strongest man in the world. Again Kalidas, who was jeered at even by his wife for his illiteracy, became the greatest poet in ancient India.

Again, the curriculum should not be so bookish. It should be so designed as to provide the pupil with ample opportunities in school for actualising their inner aptitudes. The introvert should be encouraged to take part in co-curricular activities of the school.

Moreover, there should be efficient *counselling service* in every school to help the students, as well as their parents. Over-expectation of parents, who want their children of low intellect to become genius, should be tempered through proper counselling.

Lastly, our scriptures and prophets teach us to surrender ourselves to the feet of the Almightly, who will give us solace in all our mental agony. So, moral instruction and prayer in school assembly should form a part of our school activity.

Summary

1. Causes of Suicide :
   (a) Repression of sex urges.
   (b) Deprivation of love in family.
   (c) Over-expectation of parents, who want their children to become sophisticated robots.
   (d) Overloaded curriculum in schools.
   (e) Failure of schools to provide value-education.
   (f) Frustration.
2. Remedies :
   (a) Sublimation of sex instincts through physical and social activities.

(b) Peace and harmony be maintained in family. Children should have love and proper care.

(c) Children should be allowed freedom to work according to their capacity. They should not be burdened with the parents' unfulfilled desires. Do not impose high a standard to be achieved by children.

(d) Unhealthy curriculum should be scrapped. Teach curricular subjects through co-curricular activities. Avoid competition through examinations. Promote cooperation through team activities.

(e) Teach moral and religious values. It would not impair secular character of the state.

(f) Counselling and guidance to avoid frustration.

References

1. Freud, S. : *A General Introduction to Psycho-analysis,* New York : Live Right, 1935.

2. Symonds, P. : *The Dynamics of Human Adjustment,* New York : Appleton, 1946.

Questions and Assignments

1. What are the causes of suicide? Suggest how it can be prevented.

2. Can you cite any case of suicide? Why school students commit suicide?

3. Discuss the psychoanalytic view of suicide.

Chapter 27

Psychology of Thinking and Reasoning

Introduction : Man is superior to all other creatures because of his superior ability to think and reason. He is endowed with the faculty of thinking reasoning, hence is called a rational being. These powers of human being have produced a vast domain of culture, science and systems of knowledge. Thinking of man has been an inevitable factor in the welfare of individual and society. It is the main object of education to develop capacity for independent thinking in children.

27.1 Nature of Thinking

Broadly speaking, thinking includes all forms of cognition. It includes perception, imagination, memory and concept formation. But in a restricted sense, it is considered as symbolic behaviour. C.T. Morgan regards thinking as a sequence of symbolic processes. Munn also regards thinking as a sequential arousal of symbols. Thinking is manipulating the world internally with the aid of symbolic processes. It makes use of memory, imagination and reasoning or problem-solving.

Thinking is ideational activity which is deliberately controlled by a purpose. It is mental exploration of data in order to deal with the environment effectively.

Thinking has a *motive* behind it. It cannot be studied apart from purpose, needs and drives. For example, when there is an accident, the individual at once starts thinking what should be done. Thus, thinking enables the individual to solve the problem of his adjustment.

Thinking is *connative* in nature and occurs when some difficulty crops up that requires the individual to make new adjustments.

Thinking, according to Gilmer (1970), is a problem-solving process in which we use ideas or symbols in place of overt activity. The most orderly process of thinking in problem-solving. It is the highest form of thinking.

According to Woodworth, thinking consists of the following elements :

1. Orientation towards a goal.
2. Recall of previously observed facts.
3. Grouping those recalled facts into new patterns.
4. Inner speech movement and gestures.

Thinking involves both the processes of analysis and synthesis.

To get a clear idea of a problem we mentally analyse its pros and cons and synthesise its different aspects. Without the help of these two processes we cannot have a complete picture of a problem.

According to Woodworth, thought involves Hind sight as well as Foresight. While thinking we utilise past events. This is hind sight. Thinking also involves foresight, which prepares us for future consequences.

Sometimes thinking involves transfer. A principle or rule acquired from past experience is applied to solve a new problem. This is called transfer.

Thus, thinking has the following features :

1. It is essentially a cognitive process.
2. It is goal-oriented. Discovery and invention are the goals of thinking.
3. It is a problem-solving behaviour.
4. It involves analysis and synthesis.
5. It involves both Hind sight and Foresight.
6. It is mental exploration rather than motor exploration.
7. It is a symbolic activity.
8. Thinking is subvocal talking. It involves inner speech.

27.2 Types of thinking

Thinking may be classified into the following categories :

1. **Associative Thinking :** This type of thinking is non-directed and without goal. For example, the burnt child dreads the fire. Here associative thinking works. The sight of the fire awakens the experience of pain in his mind. As a result, the child refrains from touching fire.

   Again delusion, day-dreaming and fantasy also fall in the category of non-directed thinking. Delusion is persistent, absurd thought. An individual under the influence of such delusions may think that he is the lord of the universe. In day-dreaming and fantasy a child may think of becoming a renowned cricket player.

2. **Perceptual Thinking :** Perceptual thinking is carried out on the perception of concrete objects. This is the simplest form of thinking.
3. **Conceptual Thinking :** Conceptual thinking is an abstract thinking where concepts are used. It economises effort in understanding and problem-solving.
4. **Creative Thinking :** A creative thought travels its own way and aims at creating something new. No pre-established rules or conventions restrict creative thinking. There are four phases of creative thinking : preparation, incubation, illumination and verification. At the preparation stage there is focussing of consciousness upon the problem and organisation of the data.

   At the incubation stage, the problem is temporarily forgotten. Mind works on it occasionally before it develops into a usable product.

   At the illumination stage, the central idea appears all on a sudden in a flash of insight.

   At the verification stage, the refining and polishing of the central idea occurs putting it into finished form.
5. **Wishful Thinking :** Often our wishes, needs and desires force us to think in the ways of their own satisfactions. This results in an incorrect thinking.

27.3 Tools of Thinking

The following are the tools of thinking : 1. Images. 2. Concepts. 3. Languages and 4. Muscle activities.

1. **Images :** Thinking involves images of objects actually seen. The images rather than the real objects are usually manipulated in thinking.
2. **Concepts :** Concepts have been described as general ideas, symbols and names referring to the general class of a particular object. When similar objects are perceived in different contexts, they are segregated as a class and named by the subjects. Concepts simplify the process of thinking by reducing the number of the objects of thought. Concepts classify things and economise thought. They are indispensable for reasoning.
3. **Language :** Generally, thinking is expressed in language. When we think over a difficult problem, very often we talk to ourselves internally. Language is the expression of thought and thought is aided by language.
4. **Muscle activities :** Thinking involves muscular movement. There is positive correlation between the thinking and muscular activities of a person.

Concepts : Concepts are tools of thinking. It is defined as the name of a class of objects or their common qualities. Thus dog is a concept, which is the name of a class of animals. General ideas are called concepts. "It is the sum total of what you know about the object" (Woodworth). When a child observes different kinds of birds and notes that they are called by a particular name, he forms the concept of the bird in general.

27.4 Formation of concepts

Formation of concepts takes place through following phases :

1. **Comparison :** In order to form concepts about an object, the first step is to observe the characteristics of the objects of the same class. Then comes analysis of the qualities of each of them. The points of their similarity and their points of differences are noted. For example, to form the concept of a bird, one has to observe the similarities and differences of different kinds of birds.

2. **Abstraction :** In this stage, the concrete details of sense perception is eliminated and general features of objects are separated.

   For example, all kinds of birds have two wings, two legs and a beak. These features, which are common to all birds, are fixed and other qualities such as colour, size etc. are eliminated.

3. **Generalisation :** The idea that the special features which have been separated through analysis will be found in each of the object of the class is called generalisation. The bird which we have not seen must have also two wings, two legs and one beak. This mental process is generalisation.

4. **Naming :** Lastly, for the expression of the concept we need naming the object. That is, the creature which has two wings, two legs and one beak is a bird. Naming completes the concept.

   Thus the concept of whiteness is formed after observation of many white objects and comparing them with those having other colours. Here, as in other cases, the analysis is followed by synthesis.

27.5 Development of concept

The process of concept formation emerges from a big, buzzing, booming, confusion in which the child is born. The child gets the knowledge of the external world through sense organs. The building of concepts starts with the process of sensation and perception.

From the first year of life of the child, development of concepts begins. The behaviour of the child suggests that even before he can talk, he has already formed some rudimentary concepts. He recognises a feeding bottle and expects to suck milk from it.

When the child begins to understand words and, soon after talks, he certainly forms concept.

Between the ages of three and ten, the child develops animistic concepts of physical objects. He forms animistic concepts of the sun, the moon, the rain and storm and other physical phenomena. He has animistic concepts of a ball, a balloon, a doll etc. But as he manipulates them, he gradually develops mechanical concepts of them.

The child passes from egocentric concepts to objective concepts. He forms concepts of physical objects as related to himself. Then he forms concepts of them as related to one another. For instance, the child sees the moon move with him when he walks. At first, he thinks that the moon follows him. However, he soon forms objective concept of the moon.

Objective concepts are gradually developed in conformity with the physical environment and social environment. When a child sees different types of dolls and notes that they are all called by a particular name, he forms the concept of doll in general. For the child, these dolls are things to play with. This common quality is abstracted by the child unknowingly and the concept of doll thus stands for anything that can be played with.

The variety of concepts and their quality depends upon the experiences the child receives in his social environment.

27.6 Concept formation and Role of the teacher

By the age of five years, the child is generally admitted in a school. The function of the teacher is to sharpen and modify the already formed vague concepts. He has to teach new and complex concepts to the child.

The most effective method of developing concepts is to provide the child with direct experience of the object. To have clear concept of mountain or ocean, one must have the experience of seeing these. So, to give the students first-hand experience of these things, the teacher has to organise educational excursions. But it may not be always possible to organise such trips. Therefore, the teacher must provide indirect experiences to students of such objects through charts, diagrams, models and other audio-visual aids. Students should be provided with various examples of the concept and they should be encouraged to define the concept verbally.

27.7 Thought and Language

Human being is superior to all other beings because he can think. Not only he thinks but he can express his thought in language. So, there is a close link between thoughts and language.

1. **Language is the expression of thought :** Language is the most important element of thought. When we think over a difficult problem, often we talk to ourselves internally. If we are alone, we may talk aloud with gestures. Language is the expression of thought. And thought is aided by language. Thinking and talking develop through social interaction.

2. **Language is the means of communication of thought :** We can record our thoughts in language and communicate them to others through it. When our thoughts are recorded in language, they may be used by us in future, or they may add to the knowledge of others.

3. **Language is an aid to thought :** The more we give expressions to our ideas, the more our ideas become clear. Discussion and argument stimulate our thinking capacity. When a teacher explains to his students a complicated topic, not only students' ideas become clear, the ideas of teachers are also stimulated through interaction.

4. **Language is an aid to recall :** Facts and principles which are expressed in language are easily retained and readily recalled. We can easily recall those facts to which we have assigned definite names. Abstract ideas such as affection, pity, beauty etc. cannot be formed without language.

5. **Language is a thought-saving instrument :** Language is a system of symbols which stand for facts and principles. They can be more easily manipulated than the facts. Progress of science and mathematics have become possible only by the use of symbolical language. Chemical reactions cannot be retained in our mind without chemical symbols and formulae.

6. **Language and thought develop together :** Development of thought takes place simultaneously with the growth of language. Development of language greatly depends on the development of thought. Precise thoughts lead to precise expressions. Precise expressions make for greater precision of thought.

In fact, nowadays language has become so closely linked up with the social environment that without the help of language we cannot think of the worldly affairs. At present, the news of the world are communicated either in verbal or written language, so, thought processes will not develop if language is excluded and simultaneously, advancement of knowledge will be thwarted.

27.8 Is thought sub-vocal talking?

Watson and other Behaviourists hold that thinking is identical with implicit or explicit speech movements. This appears to be true, because we talk to ourselves more or less, while thinking. We often mutter words while we carry on thinking. A child loudly says what he does. But when he grows up, he gives up this practice under social pressure and resorts to inner speech. This inaudible inner speech is identical with thinking. With the finer scientific measuring instrument it has been observed that our vocal apparatus including tongue become active during our thought process. These facts show that thinking and inner speech very often go together. But they can by no means prove that thinking is identical with inner speech. Thinking does not take place by the simple movement of the vocal apparatus.

Sometimes thinking is carried on without language. When thought is very active, speech becomes fragmentary.

Often we think of an object, but we fail to recall its name. Sometimes we deliver a set speech without the corresponding thinking. A child may recite a poem without thinking a word of it.

Often when we deliver a speech extempore, our thinking runs ahead of the speech. Thinking goes ahead and speech follows it.

We often get stuck for even a familiar word. We feel difficulty in finding out the exact word required to express a meaning which we certainly have in mind.

All these facts clearly indicate that thinking precedes speech and is not identical with it. In fact, it is absurd to hold that thinking = speech.

27.9 Thinking and Imagination

On the cognitive side, thinking includes all forms of mental activities such as perception, memory and imagination. But thinking is different from imagination. Imagination is mental manipulation of past experiences resulting into something new, while thinking is mental exploration of new relations resulting into solutions of the problems. For example, in imagination we mentally manipulate tables and chairs and arrange them for a tea party without actually handling them. But suppose you have lost your money bag. Without actually searching for it here and there, you think out the clues and guess where you put it last. This is mental exploration.

Thinking has a *motive* behind it. It is directed by the goal purpose. Thus the goal or purpose controls association. Thinking, therefore, involves controlled association. But undirected imagination, like day-dreaming, involves free association. While, pragmatic imagination is goal-directed and involves controlled association. Thus, thinking always involves controlled association, whereas imagination involves both free association and controlled association.

Thinking is a higher mental process than imagination. It is more realistic than fantasy. Thinking is a systematised process, while imagination is an isolated mental process.

However, thinking and imagination cannot be easily separated as both go together in almost all situations.

27.10 Is imageless thinking possible?

Thinking makes use of images. A sensory image, visual or auditory, is often a tool of thinking. Very often a verbal image is a tool of thinking. A memory image also is a tool of thinking. The memory image of your dead friend sets you thinking of his honesty and sincerity.

Previously, the Introspectionists had thought that thinking could not be carried out without the help of images. But Kulpe, Marbe and other psychologists do not consider that the use of images in all kinds of thinking is indispensable. Thinking—which is generally carried on through sensory or verbal images, may be carried on without them.

Imageless thinking is possible in following cases :

1. Abstract thinking is imageless. It is carried on with the aid of imageless concepts.
2. In very fast thinking, images do not appear. In quick response also, images do not find time to appear.
3. Thinking in unconscious mind is carried out without images. For example, the solution of a mathematical problem may flash upon a person when he is otherwise engaged.

In fact, excessive use of images thwarts our thought process. The philosophers and mathematicians often think without the aid of images.

27.11 Effective thinking

In order that thinking may be effective we should be conscious and try to avoid those factors which drag us into wrong thinking. They may be described as follows :

1. Our desires and needs often force us to think in a particular way. Thus, our wishful thinking results in an incorrect thinking.
2. Incorrect thinking occurs when either there is no motivation or undesirable motivation.

3. There may be a number of variables of consequence. Failing to control these may result into fallacious thinking.
4. Habitual methods of attack often restrict right thinking.
5. Strong emotion often blocks correct thinking.

For effective thinking our efforts should be to check the above factors. Following conditions are also necessary for proper thinking :

1. Strong motivation.
2. Wide range of knowledge.
3. Alertness.
4. Sufficient time for incubation.
5. Freedom from false assumption.

27.12 Reasoning

1. **Nature of reasoning :** Reasoning is typical thinking. It is different from thinking because it involves a sequence of symbolic activities directed towards the solution of a problem. It resembles a trial and error process like motor exploration.

   Reasoning is the tool of thinking in problem-solving. It is stimulated when there is a problem to solve. According to Garrett (1968), reasoning is stepwise thinking with a purpose or goal in mind. It is highly specialised thinking which helps an individual to explore mentally the cause-and-effect relationship of an event. Like thinking, it is also an implicit act and involves the use of one's previous knowledge and experiences.

2. **Steps in reasoning :** Reasoning is reflective thinking. It aims at the solution of a problem. In case of complex problem, the solution is not ready at hand. So reasoning follows the steps mentioned below :

   (a) **Gathering the data :** In the first step of solving a problem one uses previous knowledge and experiences. The data thus obtained from past experiences are combined together.

   (b) **Seeing the implications of the combined data :** In this step, careful mental analysis of the available data is done and relations amongst them are perceived.

   (c) **Formation of hypothesis :** Then a hypothetical solution is formed on the basis of the most appropriate possibility.

   (d) **Verification :** The tentative hypothesis is then verified by deducting consequences from it and comparing them with observed facts.

   (e) **Inference :** Inference is the crucial step in reasoning. From the inference, new truths may be deduced.

27.13 Is reasoning a trial and error process?

The behaviourists hold that reasoning is a trial and error process at the ideational level. Reasoning resembles a trial and error process. In the trial and error behaviour, we find that an animal is set for a certain goal (e.g., coming out of a cage and getting food), but it does not see the path to the goal clearly. It explores the situation, finds, certain leads and tries them—one after another. Finally, it finds a good lead and reaches the goal by overt movements.

Reasoning consists in mental exploration of the data and finding out a new relationship among them. Reasoning does not involve overt muscular movements, nor does it always involve actual perception of the leads.

Reasoning is creative and reflective in nature. It involves trial and error and also insight. In reasoning, as contrasted with T–E learning, one's past experience play a crucial role.

27.14 Types of reasoning

There are two broad types of reasoning : Inductive reasoning and Deductive reasoning. In inductive reasoning, a general principle is derived from particular acts observed. For example, Ram is mortal, Shyam is mortal, Jadu is mortal. Therefore, all men are mortal.

In deductive reasoning, a general principle is applied to a particular act. For example, Man is mortal. Ram is a man. Therefore, Ram is mortal.

27.14.1 Fallacies in reasoning

Fallacies in the process of reasoning occur owing to the violation of the rules of logical reasoning. For example :

All thieves are men;

All poets are men;

∴ All poets are thieves.

In this reasoning, the middle term men is undistributed, and so it is fallacious.

Again fallacies of reasoning arise from the ambiguity of the major term, the minor term or the middle term. For example,

Light travels fast;

Cotton is light;

∴ Cotton travels fast.

In this reasoning, the middle term light has been used in two senses. Hence this reasoning is incorrect.

27.14.2 Training students in reasoning

Training in reasoning is very important in education. Teaching should improve methods of reasoning and critical thinking should be stressed in all fields of education. Parrot learning should be discouraged.

One of the important objectives of education is to develop in children the power of independent thinking and reasoning. The teacher should place the problems before the students and ask them to think about the problem. When the students fail to find out the solution independently, the teacher will help the students to determine the relevant data, and to analyse them. The students should themselves make an effort to find out the clue to the solution. They may take recourse to trial and error method. The mental activity involved in trial and error to get the clue is the real training in reasoning.

Training in reasoning consists in allowing the student to make mistakes and correct himself. He should again and again analyse the data to find the solution, manipulating it in different ways. The solution thus obtained becomes his own possession. He gains self-confidence when he attains the solution by his own effort. In the Heuristic method, the students are guided to investigate causes of inexplicable phenomena of science.

Thus, in the training of reasoning, emphasis should be made on the need of stimulating the spirit of searching out the explanation by the students themselves. They should be encouraged to be self-reliant in their quest of knowledge.

Real thinking and reasoning depend on perfect observation, concept formation and language development. The teacher should see that these develop properly in children. Through a set of questions, he should help the students to analyse a problem and correct them if there is any error in reasoning.

The teacher should initiate the problem and guide the child in the solution of it, giving as much freedom as possible. Thus, through such Psychological methods as Project method, Problem-method, Heuristic method, the teacher should train students in proper thinking and reasoning.

27.14.3 Problem-solving

Problem-solving is a deliberate act involving the use of higher thinking and systematic planned steps for achieving the set goal.

According to Skinner (1968), problem-solving is a process of overcoming difficulties that appear to interfere with the attainment of a goal. It is a procedure of making adjustment inspite of interferences.

Today everybody in this world has some problem, simple or complex, theoretical or practical. There are various needs to be satisfied. In an attempt to realise the goal, the individual experiences obstacles. The individual is confronted with a problem situation when he has to think and find out solution to reach the goal. The solution is not ready at hand. So the perplexing situation initiates reflective thinking or problem-solving behaviour.

27.15 Nature of problem-solving behaviour

Problem-solving behaviour has the following features :

1. Problem-solving behaviour arises only when the goal is purposeful and essential for the individual.
2. It arises when there is serious obstruction in achieving the goal.
3. The individual engages himself in serious mental exploration by systematically following certain planned steps to remove the obstacles.
4. Problem-solving behaviour helps the individual to ultimately remove the obstacles and reach his goal.
5. Problem-solving behaviour helps an individual to attain a state of satisfaction when his endeavour is crowned with success.

27.16 Processes of problem-solving

Psychologists have mentioned two types of processes to problem-solving : (a) Trial and Error and (b) Insight.

1. **Trial and error :** In the trial and error behaviour, an organism is set for a certain goal. It explores the situation, finds certain leads and tries them one after another, fails several times, and, finally, finds a good lead and reaches the goal. This process may involve motor exploration or mental exploration. For example, suppose a person has lost his way in a new place. Without being puzzled, either he will try to find his right way by walking this side or that or he may mentally explore the way leading to the goal. This process of mental exploration or reflective thinking is termed problem-solving.
2. **Insight :** The Gestalt psychologists emphasise the importance of perception of total situation. The classical experiments of Kohler on chimpanzees show that solution of problem is achieved all of a sudden through insight into the situation.

Harlow (1959) tried to synthesise the two processes of T–E and insight in solving a problem. According to him, in the beginning, animals show trial and error behaviour to solve a problem and acquire a learning set.

This learning set is transferred positively to other problems of similar type and appear, to be insightful learning. Learning becomes simple and effortless in the later stage.

27.17 Steps in problem-solving

Psychologists have suggested different steps involved in the process of problem solving behaviour of animals and human beings. Briefly they are as follows :

1. **Understanding of the problem :** Firstly, the problem should be clearly comprehended, otherwise it cannot be solved. It should be completely understood in all its bearings. All the obstacles in the path of the goal should be identified in the beginning.
2. **Collection of the relevant information :** Then the individual collects all relevant information about the problem from different sources.
3. **Formation of hypothesis :** In this step, the individual attempts to think out the various solutions to the problem. These hypothetical solutions are then closely analysed and evaluated. The individual finds out whether the solution tallies with accepted facts and investigates for any negative aspect which may vitiate the conclusion.
4. **Verification of the hypothesis :** The deduced results are then again verified by applying it in the solution of various similar problems. The final testing may necessiate certain changes in the original conclusion. Thus verified, the final solution becomes a useful product of the individual's problem-solving behaviour.

However, it may not be necessary to pass through all the above steps in every problem. The process of problem-solving in a case depends upon the nature of the problem, mode of research for the solution and on the individual's intellectual ability.

27.18 Role of the teacher in problem-solving

Helping the students in problem-solving is very important in the field of education. The teacher should try to develop a scientific attitude in students to solve problems related to academic as well as social life. Although no universal doctrine can be formulated for solving all types of problem, a few useful suggestions for teachers may be offered here :

1. **Motivation :** The teacher should motivate the students to find out the solution independently. When the students do not themselves make effort, the chance for solving problems is remote. By using various techniques, the teacher can motivate the students to a great extent.
2. **Analysis of data through questioning :** The teacher, through a set of questions, should encourage the students to analyse the data to discover the clue to the solution.

3. **Presentation of problems as a whole :** The teacher should present problems in the class as a whole and not by parts. This will help the students to have a perception of the total situation.

4. **Divergent thinking :** The teacher should encourage divergent thinking in his pupils, so that they learn to tackle the problem in various ways.

5. **Use of teaching aids :** Abstract problems should be concretised by using charts and diagrams and other teaching materials.

6. **Enough practice :** The students should be given enough drilling on variety of problems so that they develop proper mental set to solve similar kinds of problem, which they may meet in future.

7. **Maturity level :** The teacher should present the problem keeping in view the maturity level of the students. The problem should neither be too easy, nor too difficult for the class.

Summary

Thinking refers to ideational activity which is deliberately controlled by a purpose. It is mental exploration of data in order to deal with the environment effectively.

Tools employed in the process of thinking consists of images, concepts, languages and muscle-activities.

Thinking may be classified into associative thinking, perceptual thinking, conceptual thinking, creative thinking. To this, we may add one more category in the form of wishful thinking.

Thinking includes all forms of mental activities : perception, memory and imagination. Thinking is a higher mental process than imagination. It is more realistic than imagination.

Reasoning is typical thinking. It involves well-organised systematic steps for the mental exploration of a cause-and-effect relationship for solution of a problem. It is different from thinking because it involves a sequence of symbolic activity directed towards the solution of a problem.

Reasoning is of two types : (a) deductive and (b) inductive. In deductive reasoning, a general principle is applied to a particular act, while in inductive reasoning, a general principle is derived from particular acts.

Problem-solving behaviour arises when the goal is purposeful and when there is serious obstruction in achieving the goal. Helping the students in problem solving and scientific thinking is very important in education.

References

1. Bartlett, F. : *Thinking*, New York : Basic Books, 1958.
2. Bruner, J.S., Goodnow, J.J. and Austin, G.A. : *A Study of Thinking*, New York : John Wiley, 1956.
3. Bhatnagar, R.P. : *A Study of Educational Psychology*, Vishwavidyalaya Prakashan, Gorakhpur, 1959.
4. Chauhan, S.S. : *Advanced Educational Psychology*, Vikas Publishing House Pvt. Ltd. New Delhi, 1997.
5. Garrett, H.E. : *General Psychology*, New Delhi : Eurasia Publishing House, 1968.
6. Gates, A.I. : *Educational Psychology*, New York : Macmillan, 1946.
7. Munn, N.L. : *An Introduction to Psychology*, New Delhi, Oxford, 1967.
8. Norman, R.F., Maier : *Problem-solving and Creativity*, Brooke Cole Co. Belmount, 1970.
9. Sinha, J.N. : *A Manual of Psychology*, New Central Book Agency (P) Ltd. Calcutta 700 009.
10. Skinner, B.F. : *Verbal Behaviour*, New York : Appleton-Century-Crofts, 1957.
11. Woodworth, R.S. : *Psychology*, London : Methuen, 1945.

Questions and Assignments

1. What is meant by thinking? Discuss the relation between image and thinking.
2. Discuss the relation between language and thought. Do you agree with the statement : Thinking is sub-vocal talking?
3. What is the difference between thinking and imagination? What is an image? Is imageless thinking possible.
4. What is reasoning? How is reasoning developed among students?
5. Give an account of psychology of reasoning and problem-solving. Suggest a plan of education for developing these powers.
6. What is concept? Discuss the various steps of concept formation.
7. What are the various methods which can be used to develop concept in students?
8. What is problem-solving? Describe the steps in problem-solving.

9. How would you teach a class the meaning of abstract concepts? Show by concrete examples.
10. Take a problem in Geometry to illustrate how a teacher may develop the power of original thinking among students while helping them in solving it.

Chapter 28

Micro-teaching and Educational Technology

Introduction : In 1963, a group of teacher-educators and educational research workers at Stanford University developed a new procedure called micro-teaching. Dr. D. Allen named as it micro-teaching.

28.1 What is micro-teaching?

Micro-teaching is a systematic training system in which the latest principle of learning theory have been incorporated. It is based on the teaching theory underlying programmed learning and computer assisted instruction.

Other concepts of learning theory such as reinforcement and feedback are adopted in this procedure. Micro-teaching is a scaled down sample of teaching (D.W. Allen).

28.2 Purpose of micro-teaching

Micro-teaching procedure aids at simplifying the complexities of the regular teaching process by engaging the trainee in a scaled down teaching situation. It is reduced in terms of class-size, length of class time and teaching task. The length of the lesson is also reduced to ten minutes or so.

28.3 Method of micro-teaching

In micro-teaching, length of lesson, scope of the lesson, number of trainees (5–6), teaching time (7–10 minutes) have been reduced.

In micro-teaching, following steps are undertaken :

1. For successful teaching, the nature of a desired skill is explained before the teacher-trainees. Why such skill is to be acquired?

   What is its necessity in the field of training? These are to be discussed.

2. The teacher-trainee then demonstrates the lesson before the students. At this time video, tape recorder or film strips may be used.

3. Then on the basis of the skill desired, a lesson plan is prepared. This is known as *Plan session.*

4. One of the teacher-trainees, in an artificial situation, gives demonstration to a small group. The supervisors along with others watch the demonstration carefully and note down its defects.

5. Along with the demonstration, feedback may be provided either with tape recorder or video tape. In order to make this demonstration free of defects, the supervisors criticise it threadbare. This is called the *critique session.*

6. In order to make the skill of teaching effective, feedback is provided in the light of criticism and necessary modifications are made in the plan, or a replan may be necessary.

7. Corrected lesson is again given on a similar small group and it is supervised. In the reteaching stage, again feedback is provided. This session is called feedback session.

Thus, a micro-teaching cycle is produced comprising plan, feedback, reteaching and refeedback. Until the teaching efficiency is sufficiently improved, this cycle of micro-teaching continues.

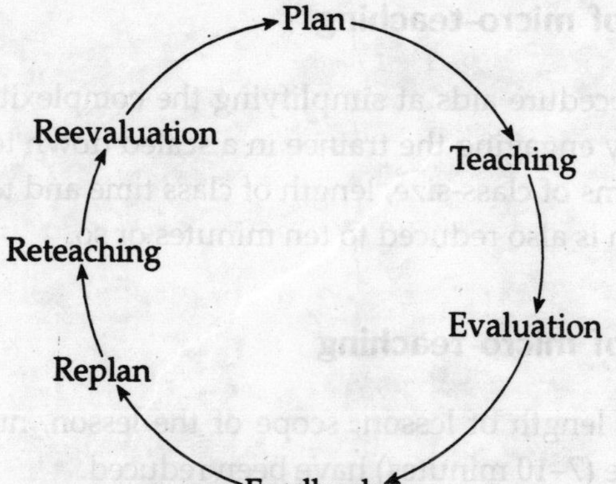

Fig. 28.1: Microteaching cycle.

28.4 Application of micro-teaching

The effectiveness of micro-teaching method has been proved by several studies in U.S.A. in the field of pre-service teacher education, in-service teacher education, counselling, medical education, industry, commerce salesmanship, armed forces, psychotherapy and human-relations and in higher education.

In India also, researches have been conducted to determine the utility of micro teaching. For instance, centre of advanced study, Baroda, has conducted research on micro-teaching and the research findings reveal the effectiveness of micro-teaching.

28.5 Education technology

By Educational Technology we mean the behavioural science associated with the teaching learning process.

In recent years, many countries have introduced technology into the basic curriculum for all children. For example, under the law of December 1985, manual and technical subjects in secondary-school education are being replaced by a program of technology education which includes informatics, electronics, machines and nutrition (UNESCO, 1986).

Technology is being integrated into the school curriculum in a number of ways, which include the following :

1. Technology as a separate subject.
2. Technology linked with science.
3. Technology linked with other subjects of the curriculum, such as history and social studies.

28.6 Scope of educational technology

The role of educational technology is to develop the application of the behavioural science to education. Educational technology utilises the concept and knowledge of modern technology, psychology, sociology, communication process, linguistics and other subjects. Besides these, it uses the management principles of cost effectiveness and successful utilisation of material and human resources.

Often we wrongly presume that educational technology is nothing but the use of audio-visual aids. But this is not all though they are used occasionally in the class room teaching.

In fact, educational technology includes : The development, application and evaluation of systems, techniques and aids in the field of learning. That is, aims of teaching, media, special features of the media, principle of selection of materials and media, management of resources and their evaluation come under the purview of educational technology.

In brief, all kinds of important techniques helping teaching-learning process fall within the scope of educational technology. Education is a life-long process. It is not limited within the four walls of the school. Today education is to be regarded as a science of training man. This is why use of complicated scientific machines, e.g., computers, is unavoidable in the teaching-learning process.

Pupils learn directly from School, Library, Museum, etc. However, they learn many important things indirectly from Cinema, Newspaper, Radio, T.V. and other mass-media.

As the use of these technological media has become indispensable in teaching-learning process, we are facing certain problems. The problem is the want of teachers properly trained in educational technology.

28.7 Role of teachers

The success of educational technology depends fully on the role of teachers. He has to use audio-visual aids wisely. He must know when and in what context these aids are to be used. He must have proper training in handling these instruments.

28.8 Equipment of educational technology

Some of the equipments of educational technology are :

1. Visual aids.
2. Audio aids.
3. Audio-visual aids.
4. Computer.
5. Micro-teaching.
6. Programmed Instruction.
7. Teaching machines.
8. Satellite communication.
9. Demonstration in classroom etc.

Visual aids : Some of the visual aids are : Black-board, Flannel board, Bulletin board, Globe, Picture, Flash card, Chart, Poster, Diagram, Specimen, Graph, Model, Photograph, Magic lantern, Epidiascope (projector), Motion pictures, etc.

Audio aids : Important Audio aids are : Tape Recorder, Radio and Gramophone.

Audio visual aids : Include motion pictures and television. For learning language, language laboratory is another example of educational technology. At present, learning of important matters have become possible through satellite communication.

The application of computer in the field of education has revolutionised our educational system. It has become a powerful medium for corrected and rapid transaction of educational informations. At present, scoring of tests are being done through computer.

Precautions : Technology is a complex integrated organisation of man and machine. So, the teacher has to take certain precautions while using these teaching aids. The teaching aids should be closely related to the contents of teaching. The teacher should not use them at random. The audio-visual aids should match the age and intellectual abilities of the pupil.

However, the teacher must be conscious about the limitations of the use of these aids. These aids cannot take the teachers' place. They simply supplement class-room teaching.

Importance of educational technology : We acquire knowledge through our senses. Learning lasts longer when both of our eyes and ear combine together. Many abstract ideas are concretised through audio-visual aids. In fact, use of educational technology makes learning lively and joyful.

Conclusion : In recent years, there has been an explosion of knowledge. So, with the explosion of knowledge, we need explosion of education too. In developing countries, particularly in India, total eradication of illiteracy has become a serious problem. Here educational technology comes to our aid. In recent years, open school and open university have come forward with technological media to educate our people. Thus, audio-visual aids are not only medium of our pleasure, it has thrown open the possibilities of complete eradication of mass illiteracy from this country.

Summary

The object of educational technology is to benefit more pupils with less number of teachers and to obtain quality education. Some of the equipments of educational technology are visual aids, teaching machines, satellite communication, micro-teaching, computer, programmed instruction etc. The effectiveness of micro-teaching has been proved in counselling, in pre-service and in-service teacher education, psychotherapy etc.

References

1. Fry, Eduard B. : *Teaching Machine and Programmed Learning*, McGraw Hill. New York : 1963.

2. Edward, F.O'Day : *Programmed Instruction*, Techniques and Trends. Appleton Century. New York : 1971.

3. Chauhan, S.S. : *A Text Book of Programmed Instruction*, Sterling Publishers (P) Ltd. New Delhi : 1985.

Questions and Assignments

1. What is micro-teaching? What steps are taken in micro-teaching?
2. Describe some of the applications of micro-teaching.
3. Describe the scope of educational technology.
4. Discuss the role of teachers in educational technology.
5. Describe the importance of educational technology.

Chapter 29

Education of the Exceptional Child

Introduction : The exceptional children deviate from the average or normal children in physical, mental, emotional or social traits. These distinct class of children need our special attention. They require special educational facilities to develop their maximum capacity. They do not benefit much from a regular classroom program and, therefore, need special treatment in school.

According to Telford and Sawrey (1977) : "The term exceptional children refers to those children who deviate from the normal in physical, mental, emotional, or social characteristics to such a degree that they require special social and educational services to develop their maximum capacity."

29.1 Characteristics of Exceptional Children

Dunn (1963) describes the characteristics of the exceptional children as : "Exceptional pupils are those who differ from the average to such a degree in physical or psychological characteristics that school program designed for the majority of children do not offer them opportunity for all-round adjustment and optimum progress and who therefore need either special instruction or in some cases special ancillary services, or both, to achieve at a level commensurate with their respective abilities."

Thus in brief, the special characteristics of the exceptional children are :

1. They differ from the average or normal children.
2. They do not benefit from normal school program.
3. They need special services in terms of care and education for their optimum growth.

29.2 Types of Exceptional Children

We may classify exceptional children into following categories from intellectual, physical, emotional and social point of view :

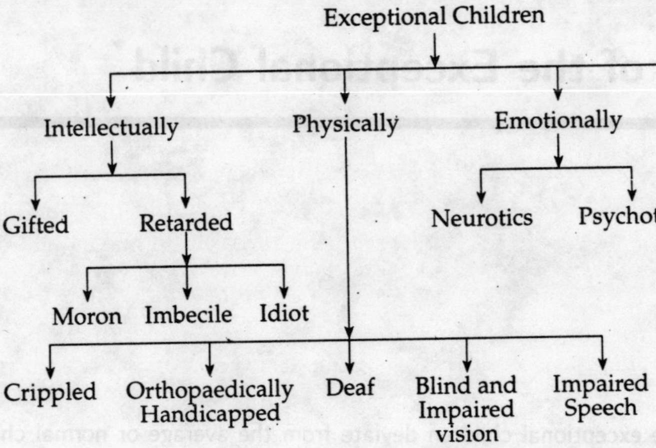

Fig. 29.1

29.3 Need of Special Education

It may appear to some that when the vast majority of normal children in this country are illiterate and deprived of adequate education for lack of resources, it is of no use speaking about education of a few exceptional children. In fact, before independence there were a very few special type of institutions in this country that could cater to their needs. However, after 1947, the necessity of educating exceptional children has been strongly felt by educators and parents. The Indian Commission (1964–66) has emphatically stated that their education has to be organised not merely on humanitarian grounds, but also on grounds of utility. Article 45 of our constitution advocates equality of educational opportunity including these who are physically and mentally handicapped.

Equality of educational opportunity, however, is attained through enabling each child to progress according to his own pace and his potentialities. Dunn thinks that the true meaning of equality of opportunity lies in diversified rather than similar school program. That is, education for exceptional children should be organised according to their needs and capabilities, because they do not benefit from regular classroom instruction. For example, the gifted children with high I.Q. do not get proper motivation in regular classes with children of average intellect.

Moreover, mentally and physically handicapped—like the deaf, dumb, blind or idiot—who cannot adjust in ordinary school, require special type of schools with different curriculum, methods of teaching and special type of trained teachers. These exceptional children, if left unattended, often develop behaviour problems and become liabilities to the nation. At present, National Council of Educational Research and Training (NCERT), New Delhi, conducts National Talent Search Test and awards scholarships to selected students to pursue higher education.

29.4 Gifted children : Who are gifted?

Those with special talents in some specific areas such as in science, fine arts, leadership, etc. may be denoted as gifted. Giftedness has been defined by psychologists from different angles. Some psychologists emphasise the role of Intelligence Quotient (I.Q.) and achievement test score, while others on social performance.

1. **Intelligence Quotient (I.Q.) :** Terman (1925–1959) classified human intelligence in terms of I.Q. in the following way :

Class	**I.Q.**
Genius	above 140
Very Superior	121–140
Superior	111–120
Average	91–110
Dull	81–90
Border line	71–80
Feeble-minded (Moron)	51–70
Imbecile	26-50
Idiot	0–25

   Thus, Terman fixed I.Q. 140 as the lower limit of giftedness. While Bentley (1937) lowers it to 110. Thus there is no universally accepted line of demarcation for gifted children.

2. **Social performance :** An individual may have average I.Q. but he may show remarkable performance in creative writing, music, dramatics, art, social leadership and other spheres of activity. This type of persons may also be regarded as gifted. Individuals with wide range of creativity and talent are asset to every society. They can contribute best to the promotion of science and art.

29.5 Identification of Gifted Children

The progress of a country largely depends on the proper education of gifted children who will one day provide leadership to the nation in all walks of life.

Therefore, early identification of gifted children is very important. But as there are varieties of giftedness in children, it becomes difficult to ascertain giftedness by means of a single tool.

There are several methods of identifying capable students :

1. **Teachers' Opinion :** Teachers observe the behaviour of children in the classroom and form certain opinion about their competence. But opinion differs and the diagnosis by teachers may not be always correct.
2. **School Record ;** Cumulative record cards maintained by school indicate to some extent giftedness of children. In a cumulative record card child's intelligence quotient, achievement quotient, results of periodic examinations and trends of personality etc. are recorded.
3. **Intelligence Tests :** The Minnesota Test of creative thinking is used for identifying creativity or giftedness among school children. Terman-Merrill's standardised Intelligence Test (L–M forms) is used to determine high intellect of children.

   Group Intelligence Tests may be employed for the purpose of screening. While individual intelligence test is more reliable than group tests, it is expensive and time consuming.
4. **Aptitude Tests :** A number of Aptitude Tests have been devised to determine high aptitudes of children in different fields. Some of them are : Stenquist's Mechanical Aptitude Test, Seashore's Musical Talent Test, Moore's Engineering and Physical Science Aptitude Tests, etc.
5. **Achievement Test :** A standardised achievement test is useful in identifying gifted children. A large number of standardised achievement tests have been devised to identify children of high competence. Some of these are :

   (a) Durrel-Reading Achievement Test.

   (b) Stanford Achievement Test.

   (c) Modern School Achievement Test.

   (d) California Achievement Test.

29.6 Characteristics of Gifted Children

Terman (1928), Paul Witty (1955), Kirk and others have studied physical, mental, social and emotional characteristics of gifted children. According to them, gifted children are endowed with a variety of intellectual traits. Some of them are :

1. The gifted children have keen power of observation and they learn more rapidly than average children.
2. They show much curiosity in questioning.
3. They display rich common sense.
4. They think logically and coherently.
5. They show rapid physical and mental growth.
6. They have good memory and power of retention.
7. They have great ability to generalise.
8. they have a rich vocabulary and good fund of general knowledge.
9. They have a desire to excel and they are ahead of their fellows.
10. They have many sided interests. They enjoy reading.
11. They possess originality and unusual ideas. They invent and develop ideas. They have strong urge to explore and to create.
12. They have a rich personality. They are more ambitious, more hard working and more self-confident than average children. According to Goddard, "Gifted children are made of finer stuff than the majority." They are more alert and quick in their thinking.

29.7 Needs of the Gifted Children

Gifted Children are the asset of a country. In addition to basic needs like food, love and security, they have certain special needs. These needs are :

1. **Need for knowledge :** Thirst for knowledge is very strong in gifted children. The method and standard of teaching in ordinary schools suit a normal or average boy. Teachers usually plan work for an average child. In such system, the genius suffers due to want of opportunity for putting forth the best in him. Within a short span of time, he completes his assignment and the rest of time he spends in acts of indiscipline in the classroom.
2. **Need for diversified interest :** The gifted child has diversified interest. He is exceptionally curious. He has many-sided interests. But these cannot be satisfied in normal system of schooling. He neither gets appreciation from his teachers nor from his classmates. Rather, he faces a sort of social rejection.
3. **Need for self-expression :** The gifted child wants recognition for his ingenuity in a scientific field or in the field of arts. He has a desire to excel others. But he is misunderstood and snubbed by the teachers. This results in emotional disturbance and problem behaviour.

4. **Need for creativity :** The gifted child has a strong urge to create and to explore. He is unwilling to accept the routine solutions of problems. He has his own vision of creating something new. The creativity of such children suffers in schools where proper environment for nurturing creativity is lacking.

In fact, the gifted child has greater ingenuity, power of thinking and judgement, practical knowledge, emotional maturity and superior intellectual ability than average children. As a result, the gifted child has certain special needs like the need for knowledge, need for diversified interests, creativity and ingenuity, and need for self-expression. If these needs remain unfulfilled due to lack of suitable environment and adequate facilities in the school, the gifted child is exposed to the risk of becoming emotionally maladjusted and abnormal.

Thus, instead of allowing their superior talents to go waste, we have to take special care for their educational needs, so that they can make valuable contributions to the welfare of the country.

29.8 Education of the Gifted Children

In our present system of schooling and limited resources, it is really a difficult problem to make provision for the education of gifted children. The program for gifted children should provide a stimulating teaching learning environment, lay emphasis on creative thinking, promote basic skills and the classwork should be challenging for their maximum intellectual growth. Kirk suggests three ways to tackle the problem of gifted children : (i) to organise special classes, (ii) to provide opportunities for accelerated promotion, (iii) enrichment in the regular grades.

Like Kirk, the following plans of special education for the gifted children have been put forward by different educationists :

1. Separate schools for gifted children.
2. Special classes.
3. Grade acceleration.
4. Enrichment programs.

1. **Separate Schools :** Probably the best thing would be to set up separate schools for gifted children. Where adequate facilities will be available for them. But such segregation is not desirable in a democratic state, because pupils educated in these institutions develop superiority complex and the gulf between the privileged and the unprivileged widens.

2. **Special Classes :** For effective teaching and learning, some educators have proposed special classes for gifted children within the same school. This plan involves grouping of children according to their ability. Such a group has the advantage of providing rapid growth through mutual stimulation. But such segregation on the basis of I.Q. is not feasible because it involves

huge expenditure. Again, the mental tests used to screen out the gifted are not quite reliable and perfect. Moreover, the students who do not get opportunity to get admitted in such classes will suffer from inferiority feeling. The parents of such children also will decry such arrangement.

3. **Grade Acceleration :** Gifted children learn faster than average children. So they should be allowed double promotion or acceleration by skipping a grade at the end of the term. They should also be allowed early admission in the school. The advantages of such acceleration plan are :

   (a) This saves time and money.

   (b) The gifted child can start his career earlier and contribute to the society at an early age.

   The plan, however, suffers from a serious defect. The child will find it difficult to adjust with his classmates who are senior to him in age and more mature emotionally and socially.

4. **Enrichment Program :** Enrichment program is another proposal to meet the need of gifted children. This seems to be the most suitable plan for the education of the gifted children in our country. Kirk, Conant and others recommended certain additional educational provisions for gifted children. Some of them are as follows :

   (a) Provide counselling and guidance services in every school for gifted children.

   (b) Flexibility in selecting subjects should be provided. Extra courses should be provided for gifted children.

   (c) Advanced classes in Science, Mathematics, Language and social studies should be organised for gifted children.

   (d) Extra-curricular activities such as, science club, hobby club, students self government etc. should be arranged for gifted children.

   (e) Special correspondence courses should be started for the able children.

   (f) Summer school for the bright students should be organised.

   (g) Work on independent projects may be initiated for the gifted children.

Conclusion : The aim of education for all children, particularly gifted children, should be to develop creative thinking and not mere mechanical memorisation. The education for able students at primary and secondary stages should be different from ordinary average pupils. Obviously, while special classes, enrichment or acceleration may not be required for an average pupil, for gifted children it is a necessity. Thus, in spite of our limited resources, some of the provisions mentioned above can be made for the bright and gifted children in our present set up of education to draw out their best potentialities.

29.9 The Mentally Retarded

Mental retardation is the general term applied to children who have slow rate of maturation, inadequate social adjustment and reduced learning capacity.

According to Rosen, Fox and Gregory, Mental retardation refers to a chronic condition present from birth or childhood which is characterised by slow rate of maturation, reduced capacity for learning impaired intellectual functioning, impaired adaptation to social environment. Simply it can be defined thus : A mentally retarded person is one who does not grow up mentally to meet the average standards. Estimates place the figure of mentally defectives at about 2 to 3 percent of the total population.

Mentally retarded children are also called mentally handicapped, slow learners, feeble-minded, educationally backward etc.

In terms of I.Q. William Stern suggests classification of the retarded children as follows :

Mental Retardation	I.Q.
Moron (feeble minded)	51–75
Imbecile	26–50
Idiot	0–25

29.10 Characteristics of Mentally Retarded Children

Mentally handicapped children are slow learners. They have poor powers of abstract thinking. They cannot relate cause and effect ideas. They are incapable of fitting parts into an integrated whole.

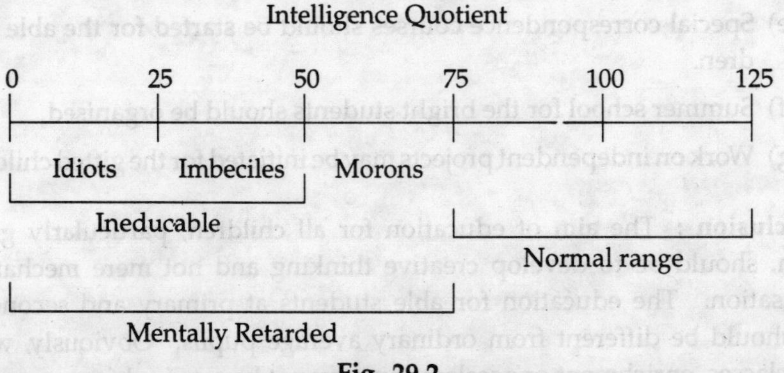

Fig. 29.2

The morons, who have I.Q. from 51–75 are educable. The imbeciles, who have I.Q. from 26–50, are almost ineducable and the idiots having I.Q. below 25 are not educable at all.

1. **Morons :** The morons are educable within limits. They can learn simple routine tasks without constant supervision. They can make beds, run errands etc. Some high-grade morons can be trained to do some remunerative jobs such as tailoring, tending animals, carpentry etc. However, they cannot successfully cope with a novel situation or solve a complicated problem. In regular classes, the morons have the adjustment problems. They lack motivation to learn a new thing. In fact, the common school environment provides them no motivation for studies. They are regarded as backwards and mentally deficient by their teachers. Their I.Q. varies from 50 to 75.
2. **Imbeciles :** Imbeciles are more defective than morons. They cannot be trained to do much useful job. Some of them in the upper limit can learn to dress, wash and feed themselves. They can learn only the simplest tasks under constant supervision. They cannot learn complex actions and they lack physical skills and communication ability. Their I.Q. varies from 25 to 50.
3. **Idiots :** Idiots lack physical coordination and proper sensory development. They require constant supervision for their very existence. The most deficient idiots cannot attend to their physical needs. They cannot learn to eat or to drink. They cannot learn to eat or to drink. They cannot be trained to wash or dress themselves. They cannot talk beyond a few mono-syllables. They cannot even avoid the common dangers of life. They are too stupid to avoid fire or a running bus. Their I.Q. varies from 0 to 25.

29.11 Identification of Retarded Children

Great care should be taken for the identification of retarded children. Mere physical appearance or low intelligence quotient are not sufficient for detection of mental retardation. We should consider the following for identification of retarded children :

1. **Observation of behaviour :** Behaviour of the children should be closely observed for detecting deficiencies in their daily activities. Teachers can detect retardedness easily through their daily observation of the behaviour of the children in or outside the class.
2. **Achievement tests :** Achievement tests in different school subjects reveal the level of educational retardation.

Achievement quotient is found out thus,

$$\text{A.Q.} = \frac{\text{Educational Quotient (E.Q.)}}{\text{Intelligence Quotient (I.Q.)}} \times 100$$

$$\text{E.Q.} = \frac{\text{Educational Age (E.A.)}}{\text{Chronological Age (C.A.)}} \times 100$$

$$\text{I.Q.} = \frac{\text{Mental Age (M.A.)}}{\text{Chronological Age (C.A.)}} \times 100$$

$$\therefore \quad \text{A.Q.} = \frac{\text{E.A.}}{\text{M.A.}} \times 100.$$

According to Burt, the A.Q. of the retarded child is below 85.

3. **Intelligence tests :** For confirmation of mental retardation, standardised intelligence tests should be used.

29.12 Classification of the Mentally Retarded Children

In classifying the mentally retarded children we need to consider their : (a) Low Intelligence Quotient, as well as their, (b) Deficient Adaptive Behaviour.

Thus on the basis of intelligence and adaptive behaviour, we can broadly classify mentally retarded children as follows : (i) Severely Retarded, (ii) Moderately Retarded and (iii) Mildly Retarded.

Severly retarded children (custodial children) show acute speech and sensori-motor deficiency. They have retarded growth and physical deformities. They are unable to manage their own affairs. They are dependent on others and need to be institutionalised. Nearly 5 percent of all retarded children suffer from severe mental retardation.

Moderately retarded children are dull and clumsy in physical appearance. Their rate of learning is very slow and they are practically ineducable. They require constant supervision and support and hence need to be institutionalised. Nearly ten percent of retarded children have moderate mental retardation.

Mildly retarded children are detected in schools as backward. They show slow physical growth. They have poor muscular coordination and speech defects. They lack the ability of abstract thinking and reasoning. They lack motivation to learn and normal school environment does not provide them motivation to study. However, they are considered to be educable and with the help of special classes and trained teachers, they may reach elementary school education level.

The teacher with proper understanding can guide such a mildly retarded child and his family to enable him to do simple jobs and earn livelihood. Nearly eighty-five percent of the retarded children are only mildly retarded.

29.13 Causes of Mental Retardation

In a mentally retarded child, the brain is damaged either : (i) in utero; (ii) during delivery or (iii) post-natally. Pre-natal causes include : (a) Genetic causes, (b) Chromosomal aberration and (c) Environmental factors, e.g., Pre-natal causes include: Birth trauma, Hypoglycemia. Post-natal causes include: Encephalitis, Cerebral haemorrhage, Cerebral trauma etc.

29.14 Some clinical disorders associated with mental retardation

1. **Mongolism or Down's syndrome :** Lang Down (1866), first described this syndrome in connection with mentally retarded people. The Mongoloids have short necks, small round heads, short broad hands, a small mouth with narrow, arched palate, large protruded fissured tongue, poorly developed dental structure, prominent abdomen and narrow eyes. A typical Down's syndrome child is short and fat and markedly over-weight for his height. The I.Q. of these children varies between 20–50 (Imbeciles). They can learn routine manual skills. The causes of Mongolism may be due to chromosomal anomalies.

2. **Microcephaly :** The microcephalic has very small head. He is of short stature with cone-shaped skull and receding forehead. The brain of the true microcephalic is extremely small and the convolutions of cortex is markedly simplified. Practically there is no effective treatment for microcephaly.

3. **Acrocephaly :** The acrocephalic has pointed and high head. In this case, sometimes mental retardation is associated with visual impairment. Correction of such deformities by surgical means have been attempted but the results are not encouraging.

4. **Hydrocephaly :** Hydrocephalus literally means water in the head. Hydrocephalic results from the accumulation of excess cerebrospinal fluid within the cranium causing enlargement of the skull. There is a very high risk of mental deficiency consequent on the gross destruction of brain tissue. Often the disorder develops during infancy. Modern neurosurgical treatment shows favourable results in checking damage to the brain tissue to some extent. But the acute and advanced cases do not respond to any treatment.

5. **Phenylketonuria :** This is an inherited disease that was first described by Folling in 1934. In this case, phenylalanine and phenylpyruvic acid accumulate in the blood producing toxic changes in the brain and causing mental deficiency. There is often poor growth in development and symptoms like EEG abnormalities, muscular hypertonicity, microcephaly, eczema; seizures are common with this disorder.

Fòr treatment to be effective, it must be started very early in life and the earlier the better before irreparable brain damages has occurred degenerative changes in the brain can be prevented by suitable phenylalanine-free diet from an early age.

6. **Autism :** The disorder was first described by Kanner (1943), who described the central features as a lack of responsiveness to other people. The autistic children show normal development but may not develop speech at all or acquire this faculty very late. There may be echolalia or other mannerisms of use and diction. They may appear deaf and prefer to be recluse. Difficulty in mixing and playing with other children is an outstanding feature. Some degree of destructiveness may be present. The disease affects boys more than girls (4 : 1). Most of such children are mentally handicapped. Often they are good looking but as they grow older, their features often become much coarser.

The disturbance present in these children seriously interferes with the normal teaching learning processes. They need residential care.

29.15 Needs of the mentally retarded

Like normal children, mentally retarded children also have the same kind of physical as well as emotional needs. But mentally handicapped children have certain special needs. As they are not able to adjust properly to their environment, some one else has to take care of them. According to D. Gordon (1975), the special needs of the mentally handicapped and their families can be enumerated as follows :

1. Early identification of the metabolic disorders.
2. **Complete assessment and prompt treatment :** It is necessary to examine the whole child, paying particular attention to the special senses. A team including doctor, a specialist, a psychologist, a social worker, a physiotherapist, a special therapist and an educationist should assess the child as a whole.
3. Prompt treatment of anything that is treatable.
4. Social setting to give love and security to allow maximum development of the personality.
5. Suitable education adapted to the individual's complex handicaps.
6. Appropriate social contacts and leisure time activity.
7. Follow-up and continuous assessment.
8. Family guidance and support.

29.16 Treatment of Mental Retardation

Prevention is undoubtedly the best form of treatment, as there is no cure for mental deficiency. In fact, no amount of medical care can turn a mentally retarded into a normal individual. But this does not mean that there is nothing to do.

Some preventive measures such as proper care of the mother and child. Provision of normal and congenial environment after birth and provision of public education to educate the masses, may be adopted.

Medical treatment

Though there is no complete cure for mental deficiency, the following medical measures may be adopted to control the occurrence and development of mental retardation in some cases :

In case of epilepsy in the mentally retarded, anticonvulsant medication may prove helpful.

Cretinism may be controlled by administration of thyroid to the cretin.

To control abnormal behaviour in mentally retarded, tranquillisers may be used.

Surgical treatment is found to be useful in the treatment of hydrocephalus.

Psychotherapy is to some extent useful for the treatment of less severely handicapped.

The technique of rewarding to reinforce acceptable behaviour has been used to toilet training with success (Azrin and Foxx, 1971).

Operant conditioning has been used to promote co-operation and communication in mentally retarded children.

In case of speech difficulty in mentally deficient, speech therapist should be called in as early as possible.

Counselling : The advent of a mentally retarded child in a family does not make anyone happy. Either such child is rejected outright or over-protected by his parents. Therefore, the parents need proper counselling. It is essential that parents realise the truth about their child and they should accept the child's limitations. If needed, they have to send their retarded child to a special school or to a hospital/clinic/institution meant for mentally handicapped.

Provision of special education : The mentally handicapped may be educated in special classes attached to normal schools or in schools devoted entirely to the training of the mentally retarded. Parents often prefer to admit their retarded children in normal schools with special classes, rather than in schools meant exclusively for mentally handicapped. Such institutions should have a nuclear team comprising a pediatrician, psychologist, social worker, physiotherapist, speech therapist and an educationist. A specially trained educationist is considered an important member of the team responsible for the care of the mentally retarded. He has to teach them practical skills which aid self-help. He should make every effort to teach communication skills by developing language ability in the mentally handicapped. They should be encouraged to co-operate with each other through various social activities.

The mentally handicapped children should be motivated to learn through audiovisual aids and other modern techniques. But the sincerity and devotion of the educator is more important than the use.

The institution for mentally handicapped should provide vocational education, as increasing vocational competence is the ultimate aim for the mentally handicapped children. The educable mentally retarded children can learn vocational skills, of semiskilled or unskilled nature, if the instructions and the atmosphere for learning are appropriate. The teacher should also teach them the habit of work, responsibility and getting along with others. The teacher also should teach them the rules of conduct, safety measures, first-aid, and management of materials, money and time.

29.17 Backward child

A backward child is one retarded in educational attainments. He deviates from other students in school achievement. The backward child may be intelligent enough to do average work but may be lacking simply in persistence. According to Barton Hall (1947), the term backwardness is applied to cases where their educational attainment falls below the level of their natural abilities. Unlike mentally retarded, a backward child may have high I.Q. but he may be indifferent towards school-work. He lacks motivation to learn and has adjustment problems in regular classes.

29.18 Causes of backwardness

Educational backwardness may be due to a complex of causes. Some possible causes of backwardness are :

1. **Home environment :** Adverse home environment influences children's educational attainment. Children of poor families suffer from malnutrition due to want of proper food. They do not get proper education at home. Poverty, illiteracy of parents, frequent conflicts and quarrels amongst family members, alcoholism and homes broken by divorce or death of parents contribute towards educational backwardness of the children.

2. **Social environment :** Besides home, other social agencies like clubs, television, radio, religious and other social places greatly influence the scholastic attainment of the children.

3. **School environment :** Defective examination system, uninteresting methods of teaching, lack of proper guidance and motivation often make a child truant from school. Prolonged absence or irregular attendance in school contributes to the backwardness of the child. Burt (1950) found that bad school-conditions was the cause of backwardness in 8% of the cases he studied.

4. **Defective intelligence :** Burt found that low 'g' was the cause of backwardness in 60% of the cases he studied. Schonell (1948) found only 8% of the backward children intelligent enough to do average work.

5. **Physical defects :** Physical deformities, poor health, faulty hearing, defective eyesight and impaired speech seriously interfere with children's educational attainment.

29.19 Identification of Backward Children

1. **Observation :** The child's behaviour in the class and outside the class should be closely observed by the teachers and parents. The teacher, on the basis of his daily observation of the performances of the students, can judge in which subject or subjects the students are weak and backward.

2. **Intelligence tests :** The intellectual standard of the backward children can be ascertained by standard tests of intelligence. Children having an I.Q. on the range from 60 to 75 may be regarded as backward.

3. **Achievement tests :** Achievement tests and diagnostic tests may be applied to ascertain the extent of backwardness in specific school subjects. According to Burt, the backward child is one whose A.Q. is as low as 85.

4. **Medical examination :** To determine the physiological condition of the backward children, a thorough medical check-up is essential. It is often found that educationally backward children suffer from some kind of physical deformities.

5. **Case history :** The child's case history from infancy should be thoroughly studied along with the socio-economic status of the family and the nature of the association or gang with which he mixes.

29.20 Education of the Backward Children

After determining the possible causes of backwardness, our primary duty should be to plan how we can help the child to get rid of his backwardness. As each case of backwardness is unique in itself, no single remedy can be prescribed for all. In fact, each case of backwardness needs individual care and attention.

Considering the nature and extent of backwardness following provisions may be made for the education of backward children : 1. Provision of special schools. 2. Provision of special classes.

1. **The special schools :** Some educationists think that if a backward child is kept with normal children in a regular class of an ordinary school, his chance of improvement is remote and he will become more and more backward and frustrated. Obviously, sufficient individual attention cannot be rendered to backward children in large classes of modern school systems. However, these special schools should have specially trained teachers and a special curriculum. The curriculum should be more practical and life-centric and methods of instruction should be based on concrete experiences with appropriate aids.

   However, the complete isolation of backward children from normal and bright students are not favoured by parents and others. They think that their children should not be deprived of the opportunities of mixing freely with bright and average students and labelled as block headed or dumb-bells. This is why some educationists suggest special class arrangement for the backward children within the same school.

2. **The special classes :** To render sufficient individual attention provision of special classes should be made for the backward children. In such small classes, the teachers—through individual attention—understand their needs and problems. They can also adopt appropriate psychological techniques of teaching.

29.21 Education of Physically Handicapped Child

Children having speech-defects, impaired hearing, impaired vision and those who are orthopedically disabled come under the heading physically handicapped.

29.22 Hearing Impairment

Hearing is vital for the development of speech and verbal communication. Deafness, partial or complete loss of hearing, is one of the most serious handicaps of childhood. Hearing impairment is determined by an instrument called *audiometer.* Many degrees of hearing impairment exist between the deaf and the normal. The different degrees of hearing impairment are defined in terms of decibels :

Hearing deficit	Decibel range
Mild hearing loss	20–40
Moderate hearing loss	40–65
Serve hearing loss	65–85
Profound	Over 85

Children suffering from hearing impairment are wrongly regarded as mentally retarded.

Those children who suffer from severe hearing losses during the early stage of life experience speech difficulties also. It has been estimated by audiometric surveys that about 9 to 15 per cent of school children are partially or totally deaf.

Causes : Studies made in India show that mumps, measles, chicken-pox, small-pox, cholera and malnutrition, particularly deficiency of B-complex factors, are common causes of defective hearing among school children.

Treatment : With the invention of electronic audiometer, hearing aids and effective medication, great advances have been made in the field of audition in recent years.

Mental retardness may be cured through removal of hearing impairment by using improved hearing aids. The children needs (i) early detection and proper diagnosis, (ii) vocational rehabilitation and (iii) educational rehabilitation.

A careful history must be obtained from parents regarding the hearing abilities of the child. All relevant details of the family must be properly recorded. An accurate record of the child's health, especially such important details like jaundice after birth, convulsions etc. prove invaluable.

Poor school performance, lack of attention and concentration also indicate hearing impairment of child.

Speech normally develops in the second year of life and becomes fixed by three years of age; so the diagnosis of hearing loss and therapy must be started before three years of age. Speech therapy has a useful role to play in the training of partially deaf children and this form of service should beneficially be utilised in such cases.

A deaf child should be fitted with hearing aids by an expert and when the child has learned to communicate with people with normal hearing, he may be placed in a regular class, suitable to his level of achievement with normal children.

Blindness : Blindness has been defined in various ways in different countries. In Britain the standard is 3/60 or less whereas in U.S.A. and Canada, the limit is 6/60. In India, the standard used by Somerset and Ghosh (1951) was inability to count the fingers of the hand held up at about 1 meter/yard distance.

The eye is well developed at birth and continues to grow up to 14 years of age with the greatest post-natal growth during the first three years of life.

Testing of visual acuity can be accomplished in children beyond the age of 3 years by the use of Snellen's test cards or E. Charts.

Disorders of the eye : Some of the disorders of the eye are Cataracts, Squints, Traumatic lesions, Conjunctivitis, Trachoma, Corneal ulcers, Myopia (Near-sightedness). Hyperopia (Far-sightedness), Astigmatism etc.

Causes of blindness : The commonest causes of blindness in our country are : Small-pox, Tuberculosis of the eye, Trachoma, Avitaminosis, Venereal diseases etc. Other causes are :

1. Infections : conjunctivitis.
2. Eye injuries.
3. Squint.
4. Glaucoma.
5. Severe measles.
6. Congenital anomatlies : Cataracts, Optic atrophy.
7. Leprosy.
8. Hereditary diseases.

Blindness in India : Of estimated 30 million blind persons in the world, 6 million are in India. So one out of every 5 blind persons is an Indian! According to available data, 30 p.c. of the blind in India lose their eyesight before 21 years, most cases occurring during the first five years of life. This is distressing state of affairs since the vast majority of these are due to preventable causes.

29.23 Treatment and Educational Adjustments

The keynote of treatment is prevention by simple modern treatment and dissemination of knowledge of principles of nutrition.

Prevention of conjunctivitis can be achieved by antibiotic drops or ointments. The dreaded trachoma can be successfully treated by Sulfa drugs and Glaucoma can be reduced by early drug treatment or by surgery. Adequate intake of vitamin A in the diet should be ensured.

Parents of blind children should receive special training and regular ophthalmological care will go a long way to minimise the disability of blindness.

Blind children should be taught to read and write in Braille. Braille material can now be reproduced on a multi-copy machine. Braille material may be supplemented by phonograph or tapes. In most classes for the blind, three-dimensional models are used to give an idea of solid figures. But it is difficult to give a blind child the idea of a mountain, sky, ocean or colour of flowers. It is difficult also to give them the sense of direction. Walking canes are being used by a blind person to help him to move about.

29.24 The Orthopaedically handicapped

Cerebral Palsy : Cerebral Palsy is a crippling neuromuscular disorder in children. The predominant neurological deficit is a motor disability. In addition to the motor disability, cerebral palsy, patients often have other handicaps :

1. Speech disabilities.
2. Mental retardation.
3. Impaired vision and hearing.
4. Psychological disabilities.
5. Seizures.

Etiology : Clear proof of etiology is seldom obtained. In most instances, there are multiple etiological factors. However, most of the cases are congenital, caused by pre-natal abnormalities, such as maternal toxemia, maternal infectious disease, mechanical injuries, hemorrhages etc.

Types of muscle disorder found in cerebral palsy include spasticity, rigidity, athetosis (bizarre involuntary movements), ataxia and flaccidity.

Cerebral palsy is the largest cause of crippling of children being variously estimated to have an incidence of 1 to 2 per 1,000 population.

Educational planning : Children with cerebral palsy can be broadly divided into : (a) those who have only minor disability—they can be sent to ordinary schools, (b) those who have combinations of several major handicaps may be sent to special classes and schools. The school program should be highly individualised to meet the needs of each child. It should include physiotherapy (massage, muscle training etc.), speech therapy by a fully-trained and qualified speech therapist, psychological treatment and surgical treatment. There is also need of drug therapy to ameliorate spasticity. Fits are controlled with routine use of anti-convulsants.

An important aim of training children with cerebral palsy is to let them learn to be as independent as possible. One should not do things for them that they can do for themselves.

Epileptic seizures : Epilepsy is commonly found in association with mental handicap. The cause of epileptic seizures is not always clear. Seizures of known etiology are due to structural damage of the brain, which may be due to pre-natal, pre-natal and post-natal factors.

It has been estimated that 4 per 1,000 of the population suffer from some form of seizures. Most of the convulsive disorders have their onset in early life. About 5 p.c. of children under 5 years of age have a fit sometime or other in their lives.

There are several types of epilepsy such as grand mal, petit mal and pyknolepsy. However, there are two specific epileptic conditions associated with mental-handicap : (a) Lennox syndrome and (b) infantile spasms (Salaam type).

In Lennox syndrome there is progressive mental deterioration starting during the first 6 years of life. Such cases may respond to Diazepam.

In Sallam type of infantile spasms, the infant will bend at the waist suddenly falling forwards and prostrating himself in the prone position. The control of this type of disorder is usually readily obtained by the administration of steroids but the long-term prognosis is not good.

The treatment of epilepsy in the mentally handicapped does not differ from that of epilepsy in the intellectually normal except that the control of the epilepsy is often more difficult in the mentally handicapped.

Rehabilitation and adjustment of the handicapped : The question of rehabilitation arises only in children who present with problems due to brain damage, mental deficiency, speech defects and cerebral palsy. Some of these may be directly related to epilepsy and may be alleviated by anti-convulsant therapy. Other avenues of rehabilitation like physiotherapy, speech therapy etc. should not be ignored.

It is important to treat all these children as normal children and excessive concern by parents must be avoided. Restriction of the child should be to the minimum, commensurate with the state of his disease. In the social adjustment of the child, the cooperation of the teachers and others must be enlisted.

Disability caused by impairment restricting or stopping normal functioning of any part of the body does not necessarily make a man handicapped. Disabled person, deprived of opportunities to interact with persons without disability in the society, becomes really handicapped. A child with slight impairment in the part of his brain in unable to sit up on his own. Now, if this child is not permitted in a normal school, even if he is provided with a chair specially made for him, it is a society which labels this child as handicapped.

In a country like ours where nearly 2% of the total population are suffering from one or other traumatic disability, integration or main-streaming appears to be indispensable to reach the goal of universalisation of elementary education.

Our National Education Policy as well as The Ashok Mitra Commission on Education, recommended for integrating or main-streaming as well as special schools to match the needs of the children with different types of disability.

As the Orthopedically handicapped are mentally same as the normal students, same syllabus may be followed. For this kind of students, however, games and sports requiring heavy physical exercises may be relaxed.

Education for the handicapped children is definitely a multi-disciplinary work and calls for a joint effort by the government as well as the Non-government Social Organisations in the matter of shouldering the responsibility. Coordination among Health Department, Social Welfare Department,

Public Health Engineering Department and the Education Department of the Government should be established for promoting main-streaming as well as setting up of special schools for the disabled children.

Summary

The exceptional child deviates from the normal child in physical, mental, emotional or social traits. He needs special treatment for his upbringing and adjustment.

Gifted children are those children who have special talents in some specific areas. The progress of a country depends on the proper education of gifted children. Therefore, early identification of gifted children is very important. Enrichment program seems to be the most suitable plan for the education of gifted children in our country.

Mentally retarded children have slow rate of maturation, a low I.Q. and impaired adaptation to social environment. The morons—who have I.Q. from 50–75, are educable. The imbeciles, who have I.Q. from 25–50, are almost ineducable and the idiots, having I.Q. below 25, are not educable at all.

Some clinical disorders associated with mental retardation are : Mongolism or Down's syndrome. The Mongoloids have small round heads, prominent abdomen, short broad hands and narrow eyes. The I.Q. of these children varies between 20–50. They can learn routine manual skills. The microcephalic has a short structure with a very small head. There is no effective treatment for microcephaly. The Hydrocephalic has high risk of mental deficiency consequent on the gross destruction of brain tissue. There is often poor growth in development and symptoms like microcephaly, muscular hypertonicity and seizure are common with the disorder of phenylketonuria. The central feature of Autism is the lack of responsiveness to other people. The autistic children show normal development but may not develop speech at all or acquire this faculty very late. Most of such children are mentally handicapped.

Backward children are slow learners whose educational attainment falls below the level of their natural abilities. They may have high I.Q. but they may be indifferent towards schoolwork. Considering the nature and extent of backwardness, provision of special schools and provision of special classes may be made for such children.

Children having speech-defects impaired hearing, impaired vision and those who are orthopedically disabled are physically handicapped. Epileptic seizures and cerebral palsy (crippling neuromuscular disorder) are commonly found in association with mental handicap.

Education for the handicapped children is definitely a multi-disciplinary work and calls for a close link between Public Health Department, Social Welfare Department and the Education Department of the government.

References

1. Dutta, Tirthankar : *Pediatrics* (2nd ed.), Books & Allied (P) Ltd., Calcutta, 2000.
2. Achar, S.T. and Viswanathan : *Text-book of Pediatrics,* (2nd ed.) Orient Longman, Calcutta, 1982.
3. Bentley, J.E. : *Superior Children,* New York. W.W. Norton, 1937.
4. Page, James, D. : *Abnormal Psychology,* New Delhi : Tata McGraw-Hill, 1976.
5. Terman, L.M. and Oden, M.H. : *The Gifted Child Grows Up,* Stanford, California, Stanford University Press, 1947.
6. Heck, A.O. : *The Education of Exceptional Children,* New York : Mc Graw Hill.
7. Hutt, M.L. and Gibby, R.G. : *The Mentally Retarded Child,*
8. Robins, L.N. : *Deviant Children Grow up,* Baltimore. Md : Williams & Wilkins, 1966.
9. Robinson, H.B. and Robinson, N.M. : *The Mentally Retarded Child,* New York : McGraw-Hill, 1976.
10. Seminar on Primary Education for Children with Special Needs. Prepared by SCERT, West Bengal, Calcutta, December 1996.
11. Burt, C : *The Backward Child,* London : University of London Press, 1950.
12. Burt, C. : *The Young Delinquent,* London : University of London Press, 1953.
13. Dutton Gordon : *Mental Handicap,* Butterworths & Co. (Publishers) Ltd., 1975.
14. Dunn, L.M. (Ed.) : *Exceptional Children in the Schools,* New York : Holt, Rinehart & Winston, 1963.
15. Kirk, S.A. : *Educating Exceptional Children,* Quoted in S.S. Chauhan, Advanced Educational Psychology. New Delhi : Vikas Publishing House, 1984.
16. Robinson, H.B. and Robinson, N.M. : *The Mentally Retarded Child,* New York : McGraw-Hill, 1976.
17. Rosen, E. Fox and Gregory Ean : *Abnormal Psychology.* Saunders International Student, Edition III, 1972.
18. Telford, C.W. and Sawrey, J.M. : *The Exceptional Individual,* Englewood Cliffs. N.J. : Prentice-Hall, 1977.

Questions and Assignments

1. What is meant by special education? Why provision for special education should be made?
2. Who are gifted? What provisions should be made for the education of such children?
3. Define backwardness. How will you identify backward children?
4. Define mental retardation. What are the causes of mental retardation?
5. Who are physically handicapped? How should children with hearing impairment be treated?
6. Write notes on:
   (a) Cerebral Palsy.
   (b) Epileptic Seizures.
   (c) Orthopedically handicapped.
   (d) Blindness.
   (f) Autism.
   (g) Phenyl Ketonuria.

Chapter 30

Psychology of the Group

Introduction : A group is defined as a number of persons interacting with each other so as to behave as a collective unit. According to Mills (1967), the group is a unit composed of two or more persons who come into contact for a specific purpose. It consists of persons sharing in common the group interest and the group goal.

30.1 Group characteristics

Marked changes in the behaviour of the individual result when he is in the midst of some group of persons. In the group, the individuals think, feel and act together. But the thinking, feeling and acting of the group as a whole are different from the normal thinking feeling and acting of the individuals who compose it. According to Le Bon, when human beings have been transformed into a group it puts them in possession of a sort of *collective mind* which makes them feel, think and act in a manner quite different from that in which each of them would feel think and act were he in a state of isolation.

Following factors are essential for organised group life :

1. **Group objectives :** The members of a group share common objectives, interests, similar attitudes and sentiments.

2. **Group norm :** A norm or a standard of behaviour is set by the group and the members of the group are expected to act in conformity with it. Norms enforce solidarity of structure and conformity of behaviour of a group. Members, who deviate from the group norm act to disintegrate the solidarity of the group.

3. **Group consciousness :** Group consciousness consists in thinking of oneself as a member of a particular group. The members have an idea of the nature, composition, functions and utility of the group. The group spirit holds the group together.

4. **Group loyalty :** Group loyalty is the very heart of the group life. It is a sentiment involving a sense of obligation to the group, a readiness to sacrifice for the group.

5. **Group leadership :** The leader of the group inspires, leads and unites the members together. The group morale is centred round how the group leader engineers the structure, the goal and the activities of the group which he leads.

6. **Group structure :** The structure of the group may be democratic or authoritarian in nature. In democratic structure, the power is vested in different members of the group. The democratic leader is more of an agent than of the master of the group. He is there to serve and not to dominate it. He gives the members to understand that group administration is for them and run by them.

In authoritarian group the power is vested in the leader of the group, who enjoys the absolute right of planning and executing the plans, policies and objectives of the group. Under such leadership group morale cannot be firmly established.

30.2 Types of Groups

Groups may be classified in various ways. Drever gives the following types : 1. The Crowd type. 2. The Club type and 3. The Community type.

The crowd has no permanent existence. Its modes of feeling, thinking and acting are temporary. The crowd may turn into a mob under the excitement of an emotion. The club-type possesses common interest, sentiment and ideal, whereas the community-type has a comprehensive common purpose and it has continuity and permanence.

Groups may be classified also into (a) primary and (b) secondary primary group.

(a) Primary Group : It is comparatively small in size in which the members come to know one another in a face-to-face manner as distinct individuals. Family, play group, peer group, the neighbourhood etc. are examples of primary group. There is a direct interaction among the members of the group. The classroom teaching belongs to this category as the members of the class have face-to-face intimacy.

(b) Secondary Group : Secondary groups are associations of individuals whose contacts lack personal intimacy. The examples of the secondary group in which the points of contact are mostly indirect are trade unions, the political party, municipal organisation etc.

30.3 Group dynamics

Group dynamics means the change of behaviour through interaction in the group. The group is no static entity. It is active or dynamic in nature. Kurt Lewin (1890–1945) studied dynamics of group behaviour, which is based on the basic concepts of physics and geometry.

A group according to Lewin is a field or organisation of forces acting and reacting upon each other so that any change in any part within it brings about change in the total group-field. The interactinal process within the group may assume authoritarian or democratic structure.

Group dynamics may be studied by sociometry, which was devised by Moreno (1934).

30.4 The Group Mind

Behind the individual behaviour there lies an individual mind. In the same way, we may assume a collective mind behind the collective behaviour of a group. An organised group has a mind in the sense that the behaviour of the group is determined not by the individual consciousness but by the collective consciousness. The individual is influenced by his group milieu. Therefore, groups should be organised on a higher level, having a higher purpose and lofty aim for the welfare of the society.

30.5 Significance in Education

The school is a place where a number of individual students assemble for common purpose of achieving knowledge and skill. In this sense, the school is an organised social group. Therefore, the success of a school depends upon the working of the forces of the group psychology.

The desirability of cultivating a group mind in the school is of great importance. It is the group mind of the school that will shape the character of the individual students. The group mind is a very effective force in determining the behaviour of the students who compose the group. Therefore, if we are serious about the uplift of the nation, we must organise the schools on a higher level, having a higher purpose and lofty ideals for the welfare of the society. With this end in view, the following points are to be noted :

1. We should raise the school morale and the tone of the schools.
2. There should be free mixing and free interaction amongst the pupils and the teachers.
3. The students should be helped to develop a group consciousness. This may be done through various co-curricular activities, such as games, sports, old boys' clubs, competition and excursions.

30.6 Teachers' Role as a Leader

Everyday the teacher has to deal with groups of pupils, who come to school from different socio-economic background. Therefore, the teacher must have adequate knowledge of group dynamics so that he can provide better guidance to the students for successful adjustment in the class and outside the class. He is naturally the group leader and guide of the students. The group morale is centred round how he engineers the structure, the goal, the ideology and the activities of the group which he leads.

As a group-leader, the teacher should have the knowledge of the process of interaction among different groups of students. From the sociometric studies the following patterns of relationship among the students of a class have been found out :

1. **A star :** A star is an individual student who is liked or preferred by many students.
2. **A clique :** A clique means a sub-group or a group within the same group of students.
3. **A mutual pair :** A mutual pair is a two-individual sub-group. There is reciprocal relationship among mutual pair of pupils.
4. **An isolate :** An isolate is liked by none, eking out a lonely existence of his own within the group.

The teacher should find out such isolates, discuss with them their problems and help them to adjust with one another. He should also provide certain skills and activities which would interest them.

The role of the teacher as a leader in the classroom teaching is very important and, therefore, the selection of efficient teacher is essential to the maintenance and enhancement of group morale. The teacher, as a leader of the student-group, should be endowed with special gifts and talents. He has to set a model of behaviour to be emulated by all group members. The teacher is a parent substitute and the student group should look upon their teacher leader as father figure. He lays down the goals, objectives and plans of group activities and sees that these are executed in practice.

30.6.1 Types of Leadership

In classroom teaching, the teacher as the leader of the class can play two types of roles Authoritarian leadership or Democratic leadership.

Authoritarian leadership in the class implies that the teacher enjoys the absolute right of planning, policy-making, executing the plans, policies, goal and over-all authority over the students.

The second type of leadership in the class is democratic. The teacher is there to serve and not to dominate the group. He gives the students to understand that he leads the students for their own benefit. He shares planning and decision making with the class. He encourages group participation as much as possible.

Psychologists have studied the effects of Authoritarian and Democratic leadership. However, most of the studies confirm that Democratic leadership is better in the classroom teaching. A high group morale is more facilitated by Democratic than Authoritarian leadership. The teacher can create a democratic climate in the class by free discussion to solve a problem. He can invite suggestions from students to determine policy matters and encourage group participation as much as possible.

Summary

A group is a number of individuals welded together into a unity. It should have common objectives, a set of norms and a well-organised structure. In authoritarian group, the power is vested in the leader. An authoritarian leader determines policies, goal and objectives of the group. Under his leadership, the group morale cannot be firmly established.

On the other hand, a democratic group is dominated by *we feeling* and the democratic leader serves the group and does not dominate it. He rules out hierarchical chains of intermediaries between himself and the members. In fact, a high group morale is more facilitated by democratic than authoritarian leadership.

As a leader of the class, the teacher should have adequate knowledge of group dynamics. The knowledge of group dynamics helps the teacher to improve intra group relations and to maintain high morale of the class.

References

1. Bhatnagar, R.P. : *Educational Psychology,* Vishwa Vidyalaya Prakashan, Gorakhpur.
2. Harry, Kaufmann : *Social Psychology,* Helt, Rinehart. New York, 1973.
3. Kimbal Young : *Handbook of Social Psychology.*
4. Krech, D. and Crutchfield, R.S. : *Theory and Problems of Social Psychology,* Part 2.
5. Ginsberg, M. : *The Psychology of Society,* 1964.
6. McDougall : *An Introduction to Social Psychology.*
7. Drever : *An Introduction to the Psychology of Education.*

Questions and Assignments

1. What is a group? Mention its characteristics.
2. Define a group. Describe different types of groups.
3. What is meant by group dynamics? Why should a teacher study group dynamics?
4. What is group leadership? Distinguish between authoritarian and democratic leadership.
5. Define a leader. Describe the teacher's role as a leader.
6. Write notes on:

   (a) Democratic leadership.

   (b) Primary group.

   (c) Group norm.

   (d) Group dynamics.

   (e) Group mind.

Chapter 31

Play and Education

Introduction : Play is a strong innate tendency. Not only every child plays, adults too like to play. According to McDougall, play is an innate tendency necessary for the physical and mental growth of the child. The impulse to play is just the impulse to carry out certain instinctive actions (Thomson).

Play is defined by Prof. Nunn as a profound manifestation of creative activities. There is an inward urge placed in the child by Nature to play. Just as a musician cannot restrain himself from singing, so the child too cannot restrain himself from playing. Play is a voluntary self-constrained activity (Stern).

Thus, play is a pleasurable, spontaneous, inborn activity taken for its own sake.

Another important feature of play activities is the presence of make-believe in them. A child puts a stick between his legs and runs, imagining the stick to be a motor car. The stick becomes a motor car through make-believe.

31.1 Difference between play and work

Play and work are considered as two distinct activities. The points of difference are given in the Table next page.

Play	Work
1. Play is an innate tendency. Securing pleasure is the only aim pursued for its own sake.	1. Work is imposed upon the individual, who sticks to it by a sense of duty. Work has a definite aim.
2. It is free, spontaneous and voluntary.	2. Often done under outside pressure.
3. Results of playful activity have no permanent importance.	3. Results of work are more or less permanent.
4. Play is connected with the world of fancy and imagination.	4. Work is connected with the world of reality.

However, the distinction between work and play is not strictly maintainable. The highest form of work, when done freely and spontaneously, is in essence a play. All artistic creations take the nature of play.

31.2 Theories of Play

Why does a child play? This has been explained by different psychologists in different ways. They have put forward the following theories.

1. **Surplus Energy Theory :** Schiller and Herbert Spencer put forward this theory. According to this theory, play is an expression of surplus energy. Children play because too much energy accumulates in them.

   But we find children playing even when they seem to be extremely exhausted. Again, this theory cannot explain why there is no uniform pattern of play. Moreover, play activities are conducive to the physical and mental growth of the child. Thus play is not simply letting off superfluous energy uselessly.

2. **Recreative Theory :** According to this theory, play recreates energy. Play is necessary in order to recouperate the energy spent after arduous labour. Lazarous, Lord Kames and G.T.W. Patrick are the supporters of this theory.

   Recreative theory is also one-sided. This theory represents the views of adults, who want to forget the rigours of life through play. But it is not proper to look upon children's play as escapes from the tedium of monotonous routine work.

3. **Anticipatory Theory :** This theory was developed by Carl Groos. According to this theory, play is an anticipation of the future needs of the individual. Thus play has a great biological utility. Stern observes, "Play is indeed to life as maneuver to warfare." A kitten plays how to prepare itself to hunt a mouse in future and a puppy chases another puppy in its play because in later life it will have to chase its prey. Carl Groos is of the opinion that the longer the young ones of any species play, the greater the perfection they attain. As man has to learn much, the period of play is also very long in his case.

   However, this theory has also been criticised because it does not explain how the young child could have an idea about the problems of their future life in present play activities.

4. **Recapitulation Theory :** Stanley Hall advocates this theory. According to Hall, "Children recapitulate the early stages of the growth of human race in play activities : Hide-and-seek, chasing, hunting, fishing, stone-throwing, building of houses all remind us strongly of the youth of the race" (Ross).

5. **Cathartic Theory :** It holds that the child plays because, "It provides an outlet for certain pent-up instincts and emotions which cannot find expressions."

However, no theory of play is perfectly true but each of them contains some truth. Sir T.P. Nunn has produced a synthesis of all these theories. In fact, the different theories have their own significance in different fields.

31.3 Types of Play

The plays of children vary according to age, sex and environment. Play may be broadly classified as follows :

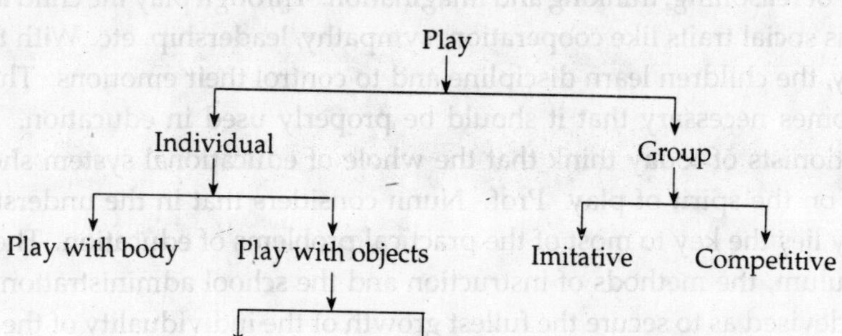

31.4 Individual Plays

The young child of 5 or 6 months plays alone. His muscles and nerves develop as he makes movements with his body. From 8 months to 2 years, he tries to crawl, to stand and to walk.

After the control of the body, the child plays with the objects. Grasping objects, taking them to his mouth and throwing them away are his playful activities. He tries to see a thing and then breaks it to produce sound out of it. The child plays the destructive games to acquire knowledge. In fact, destruction and construction go on simultaneously. Boys build homes, make tunnels in the sand and girls prepare kitchen and dolls.

31.5 Group Plays

After a certain stage of development, children like to play in groups. Group games arise because of the development of social instincts such as gregariousness and imitation. In the beginning, plays are mainly imitative. Instinct of imitation is very prominent in plays from 4–8. Imitative and make-believe plays are popular at this stage. Children imitate adults or children of their own age group. Later on, children become interested in competitive group games such as football, cricket, hockey etc. In these games, a child does not merely imitate others but he thinks out tricks to defeat the rival group. Competitive instinct is very prominent in plays from 8–12.

31.6 Importance of Play in Education

Play is a strong natural tendency found in all children at all levels of age. It helps proper physical, intellectual and emotional growth of the child. It develops his power of reasoning, thinking and imagination. Through play the child acquires various social traits like cooperation, sympathy, leadership, etc. With the help of play, the children learn discipline and to control their emotions. Therefore, it becomes necessary that it should be properly used in education. In fact, educationists of today think that the whole of educational system should be based on the spirit of play. Prof. Nunn considers that in the understanding of play lies the key to most of the practical problems of education. The school curriculum, the methods of instruction and the school administration should be so devised as to secure the fullest growth of the individuality of the child.

Our present school curriculum is wholly book-centric and does not pay much heed to the demands of the child nature. Therefore, such activities like scouting, gardening, excursions, dramatic performances, debating etc. should be encouraged in our schools.

Our methods of instruction should be made flexible and knowledge should be communicated in interesting ways. Various audio-visual teaching aids should be used to make lessons interesting. Group work should be encouraged.

Moreover, the teacher should change his authoritarian attitude towards the students. He should try to develop discipline from within and not the forced discipline from without. The teacher should be a democratic leader of the students.

The school administration has also to undergo a change. The rigid time-table and the rigid class system should be more flexible. So the individual pupil finds his creative impulse and sufficient scope for expression. This was done by Rabindranath at his Shantiniketan.

31.7 Educational systems based on Play way

A number of educational systems have today come into vogue that emphasises the need of play way in education. They are :

1. **Kindergarten System :** Froebel (1782–1852) introduced this system in 1816. With the help of various gifts and occupations, the students are given knowledge of colour, size, shape, line, etc.

2. **Montessori System :** It was introduced (1899) by Maria Montessori (1870–1952). With the help of didactic apparatus, the child receives muscular and sense training. In this method, the child, through his own initiative, learns reading, writing and numbers.

3. **Dalton Plan :** It was introduced by Helen Parkhurst. In this system, there is no rigid time table and classroom. Classroom in this system is called a laboratory. Students move to different rooms according to their need and convenience.

4. **Project Method :** It was first introduced by H.W. Kilpatrick. In this system, various problems of real life are linked with school work. Children solve these problems according to their interests.

5. **Heuristic Method :** Armstrong first introduced this method. In this method, the child is in a way placed in the position of an original discoverer and thus he has the joy of making his own discoveries.

6. **Scouting System :** The Boy Scout Movement was introduced by Lord Baden Powel to make use of the play impulse of the child for his education. The scouts make excursions, organise rallies and do their own work by themselves.

31.8 Advantages of Play way in Education

Play way is of very high significance in education. Mr. Caldwell Cook in his book The Play way has expressed the view that education should be based on this method. In fact, this is one of the best methods which sums up the modern spirit in education.

Through play way teaching becomes very effective and the child enjoys maximum freedom. Through this method, the child's creative impulse develops and his various instincts are sublimated. The child develops power of thinking, imagination and insight.

Play way creates interest in learning activities and the children are encouraged to conduct experiment and explore the truth.

Thus play way is very important from the point of view of teaching-learning process.

Summary

Play is a very strong innate tendency. It is taken for its own sake. Play and work are considered as two distinct activities. But we cannot always distinguish work from play. The highest form of work when done freely and joyfully, in essence becomes a play. All artistic creations take the form of play. There are several theories of play of which Surplus Energy theory, Recapitulation theory, Anticipation theory, Catharsis theory are important. Play of children may be broadly divided into Individual play and Group play. Play is very important from the point of view of general health and from the educational point of view.

Today a number of educational systems have come into vogue that emphasises the need of play way in education. They are : Kindergarten system, Montessori system, Dalton plan, Project method, Heuristic method, Scouting system etc. Play way has many advantages in education. Through these methods learning becomes joyful and effective. Play way generates in the students originality, power of reasoning, imagination and insight. It creates immense interest in the learning activities.

References

1. McDougall, W. : *Social Psychology.* London : Methuen, 1908.

2. Maria Montessori : *The Montessori Method.*

3. Nunn, T.P. : *Education : Its Data and First Principles.*

4. Curtis : *Education Through Play.*

5. Cook, Caldwell : *The Play way.*

6. Kirk Patrick : *Fundamentals of Psychology.*

Questions and Assignments

1. Give the psychological nature of play. "Play is to life what maneuver is to warfare." Explain and discuss.
2. Distinguish play from work.
3. What do you understand by Play way in education? Show how some of the new movements in education embody the spirit of play way.
4. What is the surplus energy theory of play? How far is this correct?
5. Why does a child play? What explanations of this are available in Psychology?
6. What are make-believe plays of children? Discuss their value in developing the imagination of the child.

Chapter 32

Psychology of Adjustment

Introduction : The word adjustment simply means to adapt or modify one's behaviour to meet the demands of changing environment.

Adjustment, according to Gates and Jersild (1948), is a continual process in which a person varies his behaviour to produce a more harmonious relationship between himself and his environment.

32.1 Nature of Adjustment

The process of adjustment is continuous. It is a two-way process. It starts right from the birth of an individual and continues till his death.

Man is a bundle of urges, cravings, desires and needs. When any of these is aroused, tension is created in the organism of the individual. The individual tries to bring about changes in this state to overcome the difficulties in the satisfaction of his needs. Sometimes he may have to modify his needs under the pressure of social environment imposed upon him. Thus the individual tries to maintain a balance between his needs and his capacity of realising these needs. As long as this balance is maintained, the individual remains adjusted. Thus, the mechanism of adjustment involves a successful interaction between two kinds of forces—the environmental and the innate. Maladjustment is caused by two factors, the inherent lack of ability of the individual and, secondly, by the stiff conditions of the environment.

Adjustment, obviously, is a continuous process, because conditions in the environment do not remain static all the time. For example, when a student from a rural setting comes to a city for higher studies, he has to frequently change his behaviour in order to adjust to the new conditions of city life.

Most of us use the adjustment mechanisms in our everyday life in varying degrees. They are protective devices against frustration and reduce our emotional strain.

32.2 Mechanisms of Adjustment

There are two methods of adjustment for maintaining harmony between the individual and his environment : One is direct and the other indirect. Direct methods include : (i) Renewed effort, (ii) Adoption of substitute, (iii) Submission.

The principal methods of indirect adjustments are : (i) Sublimation, (ii) Withdrawal, (iii) Negativism, (iv) Day dreaming, (v) Compensation, (vi) Identification, (vii) Aggression, (viii) Rationalisation, (ix) Regression, (x) Repression, (xi) Projection.

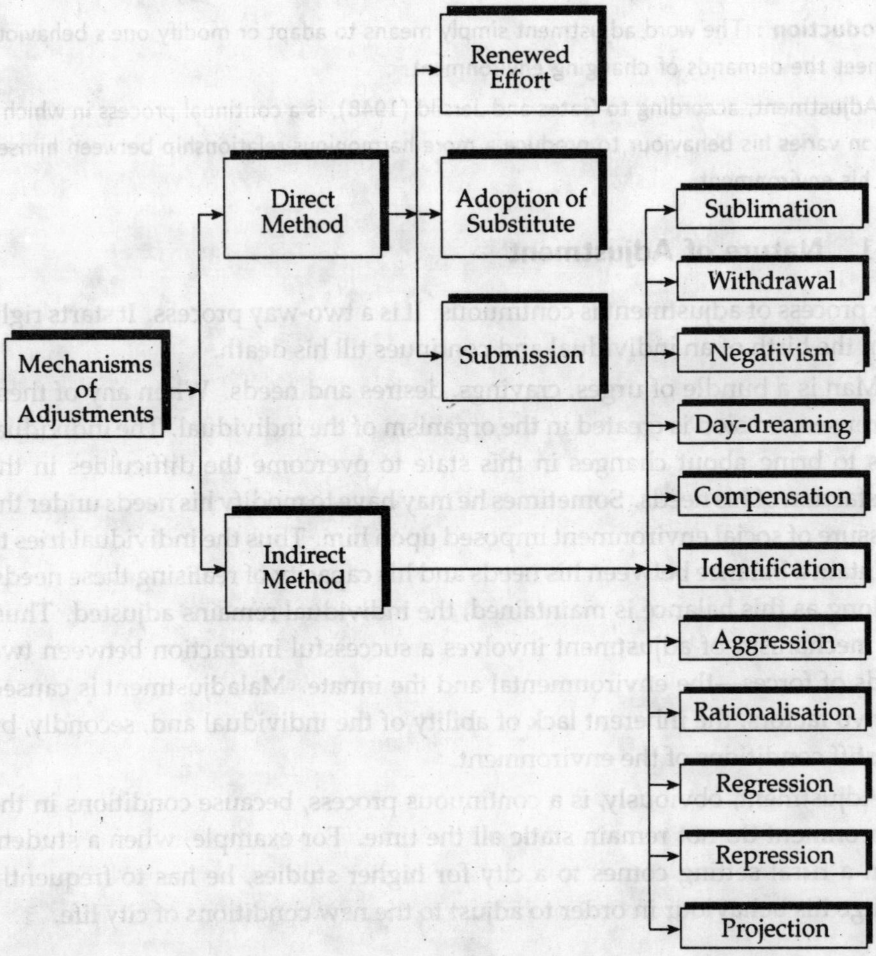

32.3 Direct Methods

Direct methods are always conscious and rational. The direct method includes the following :

1. **Renewed Effort :** A man who considers that failures are the pillars of success is never disheartened in his failure. He acts vigorously against a barrier of personal deficiency. Thus, Demosthenes, who had speech defects, became a great orator by his personal effort and perseverance.
2. **Adoption of Substitute :** A person man consider a substitute goal when attempts to reach the original goal fails. For instance, a man who wants to become an engineer, but, due to adverse circumstances, is obliged to opt for the occupation of a laboratory technician as a substitute.
3. **Submission :** When an individual finds it difficult to cope with his environment, he accepts the defeat and surrenders himself to the mighty forces of environment.

32.4 Indirect methods

Indirect methods are typically unconscious. The principal indirect methods of adjustment include the following :

1. **Sublimation :** According to Freud, sublimation is unconscious deflection of libido (sex instinct) into other more socially acceptable channels. It is the process by which unconscious and unsocial desires are channelled into socially accepted activity. For instance, a person who fails to satisfy his sex need may remove his frustration by transferring his love to dancing and fine arts.
2. **Withdrawal :** In this mechanism of adjustment a person withdraws himself from the circumstances that cause frustration. For instance, a person may shut himself in a room and may decline meeting others when he has been insulted.
3. **Negativism :** It is a tendency to do just the opposite of what is required. It is an aggressive withdrawal. It manifests itself in various forms such as refusal to speak, refusal to eat or refusal to obey command. Negativism is used as a means of gaining attention.
4. **Day-Dreaming :** Day-dreams serve to soothe mind by providing a sort of temporary relief to the unconscious tension of the repressed wish. Day-dreaming provides satisfaction to an individual who has been frustrated in the real world. We try and get for ourselves in day-dreams what we do not have in reality.

5. **Compensation :** When an individual makes an attempt to make up for a deficiency real or imaginary, he is using the mechanism of compensation. For instance, a physically handicapped person may strive hard to excel in studies. The tendency to show off is often over-compensation for feeling of fear.

6. **Identification :** In identification, a person feels himself one with another person or group. When a child tries to identify himself with the hero of a drama, he is said to have identified himself with the hero. It is good if a person identifies himself with a person of high qualities. But if identification is established with a bad person, then it shall have harmful effects.

7. **Aggression :** Aggression is a mechanism of reducing tension. It is caused by frustration or humiliation. Aggression may be of two types : (a) Direct and (b) Indirect. In the direct aggression, the act is directed against the directly responsible person. But in Indirect aggression, the act is directed against some other person. For example, a boy may attack his brother who prevents him from playing with fire. This is direct aggression. But if a wife, annoyed with her husband, starts striking her baby, then it shall be called indirect aggression.

8. **Rationalisation :** The process of self-justification is termed rationalisation. Through rationalisation, a person tries to justify his undesirable activity. The fox of the fables who could not get at the grapes said the grapes are sour. When we fail to do a job successfully, we often say, "It is of no use to work so hard on this worthless job." The opposite form of sour grapes mechanism is the sweet lemon form of rationalisation. In this mechanism, a person tries to convince himself that he has got exactly what he wanted.

9. **Regression :** Regression is the mechanism whereby an individual returns to infantile behaviour after reaching the maturity level. For instance, schizophrenic patients are often found to regress from the adult world to infancy. They are unable to dress and feed themselves.

10. **Repression :** Repression is the unconscious process which retards the painful feelings, undesirable wishes, and ideas from the conscious field. In fact, repression does not solve the real problem. It often leads to mental disorder. Repression results in complexes, which play a great role in the determination of behaviour and development of personality.

11. **Projection :** By projection an individual tries to hold others for his undesirable behaviour. A person who may not be able to play violin well, may blame the musical instrument. An aged lady complained about a young man that he wanted to elope with her and marry her secretly. On

investigation, it was revealed that the young man was quite innocent and the lady projected her own desire on the young person.

32.5 Theories of Adjustment

There are some people who can well-adjust to their environment, while some others cannot. We shall discuss below some of the theories as to the nature and causes of failure of adjustment :

1. **Theories of Charcot and Janet :** According to Charcot and Janet, mental disorder takes place because of dissociation of personality. Janet thought that neuroses develop from constitutional weaknesses and lack of energy. Fears and obsessions are the product of the weakness of the mind.

2. **Freud's theory :** According to Freud, the human mind consists of three layers—the conscious, the sub-conscious (pre-conscious) and unconscious. The unconscious mind is the greatest segment of the mind and it controls the largest fraction of human behaviour. This unconscious mind is the reservoir of primitive impulses and forbidden desires. These desires always strive to come to the level of consciousness. But the conscious mind represses them producing mental disorders. Freud postulated the imaginary concepts of Id, Ego and Superego and concluded : Goaded by the Id, hemmed in by Superego and rebuffed by reality the Ego struggles to cope with the task of reducing the forces which work upon it to some kind of harmony. When the ego is forced to acknowledge its weakness, it breaks out into anxiety. A person's behaviour remains normal so long his ego is able to maintain the balance between the evil designs of his Id and the moral dictates of Superego.

3. **Adler's Theory :** Adler, a disciple of Freud, holds that the basic urge is a striving for superiority and not sex, as Freud postulated. When this urge is thwarted the individual feels inferior and an inferiority complex results. Then he tries to compensate by asserting himself in other ways.

   Stimulated by the urge to seek power and superiority an individual adopts a distinct style of life suited to his environmental situations. In case of failure. to attain superiority, the person drifts towards acute mental disorder.

   Thus, according to Adler, first style of life of the individual is to be discovered. Then his feeling of inferiority should be removed. He should be convinced of his error and made to change his style of life and gain contact with society.

4. **Jung's Theory :** Jung, another disciple of Freud, maintains that it is not only sex that dominates life, but there are other desires too which motivate

our behaviour. According to Jung, libido includes sex impulse (Freud), will to power (Adler) and will-to-live (Schopenhauer). It is the total vital energy which seeks the goal of growth, power and reproduction.

Jung holds that Libido—the life energy—may flow inward or outward, turning a person into an introvert or extrovert. The introvert is interested in his own thoughts and feelings. He does not participate in social functions. He cannot make quick decisions. He prefers thought and planning to action. The introvert is dominated by thought and given to reflection and meditation.

The extrovert, on the other hand, is sociable, participates in social functions and can readily adjust himself to new situations. A normal and well-adjusted person always maintains a balance between introversion and extroversion. Jung recognises ambiverts, whose life energy is partly directed inward and partly directed outward. They are interested in their own thoughts and emotions and also in other persons and their actions.

5. **Karen Horney's Theory :** Karen Horney (1937) holds that conflicts and neuroses are produced by the contradiction in our culture. For instance, we teach love and cooperation but at the same time we stress the importance of competition for success in our life. There are frequent clashes between the employers and the employees, between different linguistic, religious, and cultural groups in our society. Out of such conflicts hostilities, fears, frustrations and other neurotic symptoms develop.

32.6 Characteristics of well-adjusted person

No universal criteria can be set to describe a well-adjusted person, as values and culture differ from place to place. However, some common characteristics may be described :

1. A well-adjusted person is socially accepted by others. He obeys social norms and values. He is well-adjusted to his social setting.
2. He faces the reality and solve his problems in a realistic manner. Always he thinks and acts pragmatically. He never resorts to faulty adjustments.
3. A well-adjusted person is aware of his own strengths and limitations. He knows himself, his abilities and defects. He sets up an ideal which is realisable by him.
4. He is well-integrated and flexible in his behaviour. He can adapt himself easily to changed circumstances.

5. Last but not least, a well-adjusted person should have normal physical health. He should be free from severe physical ailments and psychological disorders such as, anxiety or depression.

32.7 Detection of Maladjustment

Maladjustment is a complicated phenomenon, which needs adequate professional competency for its detection. However, at the preliminary stage, teachers may assist in detecting maladjustment of the students in the following ways :

1. **Observation Method :** In this method, the teacher has to observe keenly the behaviour of the students in the classroom as well as outside the classroom.
2. **The Interview Method :** The teacher can hold interview with parents and associates of the students to determine the nature of maladjustment. Interview method should follow a definite scheme and the aim should be to elicit relevant information.
3. **Case History Method :** The teacher has to investigate into the past as well as the present activities of the student. He has to find out his likes and dislikes, sentiments, motives, emotional status to judge the nature and extent of maladjustment.
4. **Questionnaire and Inventory Method :** These devices are used to elicit interests, attitudes and opinions from the candidate themselves. In this a number of printed questions are distributed to the candidates and are answered by them. Some of the inventories are : Bell's Adjustment inventory, Heston's personal adjustment inventory, Taylor's anxiety scale, the Mooney check list and Roger's test of Personality Adjustment.
5. **Sociometric Technique :** This is used in the measurement of social relationships. From the sociogram we can have some clues to the level of social adjustment of the candidate.
6. **Projective Techniques :** Projective technique is based upon Depth Psychology, the Psychology of the unconscious. Through this technique is let out certain unconscious dispositions that determine behaviour. Projective methods are of great value in revealing the hidden causes of tension.

   Following are some of the devices used in projective technique :

   (a) **Word Association Test :** It was devised by Jung and Kent and Rosanoff used it to detect mental disorder. The test consists of a list of unrelated words and the subject is asked to respond to these words. The Reaction Time and the nature of response tells us what lies at the back of the conscious behaviour of the subject.

(b) **Rorschach Ink-Blot Test :** This test consists of a standard series of ten Ink-blot pictures. The ink-blots themselves are meaningless. The subject is asked to look at each block and to tell what it looks like, or what it suggests to him. The subject projects into his interpretation of them, the underlying structure of his personality.

(c) **Thematic Apperception Test :** This test was devised by Murray and Morgan. It consists of 19 pictures which refer to various areas, such as fear, aggression, sexuality and parent-child relationships. The subject is asked to tell a story about each of the pictures. In the stories which he tells about the pictures, he is likely to reveal a great deal about his personality.

In the detection and measurement of adjustment, the Inventory techniques and Sociometric techniques have become very popular. The Projective techniques, however, have many limitations. They are more subjective in nature and there is a great want of standardised tests.

32.8 Sources of Maladjustment

The sources of maladjustment of an individual are his needs and urges. Air, food, water, proper rest are his organic needs. His personal needs are affection, sympathy, independence, aspiration, achievement, social approval, etc. Besides there are needs for security and sexual urge. When these needs are not fulfilled maladjustment may develop.

In fact, there are various factors in home, society and educational system, which lead to maladjustment of an individual. Poverty, broken home, parental over-protection or rejection of the child may lead to maladjustment.

Children are generally taught moral standards and religious doctrine in early life. These are often incompatible with their natural desires and may lead to emotional tensions causing maladjustment.

Lack of recreational facilities in school, defective curriculum, autocratic attitude and partiality of teachers and present system of examination create stress and strain in the mind of the pupils resulting in maladjustment.

32.9 Treatment and Follow-up

Prior to the treatment of the maladjusted individual, all available informations about him should be collected through physical examination, psychological tests and psychiatrical interview of the patient.

A conference of the different members of the clinical staff is then held and opinions about different aspects of the patient's personality are pooled together. Then, in the end, suggestions for treatment are given.

The treatment may include change of physical environment, change of activity, encouragement of hobbies, change in the attitude of parents and teachers and change in the attitude of the patient about his own self, own behaviour and problems.

The methods of persuasion and reasoning, hypnosis and suggestion, auto-suggestion, psychoanalysis, re-education or habit training, etc. have great therapeutic value in the treatment of maladjusted individual.

Summary

Adjustment is a continuos process by which a person maintains a balance between himself and his environment. The individual tries to maintain a balance between his needs and his capacity of realising these needs. As long as this balance is maintained the individual remains adjusted. Maladjustment is caused by two factors, the lack of the individual's ability and by the stiff conditions of the environment.

There are direct and indirect methods of adjustment. The direct method includes conscious efforts of the individual to increase the number of trials, improve efforts or adopt substitute goal. Indirect methods such as Compensation, Identification, Rationalisation, Repression, Projection etc. are used at the unconscious level and provide relief from the psychological tension.

Various theories have been advocated by psychologists to explain the phenomenon of adjustment. Of these, the psycho-analytic theory of Freud, Adler and Jung are very important.

There are various factors in family, society and educational system which lead to maladjustment of an individual. Before the treatment of maladjusted individual, all available informations about him should be collected and suggestions for treatment are prescribed by the professional experts. The techniques of psycho-analysis, auto-suggestion and habit-training have great therapeutic value in the treatment of maladjusted persons.

References

1. Adams, H.E. : *Psychology of Adjustment*, New York : Ronald, 1972.
2. Crow, L.D. and Crow A. : *Educational Psychology*, Eurasia Publishing House (P) Ltd. New Delhi, 1991.
3. Carroll, H.A. : *Mental Hygiene*, Prentice Hall. Inc., 1957.

4. Lazarus, Richars, S. : *Adjustment and Personality,* McGraw-Hill. New York, 1961.
5. Lind Green, H.C. : *Psychology of Personal and Social Adjustment,* Americal Book Co. New York, 1953.
6. McKinney, F. : *Psychology of Personal Adjustment,* New York. Wiley, 1941.
7. Horney, K. : *The Neurotic Personality of Our Time,* New York : Norton, 1937.
8. Shaffer, L.F. : *The Psychology of Adjustment,* Boston. Houghton Miffin, 1936.
9. Kundu, C.L. and Tutoo, D.N. : *Educational Psychology,* Sterling Publishers Pvt. Ltd., 1989.
10. Rai, B.C. : *Educational Psychology,* Prakashan Kendra, Lucknow.

Questions and Assignments

1. What is meant by adjustment? Describe the characteristics of a well-adjusted person.
2. What are the mechanisms of adjustment? Explain projection with examples.
3. Discuss the theories of adjustment.
4. What are the causes of maladjustment according to Freud, Adler and Jung?
5. How can maladjustment be detected? Describe the Questionnaire and Inventory method.
6. What are the symptoms of maladjusted children? How can they be detected?
7. What are the sources of maladjustment? How can they be treated?
8. Write notes on:
   (a) Repression.
   (b) Regression.
   (c) Sublimation.
   (d) Projective technique.
   (e) Rorschach Ink-Blot test.
   (f) Thematic Apperception test.

Chapter 33

Mental Health

Introduction : Keeping up mental health is one of the major problems of the world today. Because of rapid industrialisation and sophistication of the modern social system, an individual often fails to maintain a balance between himself and his social environment.

33.1 What is Mental Health?

A person is said to have a good mental health when he succeeds to maintain harmonious relationship between himself and his environment. According to Hadfield, "Mental health is the full and harmonious functioning of the whole personality."

Every person has certain needs, for instance, need for affection and love, need for safety and security and so on. An individual tries to establish a balance between his needs and his capacity for realising these needs. As long as this balance is satisfactorily maintained, the person remains adjusted and his mental health is retained. But when this balance is lost, he drifts towards maladjustment.

The moment satisfaction of all our needs is made the primary object of life, tension develops. The mind is stimulated by desire for more and more and consequent disturbing mental conflicts become evident.

There is a continuous struggle between the needs of the individual and his social environment. An individual becomes joyful when his needs are satisfied. He becomes sad and dejected when his needs remain unfulfilled. Thus, it is difficult to find a person having all along a good consistent mental health. However, a person with good mental health usually has certain personal characteristics.

33.2 Characteristics of Mental Health

A person having good mental health is supposed to possess the following characteristics :

1. **Capacity for Adjustment :** An individual with good mental health can maintain a balance between his needs and his capacity of realising these needs. Even in adverse circumstances, he remains undaunted. He has the courage to fight all odds.
2. **Firm Self-confidence :** A person having good mental health never loses his confidence. Even in unfavourable circumstances, he remains calm and quiet. He feels confident or himself in his everyday life and tries to solve his problems largely by his own effort.
3. **Good Physical Health :** Physical health and mental health are closely interdependent. To have a good mental health, naturally one must have a good physical health.
4. **Absence of a Critical Attitude :** A mentally adjusted individual respects himself and others. His observation is scientific rather than critical. He appreciates the goodness in others and avoids finding faults with others.
5. **Proper Intellectual Growth :** Proper intellectual growth is needed for good mental health. For harmonious relationship between himself and his environment, an individual must have capacity for thinking and reasoning. He thinks clearly and makes his own decision in solving his problems. Rational mind is an indicator of sound mental health.
6. **Proper Emotional Growth :** An individual having good mental health can easily control his emotion. Despite provocation he never becomes angry or loses mental balance. He shows proper emotional maturity in his behaviour.
7. **Growth of Proper Interest and Attitude :** A neurotic person often shows no interest in social environment and becomes introvert. But a man of good mental health shows favourable attitude and interest towards a socially useful activity. He has a variety of interests and lives a well-balanced life of work and rest.
8. **Awareness of Needs :** An individual, who possesses good mental health, is conscious of the limits of his needs. He knows all needs cannot be fulfilled. So, he reduces his needs accordingly and becomes happy and remains adjusted.

In brief, a person, who is free from nervous tension and mental conflicts and who has a balanced personality, may be said to have good mental health.

33.3 The Role of Home and School

The home and school carry great responsibilities with respect to the harmonious development of personality of a child. Therefore, the environment of home and school should be conducive to his mental health. The child should receive adequate attention, love and affection from parents. He should feel secure in the family and his legitimate needs should be satisfied.

1. **Home Environment** : For proper development of mental health of children, following measures should be taken at home by parents :

   (a) Provide conducive environment at home and avoid frequent conjugal quarrel. Drinking and use of other intoxicating substances by parents often pollute home environment.

   (b) Do not over-protect or reject the child. Deprivation of parental love either makes a child delinquent or neurotic. On the other hand, over-indulgence by parents obstructs proper mental growth of the child. Over anxiety about the future of the child is also not conducive to his mental health.

   (c) Try to meet the normal needs of the child. His basic organic needs, emotional and social needs are to be satisfied. A child has need of love and security from the parent. These needs should be met by them.

   (d) Provide guidance and advice to the child whenever necessary. A confidential relationship with the parents helps a child in resolving conflicts and making proper adjustments.

2. **School Environment** : The school plays the most crucial role in the development of good mental health of the learner. The various steps which can be taken in schools for the growth of proper mental health in children are :

   (a) School environment should be democratic and conducive to proper mental growth of the learners. It should provide opportunities for satisfaction of their needs of freedom. The atmosphere of school should be like that of a well-administered family.

   (b) The school should organise supervised games, athletic contests, debates, scouting, etc. along with curricular activities. These will provide outlets for children's social needs and also help in the development of sound attitudes.

(c) Emotional needs of children have to be met in school. The need for *achievement* is strong in every school child. But all children have not the same capacity and they are not of same standards. Instead of being primarily concerned with maintaining high standards, the teacher should help each student to progress according to his own space and to maintain his self-respect.

(d) Examinations should not be used as weapons of elimination. Instead the teachers should make it clear to the students that examinations are simple tools to discover how much progress has been made by students in the acquisition of knowledge.

(e) The school should provide a moral setting which will increase the possibilities for normal growth. It will be of great use if moral education is made an integral part of school curriculum.

(f) The school should organise child guidance clinic for prevention of mental disorders. The program of a child guidance clinic encompasses both prevention and treatment.

The most important purpose of child guidance clinics is to give direct aid to children in difficulty so that they can make better adjustments to homes and schools. The programs of the clinics also include educating parents and teachers in the principles and techniques of mental hygiene.

In fact, a joint effort on the part of the teachers in school and parents at home can only promote mental health of the children. The school environment may be conducive for learners but if the parents are indifferent then proper mental health of the learner will not develop. So there should be a joint effort by both teachers and parents.

33.4 Characteristics of a Mentally Healthy Teacher

Not only the mental health of the students but also that of the teachers play an important role in the teaching-learning process. If the teacher posseses sound mental health he can give proper guidance to the learners.

Some of the personal characteristics of a mentally healthy teacher are :

1. A mentally healthy teacher loves his teaching profession. He has sympathy and sincerity in dealing with his pupils.
2. He has wide interests in games, sports, debates, dramatics and other cultural activities.
3. He is democratic in his relations with learners and co-workers.
4. He has a good sense of humour to enjoy a joke but he refrains from sarcasm and ridiculing his pupils for their failures. He should regard their failure as a challenge and not as a defeat or humiliation.

5. He has ability to work with other staff members of the school. He is always ready to share experiences with them.

33.5 Regaining Mental Health

Mental disorders constitute one of the most challenging health problems in modern times. Parents and teachers are anxious to know different curative measures for treating their maladjusted children. In this country, people often use amulets and stones to cure mental illness. But instead of seeking treatment from an unqualified quack, they should go to a professionally trained psychotherapist, who is usually found in psychiatry and clinical psychology.

33.6 Psychotherapy

Psychotherapy is a medical term. It is the process of treatment of emotional or personality maladjustment by psychological means. Broadly, it includes all psychological methods of treating behaviour disorders in an interview situation. It involves a close relationship between two persons—the patient to be treated and the therapist.

The important functions of psychotherapy are : (a) to release pent-up feelings and emotions such as guilt and anxiety and (b) to increase the insight of the patient into his psychological disturbances. The therapist should have willingness and ability to listen. He should be deeply interested in the problems of his patient and should be sincerely desirous of helping him to solve his problems.

33.7 Types of Psychotherapy

There are various types of psychotherapy and a few of them may be discussed below :

1. **Counselling :** The principal function of a counsellor is to give counsel to students on educational, vocational and mental health problems. He will not always pass out information and give advice only. He must have sufficient knowledge to identify emotional problems if they exist and refer them to qualified psychiatrists and psychologists whenever necessary.

2. **Psychoanalysis :** The founder of psychoanalytic movement was Sigmund Freud. He developed certain methods of treatment of neurotic disorders. He suggested methods like free association, dream analysis and analysis of the daily psychopathology for the exploration of unconscious. The main purpose of psychoanalytic therapy is to release the blocked emotional feelings and strengthen the ego of the subject to face real life situation.

3. **Psychodrama :** Psychodrama is a special technique that permits a patient to act out roles, situations and fantasies in his life. Psychodrama permits a person to express himself in realistic situations by acts. It also treats the individual in social situations, which, in the past, have been the source of some of his disorders.

4. **Occupational Therapy :** In this technique, the therapist selects certain occupations on the basis of the age, sex and education of the patients. The main purpose of this technique is to detect the repressed motives of the patients. The occupational therapist is medically oriented and his skills are based on knowledge of physiology and physiotherapy.

5. **Play Therapy :** Play therapy is the most effective method of correcting the emotionally disturbed children. The child who does not tell about his own fears and conflicts, projects these feelings into his play materials. A number of play materials—such as dolls, puppets, drawing materials, running water, clay, etc.—are provided in a play room, where the child is free to handle the play materials. Play serves as an outlet for discharging pent-up emotion of the child. His behaviour in the play room is minutely observed by the therapist remaining behind a screen. Child's irrational fears and tensions are removed through free discussions and suggestions.

6. **Medical Therapy :** The most important of medical therapies are shock and surgery. Medical therapies are in the experimental stage and should be used as a last resort.

7. **Shock Therapy :** The most frequently used of the shock therapies on mental patients are insulin and electric. Insulin shock is produced by intramuscular injections of insulin. The injections are usually continued for a period of about two weeks. Following the injection of insulin, the patient becomes weak and drowsy. After three hours, he goes into a deep coma and then he is awakened by the administration of glucose. Sakel developed this technique in 1928 to treat mental patients.

   Electro-shock treatment is relatively new and the procedure consists of attaching electrodes to the head and passing through the brain of the patient, a prescribed quantity of electricity to produce convulsions. The greatest utility of electric shock therapy seems to be with depression and anxiety.

   Shock therapy (Electro-convulsive therapy) acts as sedatives reducing the overactivity of the nervous system and reducing the emotional disorder.

8. **Psycho-surgery :** Prefrontal lobotomy is one of the important forms of psycho-surgery. In a prefrontal lobotomy, small holes are made in the skull. Then some of the connections between the frontal lobes and the

thalamus and hypothalamus are destroyed. This technique is used to decrease the ability to sustain the persistent tone of psychotic states.

Psycho-surgery is generally used only in case of severe personality disorders.

Summary

An individual drifts towards tension and maladjustment when his needs remain unfulfilled. The methods of treatment of mental disorders may be classified into two groups : (a) Psychotherapy and (b) Medical therapy. There are many types of psychotherapy, such as psychoanalytic therapy, play therapy, occupational therapy etc.

The important purpose of psychotherapy is to release pent up emotions and to increase the insight of the patient into his mental disorders. The principal medical therapies are shock and surgery. These techniques are still in the experimental stage.

Mental health once lost is difficult to regain. So, effort should be made to prevent mental disorders through the maintenance of healthy conditions in the family and in the school. Parents and general public have to be educated about the nature and magnitude of mental health problems.

References

1. Achar, S.T. and Viswanathan, J. : *Text Book of Pediatrics,* Orient Longman, Calcutta, 1982.
2. Carroll, H.A. : *Mental Hygene—The Dynamics of Adjustment,* Prentice Hall Inc. Engle Wood Cliff. New York, 1956.
3. Chauhan, S.S. : *Advanced Educational Psychology,* Vikas Publishing House Pvt. Ltd. New Delhi, 1997.
4. Crow, L.D. : *Educational Psychology,* Eurasia Publishing House (P) Ltd. New Delhi, 1991.
5. Morgan, C.T. : *Introduction to Psychology,* McGraw-Hill Book Co. Inc, 1956.
6. Kuppuswamy, B. : *Advanced Educational Psychology,* Sterling Publishers Pvt. Ltd. New Delhi, 1990.
7. Kundu, C.L., Tutoo, D.N. : *Educational Psychology,* Sterling Publishers Pvt. Ltd., 1989.

Questions and Assignments

1. Define mental health and describe in brief the characteristics of sound mental health.
2. How can home help in preventing mental illness of children?
3. Describe the role of school in preventing mental disorders of children.
4. What is psychotherapy? How it can help in regaining mental health?
5. Write notes on :

   (a) Child Guidance Clinic.

   (b) Psychoanalysis.

   (c) Play therapy.

   (d) Shock therapy.

   (e) Prefrontal labotomy.

Chapter 34

Learning Process

Introduction : All living organism start learning just after their birth and this process of learning continues till their death. As soon as they come in contact with the environment they start reacting. In this process of interaction with the environment, the original behaviour of the organism undergoes change. This process of change which enables the individual to adjust itself to the environment is known as learning. Thus learning is not a passive process of absorption, but a very active process of reacting.

All living creatures learn. But while man takes lesser time to pick up new adaptations, animals take much longer time. Thus animals which could not adapt themselves to a new situation perished in the past.

34.1 Meaning and Definition of Learning

Learning is a complex process. It is difficult to give a universally acceptable definition of learning. However, psychologists have tried to define it from different point of view :

1. **H.P. Smith (1962) :** Learning is the acquisition of new behaviour or the strengthening or weakening of old behaviour as the result of experience.
2. **Kingsley and Garry (1957) :** Learning is the process by which behaviour is originated or changes through practice or training.
3. **Gardner Murphy (1968) :** The term learning covers every modification in behaviour to meet environmental requirements.
4. **Crow and Crow (1973) :** Learning is the acquisition of habits, knowledge and attitudes ... It represents progressive changes in behaviour ... It enables the individual to satisfy interests to attain goals.

5. **Woodworth (1945) :** Any activity can be called learning so far as it develops the individual (in any respect—good or bad) and makes him alter behaviour and experiences different from what they would otherwise have been.
6. **N.L. Munn (1967) :** Learning can be defined as the process of being modified, more or less permanently, by what happens in the world around us, by what we do, or by what we observe.
7. **Kimble (1961) :** Learning is relatively permanent change in behavioural potentiality that occurs as a result of reinforced practice.

The above definitions, on analysis, reveal the following facts about the process of learning :

1. Learning is a process and not a final product.
2. Learning is not a passive process. It is an active process of interaction.
3. Learning is a process of change which enables an organism to adapt itself to the environment.
4. Learning is purposeful and goal-oriented.
5. Learning develops the individual and modifies his latter behaviour and experience.
6. The scope of learning is too extensive. It covers all cognitive, affective and connative aspects of human behaviour.

34.2 Types of Learning

It is every difficult to classify learning into clear-cut types. According to J.P. Guilford, there are three kinds of learning : (1) Sensory, (2) Motor and (3) Sensorimotor. The three kinds are, however, never found in pure form. In terms of methods or techniques learning may be classified into four major groups :

1. Trial and error learning. 2. Classical conditioning.
3. Operant conditioning. 4. Insightful learning.

However, Gagne (1970) has divided learning into eight types as follows :

1. Signal learning (Classical conditioning).
2. S.R. learning (Operant conditioning).
3. Chain learning.
4. Verbal associate learning.
5. Multiple discrimination.
6. Learning of concepts.
7. Learning of principles.
8. Problem solving.

1. **Signal Learning :** Signal learning or classical conditioning was developed by Pavlov. He presented food to a hungry dog and rang a bell fifty times, and thus connected the salivary response (CR) to a bell (CS). The modification of behaviour, causing salivation to the sound of the bell, is called conditioning.

2. **S–R Learning (Operant Conditioning) :** Through his puzzle box experiment on hungry cats, Thorndike formulated his famous laws of learning. He held that learning is governed by the Law of Exercise and the Law of Effect. The rewards of a response leads to repetition of an act and the strengthening of S–R connection.

   B.F. Skinner conducted a series of experiments on animals to find out the effects of the rewards by repeating a motor response and concluded that behaviour is shaped and maintained by its consequences. It is operated by the organism and maintained by its results. This process of learning is known as operant conditioning.

3. **Chain Learning :** Often school children are asked to learn lists of material, for instance, multiplication tables, alphabets, the names of rivers in the country and so on. These learning material has some sequential or serial order.

4. **Verbal Associate Learning :** In some cases, learning takes place by reason of associations of the learning materials. For example, a child is shown a ball. When he sees the object next time, he will be able to say that it is a ball.

   The name of town like Raghunathpur is remembered due to its association with the name of Lord Rama (Raghunath).

   To have practice in paired-associate learning the subject may be presented with a series of paired words as follows :

   Door—Window, Bird—Crow, Milk—White, Tiger—Lion.

5. **Multiple Discrimination :** From the early stage, a child is able to discriminate between various stimuli in his surrounding. He learns the difference between a feeding bottle and a toy.

   Generally, discrimination depends on comparison between two stimuli and it involves higher mental processes.

   Lashley, in the tests of discrimination learning, conducted an experiment on rats with geometrical figures. The steps were as follows :

   Step 1 : Rats learned to choose the large circle as against a small circle on the two doors of the jumping apparatus.

   Step 2 : After the choice for the large circle was established, it was replaced by a large-triangle. The rats chose the triangle consistently for 200 trials.

Step 3 : Triangle and circle of equal size were then shown. The rats showed no preference.

Step 4 : Then a large circle and a small circle were shown. The circles, which were of bigger size, were consistently chosen.

[Data from Lashley, 1942, P. 258—Woodworth & Schlosberg].

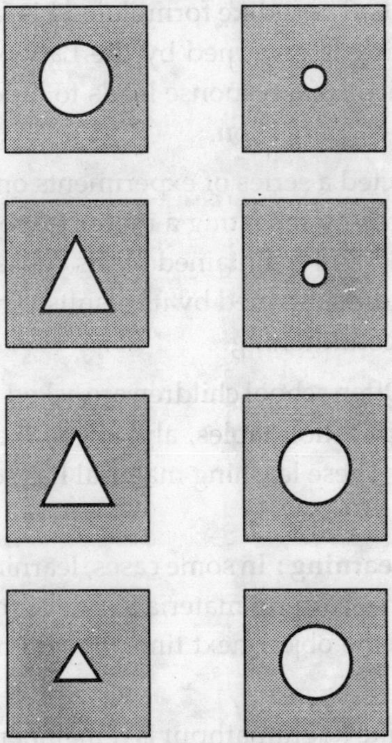

Fig. 34.1

6. **Learning of Concepts :** General ideas are called concepts. Concept represent the common qualities of many different objects. "It is the sum total of what you know about the object" (Woodworth).

   Concepts are formed through following steps :

   (a) Observation of several individuals.

   (b) Analysis of each of them into its components.

   (c) Comparison with one another to find differences and similarities.

   (d) Mental unification of the common attributes into a concept.

   (e) Assignment of a name of the concept.

   If we want to form concept about the bird we analyse the shape, size, colour and other virtues of different kinds of birds to find some common characteristics. Then we learn to discriminate them from other animals like dog, cat, horse etc. Through the process of discrimination and generalisation, concept about an object is formed.

7. **Learning of Principles :** Pupils in classroom have to learn principles of Science, Mathematics and Science to function more effectively. Principles are made by combining two or more concepts with one another.

8. **Problem Solving :** Problem solving learning indicates a higher type of learning. This learning involves abilities like insight, reasoning, thinking, power of imagination etc.

34.3 Theories of Learning

Theories of learning may be classified under two major heads :

1. **Connectionist theories :**

(i)	Thorndike's Theory;	(ii)	Watson's Theory;
(iii)	Skinner's Theory;	(iv)	Hull's Theory;
(v)	Pavlov's Theory;	(vi)	Guthrie's Theory.

2. **Cognitive field theory :**

(i) Gestalt Theory, (ii) Lewin's Field Theory, (iii) Tolman's Theory.

Edward L. Thorndike (1874–1949) was the first American psychologist to conduct experiments on learning with animals using puzzle box. Learning, according to Thorndike, is due to the formation of bond between Stimulus and Response (S → R). No doubt, this was Thorndike's great innovation.

Thorndike conducted experiments on animals like cats, dogs and monkeys with the help of puzzle box to observe their method of learning.

34.4 Puzzle Box Experiment

Thorndike confined a hungry cat in a puzzle box closed by a door which could be opened by turning a latch or a button and food was placed outside. When first put in the box, she made a large number of random movements. She tried to crawl through the bars. She clawed, bit, and scratched at the walls to go out of the box. The cat, at last by pure chance, succeeded in pulling the latch, opened the door and escaped. But one successful movement did not teach her the method of opening the door. When put in the box again, the cat did a series of random movements and again hit upon the correct response by chance. Each trial, on the average, required less time than the preceding one. After a number of repetitions, the cat would perform the successful movement at once every time she was put into the cage.

Thorndike's cat showed gradual improvement in performance. Thorndike ruled out learning by reasoning or imitation and concluded that animals learn by trial and error method. Thorndike showed that with human subjects also learning is an automatic process of connection between a stimulus and a response involving minimal awareness.

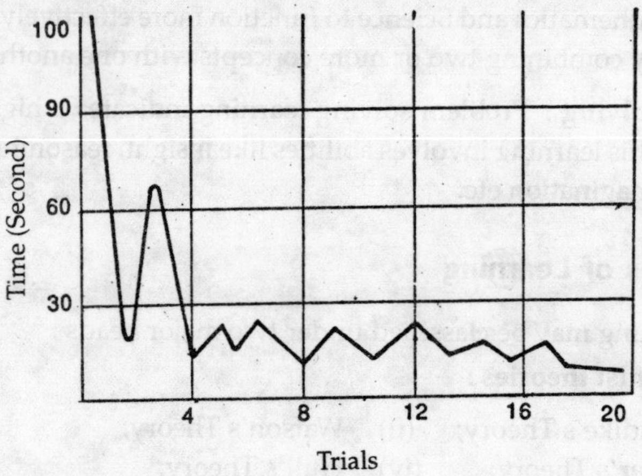

Fig. 34.2

The learning curve indicates that performance of the animal gradually improves with the number of trials.

34.5 Characteristics of T–E Learning

1. This process of learning is slow and gradual. Reasoning or imitation has no place in T–E (Trial–Error) learning.
2. There remains a goal before the animal. It attempts to reach the goal. The animal is unable to see any clear way to reach the goal.
3. The animal explores the situation blindly.
4. Learning takes place due to the formation of bond between Stimulus and Response ($S \rightarrow R$). This bond occurs through organism's nervous system. This is indicated by the formula $S \rightarrow O \rightarrow R$.

34.6 Thorndike's Laws of Learning

Thorndike formulated three major laws of learning :

1. **The Law of Effect** : This law runs as follows : "When a modifiable connection is made between a situation and response and is accompanied or followed by a satisfying state of affairs, that connection's strength is increased, and when such a connection is made and accompanied or followed by an annoying state of affairs, its strength is decreased." In other words, satisfaction tends to strengthen S–R connection and dissatisfaction

or annoyance tends to weaken it. However, later on Thorndike modified the law of effect as that satisfaction strengthens the bond but annoyance does not weaken it.

Application in Classroom Teaching : According to the law of effect, it is satisfaction that guides the behaviour of a child. Thus, for honesty, punctuality and industry, the child, if praised by the teacher, will have satisfaction and these patterns of behaviour become fixed. The teacher should not, therefore, associate anything good with something annoying to the child. He should not give home work to the students as a punishment. The teacher should use such methods of teaching that will help joyful learning. To make teaching attractive the teacher should use appropriate Audio-Visual aids. He should praise and encourage students for their good and useful performances.

2. **The Law of Exercise :** This law has two parts : (a) Law of Use, and (b) Law of Disuse.

   (a) The Law of Use states, when a modifiable connection is made between a situation and response, that connection's strength is, other things being equal, increased.

   (b) The Law of Disuse states, when a modifiable connection is not made between a situation and response, over a length of time, that connection's strength is decreased.

The Law of Exercise emphasises the need of repetition. It is said, practice makes a man perfect. Law of use refers to the strengthening of S–R connection while the Law of Disuse to the weakening of the connection when the practice is discontinued for a length of time.

Application in class room teaching : Exercise or drill strengthens connection between S–R. Learning of multiplication tables, rules of grammar or mathematical formula require intense repetition for lasting impression. Students should be given opportunities to repeat the knowledge they get in the class.

In teaching a lesson in the class repetition is needed. But repetition loses its importance as a method of learning if it becomes unpleasant. The material without meaning like nonsense syllables, is quickly forgotten.

3. **The Law of Readiness :** This law states, When any conduction unit is not in readiness to conduct, for it to conduct is annoying. When any conduction unit is in readiness to conduct, for it not to do so is annoying.

This law indicates that satisfaction follows the doing of the work for which there is preparedness in our mind. But doing a work for which there is no preparedness in our mind or not doing that for which there is preparedness is annoying.

Application in Classroom Teaching : The proverb goes, you can lead a horse to the water but you cannot make it drink. That means readiness is essential for all kinds of learning. When the child is ready to learn, he learns more quickly than when he is not ready to learn. The teacher should recognise the right moment of teaching and child's state of mind.

The child who is not allowed to answer questions which he can answer correctly feels annoyed. He feels satisfaction when he is allowed to answer.

In class teaching, the teacher should ask the students some questions on the lesson, he is going to teach in order to prepare their mind for learning new material. This is the first step for planning a lesson.

Besides the three major Laws of Effect, Exercise and Readiness, Thorndike formulated following important laws :

1. **Law of Mental Set :** Positive mental set in students is a primary condition for learning. They can perform a task properly if they have a positive attitude towards the task.
2. **Law of Frequency :** This law is a necessary correlate of the law of use. Other things being equal, the more frequently a S–R connection is exercised, the stronger the connection becomes.
3. **Law of Multiple Response :** The law states that when an organism is confronted with a novel situation it responds in a number of ways before it arrives at the correct one.
4. **Law of Recency :** The law implies that other things being equal, the more recent the exercise, the stronger is the connection between the situation and the response.
5. **Law of Analogy :** The law implies that an individual responds to a novel situation on the basis of the response made by him in similar situation(s) in the past.

Criticism : Thorndike conducted a large number of experiments to show that even human learning is an automatic and mechanistic process. But man is said to have free will and most of his behaviour is said to be governed by his intellect and reason. A child cannot learn anything simply through mechanical exercise or repetition. He needs attention, interest and awareness of the meaning of the task.

Again, in every case of learning, repetition is not required. Once burnt, a child always dreads the fire.

Some argue that bad habit which has been learned can be rooted out by repetition. Dunlop has shown that in case of typing if a particular error is repeated with perfect awareness, the error gets corrected. Here repetition or exercise helps reduction or weakening of the S–R connection.

Thorndike was criticised for methodological error in his earlier experiments. Bolles, for instance, criticised him for not using appropriate control groups in his research work.

According to Thorndike, the learning of the cat is purely a mechanical affair. It has no insight nor it learns by past experiences. Then how could it discriminate between the latch and other parts of the puzzle box? Moreover, scratching, biting and clawing responses have been repeated more than those of opening the latches. Then why these wrong responses are not strengthened in subsequent attempts?

Learning does not always depend on rewards. Learning may take place even without any reward. Hall and Bretnal have shown that learning is possible only through punishment.

According to the Gestalt Psychologists, learning is not a mechanical process of trial and error. They interpret learning as a purposive, exploratory and creative enterprise. Thorndike's theory of learning has been criticised by the Gestalt psychologists as atomistic.

34.7 Thorndike's Contribution in the Field of Education

Thorndike's theory of trial and learning has greatly influenced teaching-learning process. According to him, learning is due to the formation of bond between stimulus and response (S–R). Through drill and practice, reward and punishment, the S–R connection is to be strengthened for successful learning. Not only animal learns by this process but human learning also follows this pattern.

Thorndike also proposed the concept of reinforcement, the idea that learning occurs when a response produces satisfying state of affairs. In order to teach effectively, the educator must prepare the learner by motivating him through various means.

34.8 Human Learning

Man is a rational animal. He can discriminate right from wrong. He is endowed with the ability of thinking, reasoning and imagination and, as a result, he learns quickly and retain learned materials for a longer time than the animals.

Learning Involves : (a) Motivation, (b) Random Responses, (c) Elimination of Unsuccessful Responses and (d) Fixation of Successful Responses which satisfy the motive.

Man uses all the methods of animal learning. Like animals, young children learn motor skill by trial and error process. As they grow older, they learn more through insight. This is because man is capable of thinking with the help of language. Animal thinking is at the perceptual level. They cannot make use of language and have no power of abstract thinking. Animal learning is mostly carried on through bodily movement.

Man has greater power of observation than an animal. He can observe and analyse different characteristics of the environment, which are beyond the scope of the animal.

Man has memory and he can make use of his past experience to solve a problem. He can make use of other person's experience in attacking a problem. He has a greater power of learning by imitation than animals.

Summary

Learning is a process of change which enables an organism to adapt itself to the environment. It is purposeful and goal-oriented. Thorndike formulated three major laws of learning. The Law of Effect, The Law of Exercise and the Law of Readiness. Thorndike's theory of T–E learning has greatly influenced teaching learning process. Through practice, reward and punishment, the S–R connection is to be strengthened for successful learning.

References

1. Munn, N.L. : *An Introduction to Psychology,* Delhi : Oxford & IBH, 1967.

2. Stout, G.F. : *A Manual of Psychology,* London University Tutorial Press, 1938.

3. Woodworth, R.S. : *Psychology,* London, Methuen, 1945.

4. Ross, I.S. : *Ground Work of Educational Psychology,* London : George G. Harrap & Co., 1951.

5. Sinha, J.N. : *A Manual of Psychology,* New Central Book Agency (P) Ltd., Calcutta 700 009.

Questions and Assignments

1. Define Learning. What is Trial and Error learning?
2. What are the characteristics of T–E learning? Describe Thorndike's Puzzle Box experiment with a hungry cat.
3. Define the Law of Exercise. How can you use the law in classroom teaching.
4. What is Law of Effect? Discuss its application in classroom teaching.
5. How far human learning differs from animal learning? Discuss.
6. Write notes on :
   (a) The Law of Readiness.
   (b) The Law of Recency.
   (c) Chain Learning.
   (d) Signal Learning.

Chapter 35

Transfer of Training

Introduction : Transfer refers to the transfer of knowledge training and habits acquired in one situation to another situation (Soren Son). According to H.C. Ellis transfer of learning means that experience or performance on one task influences performance on some subsequent task. Something learned in one task may be carried over to the another task and this transfer may help the learning of the second task. Suppose an individual learns task A and afterwards attack task B and do better on B because of the previous mastery of A. Here we may infer that transfer of learning has taken place. A student learns Bengali grammar and then studies English grammar. Now if learning of Bengal's grammar facilitates the learning of English Grammar we may suppose that transfer of training has occurred.

Instead of storing knowledge, our aim of education should be to make it functional and positive. Learning can become functional only when pupil can utilise his experience obtained in classroom in another different situation. In school we teach students mathematics on the assumption that it will be used profitably in daily life to handle the problems involving mathematical calculations. In fact, those who are in charge of curriculum construction keep in view the practical utility of the subject.

Over the centuries the theories of transfer of training have greatly influenced our educational system because it was thought that what was taught in the classroom would transfer to new situations.

35.1 Theories of transfer

A number of theories have been developed to explain the phenomenon of transfer. Some of the major theories are as follows:

35.1.1 Theory of mental discipline

The theory of transfer of training is based on : (i) Faculty psychology and (ii) Formal discipline.

Faculty psychology: According to Faculty psychology our mind is composed of a large number of faculties such as, intelligence, memory, imagination, reasoning, thinking and so on. Through exercise these faculties can be improved as Locke says, "The faculties of our souls are improved and made useful to us just after the same manner as our bodies are." Thus according to some educationists the developing of power should be made the leading aim of teaching. Latin, Greek, Mathematics were thought to be the best subjects to train the various mental faculties of students.

Formal discipline : The basic premise of formal discipline was that vigorous exercise would enhance mental faculties. If the faculty of memory of a person could be strengthened by learning long poems, he would be able to memorise the dates of different incidents in History and difficult mathematical formulae. The formal discipline theory emphasised that *form of the matter* should be difficult and vigorous exercise of the different matter would increase mental powers. Thus, M.G. Glaze Brook in Teaching and Organisation says, "Memory is trained by most studies but least by language and history, imagination by all higher language teaching but chiefly by Greek and Latin Poetry." Thus the classical curriculum was dominated by the theory of mental discipline.

Criticism : Most of the educational thinkers of the present day do not subscribe to the theory of Mental Discipline or Faculty Theory. At present mind is never thought to be composed of several faculties. Again the protagonists of Mental discipline could not determine the exact number of faculties of mind. In fact, mind acts as a whole. Today the results of various experiments show that transfer of learning is not universal, and unlimited transfer is never feasible.

Experimental Evidences : A number of experiments have carried out during the last hundred years to study the problem of transfer of training :

1. **William James's experiment :** William James (1890) was the first psychologist who attacked the theory of mental discipline. He practised learning 158 lines from Victor Hugo's *Satyr.* Then he started learning Milton's Paradise Lost Book I daily for 20 minutes and memorised it in 38 days. Then he again learned next 158 lines from 'Satyr'. Due to exercise his faculty of memory should have been improved but he took more time to learn the new 158 lines. The results of his experiment thus contradicted the theory of mental discipline. It was proved that practice in memorising do not improve the memory. The result was as follows :

Table 35.1

	Material	Lines	Time in minutes
1.	Victor Hugo's Stayr	158	132
2.	Milton's Paradise Lost, Book I	Exercise for 20 mins. for 38 days	
3.	Victor Hugo's Satyr	158	152

2. **E.L. Thorndike's experiment :** E.L. Thorndike (1923) conducted experiments on 8,000 students and the time over which it was spread was one year. One group studied Latin and the other group studied Physical education. It was found that the subjects studied were of little importance in transfer of training. That is, History is as good as Latin or French.

35.1.2 Theory of identical elements

The theory of identical element was developed by E.L. Thorndike. According to him : (i) Transfer is due to the presence of identical elements present in both the influenced and influencing situation. (ii) The amount of transfer is directly proportional to the amount of identical elements.

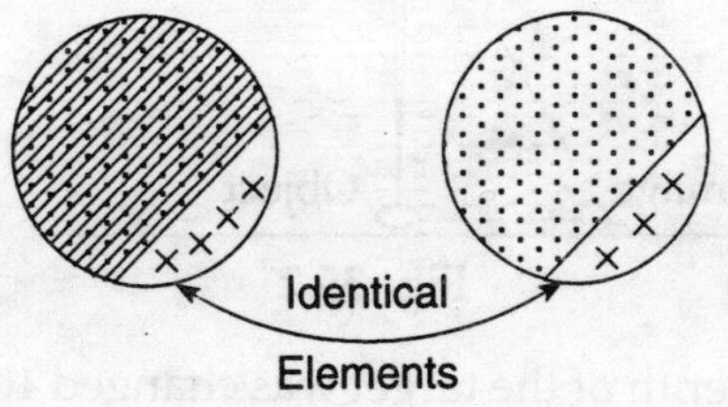

Fig. 35.1

The figure shows the transfer of common elements present in the influenced and the influencing situation. That is, as the similarity increases between two different situations, the amount of transfer increases and as the similarity decreases, the transfer also decreases in amount. According to Thorndike, the two factors—matter and method play an important role in the process of transfer.

Thorndike has also produced a biological explanation of transfer. According to him transfer depends on neural synapses along which reactions move.

Criticism : The theory of identical elements is criticised on the following grounds :

1. It is impossible to find any element of experience identical in two situations.
2. Transfer depends not only on common elements. Pupil's interest, attention, need and urge for learning also contribute to transfer.

3. Psychologists do not agree with his biological explanation of transfer. Lastly, Lashly's experiment has disproved Thorndike's biological explanation.

35.1.3 Theory of generalisation

According to Judd (1908) transfer of learning depends on generalisation of experience. In this connection he conducted an experiment. He used two groups of children : Group A (Control group) and Group B (Experimental group). Then he asked both the groups to hit the target under 12″ depth of water. Both the groups committed same type of mistakes as they were ignorant of the laws of refraction. Then he explained Laws of Refraction to the experimental Group B only.

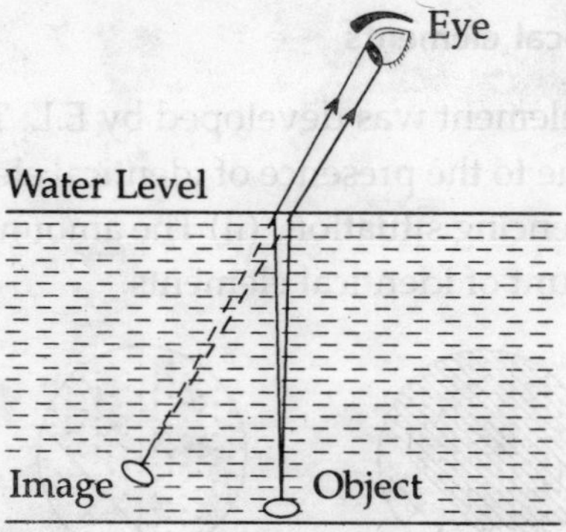

Fig. 35.2

In the final test the depth of the target was changed 108″ and the two groups were asked to hit the target. It was found that the control Group A committed the same mistakes as previously, while the experimental Group B, which was given training in Laws of Refraction showed significant superiority over the control Group A. This shows that transfer of learning depends on method of teaching, thinking, reasoning and intelligent application.

The superior performance of the experimental group was the result of applying a principle learned in one situation to the performance of a task in a different situation.

Table 35.2

Groups	Preliminary Test		Final Test
1. Experimental Gr. B	Practice in shooting 12″	Training in Laws of Refraction	Superior performance.
2. Control Gr. A	Practice in shooting 12″	No training	Depth change to 8″

Schroeder and Hendrickson (1941) repeated the same experiment of Judd. They also found that experimental group which was given the explanation of Laws of Refraction learned more quickly than the control group which was ignorant of laws of refraction. G.M. Haslerud and S. Meyers of New Hampshire University concluded experiments on transfer and concluded that :

1. Principles which are independently derived are more transferable than where the principles are given to the students by the teacher.
2. Performance under immediately guidance is no guarantee of transfer to new problems without such support.

Morrisett and Hovland after conducting a number of experiments on transfer of learning conducted that continued practice is essential to produce adequate original learning.

Relationship between Problem Solving behaviour and Transfer were studied by Schulz of State University of Iowa. He concluded that :

Reinforcement is an important variable in transfer situation. Intermittent reinforcement does lead to an increase in the amount of negative transfer in performance of another task.

The important findings of J.M. Stephens on transfer of learning are as follows :

1. Marked positive transfer is usually found when there is a mere shift from one sense organ to another.
2. In motor learning, bilateral transfer has been observed.
3. There is more transfer when there is similarity between the training task and criterion task.
4. Positive transfer occurs whenever the learner works on a series of complex similar problems.
5. Transfer occurs in extrovert than introvert students and in younger than in older students.

35.1.4 Gestalt theory of transfer

The Gestalt psychologists have stressed the importance of insight and wholeness of experiences. A Gestalt is a whole and the parts are determined by the intrinsic nature of the whole. Transfer of learning depends on establishing proper relationship between parts and whole in old and new situation. According to the Gestaltists Sultan (the Chimpanzee) perceived the relations between the parts of the learning situation on the first day and applied this experience on the second day in the same situation to solve the problem.

Thus, according to the Gestaltists insight, consistent thinking, grouping, reorganisation and structuralisation of material facilitate transfer.

35.1.5 Spearman's two factor theory

Transfer of training may be explained by Spearman's two factor theory. According to this theory the learning of a subject requires the exercise of a child's general ability (g) as well as the exercise of his special ability (s). There is transfer of training in so far as the exercise of general ability in a subject is concerned. Moreover, classics, mathematics and science require the exercise of g more than of s; whereas music, drawing, etc. require the exercise of s more than of g. Hence a training given in the former class of subjects is always of greater value than training given the latter class. Hence a training given in the former class of subjects is always of greater importance than the training given in the latter class, because in general life we need greater exercise of general intelligence rather than of special intelligence.

If the results of different experiments on transfer of learning are analysed, we find that transfer takes place in three ways :

1. Positive transfer (When performance on one task facilitates performance of second task).
2. Zero transfer (When there is no effect of one task on another).
3. Negative transfer (Performance on one task inhibits performance on a second task).

Generally, transfer is positive but the amount of transfer almost amounts to zero. It may be noted that most experimental results on transfer do not contradict earth other but only support each other with minor variation.

35.2 Transfer in school subjects

Most of the modern psychologists do not subscribe to the view that there is any real transfer of training while studying different school subjects. But according to Common Element Theory of Thorndike, transfer takes place if there are common elements in the two subjects. If they are absolutely unrelated to each other, then mastery of the one will not help in gaining mastery over the other. For instance, learning addition will help in learning multiplication because it involves the process of addition, but it will not help in learning chemical formulae. Similarly, training in learning non-sense syllabus helps little in learning sensible material.

There are many educators who still think that some subjects are superior to other in developing mental faculties and that there are certain subjects which aid transfer of desirable behaviour. Thus, M.G. Glazebrook in Teaching and Organisation says, "Memory is trained by most studies but best by language and history, imagination chiefly by Greek and Latin poetry, observation by science work in Laboratory and abstract reasoning by mathematics." But Thorndike's scientific experiment on 13,500 school students proved that the influence of the subject studied seemed unimportant. In fact, one subject was as good as another.

35.3 Role of teachers in transfer

Transfer depends upon the curriculum, methods of teaching, intellect of the pupils and the environment of learning. According to Thomson, a large number of subjects should be selected for the child's study in the school stage. The larger the number of subjects the better would be the exercise of the ability required for general use in life.

However, mechanical teaching of the school subjects by a teacher does not help transfer. The teacher can help pupils in the process of transfer to a great extent if he adopts scientific methods of teaching.

1. The teacher while teaching a subject should have a clear-cut idea about which learning experiences are to be transferred to real life situation.
2. The teacher should make learning purposeful and infuse a sense of reality in education. He should identify and highlight the important features of learning material which can be applied in new situations.
3. The teacher should emphasise the inner relations or common factors of the whole material.
4. The teacher should encourage students to learn by doing. They should be encouraged to learn by themselves through creative and experimental activity.
5. In the early stages of development of new skills and concepts, the students should be provided with enough opportunities for practice and drilling so that there may be positive transfer to subsequent tasks.
6. The teacher should adopt new methods of self-learning such as, Programmed Learning, Group Discussion, Workshop Method, Activity Method, Heuristic Method, Problem-Solving Method, etc. which will help positive transfer.
7. Instead of teaching different school subjects as different entity, the teacher should correlate each other and explain to the subjects that there is a natural relation between them. Also students should be asked to find out relation by themselves.
8. Concepts of different topics should be made clear with the use of audio-visual aids.

Summary

Previously there was a notion prevalent amongst educational thinkers that the various faculties of the child mind can be trained. It did not matter what kind of material we provide for such exercise. Thus natural science was taught to develop the power of observation, mathematics to develop reasoning and literature to develop imagination.

However, most of the psychologists and educational thinkers of today do not subscribe to the view that there is any real transfer of training. The results of different experiments on transfer show that transfer takes place in three ways namely, (i) Positive transfer, (ii) Zero transfer, (iii) Negative transfer. Generally transfer is positive but the amount is almost insignificant.

Thorndike's common element theory stresses that transfer can occur from one learning to another provided the two materials have identical elements. Judd's theory suggests that transfer of learning can be facilitated by teaching pupils general principles rather than specific solutions. According to Gestalt theory, transfer occurs because of perceptual similarities between situations and insight developed in one situation is useable in other situations.

According to Two-Factor Theory of Spearman, there is transfer of training in so far as the exercise of general ability in a subject is concerned.

The teacher can help positive transfer to a great extent if he adopts scientific methods of teaching and create interest in the subject.

References

1. Allen, J. Edwards and Scannel, D.P. : Educational Psychology, Allied Publishers, New Delhi, 1968.
2. Ausubel, D.P. : Educational Psychology, Holt, New York, 1968.
3. Chauhan, S.S. : Advanced Educational Psychology, Vikas Publishing House Pvt. Ltd., Delhi, 1997.
4. Judd, C.H. : Educational Psycholgy, Houghton Miffin Co. Boston, 1927.
5. Henry, C.Ellis : The Transfer of Learning, 1965.
6. Raymont : Principles of Education.
7. Thomson, G.H. : Instinct, Intelligence and Character.
8. Kundu, C.L. and Tutoo, D.N. : Educational Psychology, Sterling Publishers Pvt. Ltd., New Delhi, 1989.
9. Sorenson, H. : Psychology in Education, McGraw Hill Book Co., New York, 1940.

Questions and Assignments

1. What is meant by transfer of training? To what extent is such transfer of training is possible?
2. What do you mean by transfer of training? When does transfer take place? Discuss how to ensure transfer from classroom situations to life.
3. What is the theory of common element? What are its implications for classroom teaching.
4. What are the views of Thorndike in connection with transfer of training? What subjects should be included in the curriculum of studies if we give due importance to his views?
5. Discuss in the light of experimental findings when and to what extent transfer takes place. Add your comment.
6. Should mathematics be taught only for its disciplinary value? Discuss in the light of recent experimental findings on transfer of training.
7. Write notes on :

   (a) Mental discipline.

   (b) Theory of identical elements.

   (c) Gestalt theory of transfer.

   (d) Educational implications of transfer of training.

Chapter 36

Research in Educational Psychology

Introduction : Research is a systematic investigation of problems to establish facts and reach conclusions. It is a critical study for solutions to puzzling problems.

Research involves accurate observation and collection of data from relevant sources. It helps to devise certain principles which will be useful in predicting similar future occurrences. Research therefore, should be objective, reliable and valid. Finally, it should be carefully recorded and reported.

The socio-economic scenarios of a country are constantly changing. Therefore, research is indispensable for social progress.

36.1 Nature of educational research

Educational psychology is primarily scientific in nature. It applies scientific method to solve educational problems. It selects those facts and principles that are of specific significance to learning and teaching. Whenever needed educational research collects facts and informations from the allied fields of general psychology, philosophy, sociology, economics, physiology, history and statistics. Educational research adopts the general methodology of social science.

36.2 Areas of educational research

The field of educational research is very wide. This can be classified in terms of the following content areas :

36.2.1 Educational psychology

Motives and incentives in schools, interests and attitude, Breaking of bad habits, Conditions of effective learning, Factors promoting memorisation, Intelligence, Effective methods of evaluation, Measuring personality, Individual differences, Basic factors of group life, etc. are important topics of investigation.

36.2.2 Philosophy of education

Education is regarded as a dynamic side of Philosophy. A Philosophical analysis of the problem of behaviour, indiscipline delinquency, disobedience, construction of ideal curriculum, necessity of moral instruction are significant topics of educational research.

36.2.3 Sociology of education

Education is the fundamental method of social progress and reform. Various sociological factors such as, conflicts, competition, cooperation, community development, crime, causes of population explosion need to be carefully studied.

36.2.4 Economics of education

Researches in Educational expenses at various levels, Educational inputs and outputs, Optimum size of Educational Institutions, Problems of non-aided school, Grant in aid etc. may be conducted.

36.2.5 Educational administration

Educational planning, Institutional Planning, Educational Legislation, Problem of supervision, Job analysis of the Headmaster etc. are important topics of educational research.

36.2.6 Educational measurement and Test construction

Reliable and valid tests for measuring behaviour, personality, learning ability, skills and aptitudes, intelligence and achievement, attitude and interests, etc. are needed. Many standardised foreign tests are to be translated and adapted to our own situation. This is indispensable for the improvement of our educational system.

36.2.7 Teacher education

Research is needed to study the effectiveness of various methods like Programmed learning, Micro teaching, Interaction analysis, Job satisfaction of teaching, etc.

36.2.8 Curriculum construction

Construction of curriculum for different stages, adaptation of curriculum to local needs etc. are topics for intensive research.

36.2.9 Evaluation system

Traditional system of examination has been criticised for its shortcomings. Therefore, scientific and objective tests for evaluation are to be prepared for various stages through intensive research.

36.2.10 Counselling

Intensive research is needed for providing educational and vocational guidance to the pupils. For proper counselling various types of psychological tests are to be prepared.

36.3 Why research in education is needed?

Today the field of education has expanded enormously due to the advent of educational technology, new methods of teaching, educational and vocational guidance, new techniques of evaluation and so on. With such tremendous changes numerous problems relating to discipline, classroom teaching and school administration have cropped up. To meed these challenging problems in the field of education researches have to be carried out to evolve new concepts and techniques. Solution of educational problems by mere trial-error process or guess work will not yield any valid result. Demand of research in the field of curriculum construction evaluation system, creating interest and motivation, individual differences in educational performances and adjustment process, is very acute.

36.4 Steps in educational research

36.4.1 Selection of research topic

In identifying a suitable topic or a problem we have to see that the research has certain practical utility and is worth doing. The problem should have some novelty and the data on the problem should be easily available. Moreover, the time required and the cost of investigation should be taken into consideration.

In selecting a problem, a thorough review of the related literature is essential. The researcher must study research journals, books, dissertations and other sources of informations on the related topic.

36.4.2 Framing of hypotheses

After the problem has been selected, hypotheses are formulated. The hypotheses are guesses or tentative generalisation. They are partly based on known facts and partly conceptual.

Hypotheses should be clearly and precisely stated. Hypotheses should be easy to test but they should be highly significant. They should be consistent with known facts.

36.4.3 Methods to be used

Methods of educational research vary according to the purpose of research, field of research or nature of available data. Generally we may classify the methods of research into 3 categories : (i) Historical, (ii) Survey and (iii) Experimental.

Historical method is devoted to the study of the problems of the past incidence. The historical study involves documents related to legislative acts, legal decisions, official records, periodicals, journals and other literary materials concerning educational, political and social conditions of the period under study.

Survey method is employed to study a group of individuals through observation, interview, questionnaires, rating scale, case study, sociometry, etc.

Observation : In this the researcher simply observes the behaviour of the individual in real life situation. The observation can be done in two ways :

1. The observer does not hide from the subjects.
2. The observer remains behind a screen to avoid disturbance to the subjects.

To ensure reliability, the observer may repeat the observations in the same situations and record the results.

Interview : Interview may be free or standardised. In free-interview, the investigator asks the interviewee any question on the topic of study. In standardised interview the questions are pre-determined and the same questions are asked to all the subjects. To ensure reliability recently video-tape has been introduced during interview.

Questionnaire : In this a number of printed questions are distributed to the candidates and are answered by them.

These answers are analysed and the nature of their interests, attitudes, opinions abilities are determined.

Rating scales : The researchers can use rating scales to categorise their candidates on a particular traits. Suppose the researcher wants to rate the pupils of a class for honesty. They can rate the degree of this quality as, very good, good, average, poor, very poor, etc. The divisions of the scale comprise a three-point, five-point or seven-point scale.

Very Good	Good	Average	Poor	Very Poor

Case study : In this the researcher has to investigate into the past present activities of the candidate. He has to find out the likes and dislikes, emotional status, motives, interest, hobbies, etc. of the candidate. Relevant data about his ancestry, his home environment and neighbourhood are collected.

Sociometry : In this method the relationships existing among the members of a group in a given situation are determined. This technique helps the researcher to find out the degree of acceptance prevailing in the group.

Experimental method : Various psychological apparatus are used in this method to revel the attitude, interest, abilities, etc. of the candidate. To record pulse rate Sphygmograph, and to record blood pressure Pneumograph is used. In order to determine intelligence, various testing materials are used.

To elicit the unconscious and depth character of personality, Projective Techniques are used. Some of the Projective Techniques are : Word association test, Story telling, Sentence completion, Thematic Apperception Test (TAT), Children's Apperception Test (CAT), Rorschack Ink-bolt test, Picture completion test, Toy and Doll playing test.

36.4.4 Collection of data

For the collection of data proper sample is to be chosen. Then by application of different psychological devices on this sample, relevant data are collected.

Procedure of sampling : The representative proportion of the population is known as sample. According to Garrett there are four methods of sampling : (i) Random, (ii) Stratified, (iii) Incidental and (iv) Purposive.

Random sampling : In random sample every individual has equal chance of being chosen for the sample. Such a sample is arbitrarily selected in a lottery or from a carefully shuffled pack of cards.

Stratified sampling : This method is applicable when the population is composed of sub-groups or state of different sizes.

Incidental sampling : This is applied to those groups which are readily available, e.g., children in school or delinquents in Remand Home.

Purposive sampling : In the light of available evidence it mirrors some larger group with reference to a given characteristic, e.g., newspaper editors are believed to reflect accurately public opinion upon various educational and social problems.

36.4.5 Analysis and interpretation of data

It includes the selection of appropriate statistical and other techniques to be used for processing the data collected for the study.

36.4.6 Report of the research

The report of the research includes inferences, conclusions or certain generalisation.

36.5 Format of the research report

The general format of the research report is as follows :

A. Preliminary selection :

1. Title page, 2. Acknowledgments, 3. Concepts, 4. Sketches and diagrams. 5. Illustrations. 6. Preface.

B. Body of the report :

(a) *Introduction* : 1. The problem. 2. Analysis of previous reports. Relation of present problem to the previous reports. 3. Significance of the problem. 4. Delimitations of the study. 5. Statement of hypotheses. 6. Definitions of important terms.

(b) *Design of the study* : 1. Procedures employed. 2. Sources of data. 3. Data gathering tools. 4. Sampling and methods of collecting data.

(c) *Analysis and interpretation of the data.*

(d) *Summary and conclusion.*

(e) *Suggestion for further research.*

C. Reference section :

1. References. 2. Bibliography. 3. Index.

Summary

Today the field of education has greatly expanded and with this expansion new problems have also cropped up. To meed these problems, constant research is needed to evolve new concepts and techniques. A researcher in educational psychology will get help from general psychology, sociology, history, philosophy, economics and statistics. Educational research adopts the general methodology of social science. Educational research methods may be classified into 3 categories : (a) Historical, (b) Survey and (c) Experimental. Historical method is devoted to the study of the problems of the past incidence. Survey method includes—observation, interview, rating etc.

References

1. Carter V. Good, Barr, A.S. and Scates, D.E. : *The Methodology of Educational Research*, Appleton Century Crofts Inc., New York, 1941.
2. Lokesh, K. : *Methodology of Educational Research*, Vikas Publishing House Pvt. Ltd., New Delhi, 1984.
3. Garret, H.E. : *Statistics in Psychology and Education*, Longmans, Green and Co., New York, 1957.
4. Rai, B.C. : *Educational Psychology*, Prakashan Kendra, Lucknow, 1998.

Questions and Assignments

1. Define research and discuss the nature of educational research.
2. Why research in education is needed? Describe the scope of educational research.
3. What are the steps in educational research?
4. What are the different process of sampling?
5. Suppose you want to conduct a research on Juvenile delinquency. What steps would you adopt—Discuss.

Chapter 37

Imagination

37.1 The Nature of Imagination

Imagination consists in reproducing the contents of past experience and arranging them in a new order different from that in which they were originally experienced. In the words of Woodworth "Imagination is the process of establishing new relations in the things and objects." It is not simply thinking of the past events. It implies that something new is involved. Imagination has the following characteristics :

1. **Imagination is constructive :** It is rearrangement of the past experience into a new pattern. It reproduces the elements of past experiences and forms them into new combinations. Imagination is not exact reproduction of a past experience. There is conjunction in a new manner. You saw a bird and a horse in the past. You can combine the image of bird and horse and imagine a centaur, a creature with the upper half of a man and the lower half of a horse. Similarly, you can picture the image of a golden rose.

   Sometimes there is *separation* of the elements of past experiences you always perceived a man with a big moustache. But you disjoin the moustache from the man in imagination and picture the image of a man without moustache.

   Sometimes there is *substitution.* Some parts of the objects perceived in the past are replaced by other parts in imagination, we may imagine a woman with golden hair.

Sometimes there is *augmentation* of the contents of past experiences when we increases the size of a man ten times and picture the image of a monster, there is augmentation.

Sometimes there is *diminution* of the contents of past experiences. When we decrease the size of a man and picture the image of a Liliput there is diminution.

2. **Imagination is mental manipulation :** An individual rearranges facts previously observed and recalls at present into a new pattern in imagination. For example, a mermaid is composed of fish and woman.

3. **Imagination is motivated :** Imagination is influenced by our wishes. The child 'builds castles in the air' to satisfy his wishes.

Imagination is a process of trial-and-error activity in order to satisfy a want. It is a mode of adaptation to an ideal situation. It is device for achieving unattainable goal.

37.2 Imagination and Memory

Imagination resembles memory in some ways. Images are used in both these processes. They are also related to our past experiences. But in fact, the two processes are different. Following are the differences between imagination and memory.

Table 37.1

Imagination	Memory
1. Consists in reproducing the elements of past experiences and rearranging them into a new pattern.	1. It is exact reproduction of past experiences.
2. Imagination is productive. It is inventive and creative.	2. Memory is reproductive. It is a faithful reproduction of the original percept.
3. In imagination there is no place of recognition.	3. One of the important factors of memory is recognition.

37.3 Kinds of Imagination

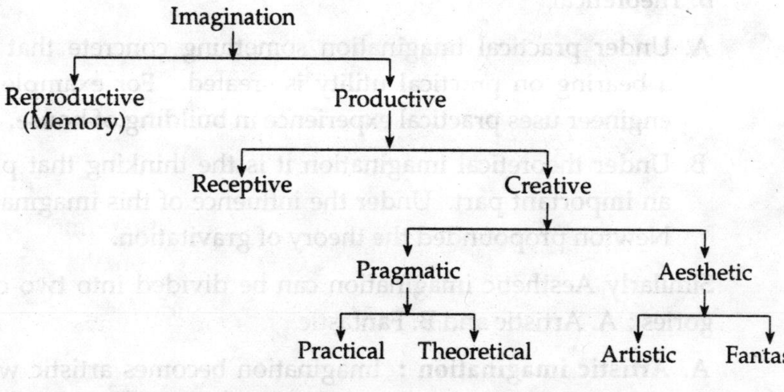

Fig. 37.2

According to Drever imagination may be classified as follows :

1. **Reproductive Imagination :** When the contents of past experience are reproduced in the same order, it becomes reproductive imagination or memory.

2. **Productive Imagination :** It is rearrangement of the past experiences into a new pattern. It reproduces the elements of past experiences and forms them into new combinations. The productive imagination is of two types : 1. Receptive Imagination. 2. Creative Imagination.

   (a) **In Receptive Imagination :** The materials of imagination and the order of their combination are suggested to the mind from without. When we read stories we have receptive imagination in which we receive the images from without.

   (b) **In Creative Imagination :** When an engineer constructs the plan of a building he has creative imagination. Here the engineer does not play according to the tunes of others. He exercises his own creative imagination.

   Creative imagination may be subdivided into two categories : 1. Pragmatic imagination and 2. Aesthetic imagination.

   (i) **Pragmatic imagination :** Pragmatic imagination serves some practical purpose. When an engineer devises a plan of a bridge or a machine, he has practical or pragmatic imagination.

   (ii) **Aesthetic imagination :** Aesthetic imagination satisfies our aesthetic impulse. It does not satisfy any practical need. The constructive activity itself gives pleasure. When a painter paints a picture, he has aesthetic imagination.

Pragmatic imagination is of two kinds : A. Practical and B. Theoretical.

A. Under practical imagination something concrete that has a bearing on practical utility is created. For example, an engineer uses practical experience in building of house.

B. Under theoretical imagination it is the thinking that plays an important part. Under the influence of this imagination Newton propounded the theory of gravitation.

Similarly Aesthetic imagination can be divided into two categories : A. Artistic and B. Fantastic.

A. **Artistic imagination :** Imagination becomes artistic when there is some purpose or direction. Writing a story or composing a poem is an example of artistic imagination.

B. **Fantastic imagination :** Imagination is fantastic when the mind has no purpose or definite aim. Day-dreaming is an example of fantastic imagination.

37.4 Imagination and Thinking

As a mental process imagination resembles thinking. But it differs from thinking in some respect. Woodworth considers imagination as mental manipulation. For example, we mentally manipulate chairs and tables and arrange them for a tea party without actually handling them.

On the other hand thinking is mental exploration. Suppose you have lost your money bag. Without actually searching for it here and there you think out and guess where you put it last. This is mental exploration.

Following are the differences between thinking and imagination.

Thinking	Imagination
1. Thinking is mental exploration.	1. Imagination is mental manipulation.
2. Thinking is generally directed by a purpose.	2. Imagination is not directed by any purpose or objective. The child falls into a day-dream and builds castles in the air.
3. Imagination is not directed by any purpose or objective. The child falls into a day-dream and builds castles in the air.	3. It is oriented towards a goal.

Thinking	Imagination
4. Thinking involves controlled association.	4. Imagination involves free-association.
5. Thinking involves voluntary attention, an effort of the will. It produces a mental strain.	5. Imagination involves no voluntary attention. Imagination of expectations is a source of delight.

37.5 Development of Imagination

Children under three have only memory of reproductive imagination. They can only revive their past experiences. At a later stage their imagination is mostly receptive. They can picture images as suggested by other persons. They cannot create images.

During the third and fourth year, children have abundance of creative imagination. They love to listen fairy tales from four to eight. From four to eight their imagination is of the fantastic type.

The child gradually develops the power of imagination. It is revealed in constructiveness, make-believe and story telling.

The child builds a house with sand, makes kites and boats of paper. He rides a stick and treats it as his horse. Gradually the child develops the power of story telling. He invents a story out of past experiences. He thinks of certain objects and combine them together according to his sweet will.

As the child grows older, he acquires knowledge of the external world and become more practical. His imagination ceases to be fantastic and becomes more pragmatic.

During adolescence fantastic imagination again becomes predominant with a strong element of emotion. It takes the form of a day-dreaming.

With the passing away of adolescence, imagination again becomes pragmatic. It ceases to be fantastic and emotion.

At last aesthetic imagination emerges. It rises above the practical needs of life and satisfies the deeper cravings of the mind.

37.6 Wrong Use of Imagination

Imagination affords pleasure to an individual. Vivid-imagination of expectations are sources to great delight. But wrong use of imagination is harmful.

Children visualise more and their images are more vivid. They often confound images with precepts. This is specially the case with children of three to six years of age. They cannot distinguish between things perceived and elements of their imagination. Often they do not deliberately tell lies but they fail to distinguish a fancy from a fact due to vividness of his mental imagery. Sometimes they fail to remember certain minor incidents that happened in the past and fill in the gaps by imagination.

Often children vividly imagine ghosts, demons or giants in the dark corner of a room at night and tremble with fear. Their vivid images are hallucinations.

The mind of an introvert child flies away from reality and lives in an imaginary world. The adolescents in particularly indulge in day dreams and substitute an imaginary world for a real world. Excessive day dreaming is undoubtedly harmful. It makes the child different and unable to cope with the world of reality. These are the misuse of imagination and should be avoided.

37.7 Abnormalities of Imagination

1. **Projection :** It consists in imagining that our own weakness is the result of the action of some other thing or person, real or imaginary. A student often attributes his failure in examination due to unfair and shift questions. A bad carpenter accuses his tools. There are persons who do not recognise their own faults, but project them to other persons and blame them for their own deficiency.

   Excessive projection may produce mental disorders.

2. **Delusion :** Delusion is the product of wrong imagination. There are two types of delusion : (a) Delusion of Grandeur and (b) Delusion of Persecution.

   (a) **Delusion of Grandeur :** In delusion of grandeur a person imagines that he is the Prime-minister of India or the President of U.S.A. The victim of such wrong imagination loses his grip on reality.

   (b) **Delusion of Persecution :** In this kind of delusion a person wrongly imagines that he is being attacked by a powerful enemy. He misinterprets all actions of others as conspiracy against him. He imagines that they are plotting to kill him.

3. **Identification :** It affords imaginative satisfaction to ungratified desires. It provides an imaginative escape from the hard facts of the real world. A boy may identify himself with a hero portrayed in television and may escape imaginatively from his rigorous study for the time being.

4. **Obsession :** An adolescent may be haunted by a fixed idea of killing his friend and does not consider it to be wrong. The idea constantly haunts him and he is almost helpless to inhibit the idea. When a person is the victim of such a fixed idea, he has abnormal imagination.

5. **Regression :** Children resort to regression when their desires are frustrated. They weep, kick objects and resort to such undesirable responses. When they are forced to take bitter medicines they revert to earlier irresponsible behaviour. Regression involves an abnormal form of imagination.

   Projection, delusion, identification, obsession and regression are abnormal modes of imagination.

37.8 Importance in Education

Imagination is a gift of the highest importance. It is the foundation of all creative thinking. Thus it has a great educational value.

Imagination precedes all kinds of inventions. Invention of Radio, Television, Gramophone, Aeroplane etc. must have followed some kind of imagination before their discovery.

Imagination is the source of pleasure. During infancy and adolescence, children indulge in day-dreaming. This gives a lot of pleasure to them.

In discontent or boredom it affords an escape into a world in which we are successful. It provides relief to an individual from the worries and hardship of the real world.

For all technical and material development theoretical and pragmatic imagination are very important.

Aesthetic imagination is inevitable in the development of higher ideals, religious sentiments and in the realisation of truth, beauty and goodness.

Play involves imagination. Fantastic imagination is essential for the playful activities of the children.

37.9 Training in Imagination

Imagination is an important power of the mind. Its cultivation is necessary for the growth of the child mind. It is the basis of other higher faculties. There can be no creative thinking without the initial power of imagination. Imagination has a great educational value. So it must be encouraged and trained. In connection with the training in imagination following are the few points that should be kept in mind :

1. Experience is the source of imagination. Elements on which child's mental images are built, are provided with experience. The teacher, therefore, should enrich the mind of the students with facts and experiences of concrete types as far as possible. While teaching he should use various audio-visual aids to enrich the child's mind and cultivate imagination.

2. Children love stories. Their power of imagination develops through listening stories. Plato advocated the use of stories to convey moral truths to children. However, Madam Montessori condemns the practice of telling stories to children, for she thinks that it encourages them to indulge in day-dreaming.

   The view of Montessori cannot be accepted because it is with the help of fairy tales and fables the moral development of the child takes place. Moreover, every community has literature of its our which reflect their social and religious life. Stories and parables are a part of this wide literature. So, to enrich pupil's experience and imagination, the role of story-telling cannot be minimised. Teachers should tell them stories of scientific inventions and geographical discoveries.

3. Teaching through dramatisation is helpful in developing the child's imagination. Dramatisation helps children to express themselves. The teacher may ask them to dramatise a dialogue or a story from their books.
4. Modelling in clay and plasticine, drawing and painting, games and excisions develop pragmatic and aesthetic imagination of the child. So, these should be encouraged in our schools. Children should be encouraged to reproduce what they have observed in their educational tour. They should be asked to write down an account of their observation.
5. Educational projects develop the pragmatic imagination of the pupils. Therefore, the teacher should encourage them to undertake various educational projects.
6. Children should be taught to distinguish between fact and imagination. They should be helped to cultivate an imagination which does not drift away from reality. Excessive indulgence in day-dreaming may result in the deterioration of adaptive capacity. It may arrest the normal growth of personality and may result in some kind of abnormality.

Summary

Imagination consists in mentally reviving past experiences and arranging them in a new order. Imagination is mental manipulation and it is constructive. There are two types of imagination : Productive and Reproductive (Memory). Creative imagination is of two kinds : Pragmatic and Aesthetic. Pragmatic imagination serves some practical purpose, while aesthetic imagination satisfies our aesthetic impulse. During the third and fourth year children have abundance of creative imagination. They love to listen, stories and fairy tales. Gradually they develop the power of imagination. It is revealed in make-believe story-telling. As the child grows older, his imagination becomes more pragmatic. During adolescence fantastic imagination again becomes dominant. It takes the form of day-dreaming. With the passing of adolescence, imagination again becomes pragmatic and aesthetic imagination emerges.

Imagination is an important gift and it is the basis of creative thinking. It has a great educational value. So it must be encouraged and trained. The power of imagination in children should be developed through story-telling, drawing and paining, dramatisation, clay modelling and educational projects. Imagination affords pleasure to the child. But wrong and excessive indulgence in fantastic imagination is harmful because it drifts away from reality and may lead to mental disorders.

References

1. Drever, James : *An Introduction to the Psychology of Education,* Middle Sex : Penguin Books.
2. Munn, N.L. : *An Introduction to Psychology,* Delhi : Oxford & IBH, 1967.
3. McDougall, W. : *An Outline of Psychology,* London : Methuen, 1949.
4. Stout, G.E. : *A Manual of Psychology,* London University Tutorial Press, 1938.
5. Woodworth, R.S. : *Psychology,* London, Methuen, 1945.
6. Ross, I.S. : *Ground Work of Educational Psychology,* London : George G. Harrap & Co., 1951.

Questions and Assignments

1. Define imagination. What is its importance in Education.
2. What can you do far healthy development of imagination in child?
3. What are the different types of imagination? Distinguish between Productive Imagination and Reproductive Imagination.
4. What steps the teacher should take to train the imagination of the pupils?
5. Discuss the value of fables in developing the imagination of the child. Comment on Madam Montessori's views in this connection.

6. Aesthetic imagination is inevitable in the development of higher ideals and in the realisation of Truth, Beauty and Goodness.—Discuss.

7. How does imagination affect practical conduct? Is 'building castles in the air' always bad?

Chapter 38

Construction of Achievement Test

Introduction : Achievement Tests measure the effect in Education or Teaching. They measure what and how much the child has learnt out of a subject. They measure present status of skill or progress in some subject and measure the result of education in a particular field, e.g., Mathematics.

Achievement tests differ from intelligence tests. While achievement tests measures the knowledge gained by a child, intelligence tests measure the innate power of the child. To measure achievement of knowledge, we find out the A.Q. or Achievement Quotient. But to measure intelligence, we find out the I.Q. or Intelligence Quotient.

38.1 Essay type of Achievement Test

Formerly essay-type of tests were the only instrument to measure the progress of students. But soon it was found out that the essay-type tests were defective and incapable of measuring students' ability correctly.

38.2 Demerits of Traditional Examination

The defects of the traditional essay-type examination are as follows :

1. **Unreliability :** It has been found that the same answer script has been scored by different examiners differently. The range of marks varied sometimes from 30 to 70 out of 100 in the same essay. Hence this type of assessment is subjective and unreliable.
2. **Validity :** The traditional examinations are meant for measuring educational achievement in different school subjects. But it has been found

that the result of the tests is influenced by rote memory, language and style of presentation of the subject. Hence the traditional examinations are invalid.

There are other defects also. The students guess the possible questions and prepare only important portions of the syllabus and leave others. Thus the purpose of the curriculum is defeated. Moreover, the time limit of such examinations is not scientific. Within three hours the students have to answer all the questions. Often a student, in spite of the knowledge, fails to answer all of them within that time-limit.

The traditional system of examination encourages unhealthy competition and cramming without trying to understand proper meaning of the subject.

38.3 New method of Achievement Test

Because of so many defects in old examination system, the new method of achievement tests or attainment tests in various subjects was introduced. These new-type objective tests are more scientific, reliable and valid.

In this system, 100–150 short questions are drawn up covering the entire curriculum. The students confine their answers to 'No' or 'Yes', by drawing a line under the answers already given. Different examiners award similar marks in the test. This makes the test objective.

As students are not required to write long essays in this system, the language, the handwriting, or writing style does not influence the examiner.

Since the questions are asked from the whole of syllabus, the students have to prepare the whole of it and there is no scope for cramming.

38.4 Forms of the new type of Objective Tests

A few models of the questions of the new type of tests are given below :

1. **True-False Test :**

   Direction : A few statements are given below. Write T against the statements which are True and F against which are false :

   (a) The highest range of the Himalays is Kanchunjangha ( ).

   (b) The founder of Moghul Empire is Babur ( ).

   (c) The only desert of India is Sahara ( ).

2. **Completion Test :**

   Direction : Fill in the blanks with appropriate words :

   (a) The staple food of the Nepalese ——.

(b) The name of the Prime Minister of India is — —.

(c) The capital of India is — —.

3. **Multiple Choice Test :**

Direction : Select the appropriate words from the given words within the brackets and fill in the gaps :

(a) We get eggs from — — (Goat, Hen, Cow).

(b) The name of Indian desert — — (Sahara, Thar, Gobi).

(c) The founder of Mughal Empire was — — (Akbar, Aurangzeb, Babur).

4. **Matching Test :**

Direction : Select words from Column A and match them with words in Column B.

	A		B
(a)	The desert of India	( )	Surat.
(b)	Present name of Pataliputra	( )	Thar.
(c)	A port on the Western coast of India	( )	Patna.

5. **Analogy Test :**

Direction : 3 words are provided in each question given below. Of these first two are related. Find out the word similarly related to the third word.

(a) Car : Driver : : Pupil : ?

(b) Cow : Grass : : Man : ?

(c) Ear : Hearing : : Eye : ?

38.5 Construction of Achievement Tests

In the construction of Achievement Tests following steps are involved :

1. Planning the test. 2. Preparing the test.
3. Trying out the test. 4. Evaluating the test.

1. **Planning of the Achievement test :** In the planning of the achievement test, first we have to determine the behavioural changes desired to be produced by a particular subject. That is, we have to determine various aims of teaching that subject.

Then a careful analysis of the courses prescribed in that subject is to be made. What is expected from the child regarding these courses is carefully determined. Planning must take into consideration the class for which the test is being constructed.

2. **Preparing the test :** While drafting the test-questions we have to see that the courses of the subject for that class are well-represented. The questions should test power of discrimination, judgement, grasping of the subject and application of knowledge. In the first draft the number of questions should be double the number of questions to be retained in the final test. Easier items should be placed in the beginning and difficult ones at the end.

Try out : At this stage we have to make a selection of most suitable questions and reject unsuitable questions. For this purpose we have to administer the test to a about 200 children representing all grades of abilities.

It is felt that often students may get chances to guess the answers of such questions. Therefore, to eliminate the effect of Guess-work following formula is applied :

$$S = R - \frac{W}{N-1}$$

[S = Score, R = Number of right responses, W = Number of Wrong responses, N = Number of responses presented for each time.]

38.6 Evaluating the Test

To determine which question should be retained in the test and which not we need to make item-analysis of the test. Item analysis involves : (a) item selection, (b) determination of the item difficulty and (c) item validity.

The initial choice of test items depends upon the judgement of competent persons or teachers as to the suitability of the material for the purposes of the test.

Items should be selected for a test which vary in difficulty from easy to hard. A test made up of items all of which are passed by approximately 50% would be the most discriminating test.

The difficulty-value of each question is determined as follows :

$$\text{Item difficulty} = \frac{\text{Correct answers}}{\text{Total No. of tests}} \times 100.$$

For instance, if an item is correctly answered by 40 out of 50,

$$\text{Item difficulty} = \frac{40}{50} \times 100 = 80\%.$$

In this way the difficulty values of all the items are calculated. Those items of the test are selected whose difficulty value is between 40%–60%.

For finding out the reliability of the whole test any of the following methods may be adopted.

1. **Test retest method :** The test is given and then repeated on the same group and the correlation is calculated between the first and second sets of scores.
2. **Parallel forms method :** Two forms are prepared of the same test and correlation is found out between their scores.
3. **Split-half method :** In this method the test is broken into two equal halves and correlation is found out between their scores.

The validity of the test is found by getting the correlation between the scores of the test and some external criterion such as, school marks of the students.

Though Achievement tests and Intelligence tests are two different things, at present both tests are used to determine the progress of the student. According to Thomson, just as the intelligence tests measure the innate intelligence, an achievement test must measure the result of intelligence plus application. The purpose of the teacher is to determine if the student is acquiring knowledge and progressing according to his intelligence. Now, if the Achievement Quotient (A.Q.) of the a child falls much below his Intelligence Quotient (I.Q.), then there must be something wrong somewhere. It may be due to disturbance in family, physical ailments or some other causes.

38.7 Finding out Achievement Quotient

Achievement Quotient,

$$\text{A.Q.} = \frac{\text{E.Q.}}{\text{I.Q.}} \times 100.$$

[E.Q. = Educational Quotient, I.Q. = Intelligence Quotient].

$$\text{E.Q.} = \frac{\text{E.A. (Educational Age)}}{\text{C.A. (Chronological Age)}} \times 100.$$

Intelligence Quotient,

$$\text{I.Q.} = \frac{\text{M.A. (Mental Age)}}{\text{C.A. (Chronological Age)}} \times 100.$$

$$\therefore \quad \text{A.Q.} = \frac{(\text{E.A./C.A.}) \times 100}{(\text{M.A./C.A.}) \times 100} \times 100 = \frac{\text{E.A.}}{\text{M.A.}} \times 100.$$

Mental Age (M.A.) is determined from Intelligence Test and Educational Age (E.A.) is found out from the results of tests in different school subject. For instance, if the Educational Age of a student is 7 and his Mental Age is 10, then his Achievement Quotient is 70. This shows that the student is backward in his class.

Summary

Formerly Essay-type tests were the only instruments to know about the progress of students. But these tests were not accurate tests of students' performance. It has been found that these traditional essay-type tests are not reliable and valid. As a result, the new method of achievement tests was introduced.

The construction of New Type Achievement Tests involve : Planning the test, Preparing the test, Trying out the test and Evaluating the test. Planning must take into consideration the class for which the test is being constructed. Questions should vary in difficulty from easy to very difficult. The test is prepared in two forms—100 items in test A, and 100 in Test B. The test is then tried out by administering the test to about two hundred students representative of all grades of abilities. The process of items analysis involves : (a) item selection, (b) determination of item difficulty and (c) item validity. Those items are selected whose difficulty-value is between 40%–60%. After this the reliability and validity of the whole test are found out.

References

1. Cronbach, L.J. : *Essentials of Psychological Testing,* New York, Harper & Row, 1970.
2. Lindquist, E.F. : *Educational Measurement,* Washington, American Council on Education, 1951.
3. Odell, C.W. : *Traditional Examination and New Type Test,* New York, Appleton Century Crofts, 1928.
4. Ruch, G.M. : *The Objective or New Type Examination,* Chicago, Scott Foresman & Co., 1929.
5. Thompson, G.H. : *The Factorial Analysis of Human Ability,* London : London Univ. Press, 1939.
6. Thurston, L.L. : *Primary Mental Abilities,* Chicago : Univ. of Chicago Press, 1938.
7. Vernon, P.E. : *The Measurement of Ability,* London Univ. of London, 1940.

Questions and Assignments

1. What is an Achievement Test? How it differs from Intelligence Test?
2. Discuss some of the important defects of the traditional system of examination and suggest how you can remove them.
3. Discuss the new methods of Achievement tests and bring out their importance.
4. Give an account of various steps involved in the construction of a test.
5. Define Reliability and Validity. Illustrate your answer with examples.
6. Write notes on :
   (a) Achievement Quotient.
   (b) True-False type Question.
   (c) Multiple Choice Test.
   (d) Objective Tests.
7. Construct an Achievement Test on History for Class X students.

Chapter 39

Individual Differences

Introduction : No two individuals are alike in the world. It is an established fact that individuals differ in physical abilities as well as in mental abilities. Some people are tall and handsome, some are short and ugly. Some are gentle, some are rude. One person may be genius with an I.Q. of 140, the other an idiot with an I.Q. of 25. In spite of many similarities we find wide variations nearly in all traits of personality and patterns of human behaviour. This lack of similarity is termed as Individual differences.

Experiments of Wundt, Jastro, Ebbinghaus and others have conclusively proved that people differ from one another in physical abilities, mental abilities, knowledge, habits, personality and character traits. Even identical twins coming from the same single cell are two quite different persons.

39.1 Classification of Difference

Individual difference is caused by a number of factors. Such differences are either acquired or innate. Social, Cultural and Educational difference amongst individuals are acquired or learned, while physical, mental and Emotional difference are innate or in born. However, such classification of individual differences are tentative. No difference can be purely acquired or purely innate. For instance, physical characteristics of an individual are influenced by both heredity and environment. Similarly, our habit and character, interests and attitude are moulded by environment.

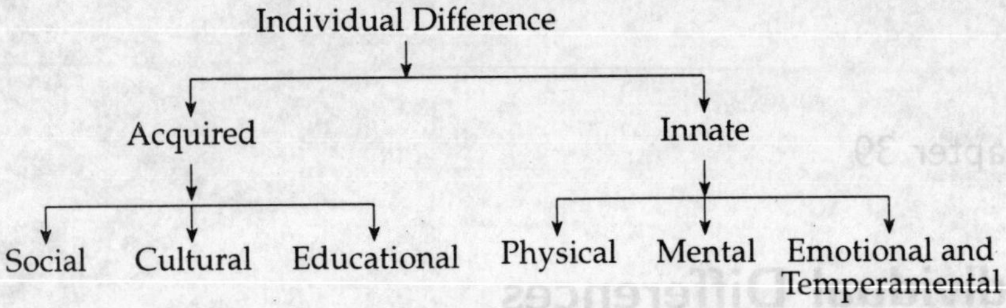

Fig. 39.1

39.1.1 Acquired Individual Difference

1. **Social difference :** Various social factors lead to individual difference. The home atmosphere, the parent-child relationship, the school environment, club, gang and political organisations exert a great influence upon the character and personality of an individual. Thus social environment is an important factor of individual difference.

2. **Cultural difference :** Culture moulds the personality and character of the individual. Children who are brought up in Muslim culture are different from those who are brought up in Christian culture. So culture is a dominant factor of individual difference.

3. **Educational difference :** All children in a school do not have the same capacity for learning. The results of different examinations prove this fact. All children do not show equal interest or equal aptitude in all subjects of the curriculum. Because of educational difference, selection of vocation also varies.

39.1.2 Innate Individual Differences

1. **Physical difference :** Physically no two individuals are alike. Some individuals are fair and tall, while the others are ugly and short in stature. Someone is fat while the other is lean and thin. Thus physical differences in complexion, height and weight are found in individuals. Again,. there is sex difference in man and woman. The individual difference in physical strength is measured by instruments like Dynamometer and Ergograph.

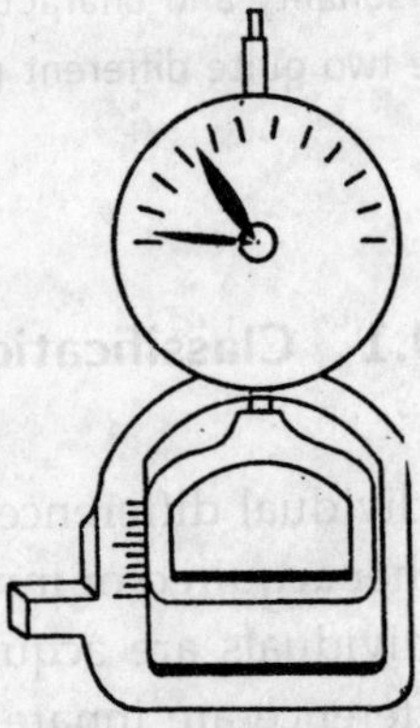

Dynamometer

Fig. 39.2

1. **Mental difference :** Mental difference is a potent cause of individual difference. The results of numerous intelligence tests show that individuals differ in intellectual ability. Terman classified human intelligence in terms of I.Q. in the following way :

Table 39.1

I.Q.	Class
Above 140	Genius
120–140	Very superior intelligence
110–120	Superior intelligence
90–110	Average
80–90	Dull
70–80	Borderline deficiency
50–70	Feeble mind (Moron)
25–50	Imbecile
0–25	Idiot

Besides general intelligence, individuals differ in special ability, such as Mechanical ability, Musical ability and Creative ability.

Individuals differ in memory, imagination, attitude, attention and interest. Power of recall, retention and reasoning are not equal in all people. Individual differences are found in memory span, span of attention, fluctuation of attention and reaction time. Reaction time of an individual is determined by Vernier Chronoscope. Interest of an individual is found by Interest inventories.

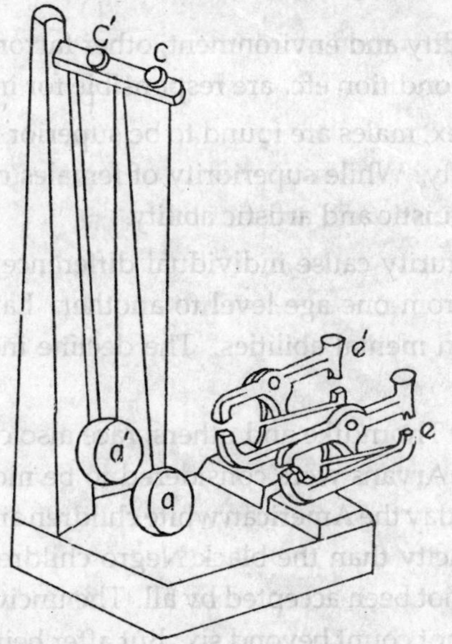

Fig. 39.3: Vernier chronoscope.

39.2 Emotional and Temperamental Difference

Emotional and Temperamental differences are found in people to a great extent. In the presence of the same object, the emotional experience of different persons may be different. Individuals differ in emotional qualities such as, love, anger and fear. Some people are rude and aggressive, while others are gentle and disciplined. They differ in emotional and temperamental traits and hence there are differences in the adjustments that they make towards their environment.

39.3 Causes of Differences

The two potential factors that cause individual difference are : (a) Heredity and (b) Environment.

(a) **Heredity :** The child receives many of his physical and mental traits from his parents. In appearance, in stature, the son resembles his parents. He also seems to inherit their intelligence, habits and character. According to genetic view, genes are the carriers of heredity traits.

(b) **Environment :** Environment is a potent factor which leads to individual difference. It is believed that the inhabitants of warm countries are lazy and people of cold climate are industrious. Climate, physical exercise and nutrition modify our growth. Well-developed traditions, customs, laws and institutions, which are part of social environment help and modify the development of the child. Social environment and education influence individuals more than the physical environment.

Besides heredity and environment, other factors such as sex, age, maturity, race, economic condition etc. are responsible for individual difference.

As regards sex, males are found to be superior in manual performance and mechanical ability. While superiority of females over males have been found generally in linguistic and artistic ability.

Age and maturity cause individual difference. The rate and character of growth differs from one age-level to another. Late in life, individuals suffer from a decline in mental abilities. The decline increases with age, especially after sixty.

According to Thorndike and others, race also causes individual difference. At one time the Aryans were considered to be more intelligent than the non-Aryans. Even today the American white children are considered to posses better intellectual capacity than the black Negro children. But this theory of racial superiority has not been accepted by all. The uncivilised Murray Islanders, for instance, could not count beyond six. But after being trained by the Scots, they developed same mathematical ability as the civilised people.

Economic condition of the family causes individual difference. Often children from poor family do not get proper training and education in spite of being quite intelligent and laborious. While children coming from well-off family can get the best possible education. Thus financial status of the parents cause individual difference.

The individual can be guided rightly only if we are able to determine the real cause of difference and measure the trait or ability that is responsible for such difference.

39.4 Tests and Methods for Determining Individual Difference

We need a thorough knowledge of individual differences, because these serve as the base upon which effective educational guidance and vocational guidance can be built. The tools that are used to measure these differences are different kinds of psychological tests, such as, Interest tests, Personality tests, Attainment tests, Aptitude test, Attitude tests, Intelligence tests and so on. Physical strength of an individual is measured by Dynamometer. Similarly, Ergograph measures the working ability of a person.

The individual difference is determined also by Case Study method. In this method a questionnaire is prepared covering different aspects of the personality and the individual is asked to answer them. From his answers the traits of personality of the individual is ascertained.

39.5 Educational Implication

The aim of education is to prepare the individual for complete living. But in traditional system of education this objective of education cannot be entirely fulfilled. The teacher thinks that all children are of equal mental ability and accordingly he adopts same method of teaching without paying any heed to individual difference. But to fulfil the objectives of education, a through knowledge of the individual difference is essential. The knowledge of Individual difference is required for :

1. Homogeneous grouping.
2. Individual instruction.
3. Adjustment of teaching method.
4. Special class and remedial teaching.
5. Proper assignment.
6. Multipurpose curriculum.
7. Co-curricular activities.
8. Educational and vocational guidance.

1. **Homogeneous grouping :** Individual differences compel us to think in terms of homogenous grouping of classes according to the level of intelligence. In certain advanced countries students are classified into three streams : Students of higher intelligence are put in A-stream, Average students in B-stream and those who have lower intelligence are put in C-stream.

2. **Individualised education :** Modern individualised education emphasises the marked individual differences of human nature. The Project method, Dalton plan, Winnetka plan, etc. attempt to adjust education to the nature of the individual.

3. **Adjustment of teaching methods :** In view of the individual differences many new methods of teaching have been devised. Individuals differ from one another as regards their interests. Now-a-days this fact has been utilised in the adjustment of teaching to the special interests of the students.

4. **Special class and remedial teaching :** In view of individual difference special classes are organised in schools. Students who are backward in certain school subjects are admitted to such classes for remedial teaching.

5. **Proper assignment :** The home assignment, which is given to the student, should be according to individual difference, The teacher should modify the assignment in amount, quality and difficulty according to individual capacity of the students.

6. **Multipurpose curriculum :** Curriculum should be constructed on the basis of individual difference. Now-a-days various types of curriculum have been devised to cater to the needs and interests of the students : Activity curriculum, Experience curriculum, Integrated curriculum, life-centric curriculum, Core and Diversified curriculum etc.

7. **Co-curricular activities :** The recognition of the fact of individual differences resulted in the inclusion of various co-curricular activities in our traditional curriculum. Children who do not find much interest in academic subjects may excel in dance, music, drama, painting or recitation.

8. **Educational and Vocational guidance :** Individual differences are of great significance for personal and vocational guidance purpose. A person should get the occupation according to his intelligence, interest, ability and personality traits. It is therefore, desirable that students in the school should get proper guidance and counselling.

Summary

Individuals differ in physical and mental abilities as well as in personality traits. Experiments of psychologists have conclusively proved it. Individual difference is caused by numerous factors. However, the potent factors are heredity and environment. Besides heredity and environment other factor, such as age, sex, maturity race or remote ancestry, economic condition of the family are responsible for individual difference.

The tools that are used to measure individual differences are various psychological tests, case study and other methods. To fulfil the objectives of education a thorough knowledge of the individual difference is essential. The knowledge of individual difference is necessary for homogeneous grouping, individualised instruction, adjustment of teaching method, formation of special class for remedial teaching, proper assignment, construction of multipurpose curriculum and vocational guidance.

References

1. Binet, A and Simon, T. : *The Development of Intelligence in Children,* Baltimore : Williams & Wilkins, 1916.
2. Thorndike, E.L. : *Essentials of Educational Psychology,* New Jersey : Prentice Hall, 1958.
3. Skineer, C.E. (Ed) : *Essentials of Educational Psychology,* New Jersey : Prentice Hall, 1958.
4. Woodworth, R.S. : *Experimental Psychology,* New York : Holt, 1954.
5. Terman, L.M. and Merrill, M.A. : *Measuring Intelligence,* Boston : Houghton Mifflin, 1937.

Questions and Assignments

1. What is meant by individual characteristics in which individuals differ?
2. What is the psychological nature of individual difference? In what respects do children in a classroom differ from one another?
3. Write a short essay on individual difference and their educational implication.
4. What are various factors that cause individual differences? Discuss the significance of this fact in education.
5. Discuss some of the individual differences and state in what way they have influenced the educational program.

Chapter 40

Educational Guidance

Introduction : Guidance means advice or direction for solving a problem. An individual may seek assistance from an experienced person to solve certain problems that arise in his life. The personal help thus given to the individual is termed, as guidance.

According to J.M. Brewer, educational guidance is concerned with the pupils' success in his educational career. The main purpose of educational guidance is to assist the students to make desirable progress in their educational career. C.E. Skinner says, "Guidance is the art of helping boys and girls to plan their action wisely."

Guidance may take various forms : Educational Guidance, Vocational guidance, Health guidance, Moral and Religious guidance, Economic guidance, Recreational guidance, Social guidance and so on.

40.1 Education and Guidance

Education and guidance are closely related. It is obvious that without proper guidance there cannot be any learning or education. The purpose of guidance is to make the individual self-sufficient and capable of solving his own problems. Guidance is a continuos life long process. Guidance helps to mould the personality of a child and makes himself a useful citizen of the country.

40.2 Objectives of Educational Guidance

The important objective of educational guidance is to aid the student in planning his educational program. The student needs proper guidance mainly in selecting the course of study he would follow. He also needs help in the method of day-to-day study.

Therefore, the purpose of guidance is two fold : (a) To select proper curriculum and study stream and (b) To assist in the proper method of study.

The pupil's success in academic field depends on his judicious selection of curriculum and of course, to a large extent on the method of study. Effective guidance will create in a pupil a strong liking for his subject.

40.2.1 To select Proper Curriculum and Study Stream

Now-a-days because of diversification of courses in Science, Arts, Commerce and Technical Education, the child has to select a proper stream according to his aptitude and capability. In order to help the pupil to select proper stream of course, his intelligence and aptitude should be properly evaluated.

1. **Intelligence test :** Binet Simon Scale, Weschler-Bellevue Test and various types of performance tests, e.g., Alexander's Pass along, Dearborn's Form Board, Knox's Cube construction, Koh's Block design, Porteus' Maze Test, Good Enough's Drawing a Man Test etc. are used to determine the Intelligence Quotient of the pupil.
2. **Aptitude tests :** Most popular Aptitude tests are Stenquist's Mechanical Aptitude Test and Seashore's Musical Test. These tests are used to determine aptitude of a pupil in different field.
3. **Sholastic tests :** These predict the future accomplishment in school-subjects like—Science, Medicine, Law, etc. For example, Iowa Placement Tests of Chemistry, Physics, Mathematics, Language etc., and the Standard Scientific Aptitude Tests are scholastic.

   By determining the results of such tests a proper stream of course may be recommended for a particular student. But for effective guidance pupil's personality, his family background, his condition of health etc. are also to be studied.
4. **Personality tests :** For effective educational guidance we have to collect facts about the personality traits of the student through different personality tests, such as Rating Scale, Sociometric Scale, Rorschach Ink-blot, Thematic Apperception Test, Word Association Test etc. The personality traits of the pupil play an important role in the educational guidance.
5. **Questionnaire and Interview :** For proper educational guidance, the knowledge of family background of the pupil is essential. For instance, if the financial condition of the pupil is weak, it may not be possible for him to pursue higher medical or engineering courses which are generally expensive. Therefore, through interview and questionnaire, collection of informations about family background and economic condition of the parents is essential.

6. **Preparation of a Schedule :** With the help of informations derived from the above tests and interviews a schedule about the student is prepared. The schedule will contain the following informations about the student :

   (a) Information about family background and its financial position.

   (b) Case history about health and physical growth.

   (c) Result of Scholastic test.

   (d) Intelligence quotient.

   (e) Results of Aptitude test.

   (f) Personality traits.

   These informations will enable the teacher or the psychologist to determine the nature of guidance required by the student.

40.2.2 To assist in the Proper Method of Study

For the purpose of educational guidance the teacher has to know the factors that influence the teaching learning process. He has to take a few psychological and external factors into consideration for effective guidance.

1. **The psychological factors :** There is a driving force behind the learning activity. This driving force behind learning activity is called motivation. Motivation may be intrinsic and extrinsic.

   To arouse intrinsic motivation, the teacher should make the subject matter meaningful and interesting. It is at the stage of introduction of the lesson that he should try to stimulate the pupils. Once the interest aroused, half of the teachers' work is done and it will take the pupils to the proper type of learning, that is, self-learning, which is the important feature of New Education.

   The extrinsic forces of motivation are rewards and punishment, praise and blame, competition, consciousness of progress, social approval and so on. The teacher should use these judiciously in the classroom teaching.

2. **The external factors :** The external factors of guidance refer to the planning of lessons, management of classroom environment and creating situations which are most favourable to the learning process as a whole. External guidance in learning eliminates chances of errors and save time. These are :

   (a) **Repeated practice and application :** For effective learning practice or drilling is essential. Things become clearer and more intelligible when actually applied. Application fixes the facts firmly in the mind.

(b) **Distribution of practice periods :** Continuous study over a long period is not conducive to the learning process. Distributed practices give relatively greater return. If one hour is to be devoted to a particular lesson, say learning a poem, it will be more fruitful to give ten minutes twice a day for three days than to study it continuously for one hour.

(c) **Active recall :** The teacher, while teaching, should frequently make use of active recall, because learning is tested by recall. After each unit of lesson has been taught, the teacher should put questions, ask students to reproduce, to fill up the blanks and so on.

(d) **Mnemonic devices :** The teacher can successfully make use of mnemonic devices when it is difficult to arrange the learning material into meaningful associations, e.g., to remember the seven colours of rainbow, the mnemonic word VIBGYOR may be used. In VIBGYOR, the V refers to violet, I to indigo, B to blue, G to green, Y to yellow, O to orange and R to red colour. Mnemonic devices are very effective for memorising unrelated words.

(e) **Methods of learning :** To make improvement in the methods of learning the teacher should take into consideration such factors as age, maturity and physical and mental condition of the pupil. After consideration of these factors the teacher should suggest the better method of memorising, better methods of reading, writing and taking notes etc. He has to suggest remedies when pupils are weak in particular subjects.

40.3 Special Guidance for Backward Pupils

There are numerous psychological and physical causes of backwardness. So, the teacher has to collect relevant data about the backwardness of the pupil from different sources. Then he has to evolve special methods of remedial teaching for such pupils.

40.4 Special Guidance for Gifted Pupils

Generally a gifted child is not satisfied with the educational activities followed in the school. These are commonly meant for average children. Therefore, certain advanced type of educational program should be developed to satisfy the inquisitive mind of the gifted child.

40.5 Vocational Guidance

One of the important objectives of education is to prepare an individual for complete living in future. For complete living one has to earn his bread and butter. In order to earn livelihood one has to undergo proper vocational training. Hartshrone remarked, "Vocational education is an education of most effective kind, for lack of which those who merely go to school, suffer all their lives." Therefore, educational and vocational guidance should be simultaneously offered. Vocational guidance helps an individual to enable him to select right type of job for himself. Moreover, when he succeeds in securing a suitable vocation he feels himself to be a worthy member of the society.

40.5.1 Aims of Vocational Guidance

The specific aims of vocational guidance are as follows :

1. To assist the pupil to choose the right type of occupation.
2. To assist the pupil to acquire knowledge of the function, duties and responsibilities of the chosen occupations.
3. To assist the pupil to discover his own abilities and skills.
4. To help the individual to achieve job-satisfaction.

Our National Policy on Education (1986) laid great emphasis on vocational education. It clearly stated : The introduction of systematic, well-planned and rigorously implemented program of vocational education is crucial in the proposed educational reorganisation. The Kothari Commission (1964–66), in order to bring education into closer relationship with productivity also recommended to give a strong vocational bias to secondary education.

40.5.2 Function of the Vocational Guide

For effective guidance, the guide should have clear idea about the individuals who need guidance. To render effective vocational guidance to the individual, informations on the following have to be collected :

1. Personal information regarding—age, sex, health, interests, personality etc.
2. Social and economic status.
3. Educational attainment.
4. Skill, aptitude and special ability.
5. Occupational opportunities.

The guide must have comprehensive knowledge about the individuals' special mental abilities, skill, education and training, interest and other personality traits. Besides these, guide must have an idea about the individual's social and economic status.

Moreover, in this age of specialisation the guide has to assist the pupil to secure a knowledge of the facilities offered by various educational institutions for vocational training. He has to provide information about admission requirements, the length of training and the cost of attendance to such institution.

Another important work of the guide is Job Analysis. He has to collect all necessary informations regarding the availability of job, age and qualifications needed for the job, rule of application and so on.

40.5.3 Guidance Personnel

The people involved in vocational guidance in a school include : 1. The teacher, 2. Counsellor, 3. Psychologist and 4. Social worker.

1. **Teacher's Role :** The teacher will keep record of every student about his attendance academic performance and his behaviour in the class. He should specially attend to the backward and problem children.
2. **Counsellor's Role :** The important function of the counsellor is to advise and assist the pupils in their personal, social, educational and vocational problems.
3. **Psychologist's Role :** The function of a school psychologist includes the use of psychological tests, determination of backwardness, finding out the causes of delinquency and suggesting the preventive measures etc. He also has to take note of the mental health of the pupils and suggest remedial measures.
4. **Role of Social Worker :** Social workers maintain contact between school and family. As directed by the psychologist and counsellor, social workers meet the parents and collect necessary informations about the child and his family.

40.6 Problems of Educational Guidance

In advanced countries educational and vocational guidance are part and parcel of the whole educational system. But in this country not much progress could be made in this field because of the following reasons :

1. Financial constraints.
2. Want of properly trained personnel.
3. Non-availability of standardised psychological tests suitable for this country.

4. *Dearth of employment* : Vocational guidance becomes meaningless if persons trained in vocation remains unemployed for a considerable period of time.

Summary

Guidance is the art of helping students to plan their action wisely. The personal help or advice given to a person to solve certain problems by an experienced man is termed as guidance. Guidance may be of various types : Educational Guidance, Vocational Guidance, Moral Guidance, Financial Guidance etc.

The important purpose of educational guidance is to aid students in planning their educational program. Because of diversification of courses, now-a-days the student has to select right type of stream as per his interest and aptitude. To select proper curriculum various mental tests, Aptitude tests, Scholastic tests, Personality tests are used. With the help of informations derived from psychological tests and interviews, a profile about the student is prepared and necessary guidance is given.

For the purpose of educational guidance the teacher has to know the factors that influence the teaching learning process. To arouse motivation, the teacher has to make the subject matter of learning meaningful and interesting through improved method of teaching.

Educational guidance is closely related to vocational guidance and they should be simultaneously offered. Vocational guidance assists the pupil to choose the right type of occupation. Persons involved in vocational guidance include : The Teacher, Counsellor, Psychologist and Social worker.

In India, not much progress could be made in educational and vocational guidance because of Financial constraints, dearth of trained personnel and lack of employment opportunities.

References

1. Crow, L.D. and Crow, A. : *Educational Psychology,* New Delhi : Eurasia Publishing House, 1973.
2. Murphy, Gardner : *An Introduction to Psychology,* New Delhi : Oxford & IBH, 1968.
3. Gates, A.I. : *Educational Psychology,* New York : MacMillian, 1948.

4. Rai, B.C. : *Educational Psychology,* Prakashak Kendra, Lucknow, 1998.

5. Skinner, C.E. : *Essentials of Educational Psychology,* Engle Wood Cliffs, New Jersey : Prentice Hall, 1958.

Questions and Assignments

1. What is meant by the term Guidance? What are the chief objectives of guidance?
2. Define Educational Guidance. On what factors educational guidance depend?
3. Discuss the need of vocational guidance.
4. "Guidance is the art of helping boys and girls to plan their own action wisely." (C.E. Skinner)—Discuss.
5. Write an essay on educational guidance. Distinguish between educational guidance and vocational guidance.
6. Write notes on :

   (a) Guidance for Backward pupils.

   (b) Vocational Guidance.

   (c) Guidance for Gifted pupils.

   (d) Problems of Educational Guidance.

Author Index

Subject Index